Machine Gun Voices

Favelas and Utopia in Brazilian Gangster Funk

Machine Gun Voices
Favelas and Utopia in Brazilian Gangster Funk

Printed in Seoul, Republic of Korea
ISBN 978-89-521-2833-1 93380

Seoul National University Press
1 Gwanak-ro, Gwanak-gu, Seoul 08826, Republic of Korea
E-mail: snubook@snu.ac.kr
Homepage: http://www.snupress.com
Tel: +82-2-880-5252
Fax: +82-2-889-0785

First Printing: October 18, 2019

This work was supported by the Seoul National University Research Grant in 2018.

MACHINE GUN VOICES

Favelas and Utopia in Brazilian Gangster Funk

Paul Sneed

SNUPRESS
Seoul National University Press

Contents

Photo Gallery

Pedra da Gávea over Rocinha
(Sergio Rivero Navaro, 1998)

Smiles in Kitchenette
(Gabe Ponce de Leon, early 2000s)

Bubble Gum (Gabe Ponce de Leon, early 2000s)

Kids on Bed (Gabe Ponce de Leon, early 2000s)

Woman with Records on Wall
(Gabe Ponce de Leon, early 2000s)

Rocinha at Night (Nino Mason, 2017)

Baile de Comunidade in Rocinha (Greg Scruggs, mid-2000s)

Boys at Baile (Greg Scruggs, mid-2000s)

Kids at Baile (Greg Scruggs, mid-2000s)

Clandestine Covers of Proibidão CDs, circa 2001-2003 (Seo Min-Gyo, 2018)

More Clandestine Covers of Proibidão CDs, circa 2001-2002 (Seo Min-Gyo, 2018)

Youths with MC Binho, in Red (Greg Scruggs, mid-2000s)

Instituto Dois Irmãos/Two Brothers Foundation
(Paul Sneed, 2009)

Rocinha Houses (Sergi Rivero Navarro, 1998)

Burnt Out Cars after Gun Fight (Sergi Rivro Navarro, 1998)

Rocinha's Mano Kacau (in Blue) and MC Binho (in Green) at Baile de Comunidade (Greg Scruggs, mid-2000s)

Roda de Funk at Cantagalo (Greg Scruggs, mid-2000s)

Thumps Up at Baile (Greg Scruggs, mid-2000s)

MC Binho at Rocinha Dance (Greg Scruggs, mid-2000s)

Polícia Militar at Roda de Funk (Greg Scruggs, mid-2000s)

Polícia Militar at Roda de Funk (Greg Scruggs, mid-2000s)

DJ at Baile de Comunidade (Greg Scruggs, mid-2000s)

MCs Júnior and Leonardo at Roda de Funk (Greg Scruggs, mid-2000s)

Rocinha Hillside (Evan Rubin, mid-2000s)

Erick Andrade Gonçalves, Paul Sneed (Author) and Sergi Rivero Navarro—Left to Right
(Unknown, 1998)

Woman in Mirror in Home (Gabe Ponce de Leon, early 2000s)

Trash Pile in Trees (Gabe Ponce de Leon, early 2000s)

Youth Group, Igreja Metodista Wesleyana da Rocinha (Paul Sneed, 2009)

Maria Clara, Anna Karolynne, Gabriel and Ana Beatriz (left to right), students at Escola Criativa (Nino Mason, 2018)

Army/Police Operation in Rocinha (Nino Mason, 2017)

International Volunteer Manuela's Tattoo (Nino Mason, 2017)

Watercolor of Rocinha by Grandpa Chan (Chan Jae Lee, 2016)

Foreword

Funk *carioca* culture originates from the young proletarians of the greater Rio de Janeiro city who united to dance to the sounds of African-American soul in the early 1970s. Unlike the English club culture known as Northern Soul, Brazilian soul people shared with their North-American peers a common African heritage, but not a common language. In the course of two decades, their musical tastes evolved with African-American music—from soul to funk, Philly soul, disco, hip-hop, electro funk, electro, Miami bass, Latin freestyle—until a hybrid of song and electronic dance music (EDM) emerged (Palombini 2014). Funk carioca arose from a club culture, but the closure of suburban venues by law enforcement agents in the latter half of the 1990s sent it back to the *favelas* where it found a new home and exploded even more.

Paul Sneed lived in the favela of Rocinha, in South Rio, as a University of Virginia undergraduate student on an exchange programme in 1990. He returned for extended stays in 1992 and 1995, for research experiences as a graduate student at the University of Wisconsin in 1996, 1998 and 2000, and for fieldwork in 2001, 2002 and 2003, adding up to some five years of residence (not including subsequent stays and research stints in Rocinha). He was thus able to gain *in situ* knowledge of the newborn music, with its early waves of popularity in the media, of which the first, in 1995, coincides with the golden age of *funk consciente* ('conscious rap'), whereas the second, in the year 2000, is coetaneous with the ascendancy of the subgenres *putaria* ('whoredom') and *proibidão* ('forbidden funk').

Proibidão is commonly described as *apologia* ('apology') with ellipsis of the object that this music would eulogize. Such an object is tacitly understood to be crime, sex or both.[1] Strictly speaking, the subject matter of proibidão is 'crime life,' where 'crime' stands for the trading of illicit substances conductive to altered states of consciousness, especially marijuana, cocaine and crack, with the exemption of those activities of this trade that take place outside the favela or are not conducted by people associated with it. The remainder of this operation is termed 'drug dealing,' so that the lower echelons of the drug business substitute for the upper ones insofar as liability to punishment is concerned. The rhetorical expenditure of this naming strategy, in which *pars pro toto* ('a synecdoche') hides behind an ellipsis, is inversely proportional to the legitimacy of the measures wherewith the music is penalized, hence the ironic hyperbole of the augmentative (the term proibidão translates as 'forbidden big thing') — yet another double figure of speech. Proibidão is best defined as the subgenre of funk carioca that deals with life on the retail end of the illicit substance trade, narrated with specific ethical concerns, from the perspective of those who experience its problems, according to a particular aesthetics of composition, performance, and musical and phonographic production.

One of the main representatives of the subgenre, MC Mascote, from the favela of Vidigal (facing the sea on the thither side of the same Dois Irmãos

1 In the case of sex, the precise name is *putaria*; see Raquel Moreira, "Bitches Unleashed: Women in Rio's Funk Movement, Performances of Heterosexual Femininity, and Possibilities of Resistance," and Mariana Gomes, "My Pussy é o Poder. Representação feminina através do funk: identidade, feminismo e indústria cultural."

rock on whose slopes part of Rocinha stands), states that the first proibidão was "Rap do parapapá," by MCs Cidinho and Doca, from the West Rio favela of Cidade de Deus, in 1994.[2] The following year, the repercussion of "Rap das armas," by MCs Júnior and Leonardo, from Rocinha, turned proibidão into a public security affair.[3] Thinly veiled allusions to *life in crime* made it onto vinyl without further ado in the 1990s, while explicit pieces, recorded live during funk dances, circulated on MDs and cassette tapes. In 1998 *Bonde do Lambari* ("Lambari Crew"), from the North Rio favela of Jacaré, was probably the first CD to feature proibidão prominently among its tracks.[4] On September 9, 1999 a copy of the CD *Proibidão do Rap* appeared when the police raided Fazendinha, in the Alemão Complex of favelas, in North Rio, and arrested 20-year old MC Sapão, who unwittingly hit the mainstream press as an alleged drug dealer in the following days ("Apreensão" 1999; Oliveira 1999, 17); on November 16th, another raid, this time in Vila Cruzeiro, in the Penha Complex of favelas, also in North Rio, led to the discovery of *Proibidão do Rap 2* ("O brinde musical dos traficantes" 1999).[5]

The year 2000 saw the proliferation of such CDs, their circulation soon enhanced by peer-to-peer file sharing networks (Soulseek), file hosting services (4shared, MegaUpload, RapidShare), social networking websites (Orkut, Facebook), webcasting, blogs, photo-logs and file-streaming services (SoundCloud). YouTube eventually became the main distribution outlet, proibidão hits reaching views in the range of eight-

2 Personal communication to Foreword's author (Carlos Palombini), August 26, 2015.

3 A radio-friendly version of "Rap do parapapá."

4 I (forward's author Carlos Palombini) am grateful to DJ Leandro Baré for calling my attention to this CD, and to DJ Pedro Fontes for giving me access to it.

5 News about these raids was discovered by Adriana Facina during archival research in the National Library and mentioned in personal communication to Foreword's author (Carlos Palombini, nd).

digit figures therein. Recorded live at Chatuba, in the Penha Complex, on July 26, 2009, "Vida bandida," by Praga, sung by MC Smith and produced by DJ Byano, epitomizes this acme, the poignancy of its refrain rendered barely bearable by DJ Byano's humorous touches: "Hoje somos festa, amanhã seremos luto" ("Our life is bandit and our game is tough, today we are party, tomorrow we shall be mourning"). Yet the extent to which this music relied on the circuit of favela dances started to become clear as the infamous Pacifying Police Unit (UPP) policy began to supress them from 2008 onwards.[6] The military invasions and occupation of the Penha and Alemão Complexes in November 2010 (Caceres, Ferrari and Palombini 2014, 160–177) as well as the illegal jailing of MCs Frank, Max, Tikão, Dido and Smith in December dealt a severe blow (Palombini 2013). The Chatuba dance, which had been the epicentre of proibidão during that decade, ceased its activities and the subgenre started to move in different directions (Facina and Palombini 2017).

In tracks like "Papo de bandido" ("Bandit's talk") and "Tá tudo monitorado" ("It's all monitored"), produced by DJ RD da NH, MC Rodson (2011, 2012) resorts to elusive syntax, ellipses and coded language; in "Rotina de patrão" ("Boss' Routine"), produced by DJs Rennan and Isaac 22, MC Smith (2011) explores the ambiguity of the bandit figure, as does MC Orelha (2013) in "Herói ou vilão" ("Hero or Villain"), produced by DJ Diogo do Serrão; in "Vida bandida 2" ("Bandit Life 2"), written by Praga and produced by DJ RD da NH, MC Smith (2013) incarnates a jailed bandit who ponders on his life. Some artists stuck to the explicitness of the old style, replacing rival criminal factions with the State as the target

6 Pacifying Police Units were designed to militarily occupy favelas located in highly valued neighbourhoods as part of preparatory efforts towards the 2014 World Cup and the 2016 Olympic Games, as well as of a wide process of urban gentrification.

of their invectives. Thus, in 2011 MC Vitinho released "Bala na Dilma sapatão" ("Bullets at [President] Dilma, the Dyke"), produced by DJ Rafael da Coruja, and in 2014 MC GEELE recorded "Na Copa do Mundo quem vai vencer é o CV" ("In the World Cup the Red Command Shall Win"), produced by Estúdio Criminoso.[7]

With his doctoral dissertation, presented at the University of Wisconsin-Madison in 2003, Sneed became the first scholar to devote his efforts to proibidão. The Master's theses of Carla Mattos (2006), Rodrigo Russano (2006), Maurício Guedes (2007), Eduardo Baker (2013) and Dennis Novaes (2016) followed suit. Some, including Guedes, have concluded that "... proibidão is the spokesperson of the drug-dealers' factions..." (Sneed 2007). Sneed's view is different. By focusing on the creation of a collective time-space of power, knowledge and existence, rather than on leaders or lyrics, in this present work (which is an outgrowth of that earlier dissertation) he reaches the insight that proibidão is a symbolic site in which the expectations of community residents vis-à-vis illicit substance retailers—and vice-versa—are both articulated and mediated. With this publication, *Machine Gun Voices* now figures alongside Carlos Bruce Batista's 2013 interdisciplinary anthology as one of the two published volumes on this music around which some of the most pressing issues of the times converge—and the first in English.

On December 15, 2010 images of the arrest of MCs Frank, Tikão and Smith by a sheriff turned into TV-star invaded Brazilian homes as an epilogue to the latest and most spectacular episode of the Global War on Drugs. Since then, a never-ending series of violations of rights has been perpetrated against MCs, DJs, sound-system owners and funksters

7 The CV is one of the three main associations of illicit-substance retailers, or *facções* ('factions'), and the one most closely associated with proibidão culture.

in general. If this can happen to artists who enjoy the love of millions, so I thought, it could happen to anyone else. In response to the popular uprising of June 2013 the middle-classes have become acquainted with a somewhat milder version of such treatment. The following year, the Operação Lava Jato (or "Car Wash Operation," the famous investigation into corruption at the forefront of Brazilian politics over the past decade) started to familiarize a selected few members of the élite with an even more polite one. Sneed's work shows one way out of the impending danger: communion with the lives, culture and artistry of those who, from time immemorial, have been suffering oppression in its crudest state.

Carlos Palombini[8]

Universidade Federal de Minas Gerais (UFMG), Brazil

8 Carlos Palombini is Professor of musicology in the school of Music of the universidade Federal de Minas Gerais(UFMG), fellow Brazils National Research Council(CNPq) and associated faculty of the graduate program at the Universidade Fedral do Estado do Rio de Janeiro(UNIRIO)

1

Funk Rio

Favela Street Party[1]

It's a muggy summer night after three A.M. on a Saturday in early 2002 in Rio de Janeiro, Brazil. At the foot of the favela of Rocinha, heavily armed gangsters are throwing an enormous outdoor funk dance party in the middle of a narrow street called the Via Ápia. Booming electronic music flows from the towering speaker stacks running along the side of the slender road, one of the primary commercial strips in the grid-like lower area of the favela. Despite the late hour, thousands of young people circle to and fro in long train-like lines, moving up and down the street as the subwoofers blast music loud enough to rattle the glass out of some nearby windows. Under a makeshift canvas awning, off to one side, drug-traffickers cluster in the dim light around tables jam-packed with money, guns and packets of cocaine and marijuana of different sizes. Others patrol in small bands, machine guns brandished as they move slowly through the crowd, serenely taking in the scene and making sure no fights break out.

This type of street *baile* is a sort of community festival that attracts people of all ages, including many who would never consider themselves

1 This description of a baile funk is offered both as one of an actual event occurring on February 8, 2002, and as a synthesis of other community dance parties taking place in Rocinha over the years of my residence there as a researcher, neighbor and community educator from the US.

funkeiros, as such, as one calls fans of Brazilian funk. Though most are in their teens and early 2000s, a significant number of those present have not yet hit puberty. Just in front of us, scattered groups of kids as young as seven and eight cheerfully perform choreographed dance moves with one another. A surprising number of middle-aged people gather along the storefronts and small restaurants lining the street—and even some elderly folks besides—drinking, laughing and playing cards in the mouths of the network of alleyways intersecting the larger road. In any case, since this *baile funk* (as these dance parties are called in Portuguese) is outdoors, there is no clear physical division or barrier between where it begins and ends. As a result, even those neighbors inside the homes up and down the Via Ápia and the surrounding areas of the favela also find themselves in its midst, like it or not. Try as they might to close up their residences, padding their doors and windows with towels and blankets, running fans, blaring their TVs, even households a considerable distance away literally tremble to the pervasive throbbing blast of the surrounding electronic soundscape.

Even when there are no dances in the Via Ápia, twenty-four hours a day it is one of the most bustling areas of Rocinha. Buildings as many as five and six stories tall line both sides of the street, which gently slopes up the base of the Morro Dois Irmãos ('Two Brothers Hill'), a famous granite-peaked, forested mountain visible from the posh beaches of Rio's Southern Zone. By day, hundreds of motorcycles, taxis, trucks and cars speedily squeeze past one another along the Via Ápia as hundreds more people enter and leave the favela on foot. At those times, countless more stand off to the sides, conversing with friends and neighbors. The street runs slightly uphill from the entrance of Rocinha past the numerous bars, restaurants and other businesses lining it along both sides, including small furniture stores, bingo halls, hair salons and stands selling hot dogs, corn on the cob and pirated CDs and DVDs. On nights when there are not dances here, skinny, unarmed teenage drug dealers talk in small groups, keeping a lookout for customers and the police.

Tonight the celebration being thrown by Rocinha's drug traffickers in the Via Apia is what funk fans in Brazil call a *baile de comunidade* ('community dance party'). It is a type of open-air baile funk held in favelas in the streets, alleyways, soccer courts or bus depots of the neighborhood.[2] I am standing shoulder to shoulder with a small group of friends from the Cachopa area of the favela, where I have lived off and on for several years during my frequent but sporadic periods of residence in Brazil. Orlando, Vítor and Cícero, all in their mid-2000s, smile as they sway gently to the beat, scanning the crowd for other friends and neighbors. The music of the baile is so loud that it forces the people at the dance to speak from a very close distance, as they hug, clasp one an-

2 At the time of my early fieldwork in the late 1990s and early 2000s, the criminal faction known as the Comando Vermelho ('Red Command'), or CV, operated in Rocinha. During subsequent fieldwork in 2004, the faction called Amigos dos Amigos ('Friends of the Friends'), or ADA, gained control. In November 2011 the government intervened with a community policing program called Unidades de Polícia Pacificadora, known as UPPs, or Pacifying Police Units. Despite some initial success, the program floundered and in September 2017 a major turf war erupted in Rocinha. At the time of writing (May 2018), friends living there report that, after initial infighting between rivals from within the ADA, the larger CV has been making a move to return to the favela. As of May 18, 2018, residents in personal correspondence with the author report that members of both the CV and ADA are in the favela, controlling different areas, along with a permanent police presence. The UPP is scheduled to be closed, along with roughly half the UPPs in the favela locations in Rio, and replaced with more conventional battalion not geared towards community policing (*O Globo*, "Intervenção"). According to news reports, as of January 2018, the related deaths of 37 persons occurred in Rocinha since September (G1, "Desde setembro"). Sporadic confrontations continue and just days ago a much-loved seventy-five-year-old man named Francisco Nunes da França, known in the community as Ciclista Pipoca ('Popcorn Cyclist'), died victim of a stray bullet (Extra Online, "Tiroteio" and UOL Notícias, "Morador").

other's hands enthusiastically and exchange *beijinhos*—as the little kisses often used by women and members of the opposite sex are called.

The crowd mixes along the narrow strip in two currents. One heads up to Rocinha's main thoroughfare, the Estrada da Gávea, where Planet Pizza and the Cabaré do Barata are doing booming business. The other stream flows down toward the entrance of the favela at the Passarela pedestrian footbridge, near the tunnel and the high-speed Lagoa-Barra freeway just below. The dense masses of people moving in either direction make it slightly difficult to breathe, let alone dance. Even so, people everywhere gently sway as they chat and smile nonchalantly. Others perform dance moves off in the small spaces to the sides and on either end, facing the line of stacked amplifiers along the edge of the street.

The heavily armed *soldados* ('soldiers'), as the armed favela gangsters are called, of the local drug cartel can be seen wading through the crowd or standing in the openings of alleyways, dressed as the other funkeiros but flashing weapons such as AK-47s, AR-15s, shotguns, pistols and Uzis.[3] One gangster wearing a rubber Osama Bin Laden mask accepts a fat, smoky marijuana joint from another, taking care to balance his assault rifle straight up in the air with his other arm so as not to accidentally shoot anyone.[4] Adhesive stickers of the Flamengo soccer club are visible against the silver plating of his weapon. The drug traffickers talk in groups as they eye the crowd, keeping watch and swaying to the thudding beat of the funk music. Fighting is uncommon at the bailes funk in

3 For a short recapitulation of the recent history of the Rocinha drug gang since the golden age of Brazilian gangster rap in Rio's favelas analyzed throughout this book, see Glenny, "One of Rio de Janeiro's Safest Favelas Descends into Violence." For a more detailed account, see *Nemesis* (Glenny 2015).

4 Bin Laden was a popular figure in the gangs at the time, which was shortly after the 9/11 Attacks.

the Via Ápia, because to cause trouble of any kind would be an offense to these same gangster hosts that are throwing the party. Still, one never knows what can happen at any funk dance party and my friends and I pay careful attention to the multitudes of people pressing against us in the ever-shifting crowd.[5]

The baile is hot and humid in the summer night, despite being outdoors, and the air hangs thick on the crowd, filled with smoke, the smell of sweaty bodies and even some gasoline exhaust from vehicles in the cramped side alleys off the Via Ápia. I'm filled with a sense of joy and expectation as people with smiling faces pass by shouting the words to the music, chanting and swaying sensually to the songs. On the small black, plywood platform by the speaker stacks, fireworks explode in flaming fountains as the stage lights flash and a smoke machine pours out columns of smoke. The MCs have not yet taken stage there and a DJ is playing the summer's funk hits. He starts with a montage titled "5 Caras" by the Bonde do Vinho. Next, we hear a familiar refrain popular in Rocinha of a song by MC Dollores (Aldenir Francisco dos Santos), one of the all-time greatest Rio funk singers and a life-long Rocinha resident. The chorus, "'O Bigode' é quem comanda a favela da Rocinha!" ("'Moustache' is in charge of the favela of Rocinha!"), makes reference to the favela drug gang's boss, Lulu (Luciano Barbosa da Silva), who was slain by police in 2004. Next comes the song "Paga Spring Love," by Fornalha, another Rocinha MC at the height of his popularity. Suddenly my friend Josivaldo, from the Cachopa area of Rocinha, appears in the crowd in front of me and clasps

5 For perspective on the urgency of such ongoing violence in this context, 2017 Rio recorded 6,590 violent deaths, the highest number in a decade. There were a staggering 61,000 total violent deaths across Brazil during the same time (Faiola and Kaiser, "A Once Trendy Slum").

my hand enthusiastically, slapping me on the back several times. He has come upon the dance on his way over to his girlfriend's house across town in Taquara and has been lingering in the street, taking in the scene and talking with friends.

The baile funk is its own kind of high. Drinking, smoking marijuana or snorting cocaine might heighten the experience for some of the people in attendance, but one need not be drunk or high to feel the energy of the masses of squirming bodies and the barrage of bass pulling the crowd back and forth to the beat. Despite the enormous volume of the music and the multitude of thousands jamming itself into the proportionally small street, the baile de comunidade in the Via Ápia is beautiful and I begin to feel a sense of great peace and belonging overtaking me. The music and the crowd itself are so loud that they somehow drown everything else out, leaving me with a quiet sense of awe. The sound of the heavy bass and electronic beats of the music echo across the slopes of the favela as those of us in the crowd blissfully swim in the sonic waves of a favela funk utopia.

With its population estimated at over 100,000, Rocinha is considered one of the largest of the hundreds of favelas in Rio.[6] Due to its size

6 Schmidt, "Estudo aponta mais 49 favelas," also cites the 2000 census conducted by the Instituto Brasileiro de Geografia e Estatística (IBGE) estimating the population of Rocinha at 56,000. In my interview on July 3, 2009 with Wallace Pereira da Silva, then president of the Associação de Moradores e Amigos do Bairro de Barcelos (AMABB, one of three neighbor's associations in the favela), he estimated the unofficial population at around 160,000. That same year, employees of the governmental XXVII Centro Administrativo da Rocinha, a branch of the City Hall, told me it was 120,000. When I first went to Rocinha in 1990, I became friends with the president of another of Rocinha's neighbor's associations, União Pró-Melhoramentos dos Moradores da Rocinha (UPMMR). Seu Pereira (Everindo da Silva Pereira), who has since passed away, helped me much with my initial research on organized crime in the favela. He told me that there were 300,000 people in the neighborhood. With such a tendency to inflate numbers, Rocinha's fabled size has become a part of

and location in one of the wealthiest parts of the city, Rocinha receives considerably more attention from the city government than most other favelas and has grown commercially at an astounding rate over the last few decades.[7] Still, given the limitation of its physical space relative to its vast population, Rocinha is one of the most densely populated places on Earth and remains sadly lacking in adequate sewage, water, electricity and educational resources.[8] Throughout much of its history, police have done little policing in the neighborhood and, instead, residents have relied upon local drug-traffickers to provide law and order.

Rocinha has always been one of the most important communities for the *movimento funk* ('funk movement') as folks often called it back then. Many of funk's most famous old-school MCs came from Rocinha, like MC Galo (Everaldo Almeida da Silva), Neném (Anderson da Silva Ângelo), Gorila and brothers Leonardo (Leonardo Pereira Mota) and Júnior (Francisco de Assis Mota Júnior)—none more exceptional than the aforementioned MC Dollores. *Funk melody*, a romantic, bubblegum version of funk, was also crucial in Rocinha, which was the home of the composer Renato Moreno and the singer Charlys da Rocinha, who performed songs in Portuguese, Spanish, English, French and Hebrew.[9] There were at least

itsambivalent mystique and, consequently, some may be disappointed to hear there are perhaps fewer residents than was previously thought. In any case, the difficulty in assessing the size of the population in of itself is evidence of Rocinha's nature as a partially informal community.

7 The official number of favelas recognized by City Hall in Rio de Janeiro went up in 2003 from 603 to 752 (Schmidt, "Estudo aponta mais 49 favelas"). Note that this excludes favelas from Rio's surrounding suburbs.

8 Whatever the number of people is, the relatively small physical space it occupies makes it quite densely populated. According to *The Economist*, "Rio's Post-Olympic Blues," the total area of Rocinha is 1km^2 with a population of roughly 100,000. Also see Bernardo Tabak, "Maior favela do país."

9 Charlys da Rocinha continues to embody such a spirit of favela versatility to the present day, most recently as a singer of Brazilian Contemporary Christian Music.

four large-scale bailes held weekly in Rocinha, each one attracting thousands of funkeiros, in addition to the events held for holidays and other special occasions. The most famous was at the Emoções club. Another was at the old samba *quadra* ('practice hall') on top of the favela at Rua Um. One took place along the open-air sewage duct of the Valão area near the base of the hill (and the most active location for illicit drug sales at the time) and the last was the baile in the Via Ápia described above.

Rio's Funk Carioca

With its booming bass and pulsing electronic beats, throaty vocal delivery, frenetic samplings and playful, sensual dance moves, Brazilian funk has much in common with its close cousin, American hip-hop, Latin *reggaetón* and Jamaican dancehall are also close relatives.[10] Though these are all Afro-Atlantic, urban electronic music styles with many common roots, funk carioca, as it is also known (*carioca* is used to describe someone or something from Rio de Janeiro), is far from being a mere imitation. It is a rich and uniquely Brazilian musical culture with its own distinctive ways of walking, talking, dancing and making music.[11] The bailes funk,

Charlys, his brothers Carlos and Alan and our friend Renato Moreno helped me immeasurably with my research over the years. MCs Leonardo and Júnior were also indispensable. MC Galo and MC Dollores were also supportive, as were countless other people associated with Rocinha's funk scene throughout (see acknowledgments).

10 For a thorough overview of reggaetón and its connections to hip-hop and other expressions of Afro-Atlantic youth cultures, see *Reggaeton* (Rivera et al 2009).

11 More often than not, Brazilians simply refer to funk carioca as 'funk.' To avoid confusion with the American musical style of the same name, sometimes the word 'carioca' is added, especially by journalists, music critics, scholars and activists. Besides those names and 'movimento funk,' as people often called it in the mid-1990s,

like the dance party described above, also have a distinctly Rio way of coming together. Incorporating counter-cultural aspects of the broader Black Atlantic world and the international Black Movement more and fusing them with the culture of the favelas of Rio de Janeiro, funk carioca, since its beginnings in the early 1970s, has evolved into a vibrant musical youth expression characterized by irony, complex masking and subversive messages and practices.[12] At once heroic and delinquent, a cry of protest and resistance, an apology of crime, a cheap and sexualized commodity and a call to gather together in community, to love, to fight and to live, Brazil's funk is a weapon in a postmodern war.

Since the later years of the twentieth-century funk carioca has maintained undeniable significance for millions of poor urban youth, who continue to identify with it to this day. Hundreds of thousands still attend the enormous funk dance parties each week in the streets and samba clubs of the favelas where they live. Indeed, these bailes funk have come to be emblematic of the world of Rio's favelas today. It is a world existing on the front lines of police violence and gang wars, poverty and stark inadequacies, yet still one made up of resilient people confronting the harsh conditions of their daily lives with humor, love, courage, perseverance and music.

Musically, Brazilian funk is a rich blend of beats and diverse pre-

people use other names like *pancadão*, (literally a 'big punch' or 'blow') *batidão* ('big beat'). In English, it's often called baile funk, which in Portuguese actually refers to the massive dance parties in which this music is played, and sometimes *favela funk* or Rio funk. For more nuanced and expansive list of names for funk and its subgenres, see *Batidão: Uma história do funk* (Essinger 2005, 11).

12 For the early history of funk carioca, see *O mundo funk carioca* (Vianna 1988), *O funk e o hip-hop entram em cena* (Herschmann 2000, 18-31), and *Abalando os anos 90*, (Herschmann 1997, 7-13), and *Batidão* (Essinger 2015) (for his exploration of Rio's Black Pride scene see his chapter "Em tempos de soul power," 15-48).

recorded samples of everything from machine gun fire and explosions to digitally enhanced voices, radio sound bites, Brazilian cowboy calls, animal noises and anything in between. It is as unashamedly eclectic as the culture of the favelas of Rio de Janeiro within which it has arisen, mixing the melodic structures of other Brazilian musical styles such as *axé*, *forró* and samba—even the Afro-Brazilian martial art/dance form of capoeira—with features of international music like R&B, techno, hip-hop, pop, rock and even Contemporary Christian Music. Rio Funk MCs perform singing more than rapping, often calling out in hoarse, throaty voices, sometimes almost yelling as they chant out refrains reminiscent of the mass cheers at soccer games in the Maracanã stadium on the north side of Rio.[13]

MCs have been singing lyrics in Portuguese since the mid-1990s, when several of the Rocinha singers first came to prominence, as did those in neighborhoods like the Cidade de Deus, the favelas of Borel and Vidigal and countless other communities. Some, like MC Galo, female MC Taty Quebra-Barraco (Tatiana dos Santos Lourenço), Deize Tigrona (earlier known as Deize da Injeção), MC Sabrina (Sabrina Lindalva da Cruz Credo, one of the early female figures associated with proibidão), Bob Rum (Moisés Osmar da Silva), D'Eddy, and Mr. Catra (Wagner Domingues Costa) performed mostly as solo artists. Others, like Cidinho (Sidney da Silva) and Doca (Marcos Paulo de Jesus Peizoto), Leonardo and Júnior, Markinhos (Marcos Ribeiro Chaves) and Dollores (Aldenir Francisco dos Santos), William (William Santos de Souza) and Duda (Carlos Eduardo Cardoso da Silva)

13 For the evolution of the musical characteristics of funk carioca, including its beats from the volt mix sound of the mid-1990s to the *tamborzão* style ('big drum') of the early 2000s and the 'beat box' sound of the 2010s—and the way these changes connected historically to developments in Brazilian politics and society—see Caceres, Ferrari and Palombini, "A era Lula/tamborzão."

and Claudinho (Claudio Rodriques de Mattos) and Buchecha (Claucirlei Jovêncio de Sousa) generally performed in duos. Others started as duos, like Mascote (Fábio de Oliveira Cordeiro) and Neném, later to perform as solo acts. MC Serginho (Sérgio Braga Manhães) sung with his transgender dancer and partner Lacraia (Marco Aurélio Silva da Rosa). Still others performed as lead vocals for backing groups often called *bondes*, like Valesca Popozuda (Valesca Reis Santos), of the girl group Gaiola das Popozudas, a group that formed in 2000 but achieved national fame beginning in 2007. Although they touched on a range of topics too broad to define, many of their songs were of a romantic, sexual, violent, humorous or consciousness-raising nature. Even in those early days, lyrics could touch on everything from appealing to violence and raw sexuality one moment to brotherly love, peace and faith in God the next. Whatever the songs of funk have been about—then or now—they have been written by and large by and for people living in Rio's favelas and the city's other low-income neighborhoods. They have been, not surprisingly, mostly about the lives of such people and their love, passion, beauty, strength, faith, sensuality, sexuality and creativity.

In that first wave of funk songs with lyrics in Portuguese in the mid-1990s, one prevalent feature in songs was to enact a radical inversion of the social geography of Rio de Janeiro. Rejecting the traditional superior value given to middle and upper-class neighborhoods like Copacabana, Ipanema, Leblon and Lagoa, commonly referred to in Portuguese as *bairros nobres* ('noble neighborhoods') songs instead proclaimed the favelas as the quintessentially Brazilian social spaces—and indeed quintessentially pan-human ones. This tendency was particularly evident through the mid-1990s through early 2000s, in what I consider the heyday of the community dance parties—like the one described in the beginning of this chapter–that took place in that favela. It was a common feature in funk songs at the time to include lengthy, fluidly arranged lists of the names of favelas. An excellent example of this tendency was in the song "Nosso Sonho" ("Our Dream"), by the bubblegum pop-funk duo Claudinho and Buchecha, a hit in 1997. The song's title, too, is well in keeping with the utopian impulse at the heart of funk carioca analyzed in this study.[14]

Beginning in the 1990s, distinctions arose between categories of the funk (pronounced 'funkee' in Portuguese). *Montagem* ('montage') used heavy samples and electronic beats with highly repetitive lyrical phrases and refrains. Rap was a lyrical form of funk which, despite the name, almost never actually included rapping, per se. *Funk melody*, the variety performed by Claudinho and Buchecha, mentioned above, was similar to the sound of Rio's *charme* scene, a close cousin of funk carioca popular in those early days. Into the early 2000s, the array of funk subgenres grew to include *proibidão*, a sort of forbidden, underground gangster rap, *putaria*, which literally means 'whorishness' (often euphemized as *funk sensua l*).[15] More recently still, it has expanded to include *funk ostentação*, ('swag funk') associated mostly with funk carioca as it has developed in São Paulo. Today one also hears of *funk de raiz*, literally meaning 'root funk,' a sort of consciousness-raising, throwback style used as a platform for a social justice agenda, and even an Evangelical Christian variety of funk carioca known as *gospel funk*.[16]

Given the richness and complexity of Rio's funk, the best sound or

14 The perfect pitch of the duo on the track is remarkable, as well, especially in the artfully crafted list of favelas and other working-class neighborhoods in its middle section. Like most songs mentioned in this book, "Nosso sonho" is readily available on YouTube.

15 For more on putaria, especially the debates as to whether or not the female MCs should be considered organic feminists, see Caetano, "My pussy é o poder: representação feminina através do funk: identidade, feminismo e indústria cultural," Moreira, "Bitches Unleashed."and *Funk-se quem quiser* (Lopes 2011, 151-210).

video recordings are not truly capable of transmitting the full experience of the musical culture but are instead more like photographic snapshots. The same is true when it comes to books like this and even TV shows, films and documentaries about funk. Even so, for those interested in getting a sense of what funk carioca is about, one might start with Denise Garcia's 2005 *Sou feia, mas tô na moda* or Wesley Pentz (DJ Diplo) and Leandro HBL's 2008 *Favela on Blast.* Despite its age and the many changes occurring in funk culture over the past two decades, Sérgio Goldenberg's pioneering film in 1994, *Funk Rio* is still arguably the best example of Brazilian funk videography, for its emphasis the lives of ordinary youths in and around the bailes funk.

One of the most widely-viewed funk documentaries, with over a million views on YouTube, is 2018's fan film Documentário Mc Zoi de Gato (A Voz da Favela), by internet influencer Kelvy Lopes. It tells the story of MC Zoi de Gato (Denner Augusto Sena da Silva), a brilliant pioneer of proibidão in São Paulo who died in a car crash, merely sixteen-years-old, in 2009. If viewers can be patient enough to sit through the meandering first hour and a half of the film, the final fifteen minutes is deeply moving, and even reminiscent of Sérgio Goldenberg's relational film style. It highlights the inauguration of a giant graffiti memorial to the MC, where Denner's mother, dona Kátia, is presented with an illustrated portrait of her son. The scene takes place as a surprise to dona Kátia, who is brought in blindfolded before hundreds of neighbors to

16 For more on funk de raiz and funk activism more generally, also see *Funk-se quem quiser* (Lopes 2011, 67-150). As the most in-depth study to date of funk carioca's role in leftist mobilization in Rio, her narrative provides detailed accounts of the partnerships between funkeiros, journalists, university professors, politicians and other activists in promoting funk and social inclusion more generally. See especially chapter three, "De funk de raiz a movimento político e cultural," 99-150.

a small plaza in the MCs community of Vila Natal, along the working class periphery of São Paulo. Meanwhile, his hauntingly beautiful underground hit "Amor é só de mãe" ("Love Is Just from Mothers") plays in the background.[17]

Ultimately, what makes it so difficult to encapsulate the culture of funk carioca in print, sound recording or video representations is that it is primarily one of live performance, despite its explosive growth in cyberspace and social media since the early 2000s. Indeed, the real space-time of funk carioca comes together in the lives of the people who join together to create it—especially within the reality of the baile funk dance parties themselves, live and in color, in the midst of thousands of sweaty dancing bodies and the thunderous bass of the wall of speakers. More than a beat or musical style, Rio funk is in many ways the transformation of the sounds and realities of the favela themselves into music, dance and song—heightened and intensified in the bailes funk. As local expressions of the larger, historical Afro-Atlantic world, over time I have come to understand these dance parties as community encounters in the everyday life, religious and musical practices of the youth culture of the residents of Rio's favelas, as African Diaspora peoples.[18] As community

17 My efforts to track down the acclaimed funk documentaries—not including feature pieces in news media—have turned up nearly a dozen (all listed in the bibliography). Also relevant are commercial productions prominently featuring funk dances, such as the Oscar-nominated feature film *Cidade de Deus* (2002), José Padilha's *Tropa de elite* (2007), *Vai Anitta* (2018) and the television episode "Sábado," from the series *Cidade dos homens* (from Fernando Meirelles, one of the directors of *Cidade de Deus*). In my opinion, this last production offers a particularly poignant portrayal of the bailes funk for its focus on the experience of everyday fans, along with *Funk Rio*, mentioned above. The latest is 2018's *Vai Anitta*, a six-part docu-series from Netflix about the funk singer turned Brazilian national diva Anitta.

18 Of particular relevance to my view in this sense is Gilroy's treatment of musical expressions in *Black Atlantic: Modernity and Double-Consciousness* (Gilroy 1993), especially chapter 3, "Jewels Brought from Bondage: Black Music and the Politics of encounters, the reality of these spaces is limbic besides, making them not only hideouts from hegemony protecting them ideologically but as safe havens strengthening them psychologically and even physiologically.[19]

Rio's funk scene has evolved over the past few decades into one of the country's most vibrant musical expressions—this in a country well-known for its rich musicality. Even so, it continues to be one of the least understood by people outside of the favelas and other poor communities where it is most famous, not only abroad but also among the greater Brazil public. Its reputation as a violent and socially irresponsible form of music involving overly explicit dance moves, superficial lyrics, low-end levels of music production and frequent references to Rio's infamous criminal factions has made it difficult for outsiders to consider funk carioca in a sympathetic light.

Amidst those booms of funk carioca in the mid-1990s and early 2000s, media representations of funk were common, though scholarly analyses were still few. Many of the initial media coverage of Rio's funk tended to either romanticize or vilify it, generally in either a sensationalist tone or an exotic one (Herschmann 2000). Funk carioca's reputation for violence and overt sexuality made it, according to the *New York Times* in 2001, "perhaps the most controversial dance scene in the world" (Strauss 2001, 29). The following year, the *Washington Post* reported that "The 'funk balls' of Rio are pantheons of pleasure and violence that have gained international renown as the world's fiercest urban dance scene. Brazilian funk—inspired

Authenticity," 72-110.

19 With the idea of 'limbic realism' in this context, I am thinking of work done in the field of psychology emphasizing such neuro-physiological interdependencies, as expounded by Flores, *Addiction as Attachment Disorder*. An earlier, even more foundational work in this vein is Thomas Lewis, Fari Amini and Richard Lannon, *A General Theory of Love*, in which the authors provide a concise summary of the nature of such limbic inter-connectedness. I consider this more closely in the Afterword.

by the sounds and styles of American gangsta rap and hip-hop but far more extreme than either—and the balls where it is played are the most controversial craze yet in Latin America's largest nation (Faiola 2001, C7)." That same year, Brazilian investigative reporter Tim Lopes—of Brazil's leading television network, Globo—was discovered by drug traffickers as he filmed their activities inside a funk dance in a favela in Rio de Janeiro. The events surrounding the brutal torture he suffered and his murder shortly after that invigorated the debate about funk and its connections to the growing crisis of violence and social exclusion in Brazil (Souza 2002).

Over the years, scholars writing about funk carioca have wrestled with its demonization in mainstream Brazilian media and society, starting with the very first research publication about funk, anthropologist Hermano Vianna's *O mundo funk carioca* (1988). A decade later Micael Herschmann provided an in-depth communications-based analysis of this issue early on in his edited volume *Abalando os anos 90* (1997) and in his single-authored follow-up book *O funk e o hip-hop invadem a cena* (2000). Over the course of time, journalists like Sílvio Essinger, author of *Batidão: Uma história do funk* (2005), and Júlio Ludemir, author of *100 Funks que você tem que ouvir antes de morrer* (2013), have also written about this problem. So, too, have leading scholars of funk today like Adriana Facina and Carlos Palombini, co-authors of "O patrão e a padroeira: festas populares, criminalização e sobrevivências na Penha, Rio de Janeiro" (2016). Funk activists, like brothers MCs Leonardo and Júnior, themselves similarly decry the problem, , as is recounted in Adriana Lopes' *Funk-se quem quiser* (2011) (see, for instance, the preface by MC Leonardo, 13-17), and in Mariana Gomes Caetano's equally penetrating—and hotly debated—Master's thesis "My pussy é o poder: Representação feminina através do funk: Identidade, feminismo e indústria cultural" (2015). Together these sources offer useful historical perspectives on the development of funk carioca, as well.

Eventually, defenders of funk carioca would take the debate all the way to Rio's legislature, where they were finally successful in getting a law passed that recognized funk as one of the city's most significant cultural manifestations. The session was presided over by the well-known human rights advocate and Rio representative Marcelo Freixo, of the Partido Socialismo e Liberdade (PSOL). Other advocates who presented arguments in favor of funk included: anthropologist Hermano Vianna, the pioneer of studies of funk, anthropologist Adriana Facina, one of the most active funk scholars/activists today; famous Brazilian white pop/ MPB singer Fernanda Abreu; MC Leonardo, renowned Rocinha funk singer from the `s. With his brother, MC Júnior, Leonardo is co-founder of Apafunk (Associação Profissionais e Amigos do Funk), an organization that, besides defending funk, advocates for the rights of prison inmates and favela residents.[20] Despite such legal recognition, however, funk carioca continues to be the most controversial musical style in Brazil today.

Machine Gun Voices

My first contact with funk carioca occurred in 1990, during my initial period of residence in Rocinha, a favela that would eventually rise as one of the cradles of the style as it is known today. At the time, I was an undergraduate student from the US researching in Rocinha; my research was not about funk, per se, but the about views of residents of Rocinha on the favela's powerful drug gang and what they called the "law of the favela." I still remember the first time I ever heard funk, one night late

20 See especially *Funk-se quem quiser* (Lopes 2011, 68-74), "No dia em que o parlamento cantou..."

as the music and live singing came booming up the hillside to the tiny home at the top of the favela where I was renting a room. I was up on the roof that night talking with Bete, the daughter of the family with which I was living. Still in her early 2000s, Bete and her family was originally from the State of Pará, in Amazonia to the north. There leaning on an unfinished brick wall about waist-high, next to a clothesline hung with drying socks and underwear, she explained to me that the song was coming all the way from the Emoções Club at the bottom of the favela. Since the house in Rua Um, quite near the top, I couldn't believe the music was coming from so far away: it was so loud! Maybe the enormous granite rock face of the Morro Dois Irmãos was somehow funneling the sound our way, I thought.

Since I had only arrived in Brazil for the very first time months earlier, my Portuguese was still quite rough. Indeed, it was more 'Portuñol,' as people often jokingly call the mixture of Spanish and Portuguese. Bete did her best to help me understand the meaning of the song. Though I was grateful for her efforts, I remember that the playfully sexualized tone of the song struck me as woefully vulgar and the singing unpolished. The cheap eroticism of the song was especially apparent in the one verse I could easily make out by myself, a gleeful cry of "*...e a mulher abre as pernas*!" ("...and the woman opens her legs!"). Bete didn't seem phased by it at all. In fact, she told me that she originally had been planning to go to the dance party herself, but something had come up. When she told me that she'd go for sure the next week I had no desire to tag along and dropped the subject. That same year, a funk carioca song became a radio hit in Rio. "Feira de Acari," produced and mixed by funk great DJ Marlboro and sung by MC Batata, was based on the famous stolen goods market in Acari, on Rio's north side. Despite the fact it was one of the first-ever Brazilian funk songs sung in Portuguese, hearing the song did little to change my view. Though I found it mildly amusing, I incorrectly assumed "Feira de Acari" was merely a low-quality rip-off of hip-hop.[21]

With my limited initial contact with it that year, I had not yet understood funk carioca as constituting an important development in Brazilian music; even though it had already been playing an increasingly crucial role in the lives of poor young people over the previous decade or two. In truth, I somewhat loathed the music at first: funk carioca was cheap-sounding and superficial. It was not as 'authentic' as the Afro-Bahian Carnival music that was at the time emerging from the more explicitly consciousness-raising *afoxés* and *blocos-afro* like Filhos de Gandhy, Ilê Ayê and Olodum. As I returned to Rocinha several times—as a researcher, social activist, community educator and neighbor, eventually coming to live there for a total of over four years-over time I slowly gained an appreciation for the significance of the music in the lives of my young friends and neighbors. Eventually, funk carioca won me over as a fan: for the music and lyrics and for the utopian intensity of those colossal community dance parties in the streets of Rocinha.

In the mid-1990s, the style underwent its first major boom, suddenly rising to a previously unknown level of exposure in television and radio, not only within Rio, but throughout Brazil, and gaining a following that cut across social classes. Songs like MC Cidinho and Doca's "Rap da Felicidade," Leonardo and Júnior's "Rap das Armas," Willian and Duda's "Rap do Borel" and Claudinho and Buchecha's "Nosso Sonho"

21 Coincidently, around the time the song was becoming popular, I visited the Acari open-air stolen goods market with one of my professors from the Catholic university where I was studying, Rio's Pontifícia Universidade Católica (PUC-Rio). Father Henri Georges D'Aviau de Ternay, a Jesuit and professor of philosophy, was attached to the parish in the favela of Acari, where we went with another student one weekend to visit his parishioners and spend time with them.

were instantly ubiquitous on radio and TV all across Brazil. I also became interested in the social and political concerns evident in the music, especially the consciousness-raising aspects regarding issues such as racial and class discrimination. Many songs from those early days also dealt with the theme of putting an end to the violent clashes occurring in the city's funk dance halls that were occurring at the time outside of favelas (in the infamous *bailes de corredor*, names for the so-called 'death corridors' formed in such dance parties).

It was in the early 2000s that funk carioca entered into its second major boom, one in which the sub-genres putaria and proibidão became central. During the mid-1990s, despite the popularity of funk acts and the radio-friendly versions of some select songs, funk parties had been demonized in mainstream society to the point they were chased off from clubs and other venues of the formal city. This vilification coincided with an effort on the part of the legal authorities to quell the collective fighting in the death corridor-style bailes. As a result, the locus of funk culture moved from clubs in mostly low-income neighborhoods to the city's favelas, where the community street dances assumed central stage (Herschmann 2000, 87-123). Such a shift placed Brazilian gangster rap at the center of the parties, too, along with the favela drug traffickers who commonly sponsored them. In those days, proibidão and putaria—usually identified as separate subgenres of funk today—were conflated, often under the name *raps proibidos* ('forbidden raps'). Originally, this prohibited or forbidden style of funk arose as an underground expression, mostly from live performances at funk dances involving alternate versions of radio -friendly songs.[22] Recordings of these songs emerged from clandestine studios to be distributed in the informal economy of favelas on cassette tapes and CDs to celebrate the names and deeds of local drug traffickers.

My status in those years as an on-and-off resident of Rocinha placed me in a position to witness firsthand these developments in that first boom of consciousness-raising-style funk in the mid-1990s and then the rise of the proibidão-style gangster rap of the second explosion in the popularity of the community dances. In the summer of 1996, I began formally studying funk, as a Ph.D. student at the University of Wisconsin-Madison. As I delved more deeply into the subject over the years, in readings, lyrical and performance analyses and broader ethnography, two central questions emerged in my thinking.

The first was about how proibidão funk functioned as one of the principal arenas through which the power and legitimacy of Rio's favela drug gangs were produced and lived. I didn't see this process as merely a top-down ideological imposition by the drug traffickers upon the other residents. It struck me instead as a complex field of negotiations, in which residents also exerted a significant degree of influence upon their would-be leaders in the gangs, from the bottom-up.[23]

Beyond the issue of violence and crime, however, it seemed to me that an even more primordial theme of funk carioca was community—in the 'live' sense of a collective encounter. In this vein, the other primary question guiding my research was that of the Afro-Atlantic aesthetics of

22 For more on proibidão, see *Tamborzão* (Batista 2013) and Batista, "Da criminalização do funk," Facina and Palombini, "O patrão e a padroeira," Novaes, "Funk proibidão," Palombini, "Funk Carioca and Música Soul" and "Funk proibido," Russano, "Bota o fuzil pra cantar!" and Sneed, "Bandidos de Cristo."

23 Today's scholars of funk, such as Carlos Palombini, generally eschew the use of terms like *traficantes* ('drug traffickers'), as well as *bandido* and the slightly different English term, "bandit," even though local people often use them. Palombini himself prefers calling them *varejistas de substâncias ilícitas* ('retailers of illicit substances,' as he does in the Foreword to this work). Instead of updating the language of my text in this book to fit the more politically sensitive jargon the current decade, however, I have decided to leave it as it would have been during the time of my primary fieldwork, whenever possible.

funk carioca. It struck me as a powerfully utopian musical practice born of the remarkably fluid hybridity of the favelas and the politics of transformation characteristic of African Diaspora peoples. For me, more than any other context of funk carioca the outdoor spaces of the bailes de comunidade embodied the counter-cultural utopian tendencies of Black Atlantic cultural expressions.[24] This focus on utopia also made it possible for me to begin comparing and contrasting funk carioca with other utopian popular cultural forms in Brazil such as Carnival, *capoeira*, Brazilian hip-hop and even the country's more literary *modernismo*. I also wondered to what degree these two questions intersected. In other words, how did the negotiation of power in the favela in ideological terms relate to the Afro-Atlantic aesthetics of the music?

With such considerations in mind, in Chapter Two of this book, "Machine Gun Voices," I explain in greater depth the motives that led me to study funk in Rio in the first place and offer a bit of my personal history in the favela of Rocinha. I also offer a summary of trends in Brazilian music at the time of the golden age of proibidão funk in the community dances and discuss the emergence of that style in regards to those trends. In Chapter Three, "Writing about Funk Carioca," I discuss several of the major studies of funk that were influential on my fieldwork and comment on the methodological procedures I employed in carrying it out. In Chapter Four, "Proibidão and Rio's Gangs," I present my discussion of proibidão funk in the context of the aftermath of the murder of investigative journalist Tim Lopes in 2002 and the debates regarding the culture of drug trafficking. In particular, I attempt to bring the dis-

24 Of particular relevance to this view is Gilroy's treatment of music in *Black Atlantic: Modernity and Double-Consciousness* (Gilroy 1993, 72-110), especially chapter 3, "Jewels Brought from Bondage: Black Music and the Politics of Authenticity."

cussion on crime and security in Rio beyond the mostly economic focus of Alba Zaluar, a well-known specialist on crime in Rio, to open up consideration of the more cultural side of hegemony in that context.

Chapter Five, "Rocinha Favela," provides a brief social history of Rocinha and offers a reading of the baile funk in the streets of the favela as a staging of their power. With Chapter Six "Crimes of Self Defense," my goal is to consider in greater detail the specific ideological strategies evident in proibidão and the ways those strategies have served in the negotiation of an image of the drug traffickers of the favelas of Rio de Janeiro as "social bandits." In Chapter Seven, "Social Bandits in Funk," I discuss the portrayal of organized crime in funk in songs like "10 mandamentos da favela" ("10 Commandments of the Favela") as comparable to the notion of the social bandit developed by E. J. Hobsbawm. Chapter Eight, "Bandits of Christ," further explores the figure of the proibidão MC as a mediator of the culture of crime in Rio's favelas, between actual gangsters and their cartels and the everyday, non-gangster residents in and around favela community funk dances parties. I expand upon this in Chapter Nine, "Trafficking Culture," undertaking additional close readings of proibidão lyrics to analyze the ideological strategies of the drug gangs evident in them, according to ideological categories suggested by Terry Eagleton.

In the tenth chapter, "Musical Survival Tactics," I move from the question of violence and organized crime in funk and favelas to an exploration of its Afro-Atlantic aesthetic dimensions as a utopian cultural practice. In Chapter Eleven, "Utopias de Favela," I follow the straightforward analytic framework employed by cultural critic Richard Dyer in his influential article "Utopia and Entertainment." In the next chapter, "Mixes from the Margins," I examine the baile funk as an example of the utopian community practices of the cultures of the African Diaspora, analyzing it considering what Paul Gilroy has referred to as the "politics of transformation." I consider the tendency of funk carioca towards hybridity through the lens of Brazil's famous cultural cannibalism aesthetics and beyond, as well as comparing it to expressions of Carnival and hip-hop in Brazil. In the final chapter, "Last Dance," I reflect on the connections between the threads of violence, utopianism and community dealt within throughout the various chapters and contemplate the significance of funk in the context of the struggle for social justice in Afro-Atlantic culture today.

To bring this study of Brazilian funk full circle, from my original observations during the time of my original fieldwork to today, I have included an Afterword reflecting back upon that golden age of funk carioca in Rocinha from my point of view today. In the interval, much has changed in Rocinha, Rio de Janeiro and Brazil, not least of all funk itself and the academic scholarship on the subject. Despite changes in the music and Rio's favelas over time, however, the representation of the power of the drug traffickers that arose in the late 1990s and early 2000s in funk continues to be central to everyday life in communities like Rocinha. Similarly, the utopian dimensions of the live outdoor community street dances continue to attract a new generation of funk fans and artists and to offer them a mode of relational collective resistance. Looking back at that pivotal time now indeed offers relevant vistas into the ongoing crisis of social exclusion and violence persisting in Brazil to this day.

In 2003, when I first defended that early dissertation form of this study, I was reluctant to publish my findings in book form. I worried that a book titled *Machine Gun Voices* might contribute to the bad reputation of Rocinha and other much-maligned favelas in Rio and throughout Brazil. As the years have gone by, I have seen how the work is relevant not only as local case study of violence and community and for its broader implications for social justice in the context of the Afro-Atlantic world. From my point of view now, the utopian aspects of funk carioca point towards an even more profound, more primordial impulse at play in the live street funk parties rooted in our pan-human needs for relationship and attachment. In a sense, I see a progression in my own thinking from the two central concerns of my original work in the 2000s—in the culture of crime and the utopianism of funk—to a Community Studies perspective.

Viewing funk in this way seems especially important to me from my current vantage point living and working here in Korea, a country that is grappling with violence and dehumanizing polarization in its own right. Internally, recent years in Korea have seen the Candlelight Revolution and the ouster of President Park Geun-hye for corruption. Externally, the threat of nuclear war in the region looms larger than ever. In the face of such challenges, like in the case of Brazil and the favelas of Rio de Janeiro there is hope here in Korea, too. The 2018 Pyeongchang Winter Olympics attest to this, as efforts for cooperation and dialogue between the Koreas intensify.

In this light, I could say that, although the title of that original work has not changed its meaning for me has. At the very least it has expanded. The "machine gun voices" in question are not merely a defining feature in the soundscape of the often brutal reality of Rio's favelas or even echoes of the gangsters' gunfire, as such. For the favela residents, those machine guns and the sounds they make are their own, both as emblems of the difficulties they face in the conditions of their lives and as symbols of their determination to forge a community and protect it through their own travail. In the sense that funk carioca is part of something larger than Brazilian culture or even the Afro-Atlantic world, for me, those machine gun voices of funk are also a symbol of the universal suffering of human beings everywhere as we hold on together for the possibility of some more profound peace and coexistence.

2
Machine Gun Voices

My Brazil is a tropical country
The land of funk, the land of Carnival
My Rio de Janeiro is a postcard
But I'm going to talk about a national problem
– "The Firearms Rap," by MCs Leonardo and Júnior[1]

As I began recounting in Chapter 1, several motives led me to study Brazilian funk. The fact that I lived in Rocinha for some four to five years off and on since I first moved there in 1990—even maintaining a permanent residence there for much of that time—greatly impacted my interest in funk carioca. It helped that ever since my initial experience living in the community, as an undergraduate student doing an independent research project on organized crime, residents of the favela always made me feel at home.[2] As the years passed and my history and identity in the

1 Portuguese: "O meu Brasil é um país tropical, A terra do funk, a terra do carnaval, O meu Rio de Janeiro é um cartão postal, Mas eu vou falar de um problema nacional" ("Rap das armas"). All translations are mine unless otherwise noted.

2 I conducted that original research as an independent study under the direction of Herbert Braun of the University of Virginia in 1990. In addition to being my first chance to live in Rocinha, that research placed me in contact with one of the favela's neighbors' associations, the União Pró-Melhoramentos dos Moradores da Rocinha (UPMMR), and its president at the time, Seu Pereira (mentioned above). Aside from allowing me to observe and even participate in his daily activities at UPMMR, Seu Pereira also put me in contact with members of the drug gang. He even took me

neighborhood evolved, I formed deep personal ties to my friends and neighbors that profoundly shaped me as a young person. Afterwards, I returned for extended stays in Rocinha in 1992, 1995, 1996 (made possible by a grant from the Tinker Foundation) and 1998. In 2000, I was a graduate exchange student at PUC-Rio. The most intensive phase of my fieldwork took place from 2001-2003, a time in which I conducted the majority of my formal interviews and visited bailes. Starting in 2000, I maintained a home in Rocinha, where I stayed afterward, too, in 2004, 2006 and 2009, conducting follow-up research.

My connection to Rocinha grew even stronger through my involvement in co-founding and directing the Two Brothers Foundation with friends in the favela in 1998. In 1999, we registered 2bros, as we called it, in Madison, Wisconsin, in the US. We obtained a Tax Identification Number (TIN), opened a bank account and applied for 501(c)(3) status with the Internal Revenue Service (IRS). The following year, we officially founded the Brazilian arm of the organization, the Fundação Dois Irmãos. Shortly afterward, we switched our name to Instituto Dois Irmãos(i2i), for legal reasons. It was a binational, non-profit organization promoting education, community service and international exchange in Rocinha. Over the years, we purchased and refurbished a community center, offered hundreds of classes and supplementary educational programs and hosted a great many residential volunteers from around Brazil and across the globe until the organization's eventual end in 2016.

to meet with Rocinha drug traffickers at their main boca-de-fumo, as one calls the points of illicit drug sales in Brazil. In those days, that boca was the *quartel general*, ('command center') for Rocinha's crime boss, Eraldo (Erlado Souza da Silva), who was said to be one of the founders of the Comando Vermelho. For better or worse, I never managed to meet with the boss personally (see "Ex-chefe do tráfico na Rocinha é preso na Zona Oeste").

Through it all, I went from starry-eyed visitor to community activist and adopted Rocinha as something of a long-term home. Of course, I'm not making any claims to have authority as a native of the community. I'm not a native of Rocinha. But my status as resident did impact my research and this book. So, too, did my role as researcher, community activist and educator. Undoubtedly, my research also has been affected by the fact I am a US-born, middle-class, white male with a Ph.D. Hopefully, instead of radical objectivity the somewhat ambivalent perspectives I have developed have strengthened my analysis in some ways, even as it has undoubtedly presented certain limitations.

When friends from Rocinha and I decided to start up 2bros in 1998, I had never heard of action anthropology or action research. It was not a conscious strategy for achieving mutuality or a higher degree of dialogue in the research process. In fact, my dissertation advisor and my father in the US expressed great concern that my efforts with the NGO would hamstring my research. Even other researchers I was friends told me I couldn't do both activities well. Looking back now, I understand their concerns, since it certainly slowed things down quite a bit.

Quite by accident, however, it turned out that my deeper involvement in the community through the NGO informed my research, just as my research affected my work as community activist and educator. It positioned me in a much more relational posture regarding my neighbors in the favela and the various styles of music that were important there, starting with funk. Eventually, this broader level of interaction led me to formally research other spaces of community encounters in Rocinha, such as a local clubhouse of Alcoholics Anonymous, a *terreiro*, as one calls centers of the West African derived animist religion *candomblé*, a martial arts groups of the Afro-Brazilian style called capoeira and a Pentecostal church. Spending time in these spaces, sometimes as a researcher and others as a participant, not only gave me a more intimate level of contact, it allowed me to engage as a community member. It also allowed me to participate in roles in which I was not a teacher or leader but a learner and group member. This polyvalent posture went a long way to helping me overcome some of my earlier biases, not so much by any plan or design by me but through the residents around me who loved me, helped me and took me in.

In the years I lived in Rocinha, a sort of epicenter for the funk movement, my opinion about Rio's funk indeed evolved. As I recounted earlier, I was bemused at best in 1990 when I first heard the blatantly pornographic references of live funk songs ringing out in the neighborhood up to the roof of my first home in Rocinha. When, in 1995, my teenage friend Josivaldo gave me a cassette of Pipo's *A volta do homem mau*, with MCs Willian and Duda's famous "Rap do Borel (Rap da Liberdade)" on it, I remember finding that it sounded unprofessional and simplistic, as well as disappointingly 'un-Brazilian.' Throughout the years I spent in and around funk living in Rocinha, though, I grew to appreciate how significant that music was for so many young people, especially the funk dances in the streets and at the Emoções club at the bottom of the hill.

As time passed, I became steadily 'funkified,' to borrow a phrase from George Yúdice in his well-known pioneer study of funk in Rio.[3] When I began actively researching funk carioca, specifically, I was 28-years-old. That made me most definitely 'old' compared to the young people typically involved in funk culture, who tended to fall within the ten to twenty-something age group, but not ancient (as I would seem to them now). By the point of my most intense fieldwork in the late 1990s and early 2000s, I

3 Yúdice, "The Funkification of Rio," 173-217. This article was the first scholarly treatment of funk carioca in English.

had been enjoying funk for years, going to the dances and buying and listening to records at home. I also came to respect many MCs and DJs of funk, as well as dancers and composers, and to associate funk with a very genuine sense of community in Rocinha. I also came to realize that of all the musical practices that form the cultural landscape of favelas in Rio, funk was and continues to be one of two musical styles to most self-consciously embrace the social reality of Rio's poor as its origin and essence. Such music includes other less controversial styles popular there such as samba, pagode, forró, sertanejo and Evangelical music.[4] The other is Brazilian hip-hop, a fascinating and energetic musical culture that deserves much more attention than it will receive in this study.[5]

At the heart of funk, I came to believe, was a revolutionary affirmation of the strength and worth of folks in favelas and other poor people in Rio. Funk is not a banal form of anti-music nor an artless apology for crime, as some suggest. With all the inherent contradictions and incoherencies of postmodern youth culture movements, funk carioca constitutes an oppositional and transformational social reality. At its core is an affirmation of community, besides being an expression of the class and racial dissatisfaction of the residents of innumerous favelas and other poor neighborhoods in Rio or even gender dissatisfaction (as I shall explore in Chapter 8). In Brazilian society, where the Globo network and its ilk bombard the spaces of mass culture with a constant flow of texts and images that serve to reinforce colonial hierarchies of race, class and gender, it is indeed rare to find a counter-hegemonic or alternative cultural

4 For more on these styles, see Bocskay, "Undesired Presences: Samba, Improvisation, and Afro-politics," *O mistério do samba* (Vianna 1995), *Forró and Redemptive Regionalism from the Brazilian Northeast* (Draper 2010), and *Rivers of Tears: Country Music, Memory and Modernity in Brazil* (Dent 2009).

5 See *Ideologies of Marginality in Brazilian Hip-hop* (Pardue 2008).

movement as impacting as funk. With this in mind, it's worth remembering a statement made by Chuck D, of the pioneering hip-hop group Public Enemy, who famously called hip-hop the "CNN of black folks."[6] In the same way, one can say that Rio's funk is the Globo network of people from Rio's favelas—black, brown and otherwise.[7] As such, the style presents one of the most direct challenges to the authority of the consensus view of the dominant social order in Brazil today.

Furthermore, the persistent vilification of funk by the media throughout the years has aided in reinforcing an age-old Brazilian ideological basis for societal discrimination of the poor. As is evident in the quotes from the *New York Times* and the *Washington Post* in Chapter 1, it is rare to see mentions of funk in the media, Brazilian or otherwise, that are not double-edged at best. References are nearly always made to things such as 'corridor of death'-style gang fights, organized crime's recruitment of soldiers in the dances and violent gang slogans used as refrains of songs. This process of vilification is a symptom of the intense and extreme prejudice against favelas and their residents that has been prevalent throughout Brazil.[8]

6 In The *Harvard Dictionary of Music* (Rendal 2003) this quote is contextualized in a way highlighting the revolutionary significance of hip-hop as a platform for countercultural discourse, in a similar way appropriated by funk carioca. The passage reads, "In the late 1980s a large segment of rap became higly politicized, manifesting the most overt social agenda of any form of popular music since the 1960s urban folk movement. Coming to prominence with their second album, 1988's *It Takes a Nation of Millions to Hold Us Back*, Public Enemy embodied this aesthetic more than any other group. In an oft quoted phrase, lead singer Chuck D referred to rap as 'CNN for Black people.' Against the backdrop of conservative political programs that were decimating the inner city, rap functioned as a voice for the community without access to mainstream media. As such, it served to promote pride and self-help, communicating a sense of Black history as positive and fulfilling that was largely absent from any other American institution," in *The Harvard Dictionary of Music*, 4th ed. 2003, s.v. "rap."

7 The Rede Globo is Brazil's longstanding leading telecommunications network.

An anecdote will help illustrate the point. Before moving to Rocinha in 1990, I had been living in a wealthy home in a gated community in Rio's chic beachfront São Conrado neighborhood. When I told Dona Helga, the kindly, wealthy, white senior woman with whom I had been living that I was moving out of her home to live in Rocinha, she asked me why on Earth I would want to live in a favela. I couldn't move there, she assured me—I would undoubtedly be kidnapped, killed or worse. When I replied that I wanted to learn about the culture of the people in favelas she laughed. "Those people don't have culture!"

She had treated me well as a resident in her home, and I was grateful, but I had to agree to disagree, as they say. I'm glad to say that reactions like Dona Helga's have become less typical in the years since. In any event, that the term *favelado*, a pejorative one used in references to folks who live in favelas, has been constructed in Brazilian society as something of a second-class citizen is at once apparent, well documented and predictable, as is the disdainful and neglectful treatment of the poor more generally. It's important to recognize the vilification of favelas for the bearing it has on funk. Indeed, for me, one of the most compelling reasons to study and write about funk has been to work against the myriad forms of discrimination that everyday people are faced with, in Brazil and around the world.

Due to similarities between Brazilian funk and Brazilian hip-hop as

8 An eye-opening account of the severe living conditions many favelas in Brazil have faced, historically—in particular those in the northeastern region—is *Death without Weeping: The Violence of Everyday Life in Brazil* (Scheper-Hughes 1992). Other studies of Rio's favelas include Perlman's classic, *The Myth of Marginality: Urban Poverty and Politics in Rio de Janeiro* (Perlman 1976) and her more recent follow-up study, *Favela: Four Decades of Living on the Edge in Rio de Janeiro* (Perlman 2010). Also see *Samba* (Guillermoprieto 1990), *Laughter Out of Place* (Goldstein 2003), and *The Spectacular Favela* (Robb Larkins 2018). For a treatment of the favela of Rocinha within the panorama of favela communities around the world, see *Shadow Cities* (Neuwirth 2005).

black urban counter-cultural musical styles, the two styles are often studied together and talked about as if they were the same thing. One must bear in mind that, in truth, such is not the case.[9] In fact, the first people to say so will be adherents of the *nação* hip-hop (the 'hip-hop nation') in Brazil—largely based in São Paulo—which is much more self-consciously political than funk carioca. Many adherents of Brazilian hip-hop, and indeed others of the world hip-hop culture originating in the US, reject Rio's funk as hip-hop's ugly and illegitimate offspring. Brazilian hip-hop is perceived by them to be the musical arm of Brazil's *movimento negro*, ('Black Movement') and an empowering critique of the system from the periphery. Funk, on the other hand, is denounced as a sort of musical form of bread and circus, a new opiate of the masses glorifying hedonistic sex and violence.

On a related note, on April 22, 2001, at the Second Annual Hip-Hop Generation conference in Madison, Wisconsin, Vee Bravo (Virgilio Bravo), then editor-in-chief of the hip-hop magazine *Stress*, made some controversial comments to this effect. At the panel discussion on Latin American hip-hop, Vee Bravo showed clips from a film he was putting

9 The anthology *Abalando os anos 90: funk, hip-hop: globalização, violência e estilo cultural*, organized by Herschmann, and *O Funk e o Hip-Hop invadem a cena*, written entirely by Herschmann, are examples of the tendency to conflate funk and hip-hop styles in Brazil. Despite their merits in bringing together a wide range of critical perspectives about funk, neither genuinely treat the subject of Brazilian hip-hop to any significant degree. *Abalando os anos 90* does include two articles about American hip-hop artists, a style even further removed from funk than Brazilian hip-hop. Perhaps this is something of a marketing strategy, as there are, of course, connections between Brazilian funk and world hip-hop and the second term is much more universally recognizable. Nonetheless, it's important to state that funk and hip-hop in Brazil do constitute two separate aesthetic styles and cultural practices—despite their shared lineage as descendants of US hip-hop. Also see Lurie, "Funk and Hip-Hop Transculture," 2001, 643-659 and Béhague, "Afro-Brazilian Traditions," 2000, 272–287.

together on hip-hop in several Latin American countries (*Estilo Hip-hop*, with Loira Limbal). He praised hip-hop in Brazil for being the best in the world at the time, saying that it was coming together within a Brazilian reality comparable to the state of things in the South Bronx of the late 70's that had given rise to American hip-hop. Unfortunately, he went on to argue quite vehemently that funk in Brazil was 'inauthentic.'[10] Apparently, the fact that he only spent two weeks in Brazil and did not speak Portuguese had not been an obstacle for him in knowing enough about funk to condemn it in a public forum. His confidence in his assessment came largely from the fact that the 'pioneers' of Brazilian hip-hop, such as Mano Brown of São Paulo's Racionais MCs and MV Bill in Rio had told his translators that funk was 'bad.'[11]

While these hip-hop artists are widely recognized activists and consecrated spokespersons for racial and justice in Brazil, and social justice more generally, a newcomer and outside observer should not rush to present their conclusions out of context or without hearing from the other side. Such criticisms notwithstanding, in general, the rift between hip-hop and funk is quite small, at least on the funk side of things. For funkeiros, there is no animosity, nothing like the famous West Coast/East Coast

10 It seems one finds snobbery in the most unlikely places at times. This reminds me of a time when an American DJ working with funk music ridiculed my simple, tribal mermaid tattoo for being overly simplistic, showing off his full sleeve tattoos, ripe with images of funk and favelas. I fully expected some people would object my tattoo, but it had never crossed my mind someone with more expensive tattoos to criticize me like that. That just goes to show that even alternative cultures often take on the same competitiveness and hierarchical biases of the dominant, mainstream culture.

11 Though he was less than sympathetic towards funk carioca, at least Vee Bravo was right about Brazilian hip-hop at the time. Another writer around the same time, Mark Schwarz, made a claim in *The Vibe History of Hip-hop* (Schwartz 1999) that hip-hop in Brazil had experienced stunted growth in the shadow of samba, a gross misunderstanding by all counts ("Planet Rock: Hip-hop Supa National").

rivalry of American hip-hop. In fact, I have never heard any distaste for hip-hop expressed by fans of funk. On the contrary, to this day Brazilian hip-hop itself is widely cannibalized by funk, which samples its music freely and even borrows from its lyrics and dress styles. Indeed, large numbers of funkeiros who don't possess a single album of Brazilian hip-hop often wear Racionais MCs and other Brazilian hip-hop tee-shirts.

My objections to the wholesale rejection of funk in these terms do not change the fact that Brazilian hip-hop does reflect a much more self-consciously political impulse than does funk carioca, even in its more 'essentialist' understanding of racial identity and its tendency to construct Afro-Brazilian subjects explicitly in terms of Blackness. The culture of funk projects ethnicity in a more fluid, less polarized fashion much less explicitly foregrounded. That the two movements do not entirely converge into just one is further apparent in the process of vilification both have undergone. Brazilian hip-hop has undoubtedly received its share of bad press and found itself at the center of controversy. Still, any defamation of hip-hop in Brazil pales in comparison to that which has occurred in the case of funk from Rio.[12]

Nonetheless, while it is necessary to avoid lumping the two cultures into one, neither can they be completely separated. First and foremost, millions of everyday people participate in both cultural currents, both of which obviously speak to and about the experiences of poor folks in Brazil in the discursive struggle for symbolic terrain—and for Afro-Bra-

12 Brazilian hip-hop has been incredibly impacting in the formation of racial consciousness in Brazil. One outstanding documentary on this subject is *Entre a Luz e a Sombra* (2009). The film recounts the story of the hip-hop duo Dexter (Marcos Fernandes de Omena) and Afro-X (Cristian de Souza Augusto), who called themselves 509-E, in honor of their cell block in São Paulo's infamous and now defunct prison Carandiru.

zilians.[13] Questions of race and class are crucial to both forms and they are two of the principal cultural expressions of resistance of poor folks in Brazil, as I have stated. Both Brazilian funk and hip-hop are the legitimate offspring of the world hip-hop movement, two hybrid forms appropriated and practiced by poor folks in Brazil as two edges of a sword in the struggle of countercultural politics. In fact, the hybrid nature of American and world hip-hop in general, and its openness to appropriate elements of other styles and cultures is one of its most essential characteristics, as Paul Gilroy repeatedly observes (Gilroy 1993, 36).

Such hybridity is indeed one of the great strengths of practices of popular culture, as communications theorist John Fiske has noted:

> The theory of popular culture that underlies this essay derives from the tradition of cultural studies. This school of thought agrees with all the criticisms of industrial capitalism sketched above (i.e., *the commodification and massification of high art leading to a 'middle-brow' conformist culture, destroying both high and popular culture and therefore any authentic human sense from which to criticize capitalist society*) but disagrees with the claimed totality of their effectiveness. It accepts the accuracy of the diagnosis of the forces with which popular culture has to cope but rejects the assumption that people have no resources of their own from which to derive coping strategies, their own resistance and their own culture. Popular culture in industrial societies does exist, even though it may never be pure and authentic, for it is always made from cultural resources that are opposed to it, it is always contradictory and inscribed with traces of that to which it is opposed. It is always, then, a culture of struggle, a culture of making do rather than one of making.

13 See Adriana Facina and Adriana Carvalho Lopes, "Cidade do funk: Expressões da diáspora negra nas favelas cariocas."

> Popular culture is typically bound up with the products and technology of mass culture, but its creativity consists in ways of using these products and technologies, not in producing them (Fiske 1995, 325).[14]

This "making do," the hybrid nature of popular culture to borrow and expropriate elements from the ideologically ambiguous terrain of mass culture, is an element that lends power and creativity to subaltern communities. Therefore, instead of labeling either Brazilian funk or hip-hop as 'inauthentic,' cheap imitations of American culture, or praising one form over the other as the legitimate heir to world hip-hop, the hybridity of both styles should be viewed as essential dimensions of their oppositional natures.

Another significant consideration that led me to study the culture of funk Brazil is the urgency of what I view as the growing crisis of social exclusion and violence that has been unfolding in Rio de Janeiro and in Brazil more generally for many years now. There is a very genuine war taking place in Brazil, albeit somewhat 'postmodern' and undeclared, occurring mostly in the favelas and other poor neighborhoods of Brazil. In his highly influential study of what he saw as the increasing divide between social classes in Rio de Janeiro in the early 1990s, *Cidade partida*, Zuenir Ventura defines the nature of this postmodern war:

> Exclusion became the biggest social problem. As long as one only

14 He continues to say on page 331 that popular culture is always closely tied to mass culture, even though they are different. They exist in a constant dialectic in which mass culture appropriates, or incorporates, popular cultural artifacts for advertisement and other marketing purposes and people 'constantly scan' mass culture to expropriate, or 'excorporate,' some elements of it as resources for their own cultural purposes.

heard the sounds of samba from Rio's hillside favelas, there was no problem. But now one hears gunshots. It's not a question of a civil war, as one sometimes thinks, but rather a war that is postmodern and economic, one involving not just arts of war but also laws of the market; it's a type of commerce. That's why there's no magic solution in sight. We know we must destroy the "vanguards"—those who practice atrocities, the drug traffickers—with unstoppable force. Exterminating them, however, might prove easier than taking down the economic circuit that sustains them and whose driving forces—production and consumption—are not located in the favelas (Ventura 1994, i).[15]

In the most immediate sense, Ventura is referring to the economic channel of the production and consumption of cocaine and other drugs, a circuit which passes through the favelas of Rio de Janeiro as drugs come in from other countries and are distributed to users who are not mostly from the favelas themselves. By linking the notion of an unbalanced economic circuit to social exclusion, however, Ventura further suggests that the rise of the power of the drug traffickers in Rio's favelas itself is a symptom of the failings of the more extensive system of consumer capitalism in Brazil in general. That system that has served to crystallize and worsen the distance between the country's rich and poor.

15 "A exclusão se transformou no problema social maior. Enquanto dos morros só se ouviam os sons do samba parecia não haver problema. Mas agora se ouvem os tiros. Não se trata de uma guerra civil, como às vezes se pensa, mas de uma guerra pós-moderna, econômica, que depende das artes bélicas mas também das leis do Mercado; é um tipo de comércio. Por isso não há solução mágica à vista. Sabe-se que é preciso destruir as 'vanguardas'- os que praticam barbaridades, os traficantes de drogas- numa operação de força implacável. Exterminá-los, porém, talvez seja mais fácil do que desmontar o circuito econômico que os sustenta e cujas pontasa—produção e o consumo—não estão nas favelas."

Ventura's words appear in the preface of his study *Cidade partida*, written in 1994 after the massacre of 21 innocent residents of the favela of Vigário Geral by a group of off-duty police officers (in reprisal for the earlier slaying of four officers). The relevance of his observations only grows as the conflict between organized crime and the government has worsened since the writing of that book. After Tim Lopes' death in 2002, and the subsequent police crackdown on drug gangs, a chain of events unfolded in Rio that has marred the city with new forms of violence. The campaign of guerrilla tactics undertaken by organized crime brought the debate about violence and social exclusion to a new level of intensity in which the demonization of both the populations of favelas and funk music worsened. I see this book as a part of the debate about the violence and social exclusion taking place in Rio de Janeiro.[16]

At the close of the introductory chapter of this book, I explained some of the ways I understand the title of this book today, "Machine Gun Voices." Now is a good time to offer a bit more perspective on how it came to me originally, when I was writing my dissertation. I was listening to what has become a funk standard, "Rap das armas," quoted at the beginning of this chapter—a song that came out in the mid-1990s as a protest about the problem of violence in society and a disclaimer of the blame of favelas. Its lyrics form a rapid-fire poem listing the firearms often found in favelas, like Colt 45, Glock and Walther PP pistols, FMK-3 sub-machine guns, AR-15 semi-automatic rifles, M16s assault rifles, Uzi machine guns and so on.

16 A now classic account of the culture of police violence in Rio is the semi-fictionalized one of Soares, Batista and Pimentel, which gave rise to the highly controversial film of the same name. Its sequel, *Elite da tropa 2: O inimigo agora é outro* (2010), portrays the culture of the city's paramilitary *milícias* (vigilante groups made-up of off-duty police and firefighters) and their nefarious control of many favelas there. One of Soares' earlier works serving as a point of reference in the field of security studies in Rio is *Violência e política no Rio de Janeiro.*

Written by Leonardo and Júnior, well-known brothers from the Valão area at the bottom of Rocinha, the hit underwent a significant process of vilification by the media in the mid-1990s falsely connecting the duo to the drug underworld.[17] As a result, the Rio police constantly harassed the brothers as they came in and out of the favela, despite the fact that their song was never intended to promote the drug gangs and that their own older brother is a police officer in Rio's Polícia Militar ('military police'). This term is a carry-over from the days of Brazil's military regime, from 1964 to 1985, though their policing activities are by no means limited to military circles but rather include maintaining public order and combatting crime. The refrain, sung by old-school funk's most famous duo, MCs Cidinho (Sidney da Silva) and Doca (Marcos Paulo de Jesus Peizoto)—of the Cidade de Deus, is a series of syllables sung to imitate machine gun fire, "Pá parrá pá parrá pá parrá claque bum ..." It quickly became a cliché in funk and the practice of singing off lists of weapons was quickly adopted as a typical feature of proibidão funk music, as was that of sampling machine gun bursts and other gunshots and explosions in funk music.

Listening to the song one day, it struck me that the practice of

17 The article "Rap exalta lema do Comando Vermelho," by journalist Letícia Helena, is a good case in point. In the article, whose title translates as "Rap Exalts Slogan by the Red Commando," she claims that "... an apology of the Red Command is the hit of the moment. Using a slogan of the criminal organization as its refrain—'peace, justice and liberty'—MCs Leonardo and Júnior explode in the funk dance party scene with 'Rap of the Guns'... and the Red Command recruits under-age youths in the bailes funk using 'raps de galera' (galera means 'groups of friends')—known versions of the songs in which the lyrics, modified, exalt the crimes of the bandits." In Portuguese, "Uma apologia ao Comando Vermelho é o sucesso do momento. Usando como refrão o lema da organização criminosa—'paz, justiça e liberdade'—os MCs Júnior e Leonardo estouraram nos bailes... com o 'Rap das Armas'... o Comando Vermelho vem arregimentando menores nos bailes funk se valendo dos 'raps de galera—versões de música conhecidas nas quais as letras, modificadas, exaltam crimes e bandidos."

vocally and digitally imitating machine gun fire in funk lies at the core of the struggle in for power in Rio at an ideological level. As an image in mainstream media, gunfire often serves as an emblem of the 'violence' and 'barbarity' of the poor and the misery of their lives in favelas. By turning the gunfire into a voice of protest and solidarity, however, funk artists perform a densely suggestive semiotic inversion that subverts this dehumanizing association and opens possibilities for new meanings. Gunfire can be a lament of the conditions of life in favelas and their abandonment by mainstream society, it can be a roar glorifying the power of the favela and its drug lords or it can be an ominous war cry warning those of the status quo that there is a storm rising.

Furthermore, as a sign in dispute, it becomes recognizable differently according to the listener's particular social reality. The artistic representation of gunfire, self-consciously and ironically affirmed as emblematic of life in the favelas, may provoke sadness in some listeners and fans or make them indignant at the general lack of social justice in Rio. It may make others feel proud to be from powerful, respected neighborhoods and it may make still others even feel threatened and scared. Whatever the reaction of the individual listener may be, funk music has made the cadence of machine gun fire and the cult of arms almost as typical in its music as the thumping beats of hip-hop and techno have become to its rhythm. These musical gunshots have become as much a part of the landscape of funk as real bullets are to the reality of the favelas and other poor neighborhoods of the city. Whether guns are seen as a problem or as a solution is a matter of debate and interpretation. But by placing gunshots and other aspects of the violence in the lives of people in favelas to the forefront of artistic production, funk music serves to interrogate and denaturalize assumptions about the climate of violence in Rio de Janeiro. Ultimately, from the perspective of people living in Rio's favelas and other poor neighborhoods, there is something about the gunfire of funk that says "It may be sad and it may be harsh, but it's *ours*. We are making it ours." It becomes a gesture of forging a community. "This is our pain. It is our power. We are here, together. Society will not ignore us."[18]

Trends in Contemporary Brazilian Music

An enormous variety of musical styles have developed in Brazil over the past century, expressions which have been influenced by international music at the same time that often they have impacted it. There is the Afro-Brazilian samba music of Carnival, and the big band versions of samba in the thirties and forties which came about as samba was chosen to be the 'authentic' national music of Brazil (McCann 2004; Vianna 1995). Then there were the smooth sounds and poetic lyrics of bossa nova in the early 1960s by such greats as João Gilberto, Tom Jobim and lyricist Vinícius de Morais. During the period of the military dictatorship in Brazil in the 1960s and 1970s, the great music festivals produced a new generation of talented progressive performers who questioned the legitimacy of the regime. Caetano Veloso and Gilberto Gil introduced the eclectic and iconoclastic tropicália movement. Other MPB (Música Popular Brasileira, a sophisticated, diverse style that mixes elements of jazz and various other world currents with Brazilian folk music and styles like samba and bossa nova)

18 Samuel Araújo has systematically raised similar questions about the role of violence and conflict in Brazilian music, including proibidão. His work partnering the ethnomusicology laboratory of the Universidade Federal do Rio de Janeiro (LE-UFRJ) with the Musicultura project of a local, community-based non-profit (CEASM, or Centro de Estudos e Ações Solidárias da Maré) has been groundbreaking. For more on this "participatory," "horizontal" and "dialogical" approach, see Araújo "Conflict and Violence as Theoretical Tools" and "A violência como conceito na pesquisa musical."

artists such as Chico Buarque and Milton Nascimento blended social commentary with elements of Brazilian popular music and world musical currents.[19]

These developments in music came about in the context of the changes in the broader Brazilian socio-political landscape that were occurring during this period of the military dictatorship, changes which reflected the growing mobilization of local groups and minorities around particular causes and concerns. Within the Catholic Church, liberation theology's CEBs emerged—the *comunidades eclesiásticas de base* ('Christian base communities'). These were intimate bible study groups organized to apply the Gospel to social and political action. Neighbors' associations also emerged in favelas; both of these focused on local forms of advancement and fighting the marginalization of the poor. Also, women's groups were created and the Movimento Negro arose for the first time since the Frente Negra Brasileira ('Black Liberation Front') of the 1920s and 1930s. During this period, protest in music was extremely significant but tended to limit itself to criticism of the military regime. MPB itself became a primary platform for voicing opposition to the government and artists, such as Chico Buarque, Gilberto Gil, Caetano Veloso and Geraldo Vandré, were harassed, censured, forced into exile, sometimes being incarcerated and tortured for protesting against the regime.[20]

As the military regime adopted a less totalitarian stance in the late 1970s and early 1980s, the mobilization of minority and marginalized

19 An excellent overview of currents of protest in MPB is chapter four of *Seven Faces: Brazilian Poetry since Modernism* (Perrone 1996). Also see Perrone's path-breaking solo work, *Masters of Contemporary Song: MPB, 1965-1985* (Perrone 1989).

20 For more about this fertile period in Brazilian popular music and the trajectories of these artists, see Dunn, *Brutality Garden*. See, too, Stroud, *The Defence of Tradition in Brazilian Popular Music*.

groups gained momentum, continuing to bring the question of citizenship to the forefront of socio-political debate. By the time civilian rule was restored in 1986, the problematic of citizenship was exacerbated by a state of crisis which overtook Brazil: inflation soared, corruption was prevalent and a surge of violent crime pervaded urban centers. Throughout this conflictual period, discourses of resistance that had identified themselves in opposition to the military regime gave way to broader strategies which problematized racial inequality and the de facto lack of citizenship of various groups of marginalized people. Reflecting these changes in this period many forms of music gained popularity for which the question of citizenship was a central theme.[21]

Localized Brazilian hybrids of world currents like rock and punk continued to grow in Brasília, Rio de Janeiro and São Paulo, and bands like Legião Urbana and singer-songwriters like Cazuza gained wide audience. Legião, something of a cross between U2, The Smiths, REM and the Cure, is the all-time most popular Brazilian rock band, combining themes of everyday life with a quiet sense of spirituality and combative political commitment. Cazuza was a hugely successful pop rock singer who combined tremendous energy and pop sensibility with intelligent and socially conscious lyrics. Sadly, both Renato Russo, the lead singer of Legião Urbana, and Cazuza died of AIDS in the 1990's. Other Brazilian rock music groups flourished, too, like Os Paralamas do Sucesso and Engenheiros do Hawaii, both of which consistently lamented social inequalities and their disillusionment with society in their lyrics.[22]

21 For a more thorough overview of the tendencies of Brazilian music of the last few decades, see *Brazilian Popular Music and Globalization* (Perrone and Dunn 2001). A resource including more recent musical tendencies is *Brazilian Popular Music and Citizenship* (Avelar and Dunn 2011).

22 For concise, thorough information on the various musical styles of this period of the

Rio's movimento funk originated in the Black Pride soul music of Black-Rio, Black-Sampa and Black-Mineiro in the 1970s. It quickly moved away from the racial specificity of its earlier aesthetics, broadening the scope of its social criticism to the question of the marginalization of the popular classes. The older artists of the MPB generation such as Gilberto Gil and Caetano Veloso also took up the problem of racial and class-based inequalities to a higher degree than before, focusing on, among other things, police violence, street children and the overcrowding of prisons. Also during the 1980s and 1990s, citizenship related themes were often treated by interpreters of more traditional styles of Brazilian music as well, by artists such as the *pagodeiro* Bezerra da Silva of Rio de Janeiro, who performed a style of samba called pagode.[23]

Unquestionably, one of the most important new tendencies in Brazilian musical culture has been the rise of new black consciousness styles of Afro-Bahian music, and Brazilian music generally, a development that has had far reaching consequences throughout contemporary Brazil. It will be helpful to outline some of the significant stages in this process to raise questions about racial identity in funk later in this study. During the 1970s and 1980s, Brazilian musical culture underwent a process of re-Africanization as *afoxés* like Filhos de Gandhy and blocos-afro like Ilê Ayê and Olodum were formed and popularized in Bahia. In the late 19th century, some black Carnival associations were in existence, such

thawing of military rule, known in Portuguese as the *abertura* ('opening'), see *The Brazilian Sound* (McGowan and Pessanha 1998). See especially, in this context, their writing on MPB (75-102) and rock (185-202).

23 For one of the most in-depth explorations of samba in recent times, see Stephen A. Bocskay's doctoral thesis, "Voices of Samba: Music and the Brazilian Racial Imaginary, 1955-1988." For a concise perspective on the relationship between samba and Black consciousness on a global scale, see his article "Undesired Presences: Samba, Improvisation, and Afro-politics in 1970s Brazil."

as the Pândegos da África afoxé, a percussion and dance group which paraded through the streets during Carnival. These afoxés borrowed their rhythm and thematics from candomblé music, presenting in their Carnival parades secular representations of *orixá* deities.

By the turn of the century, such organizations were prohibited and it was not until 1949 that a new afoxé was founded, the Filhos de Gandhy.[24] The association did not attain widespread popularity, however, until the 1970s, and until that time Carnival celebrations in Salvador were characterized by other less explicitly Afro-Bahian forms, such as the *trio elétrico* ('electric trios'), as the trucks with live bands mounted on them are called.

In 1975, Gilberto Gil, a huge star of the tropicália movement and of MPB in general, became a member of the afoxé Filhos de Gandhy. After returning from self-imposed exile in England in 1972, Gil's musical expression took a major turn towards the question of his own African roots and identity as an Afro-Bahian. Since the 1970s, Gil has been involved in many Afro-Bahian cultural and musical projects. In the 1976 Carnival, he paraded with Filhos de Gandhy, revitalized in large measure by his own participation. In 1977 Gil participated in the International African Arts Festival in Lagos, Nigeria, as did several other Brazilian musicians, and thus was able to bring a broader Pan-African vision to the forum of Bahian music. Throughout the 1970s and 1980s dozens of afoxés, such as Olori and Oju-Obá, were organized across the city, bringing together thousands of participants from the city's mostly poor Black neighborhoods.

A wave of another kind of Carnival association in Bahia also arose in the 1970s. These organizations were *blocos afro* ('Afro-blocks'), large-scale

24 For a summary of Gilberto Gil's career, see David Hatfield Sparks, (1992) "Gilberto Gil: Praise Singer of the Gods," *Afro-Hispanic Review* 11, no. 1-3 : 70-75.

street Carnival associations, often functioning as non-profit community organizations. These did not have the same connections to candomblé as the afoxés and that based their rhythm on a loose mixture of samba and reggae. Also compared to the afoxés, the blocos afros expressed the theme of consciousness-raising and challenges to the dominant order in general much more openly. In 1974, the first bloco afro was founded, Ilê Aiyê. In addition to parading in Carnival as a bloco, and releasing albums as a smaller musical group, Ilê Aiyê undertook an educational mission which was to become characteristic of many of the blocos afros that followed. Charles Perrone describes this mission:

> The group researches and represents the culture of a different African nation each year. The directors of Ilê Aiyê consider their educational work as part of a general movement of Black advancement, while resisting affiliation with more militant political groups (Perrone 1992, 46).

Of the many blocos afro that came afterward, such as Ara Ketu, Malê-Debalê and Timbalada, the best known and most influential has been Olodum, founded in 1979. Of all the Afro-Bahian groups, Olodum has reached the largest audience, both in Brazil and internationally. A smaller group version of the Carnival bloco has toured the US and Europe, as well as backing internationally acclaimed singer-songwriter Paul Simon on his album *Rhythm of the Saints*. The music of Olodum, together with the Afro-centric educational mission it carries out through lectures and discussions in impoverished communities throughout Salvador and Brazil, are means to achieve the goal of citizenship. The mixture of international Pan-African musical and cultural influences with traditional Brazilian ones, its appeal as a universal call against oppression and its beauty and communal nature as an expression of popular art have provided Olodum with a powerful means to raise the consciousness of millions of people with its message of Black Pride.[25] Throughout the 1990s and into the new millennium, these tendencies to highlight racial and class identities and general frustration with the fruits of the restored democracy have occurred side by side with the increase of globalization and commercialization of popular culture in Brazil.[26]

Several important regional and commercial musical styles have also come to dominate the scene, such as axé, pagode, forró, and sertanejo. At the same time, the number of alternative Brazilian musical practices and localized hybrids of world music continued to increase, in large part as oppositional practices denouncing the racism, poverty and violence that characterize the country's social reality. In the 1990s, Sepultura, which began as a typical American and European style death metal group, steadily evolved into a more socially conscious and anti-racist Brazilian style, blending heavy metal with Afro-Brazilian and indigenous musical elements and sometimes singing in Portuguese.[27] In the northeastern city of Recife, Chico Science and his group Nação Zumbi, along with Fred Zero Quatro of Mundo Livre, S.A. and Mestre Ambrósio, popularized the eclectic and diverse sounds of the *movimento mangue*, or Manguebeat—or even mangue bit, as people sometimes call it.[28] A vital reggae scene emerged in São Luís do Maranhão and Salvador. In Rio,

25 For more on Olodum, see Armstrong, "Songs of Olodum," 177-191.

26 For a detailed history of the rise of Afro-Bahian music in the late 20th century, see *Samba* (Browning 1995).

27 Avelar, "Defeated Rallies, Mournful Anthems and the Origins of Brazilian Heavy Metal."

28 The bibliography on mangue is extensive. For starters, see Avelar, "Mangue Beat Music," *Maracatu Atômico* (Galinsky 2002), *Do frevo ao Manguebeat* (Teles 2000), Sneed, "Chico Science + 20" and "The Coexistentialism of Chico Science" and Murphy, "Self-Discovery in Brazilian Popular Music."

groups like Planet Hemp, O Rappa and Cidade Negra created socially-conscious eclectic music borrowing from everything from reggae to hip-hop, hard-core and rock. Bands from São Paulo followed suit, like Pavilhão 9 (named for the location of the infamous prison massacre at Carandiru) the port city of Santos' Charlie Brown Jr.

In the same climate of the afterglow of the dictatorship, the favelas and slums of Rio witnessed the rise of Brazilian funk and artists such as MC Galo and Catra. And in São Paulo, purist militant hip-hop groups like Racionais MCs, Xis and 509-E exploded in popularity with their rap music, often taken to mean *Revolução Através da Palavra* ('Revolution Through Words') the first letters of which spell R-A-P, in Portuguese.[29]

Although all of these socially-conscious post-dictatorship musical styles have been important in the ever-expanding landscape of Brazilian cultural activity, funk and hip-hop occupy a position of especially urgent relevance. Not only are they concerned with the plight of the poor, the victims of violence and racism, but they are also predominantly by and for people from the low-income social realities of favelas and other poor and working-class neighborhoods. It would be easy to over-emphasize the 'North vs. South' question and minimize the importance of class and racial nuances in the analysis of globalization in Brazilian music. But it is essential to bear in mind that in Brazilian musical practices, national identity is often a secondary concern for the poor and the identification with international musical styles based on racial and class affiliations usually weighs more heavily.

29 Besides Pardue's more exhaustive work mentioned above, see Lurie's article, "Funk and Hip-Hop Transculture." For more on Racionais MCs and 509-E specifically, see Rebelo, "509-E enquadra a sociedade" and Alexandre de Maio and DJ Fábio, "Edi Rock."

Despite the wealth of MPB, for instance, in the late 1990s and early 2000s, it was quite rare to hear Gilberto Gil, Chico Buarque or Milton Nascimento in the favelas of Rio. In fact, it was also unusual to hear much music from more contemporary, alternative artists such as Chico Science, Planet Hemp or Sepultura. In the context of favelas, even relatively mainstream groups with a social consciousness like Cidade Negra, from the Belford Roxo municipality of the Baixada Fluminense, and O Rappa, remained the domain of a minority of culturally progressive residents of the low-income neighborhoods and the majority of poor youths were not likely to buy their albums.

Such is not to say that poor people at the time were not involved in all musical styles in Brazil. For instance, despite the mass commercialization and co-optation of samba, the so-called national music of the country, during the golden age of funk carioca in the late 1990s and early 2000s the music of Carnival still carried to a degree some association with the popular classes—as it does today. Likewise, poor people in Brazil continue to be a diverse group today, having varied interests in a wide variety of musical styles in their country, from rock to reggae and classical choral music to what is one of the most common artistic practices in the popular classes, Contemporary Christian Music (CCM). Indeed, forró and pagode tend to be performed by and for a high number of poor people—not to mention styles like *tecnobrega*—a sort of mixture of electronic music, *lambada* and the old *brega* romantic ballads of Belém and the interior of Pará, in Amazonia. Like funk carioca, tecnobrega is almost entirely produced and enjoyed by people from low-income communities. Still, funk and hip-hop are perhaps the two musical styles that most self-consciously embrace the reality of the daily lives of poor people in Brazil as their very essence.

As noted earlier this chapter, funk carioca and Brazil's hip-hop *na-*

cional (or 'national' hip-hop, as it is often called, as opposed to international varieties such as hip-hop from the US) have evolved as largely separate musical practices, despite somewhat common musical and social roots. Hip-hop in Brazil tends to be a somewhat somber and militant movement of social protest and personal responsibility and is prevalent mostly throughout the periphery of São Paulo. The much smaller hip-hop scene that does exist in Rio tends to follow the more intellectual and cultural lead of Marcelo D2, vocalist of Planet Hemp.

The principal Carioca hip-hop artist who has recorded in the Paulista-style is MV Bill, from the favela/projects called the 'Cidade de Deus' (the same as the neighborhood in the famous film, *Cidade de Deus*). MV Bill (Alex Pereira Barbosa), along with his collaborator Celso Athayde, is one of the most fascinating and vital countercultural figures in the Afro-Brazilian scene today. He has to his credit a variety of non-fiction books about social exclusion and violence, a highly acclaimed documentary film and persistent work with his favela-based non-profit, Central Única das Favelas (CUFA), which works to offer opportunities for young people in favelas and other low-income communities across Brazil. The MV of his artistic name stands for the *Mensageiro da Verdade*, or Messenger of Truth. In his hip-hop craft, he has combined the militancy of Paulista hip-hop with the social context of the drug traffickers of Rio.[30]

MV Bill notwithstanding, by contrast with the Paulista style hip-hop, Rio's funk carioca tends to be more playful, sensual and aggressive. Occasionally, funk singers have been known to rap—one of the defining features of hip-hop, of course—and like its cousin funk music is based upon an electronic blend of base beats, sound effects and samples.[31] Still,

30 See *Falcão: Meninos do Tráfico* (Bill, Athayde and Soares, 2006). *Cabeça de Porco* (Bill, Athayde and Soares 2005) and the film *Falcão: Meninos do Tráfico* (2006).

where the Paulista hip-hop initially tended towards the minimalist beats of old-school West Coast gangsta rap, funk initially borrowed beats from very early Afrika Bambaata tracks, Miami bass and even techno. Rapping in fact is quite rare in the raw, throaty yelling typical of funk vocal delivery, and instead vocalists almost always sing songs, whether in imitation of current pop hits, samba and forró melodies or even the call and response chants heard at Brazilian soccer games. The difference between the Brazilian hip-hop and funk carioca is significant enough that generally members of the Brazilian hip-hop nation, along with most Brazilians in general, see funk as violent, pornographic, commercial and lacking in 'consciousness.' In fact, in light of the visceral reaction funk often produces in many intelligent people across class lines who have no problem with hip-hop, one sometimes wonders if funk is in some ways, in fact, more threatening to the dominant social order than Brazilian hip-hop.[32]

31 As mentioned in chapter one, Caceres, Ferrari and Palombini have explored the evolution of the musical characteristics of funk carioca and the way these changes connected historically to developments in Brazilian politics and society ("A era Lula/tamborzão").

32 For more on contemporary Brazilian music, especially funk carioca and hip-hop, please see "Afterword."

3

Writing about Funk Carioca

Imagine when you get that rush that hits you, that big feeling. It's like you're in another place, another world.

—Paulo[1]

In the simplest terms, by posing the world as it is against the world as the racially subordinated would like it to be, this musical culture supplies a great deal of courage required to go on living in the present.

—Paul Gilroy[2]

Early Studies of Brazilian Funk

While I present many of my comments regarding scholarship on funk in the context of my specific arguments throughout this study, it is worth briefly commenting at this time on some of the central tendencies that have characterized such research. Despite the significance of funk in Brazil, even today only a relatively small body of academic work addresses it, although most studies of topics like violence and citizenship

1 In Goldenberg's 1994 documentary *Funk Rio*, favela youth Paulo describes the feeling at the climax of the infamous weekly Brazilian funk dance parties of those days as mass gang fights erupted, saying "Imagina a hora que bate um daqueles pancadão, aquela emoção grande. A gente tá em outro lugar, em outro mundo." (18:50-19:00).

2 In this passage of his seminal study of the African Diaspora, *The Black Atlantic: Modernity and Double-Consciousness* (Gilroy 1993, 36), He discusses American hip-hop, the close cousin of Rio's funk music.

in Rio nowadays do include references to funk.[3] Early research on funk carioca was carried out from a content-analysis perspective that included field visits to bailes funk, written surveys of fans and interviews with key artists and industry personalities. Such approaches from the pioneers provided keen insights into the aesthetic and cultural tendencies of funk carioca, alongside its ideological and sociological features. With a few notable exceptions, however, such studies did not reflect a deeper appreciation and understanding of the world of funk carioca in the sense of a more comprehensive, up-close understanding of the realities of daily life in the favelas. In contrast, such distance between research and practice was less apparent at that time in the case of work done on American hip-hop, for example.[4]

By the time of those early studies of funk carioca, research on other aspects of popular music in Brazil, including the musical cultures of favelas, had already been conducted in very intimate ways that give more voice to the everyday people. One example that directly inspired my early research is Alma Guillermoprieto's *Samba*, a straightforward almost conversational piece written as an ethnographic study of the favela of Mangueira and its culture of Carnival.[5] Barbara Browning,

3 Since my initial research from the mid-1990s through the mid-2000s, many more researchers have studies funk. While I have made an effort to include their findings in this study, I have decided to limit the majority of explicit comments on them to the introductory remarks in Chapters 1 and 2 and the Foreword by Carlos Palombini.

4 For examples, see *Spectacular Vernaculars: Hip-Hop and the Politics of Postmodernism* (Potter 1995) and *Black Noise: Popular Music and Black Culture in Contemporary America* (Rose 1994).

5 In 1989, Alma Guillermoprieto spent a year living in the favela of Mangueira, accompanying the yearlong preparations for Carnival of the Mangueira samba school. Her intricate book is a window into the everyday life of people in favelas, from the evangelical movement to Afro-Brazilian religions, violence and the personalities of people in the favela. It was after reading her book as an exchange student in Rio in 1990 that I made the decision to move to Rocinha for the first time.

too, conducted her research on Afro-Brazilian popular culture of such forms as samba, capoeira and the religion candomblé, from a highly participatory approach. Unfortunately, early scholarship about Brazilian funk was not typically carried out through such bottom-up strategies but rather tended to treat it somewhat paternalistically, as if it were a simplistic and massified pseudo-musical form inaccessible to middle-class, White researchers (Brazilian or otherwise).

The tradition of scholarship specifically on funk in Brazil began with Hermano Vianna's 1988 book *O mundo funk carioca*. It was an anthropological study focusing upon the infamous *corredor da morte*, or corridor of death, a practice occurring in bailes funk involving physical confrontations between large groups of young men from different neighborhoods (like those portrayed in the documentary *Funk Rio*, referenced in Chapter 1 and at the top of this chapter). Although most of the participants of such events were unarmed, gruesome injuries and even deaths sometimes resulted.[6]

His study also provides a useful history of funk up to its year of publication. Vianna, who was a Master's student in anthropology at the Museu Nacional in Rio at the time of his research, was a pioneer in the study of contemporary popular culture in Brazil who was able to recognize the significance of funk for Rio's poor from quite early on. He attended dozens of baile funk dance parties and distributed survey forms to the fans present. Also, he spent a great deal of time with DJ Marlboro (Fernando Luiz Mattos da Matta), a pivotal figure in the history of funk.

6 By the time of my days of fieldwork in the mid-1990s and early 2000s, such practices had mostly disappeared in funk culture as bailes moved from clubs in the formal areas of Rio to the favelas, where criminal factions strictly prohibited them in the community dances they sponsored.

Since most funk songs at the time of his study were in English and proibidão had not yet appeared, Vianna did not address this 'gangsta funk' or the usage of funk musical culture by drug traffickers in Rio's favelas. Since Vianna's methodology did not include focus on everyday life or less conspicuous people in the funk community, he was not able to immerse himself into the conditions of their lives outside of funk dances or interview funkeiros in their favela homes or in other poor neighborhoods from which they came. Perhaps his starting suppositions held him back a bit, in this sense. However laudable in other ways, his effort to be 'respectful' may have served to distance him somewhat from the subject. In his work, he assumes the posture that as a white middle-class observer of funk it would have been ridiculous for him to try to become a funkeiro or even dance at a baile.

As a result, Vianna offered some precipitous conclusions, like: "Ethnic identity? The ideas of Black consciousness-raising that circulated in the funk world of Rio in the days of the group Black Rio no longer remain" (Vianna 1988, 105). He went on to explain that the dances were popular: "... precisely because they are ephemeral, because in them nothing is produced, everything is pure expenditure." In the next paragraph Vianna asserts that: "In the bailes, no social norms are contested. There is no inversion of roles or values, as is said in the case of Carnival."[7] Additionally, the fact that all the songs played at the bailes at the time of Vianna's research were early hip-hop and techno in English, and therefore mostly unintelligible to the Brazilian funkeiros, led Vianna to conclude

7 In this quote, on page 106, Vianna is comparing funk to the analysis of the culture of Carnival in Roberto da Matta's article "Carnaval como Rito de Passagem." Da Matta also put forth his argument about role and value inversions in *Carnavais, malandros e heróis: Para uma sociologia do dilema brasileiro*, 157-186.

that there were no unifying articulable social concerns present in the movement which might serve as an ideological subtext—views he would resoundingly recant in his later scholarship and social activism, as one of the leading figures in the movement to recognize funk carioca.[8]

Another pioneer scholar of funk who explored connections between funk music and violence was George Yúdice, the first scholar to publish on the subject in English. In his provocative thought piece, *The Funkification of Rio*, published in 1994 and dedicated to Hermano Vianna, Yúdice argued that the rise of Rio's funk culture was indicative of a growing displacement of national identity and affirmations of local citizenship in subgenres of Brazilian music.[9] Although Yúdice's wrote his work before the widespread usage of funk lyrics in Portuguese, the connections he made between the dissatisfaction of the favela youths at the time and the popularity of funk remain relevant today. In the article, Yúdice attempted to establish a connection between the culture of funk music and the famous *arrastões*—the large-scale looting rampages that occurred along the beaches and beachfront neighborhoods of Rio's Zona Sul in October 1992.

Throughout his piece, Yúdice asserted that funk represented the rejection by the poor of the status quo vision of racial democracy and social harmony in Brazil. He argued that prior forms of Afro-Brazilian popular culture and musical expressions, such as samba, capoeira and *umbanda* (an offshoot of candomblé heavily mixed with Catholicism and Kardecist Spiritism), had been co-opted by the dominant system and therefore no longer provide means for the expression of discontent. Accordingly, he

8 See *Funk-se quem quiser: no batidão negro da cidade carioca* (Lopes 2011, 67-150). For some of Vianna's later thought on funk, see "O funk como símbolo da violência carioca" and *Galeras cariocas* (Vianna 2003).

9 Yúdice. "The Funkification of Rio," 197.

stated, funkeiros completely rejected these other forms along with the ideology that had co-opted them. Such a collective rejection of the status quo ideology by of the funkeiros came to a head in the riotous *arrastão* attacks of 1992, he argued, in which swarms of poor youths fought along the beaches of Rio's Zona Zul and robbed bystanders:

> The arrastão, however, made it patently clear that the allegiance to funk implied opting out of other musics, particularly those identified with Brazilian nationalism, or, more locally, cultural citizenship in Rio de Janeiro (Yúdice 1994, 203).

Of course, such a claim is complicated since it is difficult to prove the arrastões were directly related to funk. In any case, I would agree with Yúdice's intuition, even though the youths involved did not take the form of an official protest, nor did the young people who participated in them articulate a call for any specific demands for governmental change. To me, the arrastões provide a good example of James Scott now classic formulation of what he labeled as "everyday forms of resistance."[10]

In any event, by focusing on media events and the previous scholarship of Vianna, Yúdice perhaps exaggerated somewhat his point that the lyrics of

10 Here I am referring to *Weapons of the Weak: Everyday Forms of Peasant Resistance* (Scott 1985) and the broader notion of "political" that he embraces against the tendency to focus "…on just the kinds of movements with which social scientists in the West were most familiar—those with names, banners, tables of organization, and formal leadership" (xv). Scott argues, quite convincingly, that such a perspective ignores the majority of real political activity, which is more subtle, stating that, "Most forms of peasant resistance stop well short of outright defiance. Here I have in mind the ordinary weapons of relatively powerless groups: foot dragging, dissimulation, desertion, false compliance, pilfering, feigned ignorance, slander, arson, sabotage and so on" (xvi). Scott expands these arguments in *Domination and the Arts of Resistance: Hidden Transcripts.*

funk songs were still all in English and that it was in total opposition with other forms of nationalistic popular culture in Brazil. In fact, by 1994 a whole new movement had taken place within funk in which Portuguese lyrics had come to dominate the scene. Additionally, fans of funk by and large never wholly rejected other 'co-opted' forms like samba and capoeira but continued to actively engage in the spectrum of popular cultural practices existing in the favelas of Rio. Some interesting collaborative projects were carried out between many of the most famous MCs and sambistas, for example. Despite the problem of his distance from the culture of funk carioca, however, the strength of Yúdice's article is his fundamental observation that funk came together as a significantly countercultural space and practice.

The most comprehensive early treatment of funk was Micael Herschmann's work on the subject, whether as editor of the anthology, *Abalando os anos 90: funk e hip-hop: globalização, violência e estilo cultural*, or in his book, *O funk e o hip-hop invadem a cena*. Despite the presence of hip-hop in both titles, these works treat hip-hop only sparingly, dedicating much more space to the analysis of funk carioca. The former contains a wide range of articles, including Vianna's "O Movimento Funk" and a Portuguese translation of Yúdice's article. It also contains an article by Hershmann that would serve as the basis for his second book. The two articles related to hip-hop, one by Olívia Gomes da Cunha and the other by Tricia Rose (the ground-breaking US scholar whose work helped hip-hop gain acceptance as a field of scholarly study), are more concerned with hip-hop in the US. Livio Sansone's article on Bahian funk is an interesting comparison of a separate style of music also called funk, from the Northeastern city of Salvador, with funk from Rio.[11]

Herschmann's second work, the single-authored *O funk e o hip-hop invadem a cena*, was primarily a communications study of the process of the vilification of funk in Brazilian media sources. It included some interesting interviews with industry personalities such as funk mogul Rômulo Costa, of Furacão 2000, and DJ Marlboro. Herschmann also visited a variety of bailes in different neighborhoods across Rio and described his observations of these dances. Even so, Herschmann's book did not often directly engage texts of funk that did not come from newspaper articles such as lyrics of songs or testimonies of funkeiros. Despite the apparent distance between Herschman and the practice of funk at the street level, however, he did come to view it in a sympathetic light:

> One can affirm that Brazil, in the 1990s, witnessed the appearance of a new type of rhymed poetry, more spoken than sung, that has since influenced and been influenced by other musical rhythms. A form of music that mixes the live with the pre-recorded, the 'new' with classic base beats, lyrics and songs, clearly constituting a sort of 'intertextual artifact.' Its singers are a mixture of storytellers and chroniclers of the 'hard reality of the streets': the content of the music sometimes is an outcry and others is romantic or even playful. Besides this, the lyrics are a sort of business card for the MCs and their 'communities.' In general, besides introducing themselves at the end of their songs, these singer/songwriters give homage to their home neighborhoods, transforming them into a central theme (or secondary one) of their raps. This type of procedure seems to indicate a clear desire for recognition, for the re-inscription of their friends, of their 'world' in the city (Herschman 2000, 163).[12]

11 Tricia Rose, "Um estilo que ninguém segura: Política, estilo e cidade pós-industrial no hip-hop" and Livio Sansone, "Funk baiano:Uma versão local de um fenômeno global?" Also, see his book chapter "The Localization of Global Funk in Bahia and in Rio."

12 "Pode-se afirmar que o Brasil, nos anos 90, assistiu ao aparecimento de um novo tipo de poesia rimada, mais falada do que cantada, que vem influenciando e é influenciada por outros ritmos musicais. Uma música que mescla o ao vivo e o gravado, o 'novo' a bases, letras e músicas já consagradas, constituindo-se claramente em

Herschman's observation is a concise and intelligent summary of the underlying themes of funk aesthetics. He is correct in identifying the tendency of funk MCs to pay homage to their neighborhoods, what he calls a type of *cartão de visita* ('business card') as a significant feature in the discursive struggle underlying funk.[13]

Another thorough and well-written, relatively early history of the rise and evolution of funk in Rio was that of journalist Silvio Essinger, *Batidão: Uma história do funk*, which came out shortly after the period of my own intensive research about funk carioca, in 2005. His account provided one of the first treatments in Portuguese of the underground proibidão, gangsta-style of funk carioca. In Chapter 11 of his book, "Rap das armas," Essinger traced the history of proibidão from its beginnings in the mid-1990s within the context of the rise of Rio's drug cartels and their presence in the city's favelas. Essinger emphasized the point of view that proibidão was more of a representation of the real-life world of Rio's favelas than an apology of crime, quoting several primary proibidão MCs to that effect. Essinger's treatment of proibidão came as a serious, poignant exploration of violence and funk more generally, although it was not within his more journalistic purpose to consider the ideological dimensions of proibidão and drug trafficking more closely—or the more intimate daily lives of the funkeiros in their favela communities.

uma espécie de 'artefato intertextual'. Seus cantores são um misto de contadores de histórias e cronistas do 'cotidiano maldito': o conteúdo das músicas traz ora um discurso de 'denúncia', ora um tom romântico ou brincalhão. Além disso, as próprias letras são uma espécie de cartão de visita dos MCs e de sua 'comunidade'. Em geral, além de se apresentarem no final das músicas, esses cantores/compositores prestam também homenagem a seus locais de origem, transformando-os em tema central (ou secundário) do rap. Este tipo de procedimento parece indicar um claro desejo de reconhecimento, de reinscrição de seus amigos, de seu 'mundo' na cidade", 163.

13 I briefly commented upon this 'favela list' theme in Chapter 1.

Perhaps the most satisfying early treatment of the political dimensions of the practice of funk carioca, in my opinion, appeared in Zuenir Ventura's widely regarded book *Cidade partida*, mentioned above and published in 1994—even though funk is not the primary topic but rather figures as part of its background. As a means of underscoring his argument that there was an ever-widening gap between rich and poor in Rio de Janeiro at that time (and one that arguably continues in ways to grow to the present day), Ventura contrasted middle-class impressions of funk with a very different image revealed by funkeiros. He portrays segments of the funk world of 1993 as being possessed of, contrary to its reputation, a highly developed sense of political self-consciousness.

His analysis took place in the wake of the massacre that occurred in the favela of Vigário Geral in August 1993, when a number of police officers randomly shot 21 residents to death. In his frequent trips to that favela, Ventura often spoke with composers and singers of the local funk scene. These funkeiros were explicitly aligned to and active in grass-roots youth and social organizations and recognized their music as a means to educate and uplift the working class youth and to curb violence. He quoted one female funk singer as saying expressly, "We don't like the political parties, but we know that we are political even when we are not." Another singer, from the group As Damas do Rap, told him that her music was, "... a protest against everything that's wrong in the country and sometimes even what's wrong in the world: corruption, political abuse, war and violence."[14]

With *Cidade partida*, Ventura went to great pains to show funk composers as an essential part of the alternative intellectual community of the working class, one in close contact with educators and social activists from the favelas. Instead of merely visiting some dances and talking to a few funkeiros, he studied the socio-political context of the massacres of street kids at Candelária and residents of Vigário Geral. He spent considerable time among them talking and getting to know them and was thus able to capture some of the significance of funk as a cultural practice within the conditions of Rio's poor communities in his analysis.

Notes on Methodology

One of the reasons I have included the above summary of early research on funk carioca is to shed light on my own thinking at the time regarding how I could add new perspectives to the subject. I hoped to build upon them by conducting more comprehensive ethnographic research—in the vein of ethnomusicology—an opportunity afforded me by the happenstance of my living and working in Rocinha, a favela rising fast as one of funk's most significant epicenters. As I mentioned in my introductory remarks in Chapter 1, I also came to see my role as a long-term resident and community educator/activist as holding potential to yield more intimate glimpses into funk from angles as yet less frequently explored, in the vein of action anthropology or action research more generally. Likewise, regarding my then latent community studies orientation, such an approach already seemed promising to me as a way to consider funk less as 'content' and more as 'presence' in nexus of relationships between everyday people.

Along with these accidentally dormant aspects of my work, I in-

14 "Não gostamos dos partidos, mas sabemos que somos políticos até quando não somos [...] sua temática é de protesto contra tudo o que ocorre de errado no país e às vezes no mundo: corrupção, desmandos políticos, guerra e violência", 60.

tuitively steered towards what I later came to identify as a performance studies perspective. This approach was helpful, too, since along the way it allowed me to consider issues of community and life power in the favela in several parallel contexts to the bailes de comunidade, such as meetings of Alcoholics Anonymous, circles of the Afro-Brazilian marital art/dance/game capoeira, candomblé sessions, worship services at Pentecostal churches and classes at our own neighborhood community center, at the Instituto Dois Irmãos ('Two Brothers Foundation').[15] Though most of my research and participation in such spheres remains far in the background of the analyses presented here, seeing funk side by side with other community spaces did help me look beyond textual aspects of funk in lyrics, surveys or interviews. Ultimately, this was helpful for me to appreciate the baile funk in the light of more primordial meetings—with performance dimensions. This performance-based view of funk carioca within the time-space of live bailes funk, opened numerous possibilities for considering funk from the 'bottom-up' and in a corporal, psychological and even physiological sense, as I shall address in the next section.[16]

Early on, my chief research interest was in attempting to identify some of the ideological features of the culture of Rio's funk as a counter-

15 These community spaces were Grupo Leão XIII do Alcólicos Anônimos (Leo XIII Group of Alcoholics Anomymous), the Grupo Abadá-Capoeira da Rocinha (led by Professor Taturana, Renato de Souza), the candomblé terreiro of Pai Almir (Almir Gomes, *pai-de-santo*, or priest, of the *orixá* Xangô) and the Igreja Metodista Wesleyana da Rocinha ("Wesleyan Methodist Church of Rocinha") and PizzaLit (owned by Sérgio Soares de Almeida).

16 Today, I see this in the light of Performance Studies of the self-conscious variety, such as those espoused by Richard Schechner (see "Performance Studies: The Broad Spectrum Approach," 7-9) and Victor Turner (see "Liminality and Communitas," 89-97). In the Brazilian context, specifically, the question of performativity has been explored by Albuquerque and Bishop-Sanchez, *Performing Brazil: Essays on Culture, Identity and Performing Arts* (Albuquerque and Bishop-Sanchez 2015). See particularly Bishop-Sanchez's "On the (Im)possibility of Performing Brazil," 15-38.

cultural practice interacting with the different status quo orders in Brazil. I did not wish to seem overly optimistic about the ability of funk to immediately improve the political situation of poor people in Rio de Janeiro. Still, I did see it as a largely counter-hegemonic struggle against the conditions of social injustice and inequality in the city and an active attempt to interrogate existing notions of class, race and gender in Brazil. Similarly, in attempting to explore the complexities of the culture of drug trafficking in Rio's favelas, I did not wish to seem romantic as to either their actual intentions or their power to improve the lives of the residents of poor communities. Nor did I want to overemphasize their importance in either favelas or funk.

At the time of my years of residence in Rocinha, the question of organized crime was without a doubt one of the most relevant issues facing Brazilian society—as it is today. I hoped that my analysis of proibidão-style funk as the primary medium expression of their power might contribute to the debate surrounding the place of drug traffickers in Brazilian society. As part of this, one aim in particular was to point to the role of everyday, non-criminal residents in shaping expectations about the favela's gangsters and their duties vis-à-vis their communities. Even so, I knew the world of funk carioca and the favelas in which it had grown was infinitely most significant than mere questions about drug traffickers or even the broader crisis of violence and social exclusion in Rio. Over time, I began to hope my work could offer some glimpses beyond this issue, one so omnipresent in both media representations about the poor in Brazil and the reality of the streets, into some more universal aspects of the culture and creativity of residents of favelas and their abilities to forge instances of community.

The tradition of cultural studies offered an ample array of conceptual frameworks through which to begin conducting a nuanced survey of funk carioca. Like many other branches of scholarship at that time, it operated from a broad understanding of politics that moved beyond overtly political organizations, such as parties, governments and unions, to include the practice of everyday life and its semantic context. That field owed much to the legacy of Antonio Gramsci's notion of 'cultural hegemony,' which made it possible to analyze the relationships between dominant and subordinate groups in society in relevant ways. (Germino 1990, 26; 213; 256-257).

In this vein, the ideas of Raymond Williams were essential for me in my attempt to grasp the nuances of this ideological interaction, helping me to explore the ideological dominance of elites over subordinate groups while paying attention to the influence of oppositional cultural practices upon the hegemonic process as well (Williams 1977, 108-112). Although the hegemonic process included the ability of the dominant national discourse to co-opt popular cultural forms of protest, it also allowed room for subaltern voices to shape things from below and even force changes in the prevailing order.

Additionally, semiotics-based analyses pointed at ways for me to move away from interpretations based on the intentions of the MCs, DJs and other industry figures of Rio's funk towards an understanding of the role of the audience in the process of communication, as everyday people. Dick Hebdige, in his study of youth subcultures, pointed to the applicability of semiotics to the study of oppositional popular culture, writing that:

> Style in subculture is, then, pregnant with significance. Its transformations go "against nature," interrupting the process of "normalization." As such, they are gestures, movements towards a speech which offends the "silent majority," which challenge the principle of unity and cohesion, which

> contradicts the myth of consensus. Our task becomes, like Barthes, to discern the hidden messages inscribed in code on the glossy surface of style to trace them out as "maps of meaning" which obscurely re-present the very contradictions they are designed to conceal (Hebdige 1993, 367).

An example of this sort of "hidden message" is the semiotic inversion of the term 'machine gun' occurring throughout funk—discussed in Chapters 1 and 2—in which a pejorative meaning as a sign of barbaric, violent criminality is replaced and transformed into one of solidarity, consciousness and power.

Another attractive aspect of cultural studies for that early phase of my research was the full range of disciplines and strategies it encompassed, particularly those which contributed to strengthening the sort of bottom-up approach I wanted to pursue. Ultimately, I came to realize, funk carioca only exists as an encounter, not as a series of isolated 'texts' and songs. To begin making sense of it from an analytic perspective requires paying attention to the perspectives of its diverse actors. In other words, though MCs, DJs, composers, producers, dancers and other industry insiders are vital to funk so are countless more everyday folks of all ages and sorts. In many ways, people's understanding of their own culture *is* the significance of their practices, not some 'objective' significance ascribed to them by an observer like me. Of course, I do not disregard close readings of song lyrics or analyses of bailes funk. In fact, I try my hand at a good bit of both, as is evident in the following chapters. It did mean, however, that I hoped to carry out these readings in a manner that contextualized them to the most considerable extent possible within the culture of the favela and the perspectives of everyday people.

Putting my methodological preferences into practice was not easy for me, nor was it particularly smooth. Despite the fact that before beginning my research I had already spent some years living and working in Rocinha, the prospect of carrying out actual ethnographic fieldwork posed some unique challenges. Throughout the time I had spent living there, I had come to know a considerable number of people and had been listening to funk quite extensively, buying CDs and going to the various dances around the neighborhood. As a result, although I had a pretty good idea about how things worked in Rocinha at an intuitive level, and with funk and gangsters, I needed to take a step back and gain a more critical perspective. Even though I had done short stints of formal and informal research in Rocinha in 1990, 1992, 1995 and 1996—prior to becoming involved with our Two Brothers Foundation and the Instituto Dois Irmãos in 1998-2000—I had always managed to keep as low a profile as possible and had shied away from recording formal interviews.

To carry out my more intentional, formal research from 2001-2003, I decided it would be necessary to make something of a fresh start and to conduct research as anybody else coming to the community for the first time would. Besides reading a great deal of new material, this also meant that I would conduct more intentional research practices such as recording interviews, taking field notes on bailes and the dealings of drug traffickers, as well as carefully transcribing the lyrics of songs. I confess at first it was a little embarrassing for me to ask people—especially those I knew—to let me interview them, and to switch roles from neighbor and community educator/activist to researcher. I think this embarrassment stemmed from the way this new part highlighted underlying differences in social class and nationality between other residents of Rocinha and me, as a middle-class, White American researcher. I didn't want to jeopardize my status as an 'adopted son' of the community and be viewed as an outsider, nor did I wish to be seen as an informant or a threat of any kind to the drug gangs. Despite my hesitation, however, the response of people in Rocinha to my research was extraordinarily favorable and, in a short time, I became excited by the possibility to interact with them in this new way.

I conducted a new set of interviews about funk carioca in Rocinha, choosing as subjects a somewhat representative selection of people connected in some ways to funk. Of course, I did interview MCs, composers and DJs, as well as a professional dancer, a bouncer and the owner of the Emoções Club—people who I see as more closely related to the production and performance side of funk. I attempted to focus even more, though, on the everyday people involved in funk like the ones who attended funk dances, bought funk albums and listened to funk songs. Often, members of this second group did not define themselves as funkeiros per se, but living in Rocinha in of itself gave them ample pertinent experience.

One of the most revealing interviews was of three ten- and eleven-year-old boys who had never bought a funk album or intentionally gone to a dance. Their exposure to funk was unintentional because they had all walked through various bailes funk in the streets of Rocinha, coming home from church events or birthday parties and the like. Likewise, the boys had continuously been in contact with funk music as it boomed from the windows of neighbors' houses in the tight confines of the alleyways in which they lived. Even though these boys perhaps were not funkeiros, as such, they did have a deep, personal level of experience with funk, as well as the distinction knowing the words to almost all of the songs that were hits at the time. In fact, they had even written some of their own funk song lyrics.

Other interviews, like that of a teenage girl from the state of Ceará in the Northeast, went to funk dances almost every week, not out of any particular fondness for funk, but because they were the favorite places to go on certain nights. The majority of people I interviewed were from fourteen to twenty-four, both male and female, and people who actively identified themselves as fans of funk. I also recorded conversations with two middle-class women—one nineteen and one twenty-one, from outside of Rocinha—who had both gone to dozens of dances and had been in romantic relationships with drug traffickers. My intimate connection to people in Rocinha also enabled me to talk extensively with some gang members from the Comando Vermelho and other independent criminals who acted outside of the favela, though I never did this as formal interviews or recorded the conversations (at least not when talking about their criminal activities).

Since I had been attending nighttime festivities in Rocinha for some years, it was easy enough in September of 2001 to begin actively taking field notes after musical events. Before this, in 1996, I had started going to bailes funk, pagodes and forró venues with my friend Charlys, who later became a somewhat famous singer in Brazil known as 'Charlys da Rocinha,' and his younger brother Alan. Both were very well-known and well-liked people on the social scene in Rocinha and they introduced me to a great many good people. At that time, a young MC named Moreno, who sold bootleg recordings at the foot of the favela, also helped me considerably with his knowledge of the history of funk music.

Once I began to work with Two Brothers in 1998, I became even more active on the Rocinha community scene, particularly with the group of students and volunteers that grew up around the organization. For eight or nine months in the 2000, my office was in the back room of the PizzaLit restaurant. This restaurant was—and continues to be—one of the busiest, favorite places to eat and drink beer in Rocinha and remains open until five or six in the morning every day. Working out of the pizza place put me in regular contact with many of the more socially, politically and culturally active members of the community that frequented the pizzeria, as well as with all sorts of other community members.

During the years 2001, 2002 and 2003, I attended every baile I could, both bailes for adults and the *matinês*, as the kids' dances are called. Besides the baile in the Via Ápia described at the outset of Chapter 1, I visited a great variety of bailes funks in Rocinha on different occasions, in different locations, and on different days of the week. On Sunday afternoons, there was a matinê dance specifically for children and teenagers at Emoções Club at the foot of Rocinha, along the Estrada da Gávea. No alcohol was served at that baile but in most other respects it was identical to other bailes at the club for adults. Later that evening, Emoções hosted a much larger, traditional baile funk, put on by the Curtissom Rio sound team. Even though artists such as Galo, Dollores, Cacau, and Fornalha performed at the matinê at Emoções, often singing the same sort of gangster funk songs they sang at adult dances—with lyrics making reference to a favela's drug traffickers—no armed gangsters actually attended the party, Indeed, it was one of the few that the favela gangsters did not pay for. On Saturdays there was a large baile in the old dance hall of Rocinha's samba school Acadêmicos da Rocinha, on the Rua Um at the top of the favela, put on by DJ Marlboro's sound team, Bix Mix.

Most of the other bailes taking place in Rocinha were considered bailes de comunidade, or community dances, which tended to be paid for and attended by heavily armed drug traffickers. On Fridays, there was a smaller baile in the Valão area of the favela, along the open sewage channel that ran along its main street. Often on Saturdays and holidays there were the sorts of huge dances described above in the Via Ápia, one of the busiest commercial streets in the favela. Other dances came and went around the community, such as the baile put on by the mini sound team A Criatura in the soccer quadra of Cachopa, about halfway up the hill, or another matinê in Rua Dois. Occasionally there were large dances featuring contests between sound teams in the garage of the Amigos

Unidos bus company along the Curva do S that entail competitions among sound teams like Escorpião, Pipo's, Furacão 2000, and Curtissom Rio. Each of these bailes had its own unique personality, setting and loyal funkeiros. Often even the same baile was different in its vibe from week to week and in terms of the folks in attendance.

Outside Rocinha, I also attended the famous baile at Castelo das Pedras, an enormous dance club in Jacarepaguá known for its loud, elaborate and somewhat middle-class baile. It was not my practice to take notes at the dances; I usually waited until later that morning or the next day; instead, I danced and socialized with friends. I sometimes did seek out people I wanted to interview and make contacts. Additionally, the composer and DJ Renato Moreno, a friend of mine for many years who wrote some of the earliest funk hits (especially some of the first hits of his friends and frequent collaborators, MCs Leonardo and Júnior). I spent a great deal of time talking with him in his CD store about the funk industry and he was even kind enough to have me as a live studio guest on his forró radio show.

In addition to attending events billed as bailes funk, I also attempted to go to other musical and cultural events in Rocinha as a means of further contextualizing the place of funk within the community. I went to the street pagode on Rua Um, on Sunday nights at the top of the hill (also a hot spot with the gang members who sponsored it), and forró dances at the Varandão and Cabaré do Barata, as well as numerous late night cookouts and birthday parties across the neighborhood. I went to some special events, like the Talento da Rocinha party at Emoções, the O Rappa concert fundraiser for the Casa da Cultura da Rocinha, and a similar concert on Christmas day 2001 in the Cidade de Deus, featuring hip-hop legend MV Bill, Áfro-Reggae do Vigário Geral, Gabriel o Pensador, Fernanda Abreu and Caetano Veloso. I went to the Via Sacra on Good Friday three years in a row and other community theater performances, practices of the samba school and its parade at Carnival at the Sambódromo.

Additionally, I attended a new type of event had become popular in Rocinha at that time, one that reflected the interconnectedness of musical cultures in Rio's favelas. At these parties, there was a higher price at the door, and a person could drink—and sometimes eat—all they wanted for the rest of the night. Several different musical styles put in an appearance, typically rock, pop, funk, hip-hop and pagode. The first in Rocinha was called '100% Bagunça,' something that perhaps translates as '100% Mess,' or '100% Craziness.' Other parties followed, with names like VIP Nites and Na Gandaia (*gandaia* translates roughly as 'partying' in English, with the sense of indulging in physical pleasures considered immoral).[17]

In March of 2003, I mentioned to three friends in Rocinha that I regularly went to dances with (Alan, Orlando and Vitor), that I would pay them to help me transcribe the lyrics of the underground proibidão-style songs only available on pirated tapes and CDs. Though all three were very excited to help with the project and refused payment, Orlando, in particular, got interested and began helping me. I gave up paying him after he declined my offer several times during the days we worked together. He insisted on doing the work for free to help out with the project, for which I am deeply grateful. We ended up spending countless hours together carefully going over the often hard-to-understand words

17 Once, in December of 2001, I attended such an event put on in a relatively small and immensely crowded soccer court halfway up the hill in the favela. The street above the court had been blocked off and right in the middle of it was a long table of beautifully catered food for the gangsters. As the night went on and the party became even more crowded, the heavily armed drug traffickers began drifting in, smiling and shaking hands as they picked at the food. My friends and I were asked to move away from the area, where we had been leaning on a car talking. At most of these events, such interactions were typical and members of the drug gangs were almost always present, out in force and showing off their weapons, cash, romantic partners and general prestige and popularity, as will be discussed in detail in Chapters 4 and 5.

of the bootleg recordings, writing them down in notebooks or typing them into my laptop. Orlando also helped me select songs and took many of the CDs to his home in the Cachopa area of Rocinha, where he typed them in by himself on his own computer. Working with him was invaluable, as I realized there were still plenty of references and slang expressions in proibidão that I did not know or understand, even after living in the favela and having made it a point to ask the people I had interviewed for explanations about slang.

Hopefully, my closeness to the subject has not obscured my views on funk but has instead allowed me to understand funk more intimately. I hope that the conclusions and observations in the remainder of this study may at least suggest some unique perspectives in the work of placing drug traffickers, favelas and funk in Rio de Janeiro in a nuanced cultural context.

Asphalt versus Community

As I mentioned above, a crucial lens through which I have viewed funk carioca, especially in the street parties, is relationality, a view that has been greatly shaped by the metaphor of 'asphalt versus community' common in everyday parlance in Rio's favelas—and which is especially near and dear to the lyrics of funk songs. The distinction low-income people make between the formal city as 'asphalt' and the informal favela as 'community' has its roots in the fact that until the final few decades of the twentieth century, most favelas in Rio didn't have many of the paved roads of the officially planned areas of the city. Some favelas still do not, especially newer ones—not to mention favelas in other, less affluent cities across Brazil.

In the face of spatial hierarchies dating back to the earliest colonial times in Latin America, to characterize favelas as 'community' and to demote the formal city to a barren 'asphalt' is a gesture that works to turn traditional values of Rio's social geographies upside down. Places in Rio like Leblon, Ipanema, Copacabana, Jardim Botânico and Barra da Tijuca, conventionally referred to as *bairros nobres* ('noble neighborhoods'), are no longer the areas of greatest humanity or culture in the city. Now, it is the favela that offers 'community' as a stronghold against the cold indifference of our mass society, especially in a context of discrimination in Rio. The favela becomes the quintessentially human landscape—with all the music, creativity, faith, friendship, hard work and intelligence of its residents.[18]

The more I've thought about the asphalt versus community metaphor over the years, the more I've become convinced there is something to it on other levels besides social geography. For openers, one can see asphalt as a form of writing. In this sense, we can say that the power relations of the city, in all its components, are written in asphalt. From a cultural studies perspective, we can think of the city thus as less of a mere map and more a full-blown literary text—or performance. The 'narrative' the asphalt writes is one about the ebbs and flow of people connected to the city in different ways, according to their social status. Written this way, in asphalt, cement, bricks, steel, wood and glass, the city tells a 'story' of the workings of power regarding class, race and gender, among other things. This asphalt-writing is not merely descriptive of power relations but also serves to produce and reinforce them. The stretches of asphalt

18 The asphalt versus community metaphor often appears in song lyrics, as well, with either favela or *morro* ('hill') standing in for 'community.' It appears not just in Rio funk but also in other musical styles associated with favelas, especially pagode and other forms of samba (see Bezerra da Silva's politically charged "Desabafo do Juarez da Boca do Mato," as just one example).

throughout the city grow up as an intricate, ever-expanding network of flat walls dividing people up into haves and have-nots. In such a way, the pavement should be seen as just as much a feature of public power as jails, psychiatric wards, police stations and legislative assemblies.

Aesthetically and philosophically, I suspect that the 'asphalt' side of the equation is also more closely connected to Whiteness, Brazil's European legacy and Western rationalist thinking. The 'community' side, it occurs to me, is more indicative of the Afro-Atlantic world—as well as other alternative cultural contexts in which rationalism is less rooted, such as those throughout the pre-modern world (and even many other forms of non-rationalist Western thought). In this sense, being somewhat off the grid in more organic spaces like favelas offers a buffer against the full blast of the colonial legacy. In terms of the 'public' versus 'hidden' split, the less formalized nature of the favela gives it a certain degree of privacy to carry on life more humanely, allowing the favela to be a sort of hideout from the hegemonic, at least partially. As such, the division also points toward tensions in thinking about such things as time-space, being, consciousness, knowledge and power. It reminds me of similar dichotomies referenced in other Brazilian youth cultures of the day, like the *sistema* ('system') versus *periferia* ('periphery') split common in Brazilian hip-hop or the *cidade* ('city') versus *mangue* ('mangrove swamp') trope so central to Recife's Manguebeat music scene of the mid-1990s. It also makes me think of the division of types of knowledge in Portuguese into the more object-centered *saber* and the more relational *conhecer*.

Some years ago now, I came across a point of reference that would profoundly impact my perspective regarding the epistemological and ontological dimensions of the asphalt versus community metaphor. This influence was the work of Martin Buber, the twentieth-century Austrian-born, Jewish-Israeli philosopher and theologian often considered the pioneer figure of relational philosophy, or the philosophy of dialogue. It was because of his ideas that I came to see funk dance parties as 'encounters' in the way I have been using throughout this book—albeit as collective ones, as opposed to his notion of one-on-one meetings.Crucially, Buber's thinking helped me move from the questions of utopia throughout the chapters of this book to questions of community, more generally. Still, in the more collectivist context of Afro-Atlantic cultural expressions like street gangster funk dance parties in Rio's favelas, I have come to see the need to expand on the use of singular pronouns in his famous "I and Thou" formulation to pluralize both sides as "We and You All." Before I explain the significance of the move from meetings of two to larger gatherings, let me lay out the nuts and bolts of some of his central ideas.

Buber's thinking was based around a unique understanding of 'encounter,' or what he called *Begegnung*, in the original German. Encounter, for him, is a situation, an event, in which relationship occurs. According to Buber, human nature was twofold, having twofold attitudes with which we regard the world around other people and us. The first, which he characterized as the way of 'I-It,' was experiential. He did not employ the term experiential in the sense we often do as something one 'undergoes' but rather more literally as that which is measurable by experiments or through solid contact with observable facts of events. The other attitude to which Buber pointed, which he named 'I-Thou' (often translated as 'I-You') was relational.[19] Relationship, for him, was not just the ways parts fit together, organizationally, but being together with one another in the present, in an encounter.[20] Only with this attitude and the encounter did we truly live, he claimed—in perhaps his most often quoted passage—

19 As recently as Early Modern English, 'thou' was used as the most intimate form of the second person singular pronoun, typically rendered as 'you' today.

writing, "All real living is meeting" (Buber 2010, 11).

Though Buber recognized the I-It posture as critical to human endeavors, it was for him incomplete. Such a mode was never of our "full being," as such, and therefore not one he considered as bringing about "real living." He believed that in our contemporary world the first attitude had grievously overshadowed the second. The society we had built up around the I-It, he warned, had made it nearly impossible for us to engage in genuine dialogue or to "enter into relation" and into the "realm of the spirit" (Buber 2010, 39). As a result, we were left to skim the surface, constantly going somewhere other than the living moment of present, driven by intentionality and a will to control. But when we turn to one another as persons in the encounter, Buber proclaimed, we do so with the fullness of our being. Somewhat as with the Daoist concept of *wu wei* ('non-action' or 'non-doing'), there was no aim in this, no purposefulness, idol or will to control. Such an encounter permitted us to pass through the surface, in grace, diving into a deeper reality beyond space and time. He wrote, "The world of *It* is set in the context of space and time. The world of *Thou* is not set in the context of either of these" (Buber 2010, 100).

Because the encounter, for Buber, occurred apart from experience, the person involved did not receive any object or thing that could be known, as such. Knowing, instead, came through a transformational revelation of life, in the relationship of the 'I' with another. It was transubstantial. Buber wrote, "Man receives, and he receives not a specific 'content' but a Presence, a Presence as power" (Buber 2010, 110). That pow-

20 In his introduction to Buber's *I and Thou*, Ronald Gregor Smith preferred to emphasize "organizational" in his characterization of Buber's I-It instead of "experiential" (Smith 2010, vii). While such a term would fit well with my concern for social space and power, I believe Buber's original emphasis on experience is better suited to the broader range of analytical categories I am pointing to here.

er received in presence was life as coexistence, not merely in the sense of tolerating or of one living peacefully side by side with others but rather as 'life with,' in the collective existence of relationality, community, fellowship and love.

One of the most intriguing aspects of Buber's thought for me is that it applies not only to the way we regard other people as persons but also the world around us. This broader view includes encounters with non-human animals, trees and even mere heaps of stones (Hodes 1972, 42). For Buber, each I-Thou relationship opened up a window giving a tiny glimpse of the ultimate 'Thou' of God. Buber stated that God could only be addressed as 'Thou' and never as 'It' (Hodes 1972, 75). In this way, the life of dialogue Buber proclaimed went beyond the realm of human affairs or what we traditionally take for 'interpersonal' to embrace interconnected relationality with everything around us. Profoundly influenced by Buber's contact with the mysticism of Hasidic Judaism, his thinking is often compared with Eastern religious and philosophical traditions, especially Zen Buddhism and Daoism.[21] Martin Buber's writings are rich and complex—and numerous. I do not consider myself a particularly thorough student of his thought. Not from any comprehensive point of view, anyway. I do often find myself reflecting on his ideas, though, especially from his seminal work, *I and Thou*, from which I've drawn all my quotes in this essay.[22]

Since the latter half of the twentieth century, psychologists have explored in depth the affinities between Buber's thinking, attachment

21 Maurice Friedman, author of *Martin Buber: The Life of Dialogue* (1955), among many other works on Buber—and perhaps the all-time greatest Buber scholar—wrote extensively about Buber's interest in Daoism. See "Martin Buber and Asia," from 1976, in which he discusses Buber's lengthy essay "The Teaching of the Tao" (1911).

22 The work was first published in German in 1923, as *Ich und Du*, and in English in 1937.

theory and what they call "attachment-oriented therapy" (Flores 2004, 307-310). In the context of the "communal encounter," the terms of attachment theory take on a special relevance for the sorts of concerns about shared spatiality and temporality that have been so central to this book. In a sense, we can think of communal encounters as examples of "limbic space"—or even "limbic realism." Here, as in previous chapters, I use the word limbic in the sense that it is used by Lewis, Amini and Lannon. They relate it to our neurological make-up as organisms that have evolved with needs of affect and community as physiologically essential as our needs for food, water, sleep and shelter (Flores 2004). Those professors of biological psychiatry classify three types of interpersonal limbic activities, all of which hold important implications for collective encounters: *limbic resonance*, *limbic regulation* and *limbic revision*. Limbic resonance, for them, is "... a symphony of mutual exchange and internal adaption by which two mammals become attuned to each other's inner states" (Flores 2004, 63). Limbic regulation is the "mutually synchronizing exchange" through which mammals adjust and fortify one another's "fragile neural rhythms" (Flores 2004, 85).

Limbic revision is "revising the code that directs emotional life" (Flores 2004, 176). It is the way that mammals help each other restore the microanatomy of one another's brains, especially in the presence of trauma and emotional disorders (See 169-182 for a detailed discussion of all three categories). Psychologist Philip Flores explains the efficacy of limbic revision for group therapy, especially in the context of addiction recovery in groups like Alcoholics Anonymous and Narcotics Anonymous (Flores 2004). By extension, it's also an interesting perspective from which to consider the sorts of resistance and resilience of musical and religious group gatherings such as those familiar throughout the Afro-Atlantic world, historically and today, as moments of refuge and healing.

Thinking about Buber's relational philosophy in the collective context of the asphalt versus community metaphor—and funk carioca dance parties in the streets of favelas—brings questions of spatiality and temporality to the forefront, in these limbic terms. For his I and Thou encounter, it is all about the infinite and eternal moment, outside of space and time. Even so, there is a kernel of spatiality present in Buber's thought. Audrey Hodes, one of the best-known scholars of his thinking, explains the meeting as 'the sphere of the between,' writing:

> When a human being turns to another as another, as a particular and specific person to be addressed, and tries to communicate with him through language or silence, something takes place between them which is not found elsewhere in nature. Buber called this meeting between men the sphere of the between (Hodes 1972, 72).

It's not such a huge step, perhaps, to move from 'sphere' to 'space,' in this sense, or to 'space-time.' Indeed, Dan Avnon, another accomplished Buber scholar in his own right, makes the point, "... the reality of 'space' that is between persons is the focus of Buber's philosophy" (Avnon 1998, 5).

For our purposes here, when an encounter is between members of a group, the spatial and temporal aspect becomes more crucial—in the 'in between' and the 'limbic reality' that forms among people. There *is* a shape to such a group encounter, not in the absolute terms of content but rather in the presence of those joining together. Furthermore, just as Victor Turner claimed regarding his notions of *communitas* and *liminality*, a communal encounter is paradoxically both in and out of space and time (Turner 2007, 90). The "liveness" of a baile funk as a gathering happening in a here and now moment, in this sense, is vital. Yet, as a communal encounter of 'We and You all,' it reaches beyond space-time into the infinite and eternal, like Buber's one-on-one encounters.

When we view the epistemological and ontological dimensions of the asphalt versus community division, along with its spatial contours and time signature, it lines up with Buber's I-It versus I-Thou in intriguing ways. This is especially so when we set it as the singular I-It versus the pluralized 'Us and Y'all' (or 'We and You All') The ontological and existential aspects of the asphalt versus community metaphor become even more apparent when we add in a fundamental issue of space that all too often gets left out in much Western thinking: the present time. Space, as is now commonly accepted, is inseparable from time. It is as space-time. The asphalt versus community metaphor drives this point home in a way that challenges Western notions of space and time by emphasizing synchronicity and the present over the linear passage of time from past to future, diachronically.

If we think of the mode of the asphalt as 'experience' and that of community as 'encounter,' in this shared sense, we can derive a series of fundamental philosophical tensions between these two modal poles:

Asfalto versus Comunidade

Mode	Content-Based	Presence-Based
Space-Time	Object-Centered	Person-Centered
Consciousness	Individual	Collective
Knowledge	Acquisitional	Relational
Being	Existence	Coexistence
Power	Control	Love

Regarding space-time, the content-based 'asphalt' is the space-time of 'I and It.' Here, words merely lead to more words and space only leads to more space. The logic of the asphalt is that of the wheel, which glides in a line across the surface of the limited and temporary, from past to future, diachronically and experientially. "Man travels over the surface of things and experiences them," as Buber(2010, 5) wrote. It is intentionality and purpose, strategy and aims, experience and objects. In this mode, the best one can do it to 'acquire' knowledge. It is about isolation, separateness, (inter)objectivity and monologue. 'Community,' in contrast, is presence-based and relational, the 'I and thou.' The logic of community is that of the circle. It's coexisting in the here and now of a living moment. In the communal encounter, one is allowed to go past the surface, like walking into a room full of friends. One is allowed to be both in space-time and outside of it, in infinity and eternity. One is transformed through relational intimacy, inter-subjectively. It is an open loop in which words do not lead merely to more words but beyond words altogether. It is space not leading only to more space but beyond space and time not simply pointing to more time but past time itself.

In thinking about how to refer to this spectrum in more readily identifiable ways outside the context of 'asphalt versus community' of Brazilian popular culture, it is not clear which coupling from the table would be best suited. Since asphalt versus community takes shape as a form of oral social cartography, perhaps it would make sense to look towards its terminology for referring to space-time. Following Buber, this might be "Content" versus "Presence." By the same token, since the spectrum involves space-time pointing beyond time and space, it is tempting to evoke "super space-time." On the other hand, since all the categories listed derive from our attitudes in turning towards the world—as "modes," here—perhaps referring to it as "Experience" versus "Encounter" might even make more sense, also drawing from Buber. Otherwise, in thinking of the predicament of coexistence mentioned at the top of this chapter, focusing on "Existence" versus "Coexistence" might also be useful, primarily since this entails a communal relationality beyond the scope of Buber's one-to-one encounters.

Perhaps this added spatial and temporal dimension of the communal encounter, compared to Buber's one-on-one view of meetings, also entails an essential change in direction from his belief that all contacts with the 'thou' of a person, a tree, or a piles of rocks leads back to the encounter with the ultimate 'thou' of God. Perhaps we could say, instead, that each encounter with the 'thou' of God leads back to everything and everyone else. Because once we meet the ultimate 'thou,' not through any effort or control but in grace, our relationship to all the other possibilities of 'thou' of the world around us—with its persons, trees and stones—is forever changed. We can love, not as an act of will or control, but because we were loved first, as it says in the first epistle of John in Christianity's New Testament.[23] We don't have to master the world or dominate it, as a result, but can live together as a part of it in coexistence. The encounter with the ultimate 'Thou' of God, in this sense, is never only one-on-one. It is always a communal encounter. It is an encounter with a 'thou' connected to everything, inside and outside of all space and time.[24]

Perhaps the most salient point of connection between Buber's individual encounters and gangster funk parties in the streets of favelas is the aversion both show regarding any links between the "acquisition of

23 "We love because he first loved us" (1 John 4:19, NIV).

24 A few short years ago, I had great fun joking with my then seven-year-old son with a catchphrase inspired by this notion of super space-time, telling him playfully that, "You don't have to go *anywhere* to be *everywhere*!" To which he would cry out in fun-loving protest, "That's not logical, Papai! It's like saying 'You don't have to go anywhere to be where you already are!'" I would always pause at that as if reflecting upon some Zen *kōan* before giving him an answer that left him even more flabbergasted. "Exactly!"

content" and knowledge or being. Instead, both emphasize the transformational immersion into the "presence" of moments of communion and collective life. For both, the central idea is that a person does not emerge from an encounter the same as he or she enters (Buber 2010, 109). The same could be said regarding the communal existentialism of the Afro-Atlantic world, more generally, in music, dance and the body. Even so, from the Afro-Atlantic collectivistic relational perspectives of funk carioca and other musical, religious and cultural expressions—and everyday life—the encounter does not always happen merely in the first and second person singular together, grammatically, as Buber's 'I' and 'You,' or even primarily so. Instead, communal encounters have the potential to be even more profoundly imbued with a spirit of plurality, as "We and you all," collectively.

4

Proibidão and Rio's Gangs

Make the rifle sing!

—"I'm from Rocinha," by MC Galo[1]

Phones and Firecrackers

It's sunup on a Saturday and I'm standing on the corner with a group of four or five *olheiros*, as Rocinha's drug gang's 'lookouts' arc called. I've just recently woken up and am heading out for a run on the beach. The others rub their eyes after their all-night shift keeping watch over the little, unpaved street running between the houses and alleys of the Cachopa area of the favela. The group of boys in their teens and men in their early 2000s laugh, stretching shirtless in the quiet, early hours of the morning. They're chatting with two teenage girls who are on their way home from the funk dance at the bottom of the hill. From a nearby bakery in the basement of a small home, the smell of the first batch of bread hot out of the oven mixes with that of the cheap marijuana members of the small group are passing around. As is typical, the olheiros are armed only with walkie-talkies and roman candles, two ways to signal to their brothers from the drug gang in case another group of drug traffick-

1 Portuguese: "Bota o fuzil pa cantar!" ("Sou da Rocinha") is an often used phrase for starting songs by one of Rocinha's grandest funk singers, MC Galo—whose name means 'Rooster' in English. Full lyrics in Appendix A.

ers or the police invade. Experience has taught the lookouts that if either type of enemy were to make it this far up the hill—getting past the many other sentinels at lower positions in the favela along the way—the olheiros could wind up dead. Roman candles and walkie-talkies aren't much against semi-automatic pistols or assault rifles. Being an olheiro is a dangerous job.[2]

The baile funk dance had been a hit, the girls report. MCs Cordão de Ouro, Manda Brasa and Ruger—all three local singers—had indeed got the crowd hopping.[3] Several of the senior drug traffickers had put in an appearance, they said, armed with more than phones and fire crackers. Throughout the night, groups of gangsters called *bondes*—representing the different areas of Rocinha—had come through the dance. Brandishing AK-47s, M16s, AR-15s, Uzis, shotguns and other assorted firearms, they had come wading through the crowd of the packed street, known as the Via Ápia, past the long row of amps and speakers. The olheiros know that many of the more powerful gangsters can't leave the protection of the *Morrão* ('Big Hill') as they call Rocinha. They are wanted men, and that for these gangsters the funk dances are one of the very few options of nightlife their situation allows. Maybe that is why the higher-ups in the *boca-de-fumo*, as people sometimes call the gang (literally 'mouth of smoke'), pay for the huge *bailes de comunidade* ('community dance parties') in the streets of the favela.

2 Two eye-opening, intimate portrayals of the lives of Rio's olheiros are *Falcão: Meninos do Tráfico* (Bill, Athayde and Soares, 2006) and documentary film of the same name.

3 Whenever possible, I've chosen to use pseudonym in this case since some proibidão MCs have been arrested or suffered other reprisals from law enforcement and the criminal justice system in Brazil (Palombini 2013, 647-657). In contexts in which the MC is presented in a more legal light, I sometimes his or her real name instead of the pseudonym. My apologies to the reader for any confusion that might result.

Dunga is one of the olheiros. In Portuguese, his name can mean a tough, courageous person. It can also mean 'Dopey,' for the beardless member of the Seven Dwarfs. Either way, Dunga is a kindly and soft-spoken Afro-Brazilian kid of 17 who is skinny, with big brown eyes, heavy eyelashes and slightly enlarged, forward pointing ears. He turns to me to say he can't wait for the day when he'll be one of those big shots with a gun in his hands. Another olheiro is André, a fourteen-year-old with shiny, straight black hair to his shoulders. He would prefer just go to the beach and meet some girls, he tells me.[4] Someone turns up the boom box in our midst and together they begin to sing along with the words of a recent funk hit. It's from a proibidão CD they've been playing all night and is about Rocinha. The MC lists off the names of areas of Rocinha in the form of a poem set to music, going on to praise the power of the gang. With a nod to the gang members' religious faith, the singer boasts of their greatness as part of Rio's largest criminal faction:

> The Via Ápia, Paula Brito, Cachopa,
> Fundação, Terreirão;
> The gangs ready, always with their AKs in hand;
> Pissed off, watching your bullshit;
> Faith in God for the big Red Command ...
> —"In Charge of Rocinha," by MC Manda Brasa[5]

4 This semi-fictionalized scene is based on the group of olheiros at the corner of the alleyway near my home in the Cachopa area of Rocinha. Besides keeping watch, they also administered the soccer court there on behalf of the gang and ran a fireworks stand there on Christmas and other holidays. Folks on the block treated them as a cross between loitering thugs and night guards, mixing apprehension with appreciation.

5 Portuguese: "A Via Ápia, a Paula Brito, Cachopa, Fundação, Terreirão; Os bondes prontão, sempre de AK na mão; Boladão, observando a sua vacilação; Fé em Deus

Funk Carioca and Criminal Factions

Throughout the 1980s and 1990s, the lyrics and dance styles of funk carioca were controversial, often being criticized by its many detractors as violent, pornographic and thematically trivial. Many of its critics considered it a sort of musical bread and circus for the masses of residents of Rio's favelas and low-income suburbs (Herschman 2000, 87-123). Despite an occasional flash of national visibility and partial acceptance by the media in Brazil, funk in the late 1990s and early 2000s continued to be mostly music by and for poor youths in Rio. As a result, it underwent neither a full-scale process of commercialization nor appropriation by the status quo. Indeed the 'prohibited' or 'forbidden' underground style of illegal gangster fun—performed live at funk dances and found on pirated recordings available only in favelas—was never embraced by the media and remained largely unappreciated by outsiders. Even so, funk carioca unquestionably continued to be one of the most significant cultural expressions of the reality and identity of poor people in Rio and the largely marginalized existence they lived across the city. And the underground 'forbidden raps' side of the music that has come to be known as proibidão boomed in the favelas.

Despite its lack of broader acceptance in the mainstream, funk carioca had become enormously popular in places across the city, like the favela of Rocinha—home of funk greats Dollores, Galo, Leonardo and Junior as well as other well-known MCs like Gorila and Preto, Fornalha, and Neném. Funk's heavy bass sound could be heard in the Tijucan favelas of the Zona Norte, too, such as Borel and Formiga, home territory for the

para o Comando Vermelhão" ("Quem Comanda a favela da Rocinha"). Full lyrics in Appendix A.

raspy-voiced Duda do Borel and Mr. Catra. It boomed away by the seaside favela of Vidigal, home of MC Mascote; and in the Cidade de Deus in Jacarepaguá in the Zona Oeste, where MCs Cidinho and Doca live. In a city with hundreds of favelas, funk was the loudest and most prevalent musical style in places like Vigário Geral, Acari and the neighborhoods of some of the most famous samba schools, such as Mangueira and Salgueiro, as well as the favelas of nearby municipalities like Niterói and São Gonçalo.

During that period, the culture of funk music became one of the dominant cultural expressions through which favela residents negotiated the legitimacy of the drug traffickers within the partially alternative social order of Rio's favelas. By 'partially alternative,' I mean that the culture of favelas was ambiguous, in some ways representing a challenge to the legitimacy of the status quo order and in others resting upon some of the same ideological foundations. Indeed, the rule of the traffickers was ambiguous in similar terms. In this sense, funk was a primary discursive site in the Brazilian hegemonic process and was uniquely situated to reflect the convergences and incongruences in the dynamics of power between the status quo order, the culture of favela residents and the rule of the traffickers.[6]

For this reason, funk carioca at the time was much more than merely a youth style or a form of popular music. It was a fundamental cultural dimension of a society in which drug traffickers exerted considerable influence over informally urbanized areas of the city, including many favelas—many of which endured under siege in a war of social exclusion and class disparity. In discussing the criminal factions in this context, it's my hope to neither condemn nor romanticize the drug traffickers or

6 One should remember that the social order of Rio's favelas is complex involves much more than merely the dimension of drug traffickers or paramilitary groups, though I am focusing on this highly significant aspect in the present analysis.

their quasi-governance, much less the proibidão funk music that served to legitimize them. Instead, my aim in this chapter is to begin mapping out the ideological formation of a Brazilian subculture of favelas that had developed in that same crisis of violence and social exclusion.[7]

As I've stated previously, my focus was on the practices of funk and drug trafficking in the favela of Rocinha, situated in Gávea and São Conrado, in the Zona Sul of Rio, considered in those days to be one of the largest and most heavily armed favelas in the city and the one with the highest rate of sales of drugs.[8] To provide additional context for my analysis, I will first discuss the crisis of urban violence in Brazil at that time more generally, beginning with some of the underlying tendencies of the culture of drug trafficking in the favelas of Rio de Janeiro. Then I'll go on to take a look at some of the ways how the baile funk had become a sort of ritual staging of the power of the drug traffickers in the favela and how the gangsters supported it and utilized it to such an effect.

7 As one of the chief cultural productions of the favelas, funk music was one of the principal spaces in which the ideological negotiation occurred between the drug traffickers, other residents and the larger Brazilian society. My understanding of ideology and the hegemonic process is dialectical in the sense that it represents the sort of continuous renegotiation of power described by *Ideology: An Introduction* (Eagleton 1991). He (1991, 29) describes ideology as "a discursive field in which self-promoting social powers conflict and collide over questions central to the reproduction of social power as a whole."

8 According to *O Globo*, "O Rio está perdendo a guerra contra o tráfico?" and Werneck, "Uma juventude perdida no tráfico," the most heavily armed favelas in those days were Complexo da Maré, Complexo do Alemão and Rocinha. Rocinha was different from the other two because it was one favela, whereas the other two were groups of favelas. In the case of Maré, both the CV (Comando Vermelho) and the TC (Terceiro Comando) controlled parts, at the same time. There was only one cartel in Rocinha—the Comando Vermelho. Since the favela's location in the wealthiest part of Rio made it an excellent place to sell large quantities of drugs and as a result, however, that commando existed in the constant threat of take-over by another, causing its gangsters to make sure it was always extraordinarily well-armed and battle-ready.

Tim Lopes and Proibidão Funk

We're Red (Command) to the bone
It's peace, justice and liberty
I'm armed to the teeth, the gang is awesome
That's why we're faith in God and the gang keeps growing
Here it's us who decide if it rains or shines
I'll defend the favela my whole life long
—"We Are Red (Command)," by MC Manda Brasa [9]

In June of 2002, events occurred in Rio de Janeiro that once more brought funk music and favela drug traffickers to the forefront of the Brazilian political scene. On June 2, 2002, Tim Lopes, an award-winning reporter for *Globo* TV network, went to secretly film scenes of minors having sex for pay and the sale of drugs in a funk dance in the favela of Vila Cruzeiro, in the Penha neighborhood of Rio. Of the hundreds of favelas throughout the city, Vila Cruzeiro was one of fifteen the police classified in 2002 as inaccessible, like Rocinha, Turano, Andaraí and the Complexo do Alemão. As a result, only elite police troops like the Batalhão de Operações Especiais (BOPE) of the Polícia Militar and the Coordenadoria de Recursos Especiais (CORE) of the Polícia Civil ('Civil Police') could go there.[10]

Tragically, members of the favela's drug gang, run by crime boss Elias Maluco, discovered Tim Lopes at the dance, torturing and killing

9 Portuguese: "Somos Vermelho até o osso; É paz, justiça e liberdade; eu tô trepado até o pescoço; E o bonde está demais; Por isso a gente é fé em Deus; e o comando cresce mais; Aqui quem sabe é nós; Se caia chuva ou faça sol; Defendo a favela nem se for a vida inteira" ("Somos Vermelho"). Full lyrics in Appendix A.

10 See Araújo, "Favelas proibidas aos PMs."

him afterwards.[11] Tim Lopes' murder touched a nerve in Brazil and sparked a city-wide debate among journalists, intellectuals and politicians about what some called the *guerra contra o tráfico* ('war on drug trafficking') often framed as one waged between the state and a *poder paralelo* ('parallel power').[12] In the weeks following Lopes' murder, a media blitz ensued, protests were held, police surrounded and invaded Vila Cruzeiro and several other favelas and many community funk dances were suspended and thousands of pirated funk CDs confiscated around the city.[13] The Brazilian president at the time, Fernando Henrique Cardoso, declared an attitude of "zero tolerance" towards the drug traffickers and Rio Mayor César Maia appealed to the federal government that a "state of defense" be declared in the city.[14] These occurrences showed the deep level of frustration felt by many people in the face of the rampant violence that had been worsening in Rio over the previous decades. They also re-energized the debate about the relationship of funk music to violence and the relationship of the drug traffickers to the state.

Before that time, throughout the 1980s and 1990s, questions about funk carioca, favelas and violence had been treated from a variety of insightful perspectives both in Brazil and internationally. Typically, those early studies on violence in funk tended to focus more on a practice known as the 'corridor of death,' semi-ritualized fights that used to occurred in some funk dances, not infrequently resulting in serious injury and even death of some participants. This practice, first studied by

11 Souza offers a detailed account in *Narcoditadura: o caso Tim Lopes, crime organizado e jornalismo investigativo no Brasil* (Souza 2002).

12 As reported in "O Rio está perdendo a guerra contra o tráfico?" Here I have translated 'tráfico' as 'drug trafficking,' though the Portuguese also implies "the drug traffickers" and their organizations.

13 As reported in "Apreendidos CDs piratas e de apologia ao tráfico."

14 As reported in Dantas, "Cesar Maia pede decretação do Estado de Defesa."

Hermanno Vianna in 1988, diminished as funk evolved during the 1990s, especially as bailes funk moved from the clubs and other neighborhood concert venues of the formal city to the informal spaces of Rio's favelas.[15]

By the time Zuenir Ventura wrote *Cidade partida*, in response to the infamous police massacres of 1993, the funk artists he had portrayed had come together to form something of an alternative intellectual community from favelas and other poor neighborhoods in Rio. They engaged in funk as a form of social protest. At roughly the same period, George Yúdice was already pointing to another connection between funk and violence. He attempted to link the culture of funk and the arrastão attacks of October of 1993 in which gangs of poor youths ran along the beaches and streets of the Copacabana and Arpoador neighborhoods harassing and mugging passersby.

In response to this staining of its image, funk musicians themselves began to take up the theme of violence as lyrics in Portuguese became more common in the early to mid-1990s, as countless songs were composed calling on people to stop fighting at the dances. By the time Tim Lopes went to the favela of Vila Cruzeiro in 2002, however, a new attitude regarding violence had arisen in funk lyrics that was very different from the calls to put an end to the gang fights of the 'corridor of death' and the more general social protest of earlier ones. This new tendency of funk carioca had coalesced into proibidão, as a movement of underground songs about the power and activities of Rio's criminal factions, sung live at funk dances in favelas or available on bootleg recordings of these shows.[16]

15 See *Batidão* (Essinger 2015). Escpecially Chapter 4, "A voz do morro sou eu mesmo, sim senhor," 99-113.

16 For further information on the evolution of funk and its relationship to violence, see

By the time of Tim Lopes' murder, crime and violence in Rio had been at the center of scholarly research for some years. In addition to studies of violence in funk, several important more general social sciences studies on violence in Rio's favelas and on the city's drug trafficking criminal factions had been conducted both within Brazil and abroad, and many of these studies are still considered points of reference for such topics today. On the Brazilian side, one of the best-respected researchers was Alba Zaluar, discussed in more detail below. An anthropologist from the Univerisdade Estadual do Rio de Janeiro, she began researching and publishing on crime and favelas in the early 1980s. Currently the coordinator of the Núcleo de Pesquisas das Violências, she has more recently focused on the issue of Rio's paramilitary groups, often called *milícias* in Portuguese—one of the most problematic developments in the panorama of violence in Rio in recent years.[17] Other Brazilian specialists in the area active at the time of Tim Lopes' death included Gilberto Velho, Marcos Alvito and Luiz Eduardo Soares, who all produced essential anthologies on various aspects of crime, poverty and citizenship in Rio. Elaine Junqueira, a law professor at the Pontifícia Universidade Católica do Rio (PUC-Rio), and her husband José Augusto Rodrigues, a political scientist at the Univerisdade Estadual do Rio de Janeiro (UERJ), also wrote and lectured extensively on the issue. So did a co-founder of the non-profit Viva Rio—one of the most important non-governmental organizations in Rio—anthro-

José M. Valenzuela Arce, "O funk carioca," and Glória Diógenes, "Rebeldia urbana: tramas de exclusão e violência juvenil."

17 See Zaluar and Siqueira Conceição. "Favelas sob o controle das milícias no Rio de Janeiro." This issue is treated in the film *Tropa de elite 2: O inimigo é outro*, and in the semi-fictionalized novel *Elite da tropa 2* (Soares, Batista, Pimentel and Ferraz 2015). A related news magazine piece treating these paramilitary *esquadrões de extermínio* ('extermination squads') is Fernandes and Mendonça. "O mundo real do Coronel Nascimento," which compares the book and film to the real-life situation in the city.

pologist and author Rubem César Fernandes.

In addition, some well-known Brazilian journalists wrote on crime and social exclusion in Rio, with varying degrees of success. Zuenir Ventura's already mentioned 1994 book *Cidade partida*, which presented the world of crime and favelas in clear, accessible Portuguese, eloquently made the case that social exclusion in Rio was worsening. Ventura considered such growing inequality to be the root of violence in the city. Just as penetrating was Caco Barcellos' *Abusado*, an intimate portrayal of the life and times of drug kingpin Marcinho MV, of the favela of Dona Marta. Marcinho VP was widely known for his views on the social responsibilities of individual drug traffickers and those of criminal factions like his own Comando Vermelho.[18] Júlio Ludemir's work on Rocinha and his novel *Meu coração no comando* provide further examples of works well-grounded in research in the favelas and prisons of Rio at that time.[19] Photo-journalist André Cypriano provided a brief history of the rise of the Comando Vermelho in the Instituo Penal Cândido Mendes, on Ilha Grande in *Caldeirão do Diabo*.[20] Other attempts by journalists did not produce quite such high-quality work. For example, Percival de Souza's *Narcoditadura: o caso Tim Lopes, crime organizado e jornalismo investigativo no Brasil*, on the lists of best-sellers in 2003, sold well despite

18 Besides developing a close relationship with Caco Barcellos during that journalist's research for the book, Marcinho VP also provided crucial testimony for the path-breaking documentary by João Moreira Salles and Kátia Lund, *Notícias de uma guerra particular*. That project, in turn, gave rise to other groundbreaking film projects in Rio like *Ônibus* 174 (2002), *Cidade de Deus* (2002), *Tropa de Elite* (2007) and *Tropa de Elite 2: O inimigo agora é outro* (2010).

19 Ludemir's work provocatively suggested that the leaders in the non-governmental scene of favelas often exploited the dynamics of social exclusion and violence in their communities to consolidate a certain parallel power of their own and wield it as political bosses of the communities in which they lived and operated.

20 See also *Quatrocentos contra um: uma história do Comando Vermelho* (Lima 2001).

the relative lack of academic rigor with which it was carried out.

Also, by the time of my fieldwork, many scholars from outside of Brazil had been drawn to the topic of crime and the social organization of favelas. Elizabeth Leeds' 1996 article "Cocaine and Parallel Polities on the Brazilian Urban Periphery: Constraints on Local Level Democratization" was already a standard reference for the analysis of crime in Rio. Her formulation of *poder paralelo* ('parallel polities'), became a standard formulation in conversations about crime in Rio in the Media, scholarship and political communication. Regarding Rocinha specifically, sociologist Corrine Davis-Rodrigues (an American academic who later naturalized as a Brazilian citizen and currently teaches at the Universidade Federal de Minas Gerais) provided a series of case studies on which residents went to the drug traffickers versus other mediating groups, such as the Neighbor's Association (AM), the Balcão de Direitos of the Viva Rio NGO or the governmental Região Administrative located in Rocinha. Her works also provided a concise history of Rocinha up to the early 2000s. In an article with political scientist Enrique Desmond Arias, she disputed the sense of personal safety often reported by residents of favelas vis-à-vis the real danger they faced, given the significant limitations of the drug traffickers as a would be security force for the favelas in which they operated.[21]

Enrique Desmond Arias' dissertation, "Crime, Violence, and Democracy: The State and Political Order in Brazilian Shantytowns" offered a sophisticated understanding of political life on the periphery of Rio de Janeiro, arguing the importance of what he termed Local Associative Networks (LANs) in the democratization of favelas. In the following passage from the introductory chapter of that study, Arias described the

21 Corrine Davis-Rodrigues and Enrique Desmond Arias. "The Myth of Personal Security: Criminal Gangs, Dispute Resolution, and Identity in Rio de Janeiro's Favelas."

complexities of the socio-political terrain of the favela with an admirable economy of words. It still serves as a useful introduction to the intricacies of social life and crime in the favelas today. It is therefore worth quoting the passage in its entirety:

> Rio's favelas today experience a complex political and legal pluralism in which different organizations enforce order over different aspects of life. No longer are AMs (Neighbors' Associations) the primary leaders of communities. Rather, drug traffickers, AMs, religious groups and other social organizations all participate in the leadership of favelas. Relationships between these organizations, needless to say, are in a near constant state of flux as communities grow and state policies change. There is a general agreement among residents that certain types of violence, such as rape and theft, are not acceptable within the favela. If drug traffickers are well-organized and have good relations with the community, they will be able to swiftly punish behavior that violates these rules. If traffickers are weak, violations of these norms will be more common. Most favelas in Rio are still formally administered by an AM, which is registered with the state and the FAFERJ (Federação de Associações de Favelas do Estado do Rio de Janeiro). The leaders of AMs are supposed to be subject to regular election. In practice, however, elections are often meaningless since there is usually only one candidate who, with the support of the drug traffickers, is willing to take office. Though AMs are responsible for relations with the state, administer prop- erty transfers and resolve disputes between residents, much of the real power in the favelas lies in the hands of traffickers. With a limited monopoly on the means of violence, they work to enforce order and often resolve disputes between residents. NGO's and religious organizations also play a prominent role in favela life in building consensus among residents and in working to improve the community. Finally, different state agencies have different roles

> within the favelas. The state does not act as the unified, coherent bureaucracy in favelas, but is rather fragmented. While its agents in the favelas have the physical and financial means to make and enforce decisions which can change favela life in fundamental ways, they act independently and their activities often contradict each other. This serves to undermine government policies. In addition, many of these state agents are corrupt and actively use their influence to undermine government directives and work to protect drug traffickers and other criminals (Arias 2001, 23-24).[22]

This description of the politics of favelas strikes a careful balance between acknowledging the power of drug traffickers within their communities and recognizing the importance of other actors in the leadership of the favelas. This is crucial because it emphasizes the limits of the authority of the drug traffickers and thus moves beyond the 'narco-dictatorship' model put forth by some other analysts and so widely embraced by the Brazilian press in those days. While Arias is realistic about the dependence of the neighbors' associations upon the support of the traffickers in many cases, he makes it clear that organized crime operates within a framework of the expectations of community residents. He also demonstrates that the success of these gangsters is very directly dependent upon the satisfaction of the local population according to certain norms. This is important for my argument because I see the practice of proibidão funk as a symbolic site in which these expectations are both articulated and mediated. It fits together nicely with anthropologist Ben Penglase's ethnographically based studies on the formation of what he

22 For an updated an expanded version of his study with an amplified comparative perspective with other Latin American and Caribbean societies, see *Drugs and Democracy in Rio de Janeiro* (Arias 2006).

termed "narco-culture" in the favela in Rio where he lived and researched the Comando Vermelho (Penglase 2008).

Notwithstanding the sorts of in-depth work of journalists mentioned above, the mainstream media treatment of Rio's criminal factions at the time was, unfortunately, typically more Manichean than that of the many social science analysts and cultural critics studying violence and poverty in Rio. This problem was compounded by the fact that, despite the repercussions of social science work in some actual governmental policy, the media was of course more pervasive and generally had a broader, more immediate impact in the formation of public opinion. A series of articles published in *O Globo* soon after Tim Lopes' murder serve as an example of this tendency to flatten out and sensationalize issues such as organized crime and funk music.

In general, funk music was represented in the articles as an apology for crime exalting violence and the claim was made that funk dances in favelas were places of 'drugs, gunshots and orgies.'[23] Drug traffickers were generally portrayed in similarly simplistic, negative terms as cold-blooded killers who tortured their victims and tyrannically dominated the ignorant and powerless populations of the favelas. One article, appearing in *O Globo Online*, quoted a heavily loaded and debatable affirmation of researcher Zilah Vieira Meirelles as to the nature of drug trafficking in Rio: "The world of drug trafficking in Rio is very violent. They are trained to kill, not to defend the weak and oppressed; they sadistically torture people who go against the established norms and don't

23 See "Juizado não consegue fazer a fiscalização." The article cites a resident of the Vila Cruzeiro favela, saying "Everyone here knows there are drugs, gunshots and orgies in the bailes funk. Sometimes, they grab somebody. Maybe even six guys jump on one guy and beat him up" ("Todo mundo aqui sabe que há drogas, tiros e orgias nos bailes. Às vezes, eles arrastam alguém. Pode juntar seis batendo num cara só").

hesitate to kill whoever they want."[24] The danger of treating the subject without a deeper understanding of the underlining social currents that have created the culture of drug trafficking was that it placed the blame entirely on the criminality of the gangsters in ways that risked bringing about even greater polarization, prejudice and violence.

That particular article presented some highly questionable statistics regarding the involvement of youths in organized crime, for instance, citing a study claiming that one in four people between the ages of ten and nineteen living in favelas participated in the trafficking of drugs. Further down in the body of the story, however, the reporter clarified that only 7% of these youths actually collected a regular salary from organized crime. As for the other 93%, the author did not explain their involvement, writing instead that they carried out small tasks for the traffickers. By not qualifying either the specific type of 'tasks' these youths performed or with what frequency they carried them out, the article had the effect of making the involvement of adolescents in the trafficking of drugs seem far more widespread than it was. Instead, the title could have just as easily have read, "1.8% of Young People of the Favelas Have Salaries with Organized Crime," a headline which would have better conveyed the results of the study cited without sensationalizing the issue—even if it would have been less grabby and entertaining.

In the ten-page Sunday insert of *O Globo* from June 16, 2002, entitled "O Rio está perdendo a guerra contra o tráfico?" ("Is Rio Losing the Battle against Drug Traffickers"), there was a revealing two-page spread that

24 Antônio Werneck, "Uma juventude perdida no tráfico." The quote in Portugues reads, "O tráfico do Rio é muito violento. Eles são treinados para matar e não defender os mais fracos e oprimidos; torturam sadicamente os que vão contra as normas estabelecidas e não hesitam em matar, seja quem for."

typified this sort of sensationalized, black-and-white representation of the problem. In enormous letters, the title appeared across the pages, "O confronto entre o poder do estado e o do crime" ("The Confrontation between the Power of the State and Crime"). There was a map of the city's major favelas, showing the numbers of trafficker-soldiers and weapons in each, and a history of what it called the "parallel powers" of Rio. There was a table with job descriptions and salaries in crime, a map of the movement of drugs throughout South America and a timeline of some dominant crime personalities of the preceding fifty years. In the middle are two groups of silhouettes of weapons; those used by police and those by drug traffickers.

The most striking aspect of the spread to me was the presentation it made of what it called the *poder público* ('public power') along the left column, and the *poder do crime organizado* ('the power of organized crime') down the right-hand one. One very similar to Leeds' "parallel polities." The description of the public power, or that of "O Estado do Rio" ("the State of Rio de Janeiro"), was accompanied by photos of Benedita da Silva, governor of the State of Rio de Janeiro at that time, and leaders of various police and public security entities. The regime of the State was defined as a 'democracy' and said to be of the system of, "twenty-seven units of the Federative Republic of Brazil, which is presidential." On the other side of the spread, the 'República do Tráfico' ('Republic of the Drug Traffickers') was described and presented with pictures of several powerful crime bosses, including Elias Maluco, Fernandinho Beira-Mar and Uê. This regime was denoted as a 'narco-dictatorship,' whose system was said to be, "… tribal, characterized by the imposition of leadership by force and by the lack of institutional organization."

It may have been fair in some ways to say that Brazil was a 'democracy' and that the ruling order of the favelas was a sort of 'narco-dictatorship.' Still, presenting the complex social terrain of Rio de Janeiro with this simple dichotomy did no justice to the complexities of the issues. Most Brazilians were all too aware of the ways in which Brazil was quite far from a perfect democracy, with its chronic problems of corrupt public officials, police abuse and neglect of the poor. Even many very conservative Brazilians would have acknowledged the economic disparities and exclusion of the poor as fundamental causes of the social crisis that gripped the country. That special Sunday insert of *O Globo*, the "State of Rio" was presented in a very unproblematic way and in legitimizing terms, however, whereas the "Power of Organized Crime" was portrayed as purely repressive and despotic.

An example is the definition of 'tribal society' it offered, the term used in the article to describe the social formation of the favelas as one which is ruled "by the imposition of leadership by force." Such a definition of 'tribal society' was inadequate and harmful, ultimately distorting the picture in a way that dehumanized the favelas and their leaders—legal and otherwise. In fact, tribal relations often rely upon kinship bonds. There are also many intricate cultural norms in tribal society that do not depend directly on the use of force. Therefore, even if it could have been argued that favelas might have been 'tribal societies' in some ways, this did not necessarily mean that the use of force was the only, or even the principal, means of social cohesion there. In any event, at least regarding direct, person-to-person relationships, it's worth considering that tribes indeed may have some advantages over mass-scale modern democracies.

In the editorial pages that accompanied that 2002 insert, *O Globo* did allow for space for the views of some important observers of socio-political life in Rio de Janeiro. Journalist Zuenir Ventura and composer/musician Marcelo Yuka (of Rio's the eclectic rock band, O Rappa) both attempted to bring the debate beyond a 'war on the traffickers.' Instead, they pointed to the longstanding problem of social exclusion and violence as underlying causes of the social and political crisis taking place at the time. In a similar vein, Paulo Lins, author of the novel *Cidade de Deus* and former resident of that favela, wrote in an editorial:

> Suppose we manage to get rid of arms trafficking, drug trafficking and the bailes funk. We reduce the age limits for adult prosecution; we toughen up on sentences; we double the effectiveness of the police. Would we be happy in a country where the monetary inequality is one of the most drastic in the world? Would all the socially excluded people follow along in blind obedience with the social order? Would we eliminate conflicts? (Lins 2000).[25]

To his merit, Lins recognized that the existence of a criminal society in the favelas and the very sale of drugs sustaining it were symptoms of more complex issues. For him, the wide-scale criminal activity in Rio was directly tied to the gross economic disparity and general social exclusion that plagued his city. Unlike the view presented in the two-page spread in *O Globo*, the multi-layered social terrain of crime and poverty in Brazil could not be divided conveniently into a legitimate, 'democratic republic' and an illegitimate narco-dictatorship. Neither could it be said, as the spread in *O Globo* seemed to suggest, that the elected government officials and their police forces altruistically represented the interests of the people while the crime bosses of the favelas and their soldiers dominated their communities in egotistical and hedonistic greed.

25 In Portuguese, "Suponhamos que conseguíssemos acabar com o tráfico de armas, de drogas e com os bailes funk; diminuíssemos a idade penal; aumentássemos o rigor das penas; e dobrássemos o efetivo das polícias. Será que seríamos felizes num país onde a desigualdade monetária é uma das maiores do mundo? Será que todos os excluídos iriam seguir caninamente a ordem social? Acabariam os conflitos?"

The reason that I have focused on the death of Tim Lopes as a means of introducing my analysis of proibidão-style funk in this chapter is that his kidnapping occurred at a baile funk. Thus, Lopes' murder stands at a critical intersection between funk as a musical practice of the culture of the favela and the prominence of drug traffickers in favela communities. As a well-intended outsider who went to analyze and critique the governance of organized crime in Vila Cruzeiro, Lopes' presence there was, in ways, a manifestation of the conflict between the authority of the state—and the status quo ideology that legitimized it—and the authority of the drug traffickers and the worldview that supported it. Since the baile funk in favelas in those days had become such a critical site for the staging of the power of Rio's drug gangs and its symbolic representation, it was not a coincidence that Tim Lopes was murdered for being discovered undercover precisely there.

Following a keen reporter's instinct, Tim Lopes went to the favela of Vila Cruzeiro to do an exposé on the activities of drug traffickers in a baile funk and on the increasingly expanding role they had assumed in the governance of their favela communities. The presence of heavily armed gangsters and the abundance of song lyrics praising their power, as well as the many illegal activities going on there openly challenged the state's legitimacy. It also called into question the State's monopoly on the use of violence in the space of the favela—and affirmed in its place the authority of Rio's criminal factions in the favelas in at least some governmental capacities. Unfortunately, as a representative of the media in Rio, Lopes' presence at the dance made him in the eyes of the local gangsters a spy and a threat to their operations. The decision to torture and murder him, in addition to being an immoral and reprehensible act, inadvertently served as a sort of declaration of war by the Comando Vermelho on the legal authorities in Rio and set off a chain of events that intensified the conflict between them in the aftermath. Additionally, it was a decision that placed the baile funk and the proibidão-style funk lyrics at the heart of the issues of violence and citizenship in Rio de Janeiro.

Rich and Poor in Rio's Crisis of Violence

Funk carioca arose in the context of the growing crisis of urban violence in Rio de Janeiro—what Zuenir Ventura characterized as a sort of postmodern, economic war of social exclusion—and the broader history of the city's favelas (Ventura 1994, i). By the late 1990s and early 2000s in the heyday of early proibidão and the community funk dance parties in favelas, that crisis had become one of the most urgent facing Brazil, and it remains so today. Indeed, the period from 1990-2002 saw no shortage of media moments in that postmodern war. These included the 1992 arrastões in which crowds of low-income youths swarmed the beaches and streets in the area of Arpoador between Copacabana and Ipanema, looting and stealing as they went. 1993 saw the extermination of seven street children sleeping on the steps of the Candelária church in downtown Rio by off-duty police and the massacre in the favela of Vigário Geral—in which a group of 30 police officers shot and killed 21 random residents of that favela in broad daylight. In 1994, Operação Rio took place, in which the army was sent to occupy several of Rio's favelas. In June of 2000, the hijacking of the 174 bus occurred right next to the Globo network in Jardim Botânico, where both the hijacker and one of his hostages were slain (Sandro Barbosa de Nascimento, a survivor of the Candelária massacre, and Geisa Firmo Gonçales, a resident of Rocinha). Then in June of 2002, drug traffickers murdered Tim Lopes. They then carried out the subsequent terrorist campaign by the Comando Vermelho in which buses were burnt, buildings shot up and bombs exploded at various points throughout the city.[26]

As frightening as these high-profile events have been for the general public of Rio, most of the thousands of violent deaths occurring each year throughout the city—and throughout Brazil more generally—have taken place in relative obscurity in its country's streets, prisons and favelas. An article on the front page of the *Washington Post* at the time reported that this climate of violence was furthering the physical isolation of the rich from the poor. This was occurring, the article claimed, as a symptom of the growing economic disparity between social classes in Brazil:

> Amid rising crime and overpopulation, the rich are retrenching into hyper-insulated lives. In this sprawling nation of 170 million, sociologists call it the price of social inequity. Brazil has one of the most marked disparities of wealth in the world, with the richest 10 percent of the population controlling more than 50 percent of the wealth, while the poorest 10 percent control less than 1 percent (Faiola 2002).

According to the article, the quality of life for middle- and upper-class Brazilians had worsened as the threat of becoming a victim of crime steadily increased. Many people became afraid to go out after dark, to take a walk in the street, or to ride a public bus. Some with more money purchased bulletproof cars, hired bodyguards and began to commute by helicopter. Carjacking continued to be frequent, there was a high number of kidnappings and assaults of banks, homes, pedestrians and even buses were commonplace. The article stated that homicide rates

26 The episode of the bus hijacking is well-documented in Padilha's film *Ônibus 174* (2002) and Barreto's feature film *Última parada 174* (2008).

in the metropolitan São Paulo area had risen in the last decade to roughly 60 murders per 100,000 residents, exponentially higher than those of Washington, DC and New York City, which, it claimed, were 7.4 and 7.8 per 100,000 respectively. According to another source on statistics of homicide in the Rio metro area, the rate in that city had ranged throughout the 1990s from 50 to 75 per 100,000—with that of the neighboring Baixada Fluminense ranging from about 67 to 85. In those times, in São Paulo approximately 11,000 people were murdered every year and in Rio, a considerably smaller city, around 6,000.[27]

Of course, most of those violent deaths were not those of rich folk but of poor people who couldn't afford to live in gated communities, people who had been forced to develop different strategies for security and survival.[28] In Rio de Janeiro, many of these poor, mostly non-white people lived in favelas, partially informal communities in which municipal, state and federal governments had a limited presence. In the face of the nightmarish levels of violence in Brazil and the need for protection and social services, residents of most favelas in Rio had come to depend upon highly organized and heavily armed groups of local drug traffickers for the well-being of the community. This alternative and illegal form of power had emerged around and depended mostly upon the revenue from the trafficking of cocaine and marijuana from points of sale located within favelas, the bocas-de-fumo. The drug gangs sometimes also made income through activities such as kidnappings, bank robberies and the ille-

27 These statistics are based on studies published in the book *Violência e criminalidade no Estado do Rio de Janeiro* (Soares and Garotinho 1998). See too, Julio Jacob Waiselfisz, "Sumário executivo: Mapa de violência dos municípios brasileiros."

28 For treatment of the issue of the increasing security-based segregation in Brazilian cities see *City of Walls: Crime, Segregation, and Citizenship in São Paulo* (Caldeira 2000).

gal sale of arms. As mentioned previously, most were backed and supplied by either the Comando Vermelho (CV, which dominated most of Rio's favelas), the Terceiro Comando Puro (TCP, also controlling a large number of favelas) or the Amigos dos Amigos (ADA, the one most openly tied to the police and whose control was limited to a relatively small number of the city's favelas).[29]

Favela Gangsters as Kingpins

During this golden age of proibidão funk and the bailes de comunidade in Rio's favelas, the complex questions about the nature and role of the drug trafficker and the perceptions of those drug traffickers by the other residents of favelas attracted the attention of many scholarly observers. By the late 1990s and early 2000s, Alba Zaluar had established herself as one of the premier researchers on urban violence in Rio, having done extensive work on drug traffickers and making significant contributions to the understanding of the study of crime in Brazil. Zaluar based her nuanced understanding of the workings of organized crime on years of research and an abundance of information gathered in her fieldwork and in that of her students at UERJ. In the early 1980s she began making the argument that, despite the impressions of residents of favelas, the rule of the drug traffickers in Rio was built upon little more than the power of their firearms. For her, no class or race identities were relevant and in fact, no sort of culture of drug trafficking could be said to exist in

29 The Amigos dos Amigos later came to dominate Rocinha and to this day maintains a presence there, though since September 2017 the Comando Vermelho has undertaken a surge to retake the favela. See Glenny, "One of Rio de Janeiro's Safest Favelas Descends into Violence, the Latest Sign of a City in Chaos" and *Nemesis* (Glenny 2015).

the favelas.

On the one hand, Zaluar's argument seemed to work against the notion that the rule of the drug traffickers constitutes a parallel power, for the drug traffickers she depicted in her work were not interested in being an alternative government to the state. On the other hand, by denying the existence of any culture of crime through which gangsters and residents interact and by insisting that their control is entirely coercive, her arguments ultimately suggested the sort of narco-dictatorship model often affirmed by the Brazilian media. It is worth reproducing a long quote from Zaluar's article "Nem líderes nem heróis: a verdade da história oral" ("Neither Leaders nor Heroes: The Truth of Oral History"). It appears in her seminal study, *Condomínio do Diabo*, in which she stated some of her most basic and lastingly influential assertions about drug trafficking in Rio that recur throughout her work:

> If there's no leadership, much less can one speak of a 'government' of bandits in low-income neighborhoods or favelas. The only role they play at all like that of a government is, *in some locations, in some periods*, that of offering a modicum of protection to the residents of the area by keeping it free from attacks by other gangsters and punishing those among themselves who commit excesses. This does not keep rapes from happening by members of their groups or prevent small-scale thefts in those areas. Their lifestyle does not render them apt for the job of providing social welfare services, the way some newspapers claim. Their standards of consumption don't allow them to accumulate the sort of money necessary to carry out such services in large communities, neither do they have a political project or symbolic system through which to think one up. They are not social bandits, champions exacting vengeance on behalf of their people, they are business people of crime and its employees (Zaluar 1994, 144). [30]

Zaluar's words came in response to the argument that the drug traffickers protected and provided for the residents of their communities, a belief she identified not only among newspaper people but that she saw as very common among the people themselves living in favelas. As the result of her research, like Davis-Rodrigues and Arias, mentioned above, Zaluar knew that residents were not as safe or well protected as they thought and that the faith many had in their drug gangs was undeserved. Her emphasis on the materialist tendencies of the drug traffickers was a part of her critique of the more mainstream Brazilian social order more generally. Ultimately, she viewed the residents as being duped into believing the hype and blinded by false-consciousness. But she also saw the drug traffickers as victims. For her, they were victims of the failings of society and the prevailing consumerist/hedonist ideology she considered as having been a part of the status quo in Brazil for some time.

As another part of her criticism of the larger Brazilian society, Zaluar suggested that a new form of paternalism had emerged to supersede older ones based on personal relationships and loyalty (Zaluar 1994, 256). Throughout her career, she worked against the notion that the drug traffickers of Rio's favelas were some Robin Hood-like 'social bandits' and that they were some sort of modern-day versions of the Northeastern

30 Portuguese: "Se não há liderança, muito menos pode-se falar de 'governo' dos bandidos nos bairros pobres ou favela. A única função do governo que exercem, *em alguns locais, em algumas épocas*, é a de oferecer relativa segurança aos moradores de sua área, livrando-os dos ataques de bandidos de outras e punindo os que, entre eles, cometem excessos. Mas isso não tem impedido estupros de mulheres por parte de bandidos, nem pequenos roubos e furtos nessas áreas. E seu estilo de vida não os faz aptos a exercerem as funções de assistência social que alguns jornais lhes atribuem. Seu padrões de consumo não lhes permitem acumular dinheiro suficiente para exercê-las em bairros e favelas extremamente populosos, nem possuem o projeto político ou o sistema simbólico que lhes permita concebê-las. Não são bandidos sociais, vingadores de seus povos, são empresários do crime e seus empregados."

cangaceiro bandits like Lampião (Virgulino Ferreira da Silva, 1898-1938) and Antônio Silvino (1875-1944). She also rejected the notion that the authority of the drug traffickers in their communities was somehow related to the *coronelismo* of Brazil's past—about the big bosses of rural Brazil, like the *caudillos* of the Spanish-speaking world. Similarly, she worked to dispel the notion that the gangsters of Rio's drug cartels were comparable to the Italian and American mafias or US and Mexican street gangs, all which she saw as depending on that more traditional sort of paternalistic base. For Zaluar, the new form of clientelism of Rio's drug traffickers was based on self-interest and consumerism in a way symptomatic of capitalist society in Brazil at the time, which she described as:

> ... late, post-ethical, postmodern and post-labor, in which the effects of consumerism and hedonism have already rooted out collectivizing social values and traditional authorities to quickly transform Brazilian society without creating institutional engineering to limit the destructive tendencies of the social fabric because they were based on profit and personal interest (Zaluar 1994, 262). [31]

Along with the demise of interpersonal paternalism, Zaluar argued, the notion of authority had become inverted and was no longer that of the traditional legitimacy, "... based on social consensus about whom should be obeyed in which spaces and by virtue of what values."(Zalu-

31 Portuguese: "...tardio, pós-ético, pós-moderno, pós-sociedade do trabalho, em que os efeitos do consumismo e do hedonismo já minaram os valores sociais agregadores e as autoridades tradicionais, transformou muito rapidamente a sociedade brasileira sem criar uma engenharia institucional para limitar as tendências destruidoras do tecido social, porque baseado na busca do lucro e do interesse pessoal".

ar 1994, 113).[32] For the *chefes* ('bosses') of this new individualistic and ego-centric paternalism, she argued, the existence of violent means of coercion was the only basis for authority. The bosses of criminal factions in Rio's favelas were simply one more instance of this sort of consumerist boss and therefore no consensus was necessary for their hegemony beyond the force of their firearms. For these chiefs and their soldiers, crime offered an easy means for poor people to participate in the consumerist society already dominant in Brazil. She went on to say that, "The criminal pathway afforded a possible entrance to the consumerist society already installed in the country." (Zaluar 1994, 113).[33]

From my point of view living in Rocinha and conducting research there on crime and funk, Zaluar's argument did not seem completely on the mark. Although Zaluar may have intended her view as a way of shifting the blame for the social ills of the war of drug trafficking from the gangsters to the larger society which had produced them, the somewhat circular reasoning she used to argue her case ended up oversimplifying the problem. Beginning from Hannah Arendt's well-known boundaries of power, violence, force and authority, Zaluar said that rule was not based on violence, and since the power of the traffickers was based on violence, they had no authority. This was slippery reasoning, for in a backwards way, Zaluar was saying that since traffickers had no authority, therefore they had no authority. She had not proven the second premise of her argument—the one that says that the power of the drug traffickers' was based entirely on violence. In fact, Arendt herself states in

32 Portuguese: "... baseado em um consenso social de quem deve ser obedecido em quais espaços e por virtude de quais valores".

33 Portuguese: "A saída criminosa é a entrada possível para a sociedade de consumo já instalada no país."

On Violence that, "Violence can destroy power; it can never create it" (Arendt 1969, 56). Thus, really a more relevant application of Arendt's thought to the situation of the favelas would have been to ask some additional questions: If violence had not created the power of the trafficker, from where did it come? How had the authority of the traffickers, understood by Arendt as "... the unquestioning recognition of those who are to obey," been mediated in the community in a way requiring "neither coercion nor persuasion?" (Arendt 1969, 45).

Although on the surface Zaluar was on target in asserting that generally gangsters in Rio did not have any specific political orientation through which they seek to better their communities, her arguments suggested a false dichotomy between 'avengers of the people' and the 'businessmen of crime.' Somewhere in between being Robin Hood and a cold, calculating criminal, there was some symbolic system through which favela residents constructed the identity of Rio's gangsters, a system that formed part of the culture of favelas. This could be seen in proibidão funk music and the micro-negotiations of the taking place there, at the same time at the level of local hegemony and regarding the larger ideological processes occurring throughout Brazil, both nationally and internationally. As far as Zaluar's thinking was concerned, it seemed to me that she had based much of her argument on an overly rigid notion of consciousness. Ideology, it seemed to me, was more than explicit political beliefs but rather included a great deal of psychological and cultural influence.

In contrast to Zaluar's views, for me it seemed vital to consider that drug traffickers might, in fact, have a specific ideological orientation, one that made up and manifested itself as a sort of 'culture of drug trafficking.' It was the same one presenting itself in the practice of proibidão funk and being mediated there by the gamut of favela residents.

This culture, though not explicitly political, per se, was the sort of new consciousness that Raymond Williams wrote about involving notions of class and racial struggle essential to the legitimacy of the traffickers in their communities. Furthermore, Zaluar's claim that the hedonist lifestyles of drug traffickers prohibited them from having any money for social assistance did not seem to account for the fact that the traffickers did give significant social aid beyond protection, specifically regarding such things as sports and leisure, as well as money and medicine for the poor. This was not to say that the forms of help offered by the traffickers to their communities were the best for political mobilization and the advancement of civil and human rights in Brazil. Still, that such support of the neighborhood was ultimately paternalist and further strengthened the legitimacy of the traffickers did not change the fact that a culture of mutually understood expectations about social assistance did exist between the residents of favelas. It was one shaped by communication and actions on all sides, as gangsters and other residents of Rio's favelas interacted with one another.

Perhaps the biggest danger with Zaluar's characterization of the ethos of the drug traffickers, from my point of view, was that it risked oversimplifying the matter in a dehumanizing way by presupposing a kind of unity of personality that simply did not exist. Just as individual residents of the community had a variety of opinions regarding the nature of gangsters in their favelas, so too did the actual drug traffickers themselves have complex, sometimes contradictory views about themselves and their activities. After all, the gangsters were human beings and were likely to be just as incoherent in their beliefs and attitudes as the rest of us. They could want love, be jealous, believe in God and hate society all at the same time. They could think both that they were racially inferior to someone and more human than that same person. Maybe a drug trafficker would watch Brazil in the World Cup one morning instead of selling drugs, thereby missing the opportunity to make some money for nothing more than a love of soccer and the Brazilian national team. Or maybe the choice stemmed from a deep, subconscious association with football from his childhood and relationships with loved ones from the past. One drug trafficker might make the sign of the cross and lower his head as he walks past a church or near a boisterous street evangelist. Another might regularly listen to funk carioca, think hip-hop had a positive message, dance with country people from the rural areas of the State of Ceará at a forró party and cry upon hearing an old song by Legião Urbana.

In a similar way, some drug traffickers were drug addicts and alcoholics. Others sporadically attended Pentecostal church services. Some got sober in Alcoholics Anonymous or 'found religion' and managed to leave the life of crime. They had brothers who were pastors, police officers and delivery boys; they had sisters who worked in the mall or who were singers in a pagode band. The point is that these drug traffickers were people. Furthermore, they were people living in a postmodern, globalized world, with TVs, radios, movies, music, churches, schools, military service, samba schools and funk dances. They were not characters in a typical Hollywood movie, flattened out and internally coherent, always acting in greed and self-interest alone. To ascribe their motives to a vague notion of "postmodern, post-work-ethic, consumerist, hedonist society," as did Zaluar in the quote above, was to deny the intricacies of their personalities and the multiple aspects of often conflicting ideological currents running through them.

Just as the drives of an individual drug trafficker were not reducible to a single consumerist impulse, it seemed to me, the rule of the traffickers collectively was a human endeavor and likely to be even less coherent and unified. There was no single motive that the enterprise was built on, nor one facile explanation that accounted for the choices of tens of thousands of individuals involved in it in different places and the different contexts of their individual lives. Everyone had a story, so the groups of drug traffickers in those days were groups of life stories, all unique and different in some ways from the others. For example, Marcinho VP, the protagonist of Caco Barcellos' book *Abusado: O dono do morro Dona Marta*, was an avowed socialist. One of the most famous bosses of the 1990s and chief of the Santa Marta favela in Botafogo, he hatched a plan to rid his gang of drug trafficking altogether. Marcinho VP wanted to retain power to be able to protect, educate and empower the residents of his community without the sales of drugs as an economic base. He was probably not the only drug trafficker to romanticize his life in one way or another, just as most people do in all walks of life.

Another of Rio's drug traffickers might be like the character Bené from the novel and film *Cidade de Deus* (*'City of God'*). He was attracted to the life of crime in that community, at least in part, for the fashionable clothes and dream of living a better life with new friends and girlfriends from other places outside the favela. Maybe another person might get involved with drug trafficking because he was angry with life, hated his parents and wanted to act out aggressively. Perhaps another thought he was on a mission from God. Still, another might wish to "live fast, die young and leave a good-looking corpse," as people say. Another might have served in the Brazilian military—as poor youths often do—where he enjoyed a sense of purpose and discipline of military life. Afterwards, he sought to find an identity and someway continue that soldier lifestyle in the world of organized crime. Still other drug traffickers were likely mentally ill, from a clinical perspective. Undoubtedly the scarce resources for mental health amongst Rio's poor had left many people vulnerable and without treatment only to find their ways into the world of the city's favela gangs.

Perhaps the best way to avoid flattening out the complexities of the souls of the drug traffickers of Rio's favelas is to resist the temptation to see them as somehow entirely different from the other residents of the communities in which they live and operate. It is not so much a question of some uniform block of consumerist hedonists wielding power over other community members as one if a spectrum of beliefs and motivations both economic and cultural, driving residents one and all in diverse ways that are unique and personal. Humanizing the question in this way will place us in a much better vantage point from which to begin assessing the challenges of favela life and its cultural manifestations, as well as the means through which everyday people face such challenges.

5

Rocinha Favela

During the golden age of the community funk dances, Rocinha was not entirely typical of Rio's favelas because of its enormous size and the fact that in parts it was more urbanized and wealthier than most others.[1] Even so, due to its location between two or three of the wealthiest neighborhoods of the Zona Sul, Rocinha offered a classic example of the extreme disparities in race and social class in Brazil. Its location gave it an intense level of interaction with mainstream influences, not only through TV, film and music but through personal contact between people living in Rocinha and others living in the most prosperous neighborhoods, boosting the vibrant intellectual, political and artistic life taking place there. It also could be seen as a paradigm of the rule of the traffickers in the city. It was also one of the favelas with the highest numbers of armed gangsters and perhaps the one that sold the most substantial quantities of illicit drugs. Rocinha was also considered to be one of the primary ports of entry for the arms trade between the Comando Vermelho criminal faction and the FARC (Fuerzas Armadas Revolucionarias de Colombia), one of South America's best-armed and most prominent narco-guerrilla groups at the time.

Many organizations besides Rocinha's drug cartel provided leader-

1 For accounts of daily life in Rocinha at around that time, I recommend *Sorria, Você Está na Rocinha* (Ludemir 2004) and *Shadow Cities* (Neuwirth 2016). For more recent portrayals, see Glenny's *Nemesis* and Robb-Larkin's *Spectacular Favela*.

ship from various sectors, including churches and other religious groups, the neighbors' associations, dozens of NGOs, local newspapers, community radio stations, the performing arts, health and fitness, martial arts, and a thriving business community that even had its own commercial association. This broad-based leadership and the multiple layers of the political make-up of Rocinha made it impractical for its drug traffickers to establish any absolute narco-dictatorship. Instead, they had to operate within a complex social terrain in which their political abilities gained them as much or even more advantage than the mere force of their arms. When Rocinha's gangsters were successful in navigating this terrain, they profited; when they were not, they were overthrown and replaced (Arias 2001, 111-151).[2]

In the 1930s, a slow trickle of people began occupying the lands of an old plantation beneath the mountain known as Dois Irmãos, nestled between Leblon, Gávea and São Conrado on what was then the remote and rustic edge of the city. Some fruits and vegetables were grown and sold in the area, which came to be known as the *Rocinha* ('Little Field'). A very curvy and narrow road was built over the hill between São Conrado and Gávea, which came to be used for early automobile racing with small cars popularly known as *baratinhas* ('little cockroaches'). Over time, more and more people began to settle in the lands of *fazenda* ('the old plantation'). Many of these earlier arrivals were Black people either from around the state of Rio de Janeiro itself or from Bahia, in the Northeast. Their religion tended to be Roman Catholic, Candomblé or Umbanda. During the 1960s and 1970s, when the tunnels were built under the Morro Dois Irmãos hill and a great deal of construction occurred in Rio's Zona Sul

2 Arias offers a case study in the favela he called "Santa Ana" of a drug cartel that came to ruin due to their unpopularity with the local residents.

('Southern Zone'), a massive wave of new residents from the semi-arid *sertão* region of the Northeast came to live in the favela.

This immigration continued in the decades leading up to the periods of my residence in Rocinha, making the favela a thriving hub of Northeastern culture. On virtually every corner one could hear people speaking in Northeastern accents, along with the carioca accents of Rio natives. The Northeastern culture could be seen Sundays at the enormous open-air market in the Largo do Boiadeiro, where *repentistas* musicians played their improvisational guitar songs every week. Northeastern forró music was as popular as funk in the favela and forró parties popped up in dozens of little bars across the big hill. One could easily buy Northeastern foods and products such as *fumo-de-rolo*, a type of raw chord of tobacco, *rapadura*, a sort of molasses brick, and *buchada de bode*, a stew made from goat entrails sewn into little bags made of stomach. Newcomers who came to Rocinha from the Northeastern were often a bit afraid of the favela at first because of its bad reputation and overcrowded living conditions. This feeling usually left them as they adapted to their new favela home. Those *Nordestinos* often maintained contact with their families back in their home states, but as the distance was great and the cost of traveling back and forth high many never returned.

The question of religion in Rocinha and favelas in Brazil more broadly was a very complicated one, as it continues to be today. While Brazil was culturally a Catholic country, considered the largest in the world, it is difficult to overestimate the impact and size of the Pentecostal movement in Brazil over the decades before I came to live there. The Assembléia de Deus (Assembly of God) and the Igreja Universal (Universal Church) were two of the most significant Pentecostal denominations in Rocinha. But there were a plethora of smaller others, too, such as Deus é Amor (God is Love), the Igreja Metodista Wesleyana (Wesleyan Methodist

Church—a Pentecostal offshoot from Brazil's Methodist Church) and Maranata. These existed side by side with traditional Protestant churches such as the Methodists and Baptists, also very active in Rio's low-income communities, and the Catholic Church, which had become more popularized in recent decades with movements like Liberation Theology and the Charismatic Renovation. Rocinha itself still had a very active Catholic community. Its *Via Sacra* street performance of the Passion of Christ, for instance, attracted tens of thousands of spectators as it ran up the Estrada da Gávea each year on Good Friday. There were still many active Umbanda houses and candomblé *terreiros*, too, where the rites of these traditions were practiced. There were numerous little shops selling bibles, plaques, music, incense and statuettes related to these various religious traditions, as well.

Commercially, Rocinha was a sizeable and lucrative market and much money was made there outside of drug trafficking. There was a McDonalds, Bob's Burgers, a Brasimac appliance store, a Deplá Kodak store, two banks and the local cable companies TV Roc and TV Siri, besides countless other successful smaller businesses. There were three neighbors associations, a commercial organization of local business leaders, dozens of NGOs of various sizes, 12-step clubhouses of Alcoholics Anonymous and Narcotics Anonymous, several thriving capoeira groups, the famous samba school Acadêmicos da Rocinha, and many gyms and sports leagues. Rocinha was a Zona Sul beachfront neighborhood, a place of surfers, weightlifters, groups of jiu-jitsu fighters, women in bikinis and men in *sungas* (Speedo-type Lycra swimsuits). There was a constant flow of people walking to the beach in São Conrado to tan, swim, rollerblade, jog, play soccer and *futevôlei* (a cross between soccer and volleyball). With its residents regularly tuned in to TV networks like Globo via satellite dishes and cable, and with its proximity to the golf courses and elite shopping mall of São Conrado, few favelas in Rio are in closer contact with the Brazilian consumerist dream.[3]

Cops and Robbers Backwards

If you invade and go bang bang bang
You'll get all full of lead
Because the gang doesn't fool around
So I say, it's very well prepared
If you are an enemy, or a cop
Better not invade the favela of Rocinha
The strong gang of Rocinha is armed to the teeth
—"Slime Ball Germans (Invaders)," by MC Ruger[4]

Despite its increasing urbanization and economic significance, Rocinha's existence as a favela amidst some of the most elite carioca neighborhoods made it a classic example of the schizophrenic social terrain of

3 For a more intimate portrayal of life in Rocinha and the people living there at the time, see the three short community-driven documentaries I created with friends and collaborators from the favela and beyond, all of which are available on YouTube and Vimeo. For an overview, see *Rocinha: Em casa no morrão* ('Rocinha: At Home on the Big Hill'), which focuses on kids and teenagers of the Two Brothers Foundation/Instituto Dois Irmãos. For the story of a capoeira teacher, an addict recovering in AA and a teenage girl at a Pentecostal church, see *Atalhos e Encontros* (*Pathways and Encounters*). For the perspective of a *pai-de-santo* of candomblé regarding the pacification of Rocinha by police in 2011, see *Pacificação da Favela: Encontro com Pai Almir* (*Favela Pacification: Encounter with Pai Almir*).

4 Portuguese: "Se tu invadir e ficar de bam bam bam; Vai tomar de fuzil ou de pistola e de sadam; Porque o bonde não é papo furado; Então eu digo, é fortemente preparado; Se tu é um alemão ou então um polícia; Melhor não invadir a favela da Rocinha; O bonde forte da Rocinha anda armado até os dentes" ("Seus alemão safado"). Full lyrics in Appendix A.

Rio de Janeiro. A long history of neglect on the part of the larger society and the rise of the drug traffickers as the governing power in the favela had left a legacy of complex and challenging social organization in Rocinha. One result of this was that the drug traffickers had come to be regarded by many residents as the legitimate protectors of the community, whereas people considered the police as aggressors.

One day, three boys ten and eleven years old told me something quite typical of this view. I had known Philipe for at least four years, a neighbor of my dear friend Dona Raimunda, a kind senior who was like an adopted mother to me in Rocinha. They lived in the alleyway called Campo da Esperaça, in the Valão area near the bottom of Rocinha. He had also been our student at the English course we taught at the Escola Moranguinhos, where our NGO was based. He was an artistically gifted, highly communicative boy with a good sense of humor that always made him the life of the party in our classes. He was one of the best friends of Erick, one of the other boys.[5]

I'd known Erick since my first stay in Rocinha in 1990, when he was only one year old. He was Dona Raimunda's grandson and nephew to my close friend Socorro, who helped start the NGO with me in 1998, along with her best-friend Vivi and my friend and fellow student at PUC, Consolação. Erick and I had played together countless times, in his home, around the favela, at the beach, in the woods above Rocinha and across town at malls, bookstores and movie theaters. He was every bit as funny as Philipe, as well as being musically gifted and a good conversationalist. Indeed, through our adventures together over the years, as I saw him grow up to be a man, I came to consider him as one of my

5 A few years later, when he was fourteen, Philipe volunteered to be featured in my documentary *Rocinha: Em casa no Morrão*.

most beloved and trusted friends in Brazil.[6] Maikom was Erick's cousin. He loved to play and spend time with his friends. He and Erick helped me make my first documentary in Rocinha, an untitled and unedited film that I have not yet been able to post online.

As we talked about such things as growing up in the favela, what was good and bad about the neighborhood, music and violence, etc., the boys expressed a much higher level of trust in the drug traffickers than in the police:

> *Author*: You all see these folks every day around here (the drug traffickers), coming in and going out... Are you afraid of them? What's your reaction?
>
> *Philipe*: No! We, we're used to them... They don't hurt the residents, see? They treat people well...
>
> *Author*: So, and police officers, if you see one around here, does it scare you?
>
> *Philipe*: Oh, yes. Police officers, yes, we get scared. Because a police officer doesn't know the difference, he doesn't know who gangsters are around here, so the first person he sees he says, "Hey! That guy must be a gangster!" He shoots, kills or at least arrests you.[7]

6 Back around the time of the interview, I remember making a sandcastle with him on a São Conrado Beach. He suddenly asked me if I had made sandcastles with my father. It was striking since his own dad had divorced his mother when he was small and lived far across town, seen by his son only rarely. Time has flown and today Erick is twenty-eight. He has his own son, Vinícius, who is eight.

7 This passage is from an interview with Erick, Philipe, and Maikom. It took place March 28, 2002, at the Escola Moranguinhos, which was the base of operations for our Two Brothers Foundation/Instituto Dois Irmãos NGO at the time. Portuguese: *Autor*: Vocês vêem esse pessoal diariamente (os traficantes), entrando e saíndo. Vocês têm medo deles? Qual é a sua reação? *Philipe*: Não! A gente, a gente já está acostuma-

Throughout that conversation, the boys expressed a constant fear of the police and their activity in the favela. Not surprisingly, when I asked them if living in Rocinha was good or bad, violence and police 'invasions' were two things that immediately came to their minds:

> *Author*: Do you guys like living here?
>
> *Maikom*: The only thing uncool here in Rocinha for me is because there's lots of houses all close together all stuffy, and when the police invade we don't… I don't know… But now I know when they're coming in because they (the gangsters) shoot off three roman candles.
>
> *Author*: So what do you do then?
>
> *Maikom*: I go home, and sometimes Dona Raimunda calls me over to her house and we all stay close to her, so everyone goes into her house.[8]

Despite the fact that all three found Rocinha to be a great place to play, their underlying fear and insecurity were sadly evident in their comments:

> *Erick*: You know why I think it's just okay to live here. It's because

do… Eles não prejudicam os moradores, entendeu? Eles tratam bem… *Autor*: Então, e policial, se você vê policial aqui, você tem medo? *Philipe*: Aí, sim. Policial, sim, a gente tem medo. Porque o policial não tem diferença, ele não sabe quem é os bandidos daqui, ele, a primeira pessoa que ele vê, "Ah! Ele deve ser bandido." Atira, mata, ou então prende.

8 Portuguese: *Autor*: É bom morar aqui na Rocinha? *Maikom*: A única coisa ruim aqui na Rocinha que eu acho, porque é muita casa uma perto da outra e fica tudo abafado, e quando as polícia invade a gente não, sei lá… mas agora eu já sei quando a polícia está entrando é quando eles solta três vezes os fogos. *Autor*: Aí o que você faz? *Maikom*: Eu vou para casa, e às vezes a Dona Raimunda me chama para eu ir para casa que a gente já está perto da dela, aí todo mundo entra para casa.

> it's like this: Because there's the good part that we don't get hurt. But there's also the part that we can get hurt when the cops come here and the part that we aren't free because nobody knows when the police are going to raid. So we never know when there's going to be a gunfight. We can be playing in the street. We don't see the police are invading. So then all of the sudden a gangster goes by there in the alley where we live. He runs by and we think he's playing. But then the policeman comes and sees the guy right in front of us. He shoots. He doesn't even notice us. So he shoots. And he hits us by accident instead.[9]

The word 'invasion' itself was indicative of the relationships between the police, the drug traffickers and the community of the favela. For example, rarely do people refer to the police as 'invading' the Avenida Presidente Vargas in the center of the city or the middle-class condos of Barra da Tijuca. Perhaps in the favela people referred to the police as 'invaders' because many residents do not consider them as the legitimate protectors of the community. Of course, often individual police officers themselves came from favelas or other poor neighborhoods, where they could be liked, at a personal level. But as a corporation, just as people saw the official government of the state as being remote and somewhat foreign to the favela, so too were the police. They just did not know its residents. As a group, they tended to be regarded by the residents of favelas as

9 Portuguese: *Erick*: Sabe por que eu acho regular porque é assim, porque tem a parte boa que a gente não é machucada, a parte também que a gente pode se machucar quando os policial vêm pra cá, e a parte que a gente não tem liberdade porque ninguém sabe a hora que os policial vão invadir. Aí a gente não sabe a hora que vai ter tiroteio. A gente pode estar brincando na rua, a gente não sabe que tem policial já tá invadindo. Aí de repente passa um bandido lá no beco onde a gente mora, passa correndo e a gente pensa que é o cara brincando. Vem o policial, vê o cara bem na nossa frente, atira, não vê nem a gente, aí atira, vem bala perdida na gente.

unsympathetic and dangerous outsiders more likely to hurt someone than to help. The fact that they were frequently corrupt and complicit with the drug trafficking did little to endear them to the residents of the favelas, either, but instead further undermined their authority and emphasized the hypocrisy of the larger system.

Despite the trust the boys had that the drug traffickers would not harm them, the actual nature of the gangs in favelas and their relationship to their communities was a hotly disputed topic. Such was not only the case among intellectuals and politicians but also for residents of favelas, as well. In the case of Rocinha, although each resident of the favela had his or her own opinion about the influence of the drug gangs in their community, by and large, most accepted them as a necessary evil. Some went further, believing that the traffickers competently defended and protected the community; others idolized and loved them. There were those living in Rocinha, too, who intensely hated the drug traffickers and resented their presence in the neighborhood. In my years of living in Rocinha and interacting with my neighbors there, as well as in the interviews I conducted for this study, I saw evidence to suggest that most residents of Rocinha at least trusted drug traffickers to a much higher degree than they did the police. If they did not like a particular trafficker or found him cruel and abusive to the population, people tended to condemn that individual by comparing him to other more favorable gangsters.

During my years of residence there, the crime boss from the mid to late 1980s, Dênis da Rocinha (Denir Leandro da Silva) was still generally revered by the population of the favela. During the years from his arrest in 1987 until his death in 2001, he was always the point of reference for how a gangster boss should be, caring for the community financially, protecting and respecting residents. Most people believed he was still making the decisions and that the onsite bosses were only acting in his name.

Upon his arrest, residents held massive protests in the streets beneath the favela in which the population demanded his release and return to Rocinha. When he was murdered in his prison cell inside Bangu 1, a short time before he was to be released in February of 2001, it sent shockwaves throughout the community and more protests were held, though on a smaller scale. The period in which he was at the head of the gang was remembered as the 'good old days' when Dênis had prohibited his gangsters from openly carrying arms in the favela and using drugs in public and insisted they always used polite forms of speech when dealing with other residents. This reverence for Dênis as Rocinha's best-ever crime boss was only fortified after his death. Other bosses since Dênis also achieved a considerable degree of popularity and support within the community, especially Lulu (Luciano Barbosa da Silva), killed by police in 2004, Bem-Te-Vi (Erismar Rodrigues Moreira), slain by police in 2005, and finally, more recently, Nem (Antônio Francisco Bonfim Lopes), arrested in 2011.

Others have been greatly feared and hated. The infamous Dudu (Eduíno Eustáquio de Araújo Filho), who was boss during the mid-1990s, was associated with the *Jovem Comando Vermelho* (Young Comando Vermelho, JCV). It was a movement which relied more directly upon terror as a means of control than the culturally hegemonic approach of the traditional CV (Ludemir 2002). Dudu was said to feed his murdered victims to the two lions and a crocodile he kept in subterranean passages somewhere beneath his boca-de-fumo stronghold. Also, it is widely reported that he used to rape teenage girls—forcing them to have their first sexual experiences with him—and that he once burned a young boy to death in the soccer court in Cachopa for stealing in the favela. Even so, Dudu did cater to the image of the drug trafficker as the protector of the community and did have his admirers. Apparently, he didn't have enough admirers, for eventually his lack of popularity caught up with him and his whereabouts were revealed to police by his Rocinha neighbors. One Sunday afternoon in 1995, Dudu was surprised by police and arrested in his mother-in-law's house. Coincidentally, the very house in which I later lived off and on from 2000 to 2004.

Either way, the basic expectations of the rule of traffickers by the residents of the favela of Rocinha were considerably more comprehensive than those described by Zaluar. True, the first order of business was protection and if a resident was murdered, raped or robbed, for example, other residents expected the gangsters to find the culprit and punish him or her, generally either by permanently or temporarily exiling the offender from the favela or by executing him or her. The drug traffickers never asked residents to pay for this protection or these services—not with money anyway. Residents, in turn, expected that the same rules be applied to everyone, even the highest ranking drug traffickers. In addition to this protection, traffickers were also expected to help residents with things like giving food, medicine and money to the poor, paving roads, supporting cultural projects, etc. They also regularly paid for enormous funk dances and were sometimes responsible for such things as fixing up sports facilities and for scheduling and administering the frequent soccer matches occurring across the favela. There had been widely-known instances in which Rocinha's drug traffickers forced the *bicheiros*, the men who control a famous illegal lottery in Rio, to provide social services for the community also, especially in the 1980s when Dênis was the gang's boss.[10]

In return for this protection and these social services from the boca-de-fumo (drug den), the residents were expected to hold their tongues

10 During their heyday prior to the ascendance of the drug cartels in Rio's favelas, the bicheiros often provided similar assistance to residents, in ways providing a model early drug traffickers were expected to follow. See *Laws of Chance* (Chazkel 2011).

with the police, acknowledge the rightful leadership of the traffickers and cooperate with their various activities—from the sale of drugs to the administering of favela justice. They were expected, in extreme circumstances, to allow the sudden invasion of a home for hiding people, weapons or drugs. If a resident were to inform either the police or rival gangs about the specific dealings of the boca-de-fumo, the traffickers would do their best to kill that resident, often in gruesome ways intended to make an example of the person. Nor could the police be called upon to resolve any problems or otherwise do any policing within the community, at least not without the joint efforts of the gang members. 'Policing,' per se, in Rocinha was the duty and privilege of the boca-de-fumo, and any resident wishing to denounce the crime of another had to approach the drug traffickers who would investigate the matter, if they deemed it necessary to do so.

As a means of demonstrating the complex ways in which the roles of the state and the drug gangs got mixed up and turned around in the multi-layered political reality of the favela of Rocinha at the time, I will recount a revealing anecdote. Until the Rocinha branch of the Bank of the State of Rio de Janeiro (BANERJ) was robbed in November of 2000, it had been considered by many to be the most secure bank in the entire city. One day, however, a group of heavily armed assailants entered the bank and demanded money. A brief exchange of gunfire between the bank robbers and the security guard working inside ensued, however, and the assailants were forced to flee.

Within minutes, the street where the bank was located, the Caminho do Boiadeiro, was swarming with heavily armed gangsters from the boca-de-fumo, who were considered responsible for protecting the bank. But these gangsters were not alone. They had called the local police officers to help them find the assailants. Together, the unlikely partners were slowly walking up and down the street—gangsters and police, together—trying to get to the bottom of the matter and find the culprits. Had the guilty parties been found within the favela, they would likely have been executed, as a means of keeping the rules and affirming the authority of the boca. Such would have been the case even if the gang had caught the bank robbers in the most commercially developed areas of Rocinha.

Generally situated near the bottom of the favela, these more developed areas were still governed by its drug traffickers even as they were becoming more and more regulated by the state. Fortunately for the bank robbers, they were not found in Rocinha, though they were captured in a random *blitz* ('police blockade'), less than one kilometer away on the beachfront in São Conrado. When the identity of the assailants was ascertained, the all-too-typical end of the episode turned out to be that the bank robbers were off-duty members of the Polícia Militar serving on the other side of town.[11]

In the light of this story about the bank robbery, it would seem very difficult to explain the behavior of either the drug traffickers or the police by the sort of "exclusively-through-violent-means" thesis espoused by Zaluar. How is one to answer the question, "Why are the drug dealers protecting a bank?" The answer will certainly be at least as complicated as the answers to the questions, "Why are police officers robbing a bank?" and, "Why are other police officers working together with the gangsters to solve the crime?"

11 An eyewitness account was given to me on November 20, 2000, by the owner of a local Rocinha restaurant, PizzaLit, Sérgio Soares Almeida, a resident of the Rocinha who was inside the bank at the time of the robbery. With a wife, his son Gabriel and his newborn daughter Lorena to think of, Sérgio told me he the experience terrified him. Indeed, it caused him considerable depression afterward as he lamented what he perceived as the disorder of the Brazilian society.

I am inclined to say that the drug traffickers were protecting the bank because of the social consensus that prohibited one from stealing in the favela. Furthermore, if gangs did not protect the banks, the authority and legitimacy of the drug traffickers would be weakened as it became apparent that they could not be trusted to efficiently uphold their end of the social bargain or defend their territory.

In any event, this example suggests that the social order of the favela was far more complex than a simple tyranny of bloodthirsty drug traffickers over the residents and that their social order was much more intimately intertwined with the status quo system than is suggested by such characterizations as 'democracy versus narco-dictatorship.' I am not arguing that the traffickers were progressive-minded revolutionaries, although some may have been. Instead, I am suggesting that there was, in fact, a culture of drug trafficking that was part of the process of cultural hegemony there and that it was built upon much more complex factors than the mere threat of the use of violence. Furthermore, it may have been that the social formation of the favela was less 'parallel' to the State than it was subordinate to the status quo order in Brazil, as the cooperation of the gangsters with police in this case suggests.

Staging Power

There where I was born, you have to know how to live,
I'm talking about my CDD ("Cidade de Deus", or "City of God")
A hustler since I was kid, always in search of peace
We add, we divide, but we never come up less
Our unity is a natural thing, and its simplicity is really divine
But if you cause problems, you'll turn into roots

Mess around and you'll get killed by the gang

—"Rap of the CDD," by MCs Santos and Agostinho[12]

In the late 1990s and early 2000s, Rocinha drug traffickers typically paid for almost all of the major weekly funk dance parties, especially those considered bailes de comunidade. Every Friday there was a baile in the street known as the Valão and Saturdays, one up top on Rua Um at the *quadra*, an indoor gymnasium-like practice area for the samba school Acadêmicos da Rocinha. For events like New Year's Eve and carnival, and on other special occasions, there were dances in the busy commercial street known as the Via Ápia, as described in Chapter 1. There were also children's bailes called *matinês* in the Rua Dois area and the soccer court near my home in the Cachopa area. The traffickers would pay individual sound teams, who came with their electronic equipment and entourage of the DJs and MCs. As was the case with funk in most favelas, Rocinha had certain preferred sound teams that tended to put on shows, but guest sound teams and even 'battles of the sound teams' were commonplace, too.

Each of the criminal factions in Rio had their favorite spokesperson MCs who would perform at any allied favela but could not sing in a favela community ruled by drug traffickers of another cartel. In addition to whatever other songs were played at these dances, the MCs inevitably sung proibidão songs about the local drug traffickers—even at the matinês. Besides just paying for the dances, the sound teams and the MCs, the drug traffickers also supported the bailes by personally attending

12 Portuguese: "Lá onde nasci tem que saber viver, estou me referindo à minha CDD; Malandro desde pequeno sempre em busca da paz; Nós somamos, dividimos, mas de menos jamais; A nossa união é coisa natural, e a simplicidade é mesmo divinal; Mas se tu tá de mancada, você ver virar raiz, mexe e morre pela boca!"("Rap da CDD"). Full lyrics in Appendix A.

them. They would bring their machine guns and a general atmosphere of power, prestige and danger that fans considered an essential part of a good baile de comunidade. Additionally, the drug traffickers guaranteed the protection of those attending the dance party, where neither fighting nor excessive harassment of members of the opposite sex was allowed. If an important member of the gang was killed, traffickers imposed a *luto*, or mourning, on the favela, requiring local business owners to close shop and suspending bailes in honor of the deceased. At other times, drug traffickers held bailes to honor the memory of a dead boss, such as one I attended in July of 2009 in honor of Bem-Te-Vi (Erismar Rodrigues Moreira), an extraordinarily well-loved boss slain by civil police in Operation Trojan Horse in October 2005 (Reforço na segurança 2005).

For an MC, the choice of whether or not to accept the patronage of the drug traffickers was one of significant career consequences. On the one hand, it was a somewhat guaranteed path to at least minor success given that proibidão was perhaps the single most popular type of funk music at the time. Going down the path of proibidão assured well-liked singers plenty of work at community dance parties. On the other, becoming associated with the drug traffickers was likely to make it difficult for a performer to ever tap into the more mainstream funk market (though there are some notable exceptions, like Mr. Catra). As I mentioned above, earlier on funk occasionally had attained popularity, even to the point of becoming a national fad. In fact, several MCs and DJs had participated on Globo TV shows such as Xuxa Hits or Domingão do Faustão. These artists, such as DJ Marlboro, Leonardo and Júnior, Claudinho and Buchecha and the Bonde do Tigrão, certainly made money much faster than their proibidão counterparts. Some, such as MC Júnior, did not particularly like proibidão anyway and lamented the connections between funk and the drug traffickers. These funk artists not connected with organized crime were able to play favelas all over the city, whether they were controlled by the CV, TC or ADA.[13]

By making such a public spectacle of their appearance at the dances, the drug traffickers were able to use them to build legitimacy. In such a climate, the baile de comunidade became a platform for the presentation of the discourse of the hegemony of the traffickers. This discourse attempted to unify the favela community in racial, class and geographical terms as it sought to naturalize and universalize the rule of the drug traffickers there (as I discuss in further detail in Chapter 6). Not only were these dances free—a gift to the favela community from the boca-de-fumo—but they were stages of power for those very same gangsters. Drugs, the product that sustained the whole structure of the criminal faction in the favela, were used in abundance, and gangsters brandished their guns. They also showed off their opulent lifestyle, with their gold chains and numerous friends, groupies, girlfriends and other hangers-on.

On the night of Fat Tuesday, in the Carnival of 2002, dozens of armed traffickers were present at a baile in Rocinha—as was typical.

13 In an interview at his home in Rocinha on March 26, 2002, MC Júnior said he would not want to sing proibidão for the reasons mentioned above. Júnior and his brother, Leonardo, were two of the most famous and best-selling funk artists of all time, performing around the country and on shows like Xuxa Hits and Domingão do Faustão. In 1995, the two had been accused of being spokespersons for the Comando Vermelho for their song "Rap das armas," as reported in Helena, "Rap exalta lema do Comando Vermelho." The song includes the refrain "Paz, justiça e liberdade" ("Peace, justice and love"), which according to that reporter was a slogan of the CV. In reality, Leonardo assured me, they had composed the song in a spirit of a social protest against violence in Brazil. It was never meant to support organized crime, he said. When I asked him if he and Leonardo knew the words were one of the original slogans of the CV, Júnior laughed heartily and said that the reporter who wrote the article apparently knew more about gang culture than did they. Though their song was often sampled and imitated by singers of proibidão, Júnior and Leonardo's vision of funk was much bigger than the traffickers, he told me. It was a vision of funk as a beautiful musical style for the entire country of Brazil—and even for the world.

Wading slowly through the thick of the crowd, they stopped now and again to clasp the hands of boys they knew and give hugs and little kisses to the young women. That was typical enough. What surprised me that night was the fact that so many were wearing matching black jumpsuits. It struck me as remarkably stylish, given the unpolished, semi-improvised fashion of the street dance. The black color also helped show off the shiny silver plating of their weapons. Though many were drinking from little plastic cups and smoking joints, the whole thing came off like a parade or a walk down a fashion runway.[14]

The presence of these gangsters at the community dances—attended by anywhere from just a couple hundred to thousands of people—was a public affirmation that they were in control and that all was well in the community. In the world of the favela, the drug traffickers and their friends were the rich and famous and their fast lives were necessarily quite public. Even if they could not leave Rocinha, at the funk dance, the drug traffickers were in their element. They were the warriors of the tribe, the Special Forces, brave, responsible, sometimes well-loved, sometimes hated—and always dangerous.

Confinement to Rocinha on the part of its top gangsters still left many options for nightlife and was probably not as restricting as it might be in almost any of the smaller favelas around the city. Although funk was the main attraction in terms of sheer numbers of people attending, there was an abundance of large-scale, mostly outdoor musical events of a variety of styles in Rocinha, from funk to pagode, samba and forró. The presence of a large number of cookouts, pizza places and bar-front parties with live music created a continuously festive atmosphere in the

14 I observed this scene at a baile in Rocinha during carnival on February 12, 2002.

favela, especially Thursday through Sunday. There was the main quadra of the samba school near the tunnel in São Conrado, where practice sessions were held for Carnival. There were also the bi-weekly 100% Bagunça and VIP Nites mixed-music, all-you-could-drink events, discussed above. Large-scale charity events featuring performers such as Gabriel o Pensador, O Rappa and Padre Marcelo Mendonça Rossi (Father Marcelo, the much-loved singing Catholic priest) took place with a certain degree of regularity. It was not uncommon to see Brazilian celebrities such as soccer players, singers and actors from the Globo network passing through in cars or mixing with the crowd, also contributing to the atmosphere of glamour and excitement to the social scene of the favela gangsters.

In Rocinha, the only funk dances not directly supported by the *comando* ('command') as the gang was often called, were the ones at the *Clube do Emoções*, a large nightclub on the fringes of the favela in São Conrado.[15] Almost always, Emoções showcased pagode music on Friday nights, forró on Saturdays and funk on Sundays. A well-known night spot for Rio's working class, Emoções also attracted patrons from other favelas and low-income neighborhoods. Its location in the Zona Sul made it a convenient place for a fair number of regulars from Rio's middle-class, as well. Between its two levels, the club had a capacity of roughly 2,500 people. It had an elaborate air-circulation systems and numerous bouncers. Because it was a private club and charged admission, the drug traffickers did not pay for dances held there nor did they openly wield their weapons while in attendance. As a result, fights did sometimes occur at the club, but they tended to be quickly contained by

15 The name of the club is used with the masculine article, "o," presumably because as a club, which is a masculine word, it is often simply called 'O Emoções' and, by extension, 'Clube do Emoções.'

the club's bouncers. Some of the clashes were quite large, with fifty-plus people involved. Because those fights often continued outside the club after the troublemakers were thrown out, the owner of Emoções, Wagner, asked the police to stay near the entrance of the club throughout the night. Before the bigger 'adult' bailes, Emoções also held alcohol-free matinês dance parties for youths.[16]

Although clubs like Emoções tended to feature a more diverse variety of acts than the community bailes, often including competitions between groups of all-male dancer/singers and all-female groups, the high point of the night was almost always the performance of one or two big-name MCs representing the Comando Vermelho. No matter what dance trends and other changes came and went within the movimento funk, the MCs were the idols and heroes of funk, many who had been around since the first funk songs in Portuguese came out in the early 1990s. Their prominent place even in the dances outside of the direct control of the comando and the popularity of their raps proibidos was testimony to the importance of the world of the drug traffickers in funk. This was true as much for the matinês as it was for the adult bailes the. One night at a children's dance, I saw a toddler on his dad's shoulders as he made a gun with his little hand and shot it to the pulsing beat of a proibidão song about the power of the Rocinha gang.[17]

Considering these aspects of the bailes de comunidade in Rio's favelas, it was perhaps no coincidence that Tim Lopes was murdered trying to secretly film while inside one. In a city where thousands of people died violent deaths each year, just what was it about his tragic and bru-

16 Much of the information regarding the Clube do Emoções comes from an interview conducted on March 22, 2002, with its owner and manager Wagner Dias Beta.

17 This was observed at the matinê at the Clube do Emoções on January 13, 2002.

tal slaying in particular that touched such a nerve in Brazil? Why were people calling on the government to send the army back into the favelas, why were favelas once again being surrounded and shut off by the police, why were funk CDs that were ignored before suddenly confiscated and dances suddenly closed?

Perhaps this was because, in a sense, the growing crisis of social exclusion and violence in Rio had brought about an informal criminal welfare system in which favela residents were forced to depend upon drug traffickers for a small amount of support in meeting their needs for protection, housing, medical assistance and recreational activities. Such, at least, was the view of my friend and Rocinha resident Sérgio Soares Almeida. Owner of PizzaLit, one of the most successful eateries in Rocinha, he one day explained to me a concept that he called 'favela-as-solution.' He told me that rather than providing expensive resources for taking care of the population legally through the government, Rio society had come to prefer delegating governance to the gangs. According to Sérgio, the middle- and upper-classes understood well the extremely high levels of violence inherent in this approach. As long as the violence was limited to the low-income segments of the population—concentrated in the favela—it was lamentable but acceptable. The favela itself is the solution to the problem of violence in society, isolating and containing it, preventing it from spilling out to the broader society. Only when the failings of this 'favela-as-solution' system caused such violence to spill over into the formal city did those more affluent residents as a group become outraged and demand action.

According to Sérgio, the public outcry regarding Tim Lopes' horrendous murder made sense, in the light of his 'favela-as-solution' theory. For decades prior, Rio's residents were increasingly finding themselves forced to live behind locked doors, bars and gates. Many circulated the roads of the city in bullet-proof cars and with bodyguards. Although the increases in crime and violence were steadily making things more difficult for elites, a certain degree of limitation on their freedom was acceptable to many. But when a crime boss like Elias Maluco perpetrated such a horrendous murder in the murder of Tim Lopes, a line was crossed. When the rules of the favela were applied to a TV Globo reporter, Sérgio explained, it was as if the monster that was allowed to live in the confines of the favela was threatening to rattle loose of its chain and turn on its master.

Favelas today remain communities of people living as a part of a Brazilian system that exploits them as it forces them to the periphery. If many poor people in Rio are obliged to rely on drug traffickers for protection and social services, it may be less from a 'consumerist' impulse or a 'medieval disposition' than from their desperation to survive amidst a growing crisis of bloodshed and disenfranchisement. In any case, for the culture of favelas to change with respect to the rule of the drug gangs in those communities, the larger society of Rio de Janeiro and Brazil will have to change as well.

6

Crimes of Self Defense

And the gangsters on the job made their guns sing

Making the Rap do parrapapá real

—"Black Boots," by MCs Santos e Agostinho[1]

Pizza and Helicopters[2]

A dozen or so tables line the area under the awning in front of 100% Gostoso Beer Pizza going up the sidewalk and in front of the pharmacy next door. It's about midnight on a Thursday and some sixty or seventy people chat, drink and eat as they mill about the tables in the muggy summer heat of Rio. The pizzeria is well-lit, the TV mounted in front of the restrooms inaudible over the roar of dozens of motorcycle taxis, cars

1 This lines are from an "a cappella" introduction to the song. Portuguese: E os amigos de plantão botaram pra cantar, E fizeram realidade o "Rap do parrá pá pá" ("Bota preta"). Full lyrics in Appendix A. Note, with the mention of "Rap do parrapapá," the singer is referring to the "Rap das armas." In the studio version of that song by MCs Leonardo and Júnior, Cidinho and Doca sing the refrain. Some say the original song was Cidinho and Doca's (see Palombini's foreword to this book). In any case, perhaps the most famous version of the song is the proibidão version popularized with the release of the uncut, pirated version of the 2007 film *Tropa de Elite*. With a simple Internet search, readers will be able to locate the sound recordings and lyrics for both.

2 This opening section is a semi-fictitious representation of the conversation and social interaction occurring at Beer Pizza on a day in November 2001 when the Special Forces of the police invaded the favela and flew over the population for several hours in a helicopter, brazenly aiming rifles at various residents (including the author).

and buses continually passing by. Even at this hour, a low-grade, seemingly endless traffic jam chokes the narrow Estrada da Gávea road. At the far end of the tables, a thin young man with an electric guitar gently tilts his head left and right as he sings an old favorite by Legião Urbana called "Que país é este" ("What Country Is This?"). Several people sing along as waiters in white shirts and black pants bustle through the crowd, serving beer and pizzas.

The Estrada da Gávea, Rocinha's main thoroughfare, almost never sleeps. Even this late, people walk by on their way to and from work, coming home from night school or heading out for the remainder of the night. A group of girls from a local gym, dressed in tiny athletic Lycra shorts and sports bras, stop and hug a group of capoeira fighters relaxing over food and drinks. One of the girls sees her young friend Jacqueline, who works at Rocinha's computer lab, Estação Futuro. Letting out a joyful cry, she runs to the other young woman's table to throw a tight hug her around her neck. In another corner of the gathering, a birthday party is taking place. It's for Vicente, one of the waiters, off-duty tonight and sitting amidst a large group of friends and family members at a row of tables joined together to make room for the various celebrants. The fumes from the traffic mix with cigarette smoke in the heat of the carioca night.

"Did you see that damn helicopter this morning?" Renato Moreno leans over across our table to Charlys, who has just arrived with his girlfriend, Luciana. "Porra, mané! That thing was right on top of me! It stuck around for hours!"

Charlys answers that he wasn't in Rocinha this morning. He's just come in from doing two shows … one late last night and one earlier this evening. "Pô, cara! All morning they were flying up and down the Morrão ('Big Hill'), cara." Renato explains that the police came into the favela early with some informants in tow, X-9s as they are called in the slang of

Rio's favelas (after the popular US comic series *Secret Agent X-9*, which ran from 1934 to 1996). The informants, Renato tells us, were all dressed in black from head to foot. Masks hid their faces as the police led them along on the ends of ropes tied around their necks. The police were after "21," a well-known soldier of the local gang. But they accidentally raided the wrong house—Renato's friend's cousin's home, in fact—which they shot up by mistake. Next door, 21 heard the gunfire and came out, shot one police officer in the arm and took off running like an Olympic sprinter. Since that time, the Military Police had closed down the favela and had been stopping everyone all day long to pat them down.

"I was brushing my teeth and I heard the damn helicopter right on top of me… I opened my window to see what it was and it was right in my face! Those two cops were hangin' on it. Hangin' by belts, you know? Standing on the landing rudders or whatever. They had those big assault rifles, with the big scopes and all, and they pointed 'em right in my face, mané!" Renato drank some beer.

I took a sip from my Coca Light with ice and a slice of lime. "Tema," I said, "You were here this morning, right? Wasn't that messed up?" Nêgu Tema is a hip-hop-style rapper and community educator from the Zona Norte living and working in Rocinha. We've been working on some new ideas for a hip-hop project at the Fundação Dois Irmãos, our NGO, and I've recently introduced him to the other guys.[3]

Just then, someone opens the trunk of a car parked next to us and a

3 The original name for our NGO was Fundação dos Irmãos, which we translated as 'Two Brothers Foundation.' As our website was www.2bros.org, people began referring to the NGO as 2bros even in Rocinha. To complicate matters more, when we registered the NGO in Brazil, we used the name Instituto Dois Irmãos, which we came to refer to as 'i2i.' In referring to it by its different names in this work, I aim to convey some of that fluidity, as the various articulations came to hold slightly different meanings for the people and groups adopting them.

massive thumping bass beat filled the street. The music of the funk song drowns out the din of the crowd and the MC's voice chants a familiar refrain:

> You head's nuts, you're effed in the head
> Rocinha is Comando (Vermelho) in the vein
> If you want to take it over you'd better bring a bazooka
> —"Crazy Head," by MCs Santos and Agostinho[4]

Nêgu Tema took his knit Rasta cap off his head and let his dreads hang down. Calmly, he rubbed his head and looked across the table at me. His answer came in a deep voice and a deadpan expression. "The Third World is one great big video game."Renato and Charlys burst out laughing, nodding their heads in enthusiastic agreement.

"Não tem mais graça, cara!"Tema said, jerking his head sideways. "It ain't funny no more, man!"

The Globo of Favela Folks

I add the scene above at the pizza place, known as Beer Pizza (pronounced 'Bia Pizza' in Portuguese) to speak to the feeling of insecurity and powerlessness police tactics in Rio instilled in the general population of the favela community in those days, as they still do today. It was, of course, entirely terrifying for residents to find themselves in the sights of

4 Portuguese: "Tá com a cuca louca, tá lelé da cuca; A Rocinha é Comando na veia; se quiser tomar tem que vir de bazuka ("Tá com a cuca louca"). Full lyrics in Appendix A.

an assault rifle or caught in the middle of explosive machine gun battles. On top of that, it was humiliating to be frisked by police or ordered to step out of a house or vehicle, mainly since the vast majority of favela residents were utterly innocent of the crimes practiced by their neighborhood drug traffickers.

In another police operation occurring in March of 2003, a policeman from the Military Police's elite squad, the BOPE, kicked in the door to my home before going in and searching it. The officer was part of a large police force searching for a Chilean man known as 'Gringo,' said to be engaged in training local gang members with urban guerrilla tactics. Different from the Spanish meaning of the word gringo, which is reserved for citizens of the United States (generally with a somewhat pejorative connotation) in Brazil *gringo* refers to all foreigners, including Latinos. Since I too was a *gringo*, like the Chilean outlaw, someone had gotten us confused and tipped the police off to my house by mistake.

It was in the Cachopa area of Rocinha, about halfway up the hill. Since I was not home at the time, my neighbors, Dona Helena and Seu Antonio, intervened on my behalf. They explained to the police officer that I was from the US and headed up the small education NGO.[5] Unconvinced, he kicked the door down anyway and walked on in. Seu Antônio went in with him in to make sure he wouldn't steal any of my belongings. When I returned later that day from a short trip to Ilha Grande, a forest-covered, mountainous island a few hours down the coast, I found my door busted into scraps of wood. Despite Dona Helena and Seu Antônio's best attempts to put about half of it back together from the various pieces, there was now more open space than wood in

5 *Seu* is used before men's names as a sign of respect, something like 'Mr.' in English. *Dona* is used similarly before the names of women, like 'Ms.' or 'Mrs.'

the doorframe.

I later learned that after the BOPE officer had kicked down my door, he had nearly done the same at my next door neighbor's place. That neighbor happened to be a reasonably high-ranking drug dealer in the local gang. After one kick on the door from the police officer, the drug dealer's young wife opened the door. Standing there with her baby boy in her arms, she asked the officer what all the fuss was about. Looking disapprovingly at the multiple tattoos across her body, he pointed a finger in her face and told her to step aside. Just then, the baby took hold of the policeman's finger and wouldn't let go. Cooing and gurgling, the little guy just kept holding onto the man's finger and smiling. Something about this softened the policeman's demeanor and he said to the infant, "You're a strong one! Someday, when you grow up, you're going to be a cop!" Smiling, the man gently wriggled his hand free from the baby's little fingers and headed off down the hall and out of the building, satisfied. The drug dealer, who had been hiding in the shower just a few feet away, pistol in hand, had overheard the policeman's prediction. Deeply offended, he later told me, "The nerve of that guy! My son will never be a damn cop!" After three days of searching, the police eventually found the men they were looking for, including the Chilean man called 'Gringo.' As was typical in those times, they left the favela when their raid was over.

Police hounded me on countless other occasions over the years I lived in Rocinha. In one particularly frightening incident, two enraged officers stuffed the barrels of their semi-automatic pistols into my belly, all the while yelling at the top of their lungs that I was a drug addict and a criminal. Referring to my ponytail, tribal tattoo and goatee-style beard, one even told me once I looked like a typical *surfista drogado* ('druggie surfer')—just the sort of *Mauricinho* ('little rich kids') who were filling the classrooms at my nearby university, PUC-Rio. He was sure that I was somehow up to no good and was itching to catch me doing something illegal. After many such encounters, local beat police eventually realized I was living in Rocinha as a teacher and that I was not there to buy drugs, so they finally started leaving me alone. That didn't keep the Special Forces folks from the Military Police's BOPE or the Civil Police's CORE (Coordinação de Recursos Especiais) from harassing me, though, since they came only sporadically and never came to recognize me. No matter how unpleasant such experiences were for me, however, they were nothing compared to what many of my neighbors faced—especially the young men. Even when the police themselves were Afro-Brazilian, the darker the skin of the young men the more they were profiled and harassed.

Beyond the feeling of insecurity that such activities instilled in favela populations, they also generally served to delegitimize the State and its agents in the eyes of Rio's impoverished residents. People living in favelas tended to see the police as an invading force of outsiders who placed the safety of the everyday residents of the community at risk. Repressive police tactics made it clear that the State was more than willing to treat the residents of the favelas as second-class citizens—or even as enemies. Of course, individual police officers, whether from the Military, Civil or Federal police, had their own opinions regarding people in favelas and many were upstanding and well-intentioned. Still, with few exceptions, folks in low-income communities viewed Rio's police as brutal, corrupt, untrustworthy and dangerous.

An anecdote that illustrates this point comes to mind. One sunny afternoon in the mid-1990s, in the nearby residential area of Jacarepaguá, in Rio's *Zona Oeste* ('Western Zone'), I was at a backyard barbecue at the home of a close friend from PUC. Her father, a colonel in the army, was telling me the story of a city bus driver who had recently been dragged out of his bus and murdered in the favela of Borel, in Rio's Zona Norte

('Northern Zone'). My friend's father had been quite upset about the situation, as had most people across town, in various social classes. Then he surprised me with a shockingly candid comment. The best thing to do, the Colonel said, was to drop a bomb on the favela of Borel and wipe it off the map. I thought at first he was joking, but he assured me that he was completely earnest. Though it was lamentable, the Colonel felt that due to a question of karma, there was no other way to straighten out the mess that Borel had become other than to kill all the people living there. I wasn't sure what he meant by 'karma.' Anyway, when I protested that to do so would kill thousands of innocent people, he explained, "Sure, Paul, there are people there who are good. Lots of them are better than you or me, for that matter. For sure. But there's no other solution, don't you see? If we're ever going to make things better, we have to just wipe 'em all out."

Another reason I opened this chapter with the scene at the pizzeria was the hope that a portrayal of a proibidão funk song in the context of the discussion of the invasion would offer a glimpse of its appeal for so many young people living in favelas. In that old school proibidão, the police were portrayed as an invading enemy—one who was corrupt, prejudiced and incompetent, while the local drug traffickers were represented as powerful, crafty warriors who both confounded the police and replaced them as the legitimate defenders of favela communities. Of course, such a discourse downplays the responsibility of the drug traffickers for their side of the situation—and for the resulting climate of violence that characterized life in favelas. No matter, as long as the guns pointed at a resident were in the hands of the police and when it was the police who kicked doors down and stopped people in the streets, it was hard for a person not to see them as the real enemy. The fact that many of the bandits of the drug gangs in any given favela were residents of that community, whereas the police were not, only served to deepen this sentiment. In this context, it was not surprising that many residents of Rocinha would sympathize with 21 in his Hollywood-style escape from the bumbling police. Similarly, it should not be surprising that the funk music which praised the deeds and lives of drug traffickers would become so popular in favelas.

In the previous chapter, I described how the local members of criminal factions patronized the musical practice of funk in the favela of Rocinha, principally through offering large bailes funk in the streets of the favela and by supporting various composers and singers of proibidão funk. In this chapter, my goal is to consider in greater detail the specific ideological strategies evident in proibidão and the ways those strategies served in the negotiation of an image of the drug traffickers of the favelas of Rio de Janeiro as 'social bandits.' This meant they were cast as 'primitive rebel' avengers of the local population in a way that harkened back to a traditional social order based on patronage. This occurred both from the top down by the gangs themselves and from the bottom up by everyday favela residents not possessing firearms or otherwise directly controlling the means of violence in the community. To restate the point, the extent to which these drug traffickers were in practice actual social bandits is another matter. Indeed, Alba Zaluar made a powerful case that they were not, as discussed above. Such socially fabricated constructions should not be dismissed too quickly, even so, since it is precisely in such imaginary, ideological constructs that much of human life finds its 'reality.'

As a means to unpack the question, the ideas of historian Eric Hobsbawm on social banditry are particularly useful. They help shift the question away from one of whether or not the outlaws are indeed 'primitive rebels' towards the issue of what such a construction says about the workings of power in the context of the favela. In his view, the tendency for the rural Italian outlaws and Mafioso groups he studied was to eventually accept and pander to a view of themselves as social bandits, for the countless benefits such popularity afforded them. Once such outlaws came to see themselves in this way, he argued, it allowed for local populations to make claims upon them for justice, protection and service—if in problematic ways. In a similar manner, by focusing on the construction of Rio's drug traffickers as social bandits in proibidão funk—if not necessarily in real life practice—it's possible to glimpse the complex set of ideological negotiations occurring between those drug traffickers and the residents of the favelas and a discourse of the power of the city's criminal factions.

Whatever the agreement between the traffickers and their communities, it was informal and unwritten and how it played out in practice was in a constant state of negotiation. Additionally, there were innumerable possible expectations and interpretations of the governance of the traffickers as there was a wide range of needs of residents of favelas. Not all of these fell under the jurisdiction of the traffickers, besides, since they shared space with other institutions such as NGOs, churches, neighbors' associations and even a limited number of government organizations.[6] Some relatively clear rules and norms for the social organization under the traffickers needed to be articulated and upheld, to some extent, so that the various actors would have a notion of the workings of power within the community.

The traditional media in Brazil played only a small role in the dissemination of these 'laws' of the favelas within those communities. It was usually the case, of course, that newspapers and televisions spread information

6 For more information about the mechanisms of conflict resolution in favelas, see Davis-Rodrigues, "Favela Justice: A Study of Social Control and Dispute Resolution in a Brazilian Shantytown."

about the social formation of favelas that was more in line with the mainstream view of the larger Brazilian society, with its particular biases regarding race, ethnicity, social class, gender, sexual orientation and geographical region. Likewise, the mainstream media's tendency towards sensationalism and commercially driven infotainment-style reporting tended to work against the greater integration and inclusion of favela populations.

Not surprisingly, Rio's drug traffickers became adept at employing means outside of mainstream media to communicate about such things as their criminal activities and their relationships to the other residents in favela communities. For their part, residents also used bottom-up communication strategies—including proibidão—to express their views. As for the traffickers, they frequently communicated with investigative journalists, documentary filmmakers and even scholarly researchers like me, thus gaining additional opportunities to shape things to their advantage.

At certain times —the practice was particularly prevalent in the late 1980s—leaders of the Rocinha gang have even been known to call press conferences with mainstream reporters. That early formation of the Rocinha gang, already allied to the Comando Vermelho, would become infamous throughout Brazil and attained a high degree of popularity in the favela. Prominent gang leaders like Dênis da Rocinha, Bolado (Sérgio Ferreira da Silva), Naldo (Ednaldo de Souza), Buzunga (Robson da Silva), Cassiano (Cassiano Barbosa da Silva) and the thirteen-year-old Brasileirinho, became household name across Rio. When police arrested Dênis in 1987, massive crowds of residents of all types formed at the foot of the hill in protest to demand his release, blocking off a major thoroughfare heading from the Zona Sul to Rio's posh Barra da Tijuca neighborhood. He had brought something to the favela the police never had, people cried: law and order—and respect.

Dênis da Rocinha was succeeded by Bolado, who was shot to death soon after he assumed the mantle of boss. The next boss was Naldo, who was filmed by news crews as he fired off a fully automatic machine gun from the rooftop of a house in the favela soon after he was appointed. Summoning the press to explain his understanding of their role in the favela as social bandits, Naldo was interviewed by mainstream journalists while surrounded by his companions flashing their powerful weapons. He explained that just as Dênis, as well as Bolado, had been righteous protectors of Rocinha, upholding the social contract between the gang and the community so too would he be. The drug traffickers would continue to help the community, he claimed, and the folks in the neighborhood would help the drug traffickers, as it had been before.[7] Perhaps more so than the patronage of proibidão funk, such interactions with the media presented dangers for the gangsters, for obvious reasons. Indeed, police invaded Rocinha soon after this public announcement, forcing Naldo and his gang to flee. He and the other leaders around him were slain not long afterward in a police operation across town in São Gonçalo.

Despite the untimely demise of so many drug traffickers from that early formation of the Rocinha gang, such proclamations of social banditry remained influential in the culture of the favela. One of my first sources on the drug traffickers there, Marquinhos, offered evidence to that effect, still years before the rise of proibidão funk as such.[8] He was a promising and bright young man in his early twenties who maintained an impressive scrapbook of newspaper clippings about Dênis, Boldado,

7 For details, see "Eu era ruim," which tells the story of writer Rachel de Oliveira, ex-gangster, recovering addict and former wife of Naldo.

8 In this case, I am using a pseudonym to provide a degree of confidentiality to Marquinhos and his family members. Except in situations like this in which I have deemed the pros to outweigh the cons in so doing, I have chosen to leave people's real names. Additionally, in some phases of research, specific people preferred to remain anonymous.

Naldo and Rocinha's other gangsters from those days, mostly from the working-class, somewhat more affordable newspaper, *O Dia*. The first time I lived in Rocinha in 1990, in the Rua Um area of the favela, it was in Marquinhos' room in his home, since he was doing his military service and was usually only around on weekends. Idealizing the social views of those early gangsters, he compared them with Che Guevara, whose poster he proudly displayed in his tiny bedroom—along with a small bookshelf holding several memoirs of the Argentinian doctor turned Marxist revolutionary.

Despite Marquinho's reputation in Rocinha as a person with a bright future, he later joined the gang, reportedly as a means to woo a young woman with whom he'd fallen in love. Eventually, he rose to the rank of *soldado* ('soldier') and was known to patrol Rocinha with a high-caliber assault rifle. When he got himself into an insuperable financial debt with the higher-ups in the gang, however, he was taken off to be executed in the very boca-de-fumo that he served. His father, Seu Marcos, frantically scraped and borrowed money from anyone and everyone he knew. He marched up to the drug stronghold, hoping to pay the debt off and rescue his son. Devastatingly, however, Seu Marcos arrived too late. Only minutes before, gang members had executed Marquinhos.

There were other occasions when the gang used their firearms as a means to announce their presence and power in the Rocinha community. Each year at the New Year's party in the Via Ápia area of Rocinha, drug traffickers not only fired their guns in the air but also choose a few representative non-gangsters to shoot some shots. Often when goals were scored during particularly big soccer matches, particularly those involving the national team, gangsters fired off bullets into the air. Even the actual confrontations with police and rival gangs had a theatrical effect for the surrounding population that made those gunfights performances displaying the power and bravery of the gangsters. Such displays contributed to the prestige and hegemony of the gangs in their communities.

One evening in Rocinha in November of 2000, for instance, thousands of rounds of ammunition were fired by gang members between about 8:15 and 9:00 PM. The sounds of the shots, mixed with explosions of fireworks and even a few grenades, could be heard slowly making their way down from the top of the favela near Rua Um to the area of the Valão at the bottom. Understandably, residents—myself included—assumed this to be a horrific gun battle. Children were crying all over the neighborhood, folks ran for cover and stayed low down on the floor.

At that moment, I was teaching an English class for our NGO at the Escola Moranguinhos. Stooping over with my head down, I frantically jogged out the classroom door and down the small hallway at the center of the school, students in tow (mostly teenagers and a couple adults). In mere seconds, we reached to entry hall area of the school, where another instructor was teaching the children's class. The young woman, a college student from the US, was embracing the terrified kids in a group hug in the center of the room. When the rest of us joined the huddle, she led us in singing several children's songs in English, though most of the kids did not stop crying enough to sing. That heartbreaking scene went on for well over a half hour until finally, the gunshots died down enough for parents and other relatives to come pick up their children.

Later that night, a rumor was circulating that the police had invaded, but the next day I learned that it had not been a gunfight at all. That incredible display of power, in which gang members fired off thousands and thousands of rounds of ammunition, had been a celebration by the traffickers after they had successfully negotiated the ransom of their boss from the police, who had captured him earlier that day (Lulu, Luciano Barbosa da Silva). The whole thing had been a sort of hot lead party, but it turned so huge and so loud that inevitably we residents had gotten scared and confused. More than a mere gesture of mirth, there may have been any number of meanings to such an event from psychological and anthropological points of view. It was clear enough, however, that these gun parties also served as a form of communication declaring the power of the drug traffickers in the community.

After the days of Dênis and Naldo in Rocinha, rather than calling on the press gangsters there developed other discursive and ritual means of disseminating the rules of the favela. Within the favela, the hegemony of the drug traffickers was mostly dependent on word of mouth as residents talked to one another, recounting oral histories both remote and recent, telling neighbors what had happened on their street, what they had seen the previous night and so on. Eventually, around the mid-1990s, proibidão-style funk became one of the most crucial means of negotiating expectations about the power of Rio's gangs in the favelas of the city, both in performance in the bailes de comunidade and the lyrics. As the traditional media was to the status quo in Brazil—and the Globo television network in particular—so was proibidão to the social order of the drug traffickers in Rio. It reflected the favela even as it helped to shape it, naming names, mentioning places, reporting what was going on and the rules of how one must behave to survive in the world of Rio's low-income communities.

From the top-down point of view, proibidão funk in the favelas quickly became one the principal platforms for the presentation of the power of the traffickers and the underlying values and rules of behavior they avowed in their governance of the favela. Those rules were closely related to those of the Comando Vermelho in the prison in which the gang was born, the Instituto Penal Cândido Mendes on Ilha Grande, an island off the coast of the State of Rio de Janeiro a few hours away.

When the CV started up in the 1970s, during the days of Brazil's military dictatorship when political prisoners and regular prisoners were jailed together, its members embraced the rule of "peace, justice and liberty" mentioned in the song "Rap das armas." As a group of inmates initially set up for their protection in prison, the group valued avoiding fights among its members, punishing troublemakers and getting and staying out of jail. As the CV blossomed into Rio's largest drug-dealing criminal faction, those same concepts came to be applied to the favela territories in which they based themselves.[9]

For instance, if the drug traffickers killed a rapist but no one knew why, the performance dimension of their action would be lost. To communicate to the residents about the rules of the favela, the traffickers might instead kill the rapist in the night and leave his body in the street with a knife holding up a note on his back saying that he will never rape again—such a thing did, in fact, happen near my home in Rocinha in October of 1990. Or they might drag the alleged rapist screaming from his house, march him across the neighborhood to die in the clandestine cemetery in the woods at the top of the hill. I have heard of occasions in which they traffickers allegedly even stripped accused rapists nude and parade them around in women's underwear before killing them.

For such actions to forcefully discourage future rapes, they must not be seen as a random act but rather as being taken within some common understanding of the rules about crime in the community. In this way, the population learned the rules and became convinced that the traffickers could be trusted to enforce them effectively. On the other hand, if word got around that other rapes did occur and went unpunished, the

9 See Lima, *Uma história do Comando Vermelho* and Penglase, "The Bastard Child of the Dictatorship" and Cypriano, *O Caldeirão do Diabo*.

authority of the traffickers would be diminished. To avoid spending all of their time policing the neighborhood and punishing culprits, therefore, it was in the interest of the traffickers to invest in activities that supported and legitimized their hegemony through public ritual and discourse. Examples were the bailes de comunidade in favelas and the patronage of proibidão-style funk music, to which we turn next. Further on, I will emphasize the role of non-traffickers in the construction of the role of the gangsters in terms of social banditry, from the bottom-up.

7

Social Bandits in Funk

I'm going to tell you how it is, don't run away
The Ten Commandments here in the favela
The first commandment is not to rat
A rat can't live in the favela
The second commandment I'll tell you right now
Don't mess with the women of your friends
The third commandment I'll also say
Is to be down with the gang and not to double-cross anybody
The fourth commandment is not difficult to say
The favela is a good school but you can't rob here
The fifth commandment is that I'm pissed off
I'll cut down any son-of-a-bitch with my G3
—"10 Commandments of the Favela," by MCs Santos and Agostinho[1]

One of the most succinct examples of the representation of the power of the drug traffickers in funk is the song "10 mandamentos da

1 Portuguese: "Vou falar agora vê se não bate biela; Os dez mandamentos que tem dentro da favela; O primeiro mandamento é não cagüetar; Cagüete na favela não pode morar; O segundo mandamento, já já eu vou dizer; Com a mulher dos amigos não se deve mexer; O terceiro mandamento eu vou dizer também; E levar no brindão e não dar volta em ninguém; O quarto mandamento, não é difícil de falar; Favela é boa escola mas não se deve roubar; O quinto mandamento, boladão estou; Vou rasgar de G3 o safadão do encharcador" ("10 commandments of the favela"). Lyrics in Appendix A.

favela" ("10 Commandments of the Favela"), quoted in the verses above. This particular version was recorded live at a baile de comunidade in Rocinha in the Via Ápia or the Valão in 2001 by a duo I will call MCs Santos and Agostinho from another favela controlled by the Comando Vermelho and appears on the bootlegged CD entitled "*Dos bandy 2*" ("Of the Bandits 2").[2] The song suggests very precisely the idea that there is a consensus about what residents should expect from the governance of the traffickers, some mutually recognized code of conduct or culture of the world of the favela. While the threat of violence hangs over these commandments as the means of enforcing them, a notion of right and wrong also permeates them. The commandments themselves constitute rules that go beyond the business of trafficking drugs. Just as God was represented in the Old Testament as capable of violence but having moral authority beyond his capability to act it out, so too are the drug traffickers portrayed in this song.

The use of a religious metaphor for presenting the rules of the favela is typical of the tendency pointed out by Eric Hobsbawm, whose ideas I will discuss below, to equate the outlaw with a traditional order. The performative dimension of the song, which occurs as the drug traffickers and other residents come together in the live setting of a baile funk in a street in Rocinha, is a ritual of power and is critical to the discursive function of the song. On the one hand, it is a clear articulation of the rules of favela life under the reign of the favela's drug cartel, from their point of view. On the other, as I will suggest, the performance of the "10 Mandamentos da Favela" is more than a lecture to a group of feeble, re-

2 "Dos bandy 2" is a homophone for 'of the bandidos' in Portuguese from Rio since the number two, 'dois,' is pronounced the same as the final syllable of that word, 'dos.'

pressed residents but also can be taken as a celebration of the strength, courage, smarts and anger of the people of the favela and their leaders. As such, ultimately it represents just as much an imposition of the view of the expectations, needs and desires of everyday people who are not drug traffickers upon their would-be protectors and patrons.

Perhaps not surprisingly, the first commandment in the song refers to what people often refer to as the 'law of silence.' This law is that a person cannot inform the police or rival gangs about the activities of the local drug cartel. Such a person, referred to as X-9, Mr. M, a *cagüete* or *cagüeta*, is continuously represented in funk as public enemy number one of the favela and his or her actions the ultimate cowardice and self-centeredness.[3] The negative consequences such informants have on the business of trafficking drugs is obvious; less obvious perhaps is the way in which gang culture sees informing as destructive of the well-being of the community.

The following quote from another funk song of the same period will shed light on such a view of the informant. "Vende um X-9 pra mim" ("Sell me an X-9") is by a singer I will call MC Bocão. Born in the favela of Borel in Rio's Northern Zone, even today he remains one of the all-time greats of funk carioca. Indeed, he has enjoyed considerable mainstream success, well beyond his fame as a singer of proibidão in its classical period, and has been a fixture in bailes funk for years. The song begins with a short dialogue between a drug trafficker and a police officer who wants more money for his the *arrego* ('payoff') used to buy cooperation from police. The drug trafficker narrator angrily suggests that the police officer

3 As Professor Servino J. Albuquerque pointed out to me, the word *cagüeta*, or *cagüete*, derives from the word *alcagüeta*, which comes from *alcoviteiro*, an archaic word for a person acting as a go-between on behalf of two lovers.

sell him an informant:

Police Officer: Hey, citizen, and the pay-off time?

Gangster: What the hell, boss? Again? Shit. You're nuts.

Police Officer: With my shitty salary it's tough, you know?

Gangster: Oh, You want more dough? So sell me a rat![4]

Next, the singer denounces the falsity of the X-9, who is said to have pretended to be a friend:

He acts like your friend, he's just pretending
Son-of-a-bitch has got to get it
Because of him my homeboy died
The gang, all their work, he weakened
And he caused lots of deaths leaving unhappy
The family of the homie who died
The neighbors are dying to get him
They all have their eyes open looking for him
The Boss has been arrested and has sent us the word
The sentence we'll execute
With AK bullets[5]

4 Portuguese: Police Officer: Aí, cidadão, e o arrego? Gangster: Qual é, Chefia, de novo? Porra, tá maluco. Police Officer: Com esse salário tá brabo, né? Gangster: Hã… Quer din-din, então vende X-9 para mim.

5 Portuguese: Se faz de amigo só pra escutar; Sujeito safado tem que apanhar; Por causa dele o meu mano morreu; O plantão do trabalho ele enfraqueceu; E causou muitas mortes deixando infeliz; Famílias dos manos que eram raiz; Os moradores já querem pegar; Até grampearam o seu celular; O patrão já tá preso e mandou avisar; Que sua sentença vamos executar; É com bala de AK. Full lyrics in Appendix A.

In the song, the singer blames the informant for the arrest of the boss, the death of members of the *quadrilha* ('gang') and the sorrow of their families. Without the boss, the gang is weakened and cannot guarantee the protection of the favela. The lyrics imply other dangers as well. It's always possible that the boss's lieutenants will fight one another for leadership, bringing about a civil war within the favela community. Or perhaps gangs from other neighborhoods will seize the occasion to attempt an invasion. Whatever the case, the peace of the favela has been compromised, and the residents are at significant risk.

The clear implication of this song, like that of the "10 mandamentos da favela," is that the person who has violated the laws of the favela should be punished. Still, violence and people talking, or singing, about violence are two different things. In the end, the fact that this 'commandment' is being represented lyrically in a popular musical style and sung in a favela at a dance paid for by the drug traffickers brings it beyond physical 'violent means' into a discursive framework about violence. This discursive framework is considerably more complex than the gossip of neighbors discussing a specific murder, for the reason that the violent acts mentioned are not concrete, specific acts that have occurred but somewhat abstract general possibilities of what can happen if one provokes the ire of the drug traffickers.

The second commandment in the "10 Commandments of the Favela"—that one should not "mess with the women (wives and girlfriends)" of friends—is not one typically mentioned in funk lyrics and, in fact, is not considered to be a rule of the favela in general. In reality, this rule applies more to members of the gang than to the general public, perhaps because any ill will between members of the gang can severely weaken and jeopardize it. Still, the rule does reflect a more traditional view of sex relations than one who sees every aspect of the power of the traffickers as hinging upon the force of their arms might expect. For example, the rule could have been that the more influential members of the community could be with whatever women they want, or at least that the drug traffickers could be with any women not involved with other drug traffickers.[6] In any event, the rule does reflect a consensus about interpersonal relations in the favela. It does not prohibit other forms of involvement with women sometimes banned by different cultures, such as involvement with married women or women under eighteen. The basis of the consensus is less abstract and more directly born of the close kinship of the members of the community. If one doesn't know the husband or boyfriend of the women it is okay for a person to be involved with her, according to this rule.

Similarly, the third commandment, which states that one must respect the other residents and not do them wrong in general, is also indicative of this privileging of the personal level of actions over more abstract principles. The commandment is understood to apply only to the residents of the favela in dealing with other residents of the same favela and not as a more abstract moral code extending to the 'asphalt' of the formal city surrounding the favela. The fourth commandment also suggests this loyalty to the favela as a sort of tribe or family when it forbids theft within the community. This fourth commandment calls the favela a "good school," perhaps an inference that one can learn about theft from the residents but not carry out robberies against them. In the fifth com-

6 Such a notion is not automatic. In the mid-1990s, for instance, when the infamous Dudu da Rocinha (Eduíno Eustáquio de Araújo) was in charge of the favela, it is widely reported that he used his power to systematically rape young women in the community. Indeed, residents often told me that such behavior was a crucial factor leading to the cooperation between locals and police in his arrest in 1995. In contrast to Dudu's demeanor, the second commandment of the favela declares that even those in power must obey.

mandment, the singer proclaims the authority of the drug traffickers to kill those who violate the previous four, a sort of 'Thou shalt die.'

It may not be a coincidence that the song does not mention the remaining five commandments of the favela. In the version appearing on *Dos bandy 2*, the singers do not finish the list but, instead, go on to do a medley of other proibidão style songs. Math, no doubt, is not their primary concern, and perhaps the singers feel that they have already touched on the most important commandments with just five. In any event, it is a song sung at a live show where the aesthetics of funk and the entertainment of the crowd are also important. The point is that the 'commandments' are indicating a set of commonly understood rules for life in the community and that these are not limited to the sale of drugs. Not only is there a discourse about the 'law of the favela,' but there is also a consensus about the values of who can use violent means where and when. The fact that these rules are being sung in a song at a baile funk patronized by the drug cartel suggests that an intricate consensus is being negotiated within the favela.

This negotiation of consensus occurs through the actions of both drug traffickers and other residents as well as through the variety of discursive forms through which the significance of those actions is defined and represented. This staging of power of the drug traffickers, both in the baile funk de comunidade and the music of proibidão, indicates that at some level the acquiescence of the population and their dependency upon the drug traffickers do constitute some 'culture' of drug trafficking in which the hegemony of the traffickers gains legitimacy. The residents do have expectations that the traffickers will uphold the laws of the favela among the residents of the favela. By walking into the gang's boca-de-fumo stronghold, fully believing the traffickers will satisfactorily resolve his or her problem, a resident displays an understanding of the power of the traffickers that goes far beyond the notion of the 'law of silence.' In the same way, by writing a song that depicts rules for the drug traffickers to follow, the composer has an opportunity to mold the notion of what it means to be a social bandit in the context of the favela and therefore participates in the negotiation of the order of power in the community.

Musical Gunfire

In the famous "Rap das armas" ("Firearms Rap"), the singers explicitly turn music into gunfire. Besides the lyrical list of firearms one finds in daily life in favelas, the refrain presents a striking onomatopoeia of vocalized gunfire. "Parrapapapapapá papá papa, Parrapapapapapapá papá papa, Paparrá Paparrá Paparrá clack bum, Parrapapapapapapa papá papa." In the two songs discussed in the previous section, "10 mandamentos da favela" and "Vende um X-9 pra mim," the MCs make a battle cry warnings against people violating the rules of favela life. Although neither song uses onomatopoeia for gunfire, both make their threats in the names of famous rifles, the former with the G3 selective fire battle rifle and the latter with the AK-47. Another example of the merging of music and gunfire in funk is the verse "Bota o fuzil pra cantar!" ("Make the gun sing!"), from the song "Sou da Rocinha" ("I'm from Rocinha"), cited at the beginning of Chapter 4. It was a typical opening for funk carioca songs in the heyday of proibidão, and was originated by a famous MC from Rocinha I'm calling "Cordão de Ouro" ("Gold Chain"). Ever since, MCs often start their songs by shouting the verse to the DJ, who then unleashes the heavy beats of the song so the MC can begin singing. Together, such firearms references in funk carioca inspired the title of this book.

In the verses quoted at the beginning of this chapter, the semantic ties between gunfire and funk music work in the reverse direction. Instead of musicians making music that is gunfire, gangsters are said to make gunfire that is music:

> And the gangsters on the job made their guns sing, making the 'Parrapapá Rap' real.[7]

The "Parrapapá Rap" mentioned here is "Rap das armas," discussed above. In these two apparently simple verses, funk music and gangster violence were mixed in one complex knot that at once glorified criminal behavior and lamented the system that created it. The verses portray a gunfight between the soldiers of the favela and an unspecified invading force. In the song, the gangsters make their guns 'sing.' On one level, they are engaged in a life and death gunfight. On another, they perform a song about a life of deadly gunfights. In the heyday of proibidão when this song was popular, the equating of gunfire and music in these two directions was emblematic of the deep relation of funk to the gangs and their discourse of the drug trafficker's rule of the favela.

Though its authors originally intended the song "Rap das armas" as a protest of violence in Rio, as mentioned above, *O Globo* newspaper accused MCs Leonardo and Júnior of glorifying the Comando Vermelho. The brothers suddenly found themselves at the center of public debate as

7 Job means the armed gangsters guarding the favela against invasion by police or rival gangs. Portuguese: "E os amigos de plantão botaram pra cantar, E fizeram realidade o 'Rap do parrá pá pá'" ("Bota preta"). Full lyric in Appendix A. For more details about the song referenced in these verses, the "Rap das armas" ("Firearms Rap"), see note 1 in this chapter.

to whether or not funk itself was an apology for crime.[8] Júnior told me that they did not know that the words "peace, justice and liberty" were considered to be the slogan of the Comando Vermelho and that, in fact, they had never found proibidão to be a very compelling artistic option.

Some six or seven years after the controversy over "Rap das armas," MCs Cidinho and Doca recorded a live proibidão version of the song, originally called "*versão comando*" ("Rap das armas"), or "Firearms Rap (Forbidden Version)." Instead of making a protest against violence, the new song glorified the power of the local gang of the Comando Vermelho in the favela of Dendê, one of the largest in Rio, located on the island known as Ilha do Governador, near Rio's Galeão International Airport. To this day, Cidinho and Doca remain one of the all-time most loved funk singers, especially for their breakout hit of 1995, "Rap da felicidade" ("Rap of Happiness"). That song has endured over the past two decades as something of an archetypical anthem of funk and one of its boldest denouncements of the social injustices suffered by the residents of Rio's favelas. Even so, perhaps today the duo is ever better-known for their proibidão version of "Rap das armas," especially with the international fame it garnished in 2007 after its inclusion in an unofficial, pirated version of the blockbuster *Tropa de Elite*.

Cidinho and Doca's 2001 version of "*versão comando*" ("Rap das armas") can certainly be considered an apology for crime in a way that the original 1995 version never was. Undoubtedly, the insinuation is that the gangsters portrayed in the newer rendition were all too ready and happy to kill somebody with their guns:

8 See Letícia Helena, "Rap exalta lema do Comando Vermelho." Leonardo and Júnior were not proibidão MCs, like the two who sing verses quoted at the beginning of this chapter, whose names I will not mention.

The favela of Dendê is hard to invade

We will have fun with whoever tries

Because I'm gonna tell you how it is in Dendê

Here it isn't even easy for the DRE[9]

To go up our hill even the BOPE[10] trembles in fear

We don't roll over even for the Army,

Civil Police or Military Police

I give huge respect for my friends

But the favela of Dendê is also a land of God.[11]

In this version of the song, the gangsters, like the MCs of proibidão funk themselves, engage in singing-fighting as a counterattack. The singing-fighting presents itself as a means for them to assert themselves against an outside power. Yes, the MCs and gangsters in this context glorify violent acts.

At the same time, in their identity as the champions of the favelas, the mournful singing of their machine guns also becomes the mark of a hard life of violence and poverty. Even so, the semiotic inversions implicit in the song turn the socio-political and cultural realities of the favela on their head in a playful way. As a voice imitating a machine gun becomes

9 Divisão de Repressão a Entorpecentes, the Federal Police's elite "Division of Repression of Drugs."

10 Batalhão de Operações Policiais Especiais.

11 Portuguese: "Morro do Dendê é ruim de invadir; Nós, com os alemão, vamo se divertir; Porque no Dendê vô te dizer como é que é; Aqui não tem mole nem pra DRE; Pra subir aqui no morro até a BOPE treme; Não tem mole pro exército civil, nem pra PM; Eu dou o maior conceito para os amigos meus; Mas morro do Dendê também é terra de Deus." Full lyrics in Appendix A under MCs Santos and Agostinho. Care should be taken to find the version by Cidinho and Doca labeled as "Original," which uses the Volt Mix beat. Various remixes have come out since using beats not traditionally associated with funk carioca.

a machine gun imitating a voice, there is a certain bravado through which the MCs unify the population of the favelas. The song becomes a gesture working far past victimhood. Just as the gang is tough, crafty and not to be trifled with, so too are the other residents—and they know it! Such is true not only for the energetic, united youth in attendance at the baile de comunidade, but rather for all the residents of favelas, young and old, who are united in the difficulties and joys they face in their everyday lives.

With such blatant praise of the violence of the drug traffickers so common in proibidão funk of that time, funk was so often accused of making an apology for crime. Indeed, in its heyday proibidão did make an apology for crime, though what this meant was more complicated than one might expect. The 'crime' it defended was, of course, the culture of the drug traffickers partially governing the favelas of Rio de Janeiro who provided their communities with policing, basic welfare services and recreational activities. Proibidão funk defended and glorified these drug traffickers, representing them as being the legitimate defenders of the poor against the violence and corruption of the larger Brazilian system. The 'crime' being 'apologized' for, in this sense, was not random violence but rather a systematic 'revolt as survival tactic' by some of the people most affected by the crisis of violence plaguing Rio and indeed Brazil more generally.

Yet defending this crime, as the MCs and indeed the entire culture of proibidão did, meant something more than merely making a protest. It was a way of negotiating the use of power in the favelas in general and the hegemony of the drug traffickers, specifically. In truth, the crimes praised in proibidão often went beyond the activities of the drug gangs as defenders of everyday people and even the sale of drugs, sometimes glorifying such things as robberies, assaults, and kidnappings. Still, in the end, what appeared as merely an 'apology for crime' was also an implicit condemnation of the social norms in Brazil that had created high levels of class, race and gender disparity and produced a social welfare system dependent on organized crime for its very existence.

In March of 2002, I interviewed a very talented hip-hop artist named Nêgu Tema[12] (Cleber Pinheiro Rocha) who was living in my area of Rocinha (Cachopa) and who taught me a great deal about favelas and contemporary music in Brazil. At the time, Tema and I were planning to put together a hip-hop workshop for kids in the favela through the Two Brothers Foundation, or 2bros as we often called it (which Tema pronounced "Chew Braw-eesh" in his thick Rio Portuguese accent). Unlike most hip-hop artists and fans, who tended to dislike Brazilian funk, Tema was somewhat favorable toward it, notably toward what he identified as a spirit of indignation in proibidão. He definitely considered probidão much more legitimate as a musical expression than the more sexualized, pop variety of funk. He even wanted to get some of the big name proibidão MCs involved as teachers in our rap workshop since he much admired their songwriting and vocal technique.

Once I asked Tema to compare the older type of protest songs calling for an end to violence that had been common in funk in the mid-1990s—like "Rap das armas," "Rap da felicidade," and "Rap do Silva"—with the proibidão-style funk songs of the millennium. Surprisingly,

12 Nêgu Tema passed away in January of 2018 at age 45 after over two decades of living as a leading figure in the freestyle rap scene in Rio de Janeiro. An activist and organic intellectual from Engenho da Rainha, in Rio's Northern Zone, Tema was a major influence on a generation of rappers in Rio (Gouveia). Internet searches for A Resistência, his group with DJ Sacinho and DJ Lulinha, with the name Nêgu Tema will turn up recordings of several of his songs, otherwise a bit difficult to find online. One can also see him in numerous collaborations with other carioca artists and even a brief clip of him in Barcelona.

Tema told me he didn't see proibidão as so different:

> Funk is a protest with 'Rap da Silva,' and it's also a protest when it talks about the power of our brothers from the Comando Vermelho, and so what? That's also a protest. It's like, "Shit, they never gave me nothing, the system never gave me a chance, so, hey, I'm from Rocinha and I not scared of the Terceiro Command, wanting to disrespect me." Or like, "Yo, dog! Come sell me an X-9, grab your money and beat it."[13]

Not surprisingly, Tema linked the rebellious spirit of proibidão and the cult of the gangsters to the failings of the system for many poor youths. Furthermore, whereas some might say that the system bears the burden of half the blame for the actions of poor criminals and the individual criminal is responsible for the other half, Tema is more radical. According to Tema, crime was widespread and found everywhere in Brazil, but there are different types of crime, like the crime of the rich against the poor and the crime of the first world against the third world.

The difference, he said was that, unlike these other types of crime, the crime of the poor was in legitimate self-defense, "Our crime is one of self-defense, one of legitimate defense."[14] So by representing and glor-ifying this crime musically and artistically, singers and composers of proi-

13 Personal interview with Nêgu Tema in Rocinha, March 14, 2002. Original Portuguese: "O funk quer fazer uma crítica social quando faz o "Rap do Silva" e quer fazer uma crítica social também depois quando fala do poder dos nossos irmãos do Comando Vermelho. E aí? É uma crítica também. É, que fala, 'Porra, nunca me deu, nunca me deu oportunidade este sistema, então, ó, sou da Rocinha e não dou mole pra Terceiro Comando querendo esculachar.' Ou então, 'Ó, cachorro, vem me vender um X-9, pega o dinheiro e rala.'"

14 Interview with Tema (continued). Original Portuguese: "O nosso crime é de auto-defesa, de legítima defesa."

bidão were engaging in a strategy of protest against the unfair treatment of the poor. Tema did not see much difference between the performance of proibidão funk and involvement in more explicitly criminal activities. Unlike the rappers of West Coast gangsta rap in the US, whom he saw as mostly posturing, Tema viewed the Brazilian MCs of proibidão as actual outlaws revolting in both word and deed. The outlaw status of MCs was something positive for him, given the illegitimate nature of 'law' in Brazil. Indeed, he saw himself in a similar light. The MCs were not merely posturing but instead singing about their real lives and those of the gangsters they represented.

Interestingly enough, it was not the glorification of violence that Tema criticizes in MCs of proibidão funk music or the gangsters they sang about, but rather their lack of more explicitly revolutionary consciousness. He thought the militant spirit of proibidão—and indeed the culture of drug trafficking more generally—needed to be tempered with a broader, more radical rejection of the violence of the system:

> I consider myself a gangster. I consider myself a criminal, just like Galo, just like Catra, only a different kind of criminal, a different kind of criminal, but with more hate than them. I've never forgotten the prejudice I suffered. I haven't forgotten, brother.[15]

In Brazilian hip-hop circles in those days, people often said that the letters of the word 'rap' stood for *revolução através da palavra* ('revolution

15 Interview with Tema (continued). Original Portuguese: Eu me considero gangsta. Eu me considero criminoso, igual ao Galo, igual ao Catra, só que um criminoso diferente, um criminoso diferente, mas com mais ódio do que eles. Eu nunca me esqueci do preconceito que eu sofri, não. Eu não esqueci, mano.

through words'). Proibidão, as Tema saw it, as the rule of the drug traffickers themselves, was subversive but much less articulate and self-conscious and ultimately not fully revolutionary. Although Tema himself never said so, perhaps one could have applied his logic to say that the 'rap' in funk, instead of being a 'revolution through words' was a *revolta* através *da palavra* ('indignation in words' or even a 'revolt through words').

In the end, Tema's assertion that the crimes of the poor were committed in legitimate self-defense turned the concept of an apology for crime on its head. Poor criminals, such as the drug traffickers that governed Rio's favelas became 'legitimate defenders,' as did the MCs who advocated them. Tema's hip-hop revolution may have been more self-reflective than that of funk culture, but for him ultimately both revolutionaries and outlaws were acting on the impulse to reject the power and authority of the State.

Drug Traffickers and Primitive Rebels

While Tema's comments were both intelligent and suggestive, I do not offer them as conclusive evidence as to the nature of drug traffickers but rather to shed light on how residents of favelas often viewed Rio's criminal factions. Certainly, Tema's interpretation of the city's drug traffickers as some sort of 'primitive rebels' revolting against injustice in legitimate defense was at odds with Alba Zaluar's analysis, mentioned above. Unlike the portrayal of the drug traffickers as the legitimate defenders of the populations of favelas in funk songs like "10 mandamentos da Favela," for Zaluar, the gangsters were radically self-serving business people who imposed their rule through nothing more than the force of their arms. In addition to her claims that the scope of the gangsters' activities did not include welfare or recreational functions but rather was limited to the efficacy of the sale of drugs in the favela, she also wrote that the drug traffickers, "... always end up employing violent means to maintain their power."(Zaluar 1994, 77) She emphatically argued against the tendency of residents of favelas and newspaper reporters to view the drug traffickers as 'social bandits' or primitive rebels:

> ... one should not romanticize even more than do the residents of the area a bandit protector or a bandit hero and conclude we are looking at romantic heroes of a social movement. In spite of all the connotations of injustice that terms like revolt and indignation call to mind, the principal activity is in a lucrative trade—the trafficking of drugs—and the lifestyle is far from anti-establishment. Neither is there 'a program of defense or restoration of the traditional order of things as they should be' as is supposedly the case with bandits or outlaw peasants (Zaluar 1994, 31).[16]

Zaluar's comment that the residents of the favelas themselves were romantic about the nature of the drug traffickers is interesting. Perhaps she saw the 'romanticism' of the population of the favelas as some false consciousness. Certainly it was possible for people to have unrealistic notions about their rulers; in fact, to a large degree, such a problem is fundamental to the very concept of ideology itself. Still, one must be careful

16 Portuguese: ... não cabe romantizar ainda mais do que os moradores da área um bandido-protetor ou bandido-herói e concluir que estamos diante de heróis românticos de um movimento social. Apesar de todas as conotações com a injustiça que os termos *revolta* e *revoltado* trazem à tona, a atividade principal está num rendoso comércio –o tráfico de tóxicos – e o seu estilo de vida está longe de ser contestatório... Nem tampouco têm "um programa de defesa ou restauração da ordem tradicional das coisas tal como deveriam ser" como supostamente os bandidos ou os camponeses fora-da-lei.

in suggesting that the social scientist knows the reality of the situation better than the actual residents. I think the word "romantic" is insufficient to describe the attitudes of the much-suffering people of the favelas of Rio, people who have every reason to be very practical and realistic. In any event, by suggesting the existence of romantic notions amongst the residents of favelas characterizing the traffickers as protectors and heroes, Zaluar undermined her general assertion that the rule of the traffickers relied solely on the power of their weapons and violent means. If there was not some culture of favelas, and some accompanying discursive process through which such notions were presented and negotiated in the hegemonic terrain of the favela, how did such romantic ideas grow and take hold?

Notwithstanding the merits of Zaluar's thinking, favela residents did have notions of the relationship between those who were drug traffickers and those who were not, and they did have ideas about how the rules about violence should work. As much as these notions derived from concrete actions, they also appeared through communication between residents about those actions. To some extent, such ideas arose as people observed the activities of the drug traffickers and talked about them with one another. Residents of favelas commented on violent occurrences in their communities in which informants or thieves were killed, for example, incidents that might have taken place in their next door neighbor's house, on their street or around the corner.

They would say things like, "Wow, that was surprising!" and, "Boy, he sure had that coming," or, "My God! What's the world coming to?" The drug traffickers were, of course, aware that people discussed their actions in the neighborhood and often choose to perform those actions publicly to let people know what they were doing and why. Such behavior was a compelling aspect of the hegemonic process through which power and the authority of the drug traffickers were negotiated. This process was more than the education of the rules of favela life by the repressive machine of the drug traffickers; it also involved the expectations of the non-trafficker residents of the communities regarding how power and leadership should and should not work. On the one hand, it allowed the traffickers to institutionalize and extend the reach of their power and authority; on the other, since the non-trafficker residents of the community also had a voice in that dialogue, they could also actively participate in the development and acceptance of the consensus on power in the favela.

Distinctions like the ones made by Nêgu Tema above between revolutionary activities and more primitive revolts were fundamental to Eric Hobsbawm's classic study of social bandits, the mafia and millenarian movements of the 19th and 20th centuries. Hobsbawm's analysis focused on how pre-modern peasant communities in 19th century Italy tended to regard their outlaws as what he called "social bandits." Peasants viewed these bandits as protectors, he argued, resisting the corrupt order of the legal authorities, redistributing the wealth, righting wrongs and dealing out justice within the parameters of a traditional value system. For Hobsbawm, the pre-modern, pre-capitalist consciousness of these peasants limited them from envisioning the total overthrow or destruction of the social order in which they lived. For this reason, he considered the millenarian religious movements he also studied to be more 'modern' than Mafioso activity or banditry, precisely because the radical apocalyptic vision driving them to call for the destruction of the world as it was.

When it comes to proibidão, one of the most salient aspects of Hobsbawm's model is the way in which it emphasized the consciousness and opinion of the peasants over the intention of the criminals. For Hobsbawm, altruism was not a necessary ingredient in the make-up of the social bandit, who was rather more likely to be motivated by self-serving political sensibilities:

> It does not greatly matter whether a man began his career for quasi—political reasons like Giuliano—an Italian Mafioso studied by Hobsbawm, who had a grudge against the police and the government, or whether he simply robs because it is a natural thing for an outlaw to do. He will almost certainly try to conform to the Robin Hood stereotype in some respects; that is, he will try to be 'a man who took from the rich to give to the poor and never killed but in self-defense or just revenge.' He is virtually obliged to, for there is more to take from the rich than from the poor, and if he takes from the poor or becomes an 'illegitimate' killer, he forfeits his most powerful asset, public aid and sympathy. If he is free-handed with his gains, it may only be because a man in his position in a society of pre-capitalist values shows his power and status by largesse. And if he himself does not regard his actions as social protest, the public will, so that even a professional criminal may come to pander to its view (Hobsbawm 1963, 20).

For Hobsbawm, the lack of altruistic motives did not keep a bandit from being a 'social' one. What made him a social bandit was that he was outside the law and dependent on the support of other poor people who were sympathetic to him. Hobsbawm characterized the social bandit's decision to play up his image as being a protector of everyday people as more of an afterthought than evidence of a revolutionary consciousness or an agenda of social contestation.

Another interesting aspect of Hobsbawm's analysis is that the social bandit did not need to impose himself on his supporters. Certainly, the bandit might impose himself to an extent on his followers, but if he were too repressive the people would turn on him, and he would, therefore, lose the advantage of their protection (as in the case of Dudu da Rocinha, mentioned above). If he were smart, on the other hand, the natural affinity that many other poor people have for the social bandit would grow. The limit of the outlaws' ability to impose themselves was why, for Hobsbawm, the phenomenon of the social bandit emerged more from the attitude of his supporters than from the bandit himself. Hobsbawm expressed an idea very similar to those of Nêgu Tema, discussed above:

> For in some sense banditry is a rather primitive form of social protest, perhaps the most primitive we know. At any rate in many societies it is regarded as such by the poor, who consequently protect the bandit, regard him as their champion idealize him and turn him into a myth (Hobsbawm 1963, 13)

On the one hand the public elevated the bandit to the status of a heroic avenger and protector of the weak, and on the other hand the bandit pandered to this view. Both parties stood to gain in this construction, for if the public could get the bandit to name himself as their protector and avenger, they were likely to see at least some of his power used for their needs. In a like manner, by placing himself within this framework created by the public, the bandit gained protection against the legal authorities, greater access to supplies, a more developed system of eyes and ears and even some people willing to join his outlaw group. This mutual benefit entailed significant consequences for the dynamics of the hegemonic process and how both the top and the bottom affected the construction of power in the favela.

Hobsbawm's observation that the social bandit phenomenon was related to a pre-modernist consciousness that was not revolutionary may help to explain Nêgu Tema's dissatisfaction with the drug traffickers and with the MCs of proibidão and his feeling that they were not radical enough. In some ways, the drug traffickers and MCs of proibidão were tragic figures for Tema, as was the social bandit for Hobsbawm; their revolt was a crime of legitimate self-defense by people pushed to the edge by a socially stratified, corrupt and violent society. They might be brave, just and cunning within the landscape of the reformist battles they fought, as they might spend some of their wealth on charity for the poor and as acts of personal largesse. But the tragic nature of these bandits was not merely the result of their ruthlessness and potentially violent nature but rather because their overall aims tended to be conservative and fundamentally non-revolutionary.

In the end, although the bandits were raised up as champions of the poor, they represented more of a survival tactic, an immediate response to the failings of the larger Brazilian social order, than a forward-thinking revolutionary plan. Even to the extent they could be seen as anti-establishment figures, in this light, Rio's drug traffickers were fighting against a system in which they found themselves trapped in a parasitic relationship, a system they could never really hope to destroy, replace or escape.

8

Bandits of Christ

One of the most striking examples of the ambivalence of representations of criminal factions in Rio's proibidão funk can be found in the pair of songs "Bandidos de Cristo" ("Bandits of Christ") and "Rap do Patrão" ("Rap of the Boss"). Recorded live at a community baile in Rocinha in 2001—when the Comando Vermelho criminal faction was still dominant there—the songs were released on the clandestine CD *Raps Proibidos Volume VII* and circulated in the favela. The MC who performed these songs was one of the two most prolific and popular singers from the golden age of proibidão in Rocinha in the late 1990s and early 2000s. To protect his identity, I will refer to him as MC Manda Brasa.[1] Live at the dance parties, MC Manda Brasa usually sung the first song as a sort of introduction to the second. Both used the same stripped down version of the Volt Mix beat already going out of style at the time, though their melodies were entirely different. Taken together, the lyrics of "Bandidos de Cristo" and "Rap do Patrão" exemplified the complexity of the discourse about drug traffickers in proibidão funk music.

"Bandidos de Cristo" borrowed its melody for the song from a popular religious folk tune called "Rise and Shine" in English, or alternately "Arky Arky." In the song, God tells Noah, "There's gonna be a floody, floody," and to "Get those animals out of the muddy, muddy." At the time MC Manda

1 The nickname "Manda Brasa" suits this particular MC well, as this expression indicates encouragement and intensity, something akin to the English "Go for it!"

Brasa recorded his song, an enormously well-known and well-liked singer and Catholic priest, Padre Marcelo Rossi, had recently popularized that children's song in Brazil in Portuguese as "Erguei as mãos" ("Raise Your Hands"). By intermingling the ethos of crime with the Christian faith, the song provoked its listeners—be they residents, drug traffickers or outsiders—with a compact representation of the complexities of the culture of the drug cartels in Rio's favelas. After a list of examples of the gang's deadly firearms, it opens with its densely ambiguous refrain:

> Bandits of Christ, they have a lot of faith in God
> Bandits of Christ, they have a lot of faith in God
> For this life you gotta have determination
> Just ask the Boss[2]

The mixture of religious elements and references to the world of crime in "Bandidos de Cristo" made for a striking juxtaposition and a supreme exaltation of the figure of the gangster. The mention of "fé em Deus" ("faith in God") presented a richly meaningful play on words. Besides the obvious meaning of this phrase as a reference for a religious or spiritual attitude, "faith in God" was a slogan of the Comando Vermelho and an expression people used to identify their loyalty to that criminal faction. In practice, the religious inclinations of individual gangsters in favelas like Rocinha were greatly varied, of course, ranging from Christian ones like Catholic, traditional Protestant and contemporary Evangelical,

2 In the recorded version, MC Manda Brasa sings with another MC listed by online versions today as his former musical partner. Portuguese: *MC Manda Brasa*: "Bandidos de Cristo, tem muita fé em Deus; Bandidos de Cristo, tem muita fé em Deus; Para essa vida tem que ter muita disposição; Pergunte pro Patrão." Full lyrics for "Bandidos de Cristo" in Appendix A.

to Afro-Brazilian beliefs such as Candomblé, to other religions popular in Brazil like Umbanda and Spiritism. Some members of the Rocinha gang did not identify with any religious faith or belief. Regardless of the actual religious affinities of gang members, whatever dichotomy might be traditionally assumed between being a well-armed, violent criminal and a God-fearing religious believer faded away in the song's "Bandits of Christ" metaphor, as did the conventional distinction between the police and bandits.

In the verses that follow the refrain, MC Manda Brasa offers a condensed portrayal of the 'law of the favela' closely parallel to Hobsbawm's notion of the social bandit (to be discussed below):

> I asked,
> The Good Boss answered me
> One has to follow the great lesson
> Grenade pouch, shotgun, and defend our Big Hill3
> I don't wanna see, I don't wanna see
> The little brothers turning their backs on the big hill
> We're Red, you are, too
> We'll fire tons of shots, Heads up![4]

The implication is that the singer has asked the boss about the gang's role in the community. The boss responds that the "great lesson" is that the gang must defend the favela. The "little brothers," as he calls the traffickers,

3 A reference to Rocinha.

4 Portuguese: "Eu perguntei; O bom patrão me respondeu; 'Tem que seguir esta lição; Porta granada e escopeta, e defender o nosso morrão; Não quero ver, não quero ver; Os irmãozinhos virando as costas pro morrão; Somos Vermelho, vocês também, quero ver; Vamos dar tiro de montão,' Presta atenção!"

must not "turn their backs" on the community. They are all "Red," in that they all belong to the same 'Red Command' family (Comando Vermelho). The second song of the song pairing, "Rap do Patrão," begins a cappella. MC Manda Brasa refers to the favela crime boss as "Rebelde" ("Rebel"), a name that closely parallels Hobsbawm's notion of the social bandit. Switching melodies as he transitions into "Rap do Patrão" ("Rap of the Boss"), he sings:

> Rebel became angry and called a meeting
> I want everybody armed, and at the top of the Big Hill[5]

It is interesting to note that the name Rebelde, or 'Rebel,' was not the nickname of an actual crime boss in Rocinha, at least not one commonly known to residents. Instead, it seems to be a sort of fictitious codename used to suggest the spirit of social banditry emphasized by the MC. In any case, the verses of this a cappella stanza suggest a profoundly nostalgic flashback to a time before the police imprisoned the boss. That time is portrayed as one in which he still had been able to dutifully carry out the task of serving and protecting the community as a sort of warrior chief—one who was wise and capable on the one hand and dangerous and violent on the other. In that flashback mode, MC Manda Brasa does not explain the motive of Rebelde's anger or the reason he called his men to arms at the top of the hill. The implication, especially considering the song's pairing with "Bandidos de Cristo," is that Rebelde is a legitimate leader who loves and protects the favela population. Symbolically, he is at the top of the favela's social structure just as he is physically at the top of the "Big Hill." He paternalistically and righteously prepares his men to come down

5 Portuguese: "Rebelde ficou bolado, fez uma reunião; Quero todo mundo armado lá no alto do morrão." Full lyrics for "Rap do Patrão" in Appendix A.

like a storm, or a plague, on some unidentified guilty party to take whatever steps necessary to correct whatever wrongs have been committed.

The detailed mention of the names of the guns used by the various types of gangsters in his gang suggests Rebelde's willingness and power to undertake such vengeance, even though as a just leader his power and authority do not stop at the barrel of his gun:

> Fireworks alarm guys, AR-15, the manager with a G3
> The dealers with pistols, I'll only say it once
> The soldiers of my gang come with 762s
> The watchers with tracer bullets, the signal is two by two
> When the gang is good, the community knows it
> Rebel comes at the lead with an AK-47[6]

As the music starts up and the beat begins, MC Manda Brasa comes in with the refrain:

> I'm going up, going up, going up my big hill
> With a hello for my friends
> And a hug for the Boss[7]

Here, the Rocinha kingpin merely is referred to the Patrão, or 'Boss.' Calling him Rebelde in the first stanza and calling him Patrão in the

6 Portuguese: "Fogueteiro, AR-15, o gerente de G3; O vapor vem de pistola, eu vou falar só una vez; Os soldados do meu bonde vêm de 762; Os olheiros de traçante, o aviso é dois em dois; O contexto quando é sangue, os amigos reconhecem; Rebelde vem no comando de AK-47."

7 Portuguese: "Vou subir, vou subir, vou subir o meu morrão; Com um alô para os amigos; E um abraço pro Patrão."

refrain reinforces the way in which the song presents the boss figure as a sort of idealized and universalized drug trafficker. He is portrayed as a crime boss embodying the legitimacy and righteousness of the gangsters as the loving and just protectors of their communities. By pairing the "Rap do Patrão" with "Bandidos de Cristo," the implication is that the boss is himself a 'bandit of Christ,' as are the gangsters he leads.

The second stanza mentions the imprisonment of Rocinha gangsters, once again referred to as the *irmãozinhos* ('little brothers'), who are trapped in a sort of Babylonian exile in some of Rio's most infamous prisons:

> A hello for Bangu 1, Agua Santa and Bangu 3
> Where the little brothers live, how I miss you all[8]

In the next lines, there is something deeply tender, reverent and even messianic about the MC's declaration of faith in God that the boss would return one day, along with the other jailed friends, a day that will be one of peace, playfulness and redemption:

> When I go up the favela and pass by that place
> Where the Boss used to hang out it makes me want to cry
> But I have "faith in God" and in all that's holy
> That soon I'll see my little Boss free
> So we can hang out together across the parts of the big hill
> Celebrating the freedom of our good brothers[9]

8 Portuguese: "Um alô pra Bangu Um, Água Santa e Bangu Três; Onde vivem os irmãozinhos, que saudades de vocês."

9 Portuguese: "Quando eu subo a favela e passo naquele lugar; Que o Patrão tirava onda dá vontade de chorar; Mas eu tenho fé em Deus e na pura santidade; Que em

Once again, at the time of the song's performance, the assertion by the singer that "eu tenho fé em Deus" ("I have faith in God") would have be understood by Rocinha residents as a double-entendre referring to the slogan of the CV mentioned above.

Additionally, many Rocinha residents in those days likely would have taken the name Rebelde to stand for Dênis da Rocinha. Some thirteen years after his arrest, Dênis was still idealized, even after he had been slain in his prison cell in Bangu 1 earlier that year. In fact, until his death in January of 2001, whatever happened in Rocinha regarding the gangsters and their activities was typically said to have been authorized by Dênis, though in many cases such direct connections were doubtful. The implication that the Rebelde of the song stood for Dênis added an extra layer of context to it, not only for the nostalgia it evoked but as an implicit yet forceful protest against the abuse of power perpetrated by the gangsters behind the murder of Rocinha's most beloved crime boss.

In the third stanza of the song, even the trafficking of drugs—conventionally seen as one of the great public evils of the day—is portrayed as a supremely redemptive gesture that unifies the city of Rio and the people of Brazil. This portrayal involves a play on the words "black" and "white," which, in addition to their racial connotations, were common Rio slang references to marijuana ("black") and cocaine ("white") respectively:

> A hello for the customers of my Rio de Janeiro;
> Whether black or white it's pure Brazilian;
> For those in the North City, West City or South City

breve eu verei o Patrãozinho em liberdade; Pra gente zuar juntinho pelas partes do morrão; Festejando a liberdade dos amigos sangue bom."

East City also, the way things are going there will be one
A hug for the friends who protect the favelas
Thank you for the help that you give to them
The dealers, the fireworks alarm guys, the managers and the thieves
And to all the soldiers that protect the Boss[10]

By thanking the drug traffickers in a context which presents them as "bandits of Christ" and through such a loving, fraternal spirit, MC Manda Brasa makes himself something of a spokesperson for the gang. He elevates its members to the status of spiritual servants of a higher good and a social order that is not racially polarized or class-stratified. At the same time, as a favela resident who is not an actual member of the gang, the MC's song should also be viewed as a means through which he is setting forth the expectations residents have of gang members. By affirming the accepted notions of what a crime boss and his men should be, ordinary civilians in the favela work to shape the culture of gangs from the outside. It's as if to say, "If you gangsters do not live up to this ideal, we will not support you. We will let the police find you or allow another gang member to come along and knock you off."

This final stanza of "Rap do Patrão" is a repeat of the first, this time sung with musical accompaniment. It remains steeped in nostalgia and that ever so Brazilian quality of *saudades* (something akin to a bittersweet, nostalgic longing) as it recalls a time when the Boss was not in prison. Back then, he was powerful and just, a friend of the other residents of the

10 Portuguese: "Um alô para os fregueses do meu Rio de Janeiro; Vai de preto ou vai de branco é do puro brasileiro; Pra quem são da Zona Norte, Zona Oeste ou Zona Sul; Zona Leste também vem, pelo jeito vai dar um; Um abraço pros amigos que protegem as favelas; Obrigado pela força que vocês dão para ela; O vapor, o fogueteiro, o gerente e o ladrão; E a todos os soldados que protege o Patrão."

favela community. When understood in the light of the whole song, the verses of this stanza express a longing, too, for the "paz, justiça e liberdade" ("peace, justice and liberty") of the CV's slogan. At its core, the song conveys a sense of utopian hope for people living in the harsh reality of the favela, one left unfulfilled by the police, government or mainstream society. It can only be made a reality by the Patrãozinho, as a good and dearly beloved 'Little Boss'—together with the power of the Comando Vermelho as defenders of the people.

In this context, a particularly richly suggestive verse is "O contexto quando é sangue os amigos reconhecem" ("When the gang is cool, the community knows it"). On the one hand, the speaker could be Rebelde, who by saying this is portrayed as appreciating the worth of the support of the residents. On the other hand, it could be understood as being in the voice of the singer/composer and as merely pointing out what he considers an objective truth about the unity between the drug traffickers and the community. As I mentioned above, however, there is also perhaps a hint of suspicion in the verse that makes it tantamount to a warning, for just as MC Manda Brasa positions himself as a spokesperson for the gang, so too does he affirm his role as spokesperson of the ordinary favela residents. It is not clear which gangsters were responsible for Dênis' death in prison—it is quite likely to have been the result of internal conflicts within the CV. MC Manda Brasa's implicit message is that no matter who tries to fill his shoes, the local population of Rocinha will not accept selfish, backstabbing drug traffickers. Such low-down thugs will end up being handed over to the police, as was the case with the abusive Dudu da Rocinha (Eduíno Eustáquio de Araújo). Instead, residents expect assistance, cooperation and respect. In this way, the coupling of "Bandidos de Cristo" with "Rap do Patrão" exemplifies the attempts of everyday favela residents to define the culture of crime in the favela, particularly regarding social banditry.

In this context, the word *sangue* ('blood') in this verse is a heavily loaded slang expression of the culture of funk, *sangue bom* ('good blood'). Sangue has a certain racial connotation very significant for the construction of a subaltern favela identity and to the notion that the gang is one with the people it rules and protects. The implication of being 'sangue' in this case is that the gang is fair and righteous, not selfish or abusive. Whether the words are understood as coming from Rebelde himself or the MC as narrator, a certain consciousness is implied of some mutual advantage between the gang as sangue and the residents as amigos ('friends'). When drug trafficking came to prominence in Rio in the 1980s, it latched on to a previous culture of organized crime in the *jogo do bicho* ('animal game') a form of illegal lottery popular in Rio. Just as the *bicheiros*, as the bookies running the jogo do bicho are known, had practiced a rudimentary form of social welfare in favelas and other low-income communities, so too now would the drug trafficking criminal factions.[11] In this sense, the song portrays the mobilization called for by Rebelde on the part of his warriors, who are expected to take part in unspecified violent actions in fulfilling their role as social bandit-style protectors and champions of his favela people.

Although Hobsbawm's observations about the phenomenon of social bandits as primitive rebels are readily applicable to the song "Bandidos de Cristo," its religious dimensions take the song beyond the demarcations the British historian made between types of 'primitive rebels,' in particular those between the social bandit and the millenarian. For Hobsbawm, the social bandit, like the Mafioso, was a form of

11 For a nuanced history of the *jogo do bicho*, see *Laws of Chance: Brazil's Clandestine Lottery and the Making of Public Urban Life* (Chazkel 2011).

primitive protest largely of a reformist nature. Millenarian movements, which he saw as apocalyptic and religious, on the other hand, had a far more sweeping, revolutionary scope that made them much more modern, despite their superficial medieval appearance. For the social bandit, he argued, wrongs were righted and the order of justice reestablished. The millenarian project, in contrast, was to remake the whole world from top to bottom. For Hobsbawm, the necessary condition for either was a population with a 'pre-modern' consciousness in which other forms of protest and social organization did not exist as practical options.

It seems to me that the construction of the drug traffickers as social bandits in the song "Bandidos de Cristo" actually mixes the two impulses in a striking way, such that the bandit becomes something of a messianic figure. Hobsbawm thought the millenarian movements were mistaken by the modernized middle and upper-classes to be barbaric, that their revolutionary spirit was mistaken for the reformist impulse of primitive protests like the social bandit and mafia phenomena. Certainly, in the case of the war of Canudos, which Hobsbawm mentioned in his the preface to *Primitive Rebels*, the Brazil of the coastal region did largely view the followers of the prophetic Antônio Conselheiro as backward religious fanatics stuck in a centuries-old, medieval past. In fact, the presence of the *jagunços* ('gunmen') of the semi-arid *Sertão* region where the war took place, did lead to a conflation of bandits and millenarians in the eyes of the Brazilian republican government, as is evident in Euclydes da Cunha's master work *Os Sertões* (1902), also mentioned by Hobsbawm.

It is worth considering the following, however: if the population begins to turn the social bandit into a millenarian figure, would this mean for Hobsbawm that they are more or less pre-modern than a community that does not? We could turn the question around. Is the notion of social bandit as millenarian figure more revolutionary than the traditional type of social bandit, described by Hobsbawm? Or are the people so non-revolutionary that even a simple reformist revolt gains a messianic significance? It is possible that, in the harsh reality of the favela and the crisis of social exclusion that surrounds it, the possibility of revolutionary social transformation is so remote that any possible semblance of order becomes eschatological. It could be that, though, that the song "Bandidos de Cristo" suggests more than a symbolic revolt—one operating within conservative tendencies to restore a traditional order or right specific wrongs. Instead, it might carry the discourse of the power of the traffickers toward a more radically revolutionary dimension that sincerely seeks to turn the world on its head.

It could also be the case that the mixture of imagery typical of the social bandit with elements of millenarian longings in "Bandidos de Cristo" and in Rocinha gang culture more generally was the result of the radical cultural hybridity that existed in the favela. The social terrain of Rocinha in the new millennium was more complex than that of rural, pre-capitalist Italy, as a favela reality entailing overlapping levels of consciousness characteristic of post-industrial and pre-modern societies. As I discussed in above, for decades, Rocinha had experienced a massive influx of people from a variety of places in the Sertão backlands of the Brazilian Northeast. These people had steadily mixed into a population that included people from all over Brazil and from all sorts of socio-political backgrounds. The result was a hybrid culture in which bandits, for example, were in some ways both the ruthless and hedonistic post-modern businessmen, as Alba Zaluar argued, and the traditional patronage-based big bosses of the Sertão region. Either way, the insistence on the part of the local population on a culture of social banditry had real-life implications, not only regarding the hope this offered those residents but also in weakening mainstream Brazilian narratives. It also worked to oblige the gangsters to operate within the framework of a "ten commandments" of the favela from the point of view of non-gangster favela residents.

Who Writes the Ten Commandments of the Favela?

> Yo... Check this out. Because there's always some guy who thinks being a gangster, brother, is screwing over your friend, using other people as a trampoline, you know? The real gangster respects in order to be respected, treats people well so they treat him well. So, I going to start this one up more or less like this, yo....[12]

Thus far, I have suggested that the construction of the drug traffickers as social bandits in the culture of Rio's favelas in the golden age of proibidão was as much the doing of the ordinary population as of the gangsters who patronized the MCs and community dance parties. In the remainder of this chapter, I intend to consider a bit more closely the negotiation of the consensus about power in the favela from the point of view of gangster and non-criminal alike. To do so, I'll borrow terms

12 This excerpt is from MC Bocão, from the favela of Borel and singer of "Vende um X-9 pra mim," discussed above. The passage quoted above is a spoken introduction to track 20, "Bandido Bandeid e Quando a chapa esquenta," on the compilation CD Bonde dos MCs. Portuguese: "Já é... Se liga na responsa. Porque tem vários caras que pensa que ser bandido, mano, é desfazer do irmão, é usar o outro de trampolim, tá ligado? E na verdade o verdadeiro bandido respeita pra ser respeitado, considera pra ser considerado. Então, vou mandar mais ou menos assim, ó...." Though at least one other version of this pair of song is currently available online, the version with the lengthy spoken intro cited here is not.

for thinking about hegemonic strategies from Terry Eagleton's nuanced study of ideology: unifying, action-oriented, rationalizing, legitimating, universalizing and naturalizing.[13]

But whose strategies were these in the context of Rio's favelas in the late 1990s and early 2000s and those community dance parties that had assumed such an essential role in the workings of power there? Was proibidão the voice of the gangsters or the community? Would it be better to think of performances of proibidão music as instances of the traffickers explaining the rules to the favela population or the other way around? Just as performance and audience tend to mix together in expressions of Afro-Atlantic music and dance, destabilizing rigid hierarchies, so too do the perspectives of gang members with those of the non-criminal favela populations of which they are part. Ultimately, the discourse of power in the favela was a process of negotiation between all the residents, criminal and non-criminal alike.

In the case of power in the favelas, such questions are crucial because, no matter how close the MCs who sing proibidão might have been to the quadrilha gang, and no matter how much patronage they may have received from the gangsters, the MCs were not typically drug traffickers themselves. Of course, one or another MC may have been an actual gun-toting drug trafficker or some other kind of criminal in the past. In general, however, they were rather friends and sympathizers of the drug traffickers, often having grown up alongside them in their favela communities, and wrote and sung their music with only the indirect support of the gangs.

It's also worth noting that in employing the term strategy one could

13 For further explanations of these ideological strategies, see *Ideology* (Eagleton 1991 , 45-61).

over-emphasize the degree of self-awareness of the actors involved. It's not necessarily the case that the drug traffickers were consciously promoting themselves as social bandits through funk carioca as an explicit public relations plan. Perhaps more than recognizing the baile funk as the staging of their power gangsters simply viewed a community dance party as a chance to show off and enjoy themselves. Similarly, composers and other party-going fans were not necessarily aware of their influence in the relations between gang and community. Ideological processes do not have to be explicit or self-conscious to work. Indeed, the fact such strategies seem so natural is a significant part of what makes them work.

It's also helpful to remember that nobody forced the crowds in attendance at the bailes to be there. These were crowd-pleasing events, considered by many as great fun. It's not a question of either or. Yes, the songs of proibidão asserted the power of the gangs and warned of the danger of double-crossing them. But there were a high number of songs criticizing selfish, abusive and foolish gangsters who did not willingly embrace local standards for community defenders. This participation of the people ruled in the hegemonic process means that the question of power in the favelas was more complicated than a top-down rule by arms. Instead, strength was built like it usually is—upon the consensus of a block of people from various strata in the hierarchy of their social order. Eagleton describes this process thus:

> Ideologies are usually internally complex, differentiated formations, with conflicts between their various elements which need to be continually renegotiated and resolved. What we call a dominant ideology is typically that of a dominant social bloc, made up of classes and fractions whose interests are not always one; and these compromises and divisions will be reflected in the ideology itself. Indeed it can be claimed that part of the

> strength of bourgeois ideology lies in the fact that it 'speaks' from a multiplicity of sites, and in this subtle diffuseness presents no single target to its antagonists. Oppositional ideologies, similarly, usually reflect a provisional alliance of diverse radical forces (Eagleton 1991, 45).

The quote appearing at the top of this section was from a spoken introduction to a live song performed at a baile funk. It offers an excellent example of an MC telling the public—understood as both gangsters and other residents—of what a 'true bandit' was. Other examples of this sort of 'code of conduct' for gangsters were the many songs that give advice telling them not to be selfish and to respect the community, usually as if from the perspective of another bandit. There were also many songs that humorously ridiculed gangsters considered braggers, brownnosers, cowards or bullies. On the one hand, only the proximity of the MC to the actual gang and his credibility as a representative of the world of crime in Rio could give him the authority to speak in such a way. Attempts to define the 'true bandit' by people outside the world of crime, such as pastors, school teachers, government officials, academics, grandmothers and other hard-working folks such as bus drivers, construction workers, bankers or bakers inevitably would have carried less weight.

Still, the MCs and other composers who wrote proibidão songs were usually far enough removed from the gangs to be considered more like residents than drug traffickers. Though the distinction may have been blurry, the MC typically was not actually a drug trafficker. Although singing about crime has occasionally caused severe problems in the lives of proibidão singers, unlike actual gang members they could leave the favela and travel about freely in Rio without fear of arrest. As evidence of the fuzziness of such distinctions, throughout the history of funk carioca, some MCs have had legal troubles or suffered from police harassment for the content of their material. Even members of the criminal factions themselves often took the MCs as members of their own or rival factions. For instance, although an MC could travel the asphalt of the formal city at will, if he were known for singing about the CV he would not be able to go into favelas controlled by the TC or ADA. There he would be regarded as an enemy, as much as would an actual bandit from a rival gang.

Even if those funk carioca MCs of proibidão were somewhat liminal figures, existing as quasi-bandits, the lyrics of their music were often written by residents of the communities with no involvement in crime. In Rocinha, for example, there was a very successful composer who wrote mostly pagode, forró and funk melody songs, a composer who tended to write very pop-sounding romantic tunes having nothing to do with organized crime. This composer was also a DJ on a successful radio show and the owner of a small business who had never used either alcohol or any other mind-altering drug his whole life, nor had he committed any crimes or had any professional connection with the gangs. Such did not prevent him from writing a proibidão-style song that two of the most famous MCs tried to buy from him.[14] In the mouth of either of these MCs, both consecrated proibidão artists, the song had the potential to gain a legitimacy that the composer himself could never give it. Coming from either of these MCs, the song was likely to be taken by residents and gangsters alike as the 'real deal,' an authentic message of a warrior who represented the world of the favela and the drug traffickers. In this way, the art of a non-gangster resident of the community had the potential to be absorbed into the hegemonic discourse and ideology of the favela.

14 This composer, whose name I withhold, told me about his song in an interview taken on March 13, 2002.

When it came to the culture of crime in Rocinha in the late 1990s and early 2000s, it was not possible to break things down into neat divisions as production and consumption, such as those suggested by cultural critic Stuart Hall.[15] The moment a composer of a funk text might sit down to write the lyrics to a song, he or she did so both as a producer and as a consumer of past and present products. In other words, the song itself did not exist outside of the circuit of production and consumption but occurred as an interpretation of the culture of funk within the culture of the favelas of Rio and the rule of the traffickers. To a certain extent, how well the composer was able to interpret this culture and represent it in his or her new production would determine its relevance and, to a degree, the success of his or her work of art within the funk movement. In this sense, although funk songs as texts could be said to have reflected the reality of the culture of the rule of the traffickers, at the same time they could innovate and shape that same culture in small ways.

Traffickers did not, as far as I know, come to a composer and demand or even ask that he or she write a song about a specific topic. Still, if the composers were not friends of the gangsters or even gangsters themselves, they were at least residents of the communities and had a firsthand experience of the reality and culture of the rule of the traffickers. Because of this, I would place the MCs and other composers—and therefore the production of music about trafficker—as only partially dependent on the traffickers. Mostly, they could be said to represent both the ordinary population of favelas and the gangsters seeking to control specific communities, for proibidão composers were

15 One of the best-known texts in which Hall expounds theories about the circuit of production and consumption is "Encoding, Decoding" (Hall 1999, 507-517).

part of the population even as eventually they were patronized by the traffickers.

Still, recognizing the give and take in the construction of the tropes of crime in this way does not require one to overemphasize the power of the composer in shaping the social reality of the favelas. If, for instance, the rules his or her song were to suggest had no resonance with the public—residents and traffickers alike—no one would pay attention to the song. For instance, it would be difficult for an MC to introduce something entirely new, say that drug traffickers were to give bouquets of flowers to all the mothers of their communities on Mother's Day. They had to work within the accepted range of possibilities, even though they could stretch and shape it to some degree. So when I use the term "ideological strategy," I am referring to this process of negotiation and its representation as it occurs between people living in the favela and not some self-conscious plan.

Cachopão

It's nine o'clock on a Sunday night in the Cachopa area of Rocinha, halfway up the hill above the affluent neighborhood of São Conrado. The football court, or quadra, by the narrow little street known as Rua da Raia is bustling with activity. For the moment, no one is playing ball, although most nights games go on until roundabout midnight, sometimes the shouting of the players and the whistle of the referees lasts clear through until morning. Spaces for leisure activities are few and far between in the favela. So even when people aren't playing football in the Cachopa court, it's almost always in use for something or another. At times it's used for volleyball matches, capoeira martial arts classes, gangster dance parties or birthday celebrations. There's even the occasional launching of one of the enormous, highly decorative homemade hot-air balloons associated with the *festas juninas* ('June Festivals') held every year in Rocinha.

Despite being in such high demand, Cachopa's football court is just a patch of open concrete surrounded by four walls, rusted chain link fencing and two or three short rows of cement bleachers at one end. Currently, the group of drug traffickers based in the Cachopa area take care of its upkeep. Back in the mid-1990s, when Dudu was the big boss in Rocinha and spent much of his time in Cachopa, that same football court had fallen into a miserable state of neglect. In those times, gangsters were occasionally known to throw hand grenades there—just for fun. The blasts would shake the homes and alleyways of the whole area, terrifying residents, waking babies and setting off the barking of the countless pet dogs living there. The explosions could be heard across the hill, reverberating off the rock face of the enormous Morro Dois Irmãos looming above the favela. The word on the street was that Dudu once assassinated a former rival, Aranha, in cold blood in the quadra. Folks also told a tale of him having given the order to burn a young boy to death there after the boy was caught stealing. Indeed, the Cachopa quadra had become part of Dudu's reputation for violence and abuse that had made him perhaps the most feared and hated crime boss in Rocinha.

After police captured Dudu, the local manager of the Cachopa area's boca-de-fumo had ordered the court refurbished and repainted. The man, whose nickname was simply *Da Rocinha* ('the One from Rocinha,') then placed his men in charge of all scheduling of events taking place there. Even after police killed Da Rocinha in an invasion in 2002, the Cachopa gang of Rocinha continued the upkeep of the soccer court. Besides the opportunity the Quadra da Cachopa affords the gang for such 'soft power' initiative, of course, it also makes a strategic vantage point from which to watch the steep ramp below for police or rival gangsters and light firecrackers to warn other drug traffickers. Then again, the gangsters also like it because it's a convenient place to plug in a boom box, to socialize and even to set up their yearly fireworks stand at Christmas time. I myself once purchased a rocket there: it was nearly a meter long and shot some two hundred meters into the air!

But tonight, there's a birthday party in the Cachopa football court for an eight-year-old girl named Daiane. I'm leaning against a parked car on Rua da Raia just above the court, with my friends and neighbors from Cachopa, Alex and Nilton. We're standing about five meters down the Rua da Raia from my place, which I rent from my senior friends, Seu Antônio, known as 'the Portuguese,' and his wife, Dona Helena. From my vantage point, I see the little girl below running back and forth through the crowd in her puffy blue satin dress, beaming happily amidst the birthday decorations and the hundred or so guests. With her are her three closest friends, Kátia, Kelly and Uli, ribbons in their hair and all dressed up in party attire. On the table by the stacks of enormous subwoofers is a big cake, lots of little *salgadinho ('savory pastries')* pastries and shiny, cellophane-wrapped Garoto bonbons. A giant Styrofoam statue of Disney's *Beauty and the Beast* rises above the tables in the middle of a serpentine garland of matching gold and blue balloons.

Young and old are in attendance. As is typical of birthday parties in Brazil, plenty of little old grandmas and grandpas, middle-aged moms and dads and teenagers have come along with the crowds of boys and girls. The grown-ups balance white plastic cups and paper plates in their hands, with half-sized hotdogs and hyper-sweet balls of chocolate called *brigadeiros*. The music playing is a playful did by MC Serginho about a little horse, "Minha Eguinha Pocotó" ("My Little Horsy Clippity-Clop"), one of those rare funk songs that have become a Carnival hit across Brazil. I wonder for a moment if the song can truly be about a mare, a little mare and a donkey or if it's not in fact some sexual pun. "Pocotó pocotó pocotó pocotó, Minha eguinha pocotó" ("Clippity-clop, clippity-clop, My little horsy Clippity-clop"). I decide it really must be a song about a horse.

Just then, Daiane's nineteen-year-old aunt, Silvana, spots me and my friends leaning on the car and comes running up out of the party to offer us a tray of the little pastries. She gives all three of us kisses on both cheeks, asking us if we want cake, too, or if we're coming down to join the party.

"I've gotta go to work." Alex tosses a salgadinho into his mouth in one piece and wipes his hand. He is a waiter at the Hotel Intercontinental down below Rocinha at the beach in São Conrado. "I'm already late... Falou, pessoal!" he says, "Okay, folks!" He clasps my hand and that of Nilton. Alex takes Silvana's hand gently in his own and thanks her warmly for the invitation. She blushes a little and smiles as he gazes affectionately into her eyes.

"I'm taking off, too," says Nilton. "My uncle's waiting for me to go to work." What Nilton refers to as 'going to work,' however, is in fact just his criminal activity as a burglar breaking into houses in Recreio, an affluent, beachfront neighborhood several kilometers from Rocinha. A few nights a week, Nilton and his uncle, Gordinho—who is a professional thief from the Rua Quatro area of the favela—take a bus out to Recreio and come back by cab. Nilton justifies his criminal occupation saying that he and Gordinho, who at thirty-six is about ten years older, only rob houses unarmed. They never harm anyone physically, he likes to point out. He's never been arrested or done time in prison, either. Not yet, anyway. Still, I have a feeling that he's definitely going to get into trouble sooner or later. And to think that just a few years ago, in his early twenties, he was working for a firm across the Guanabara Bay in Niterói, taking night classes at college and working out regularly at the gym. These days, though, his scholarship has been canceled, he's out of school and unemployed. He is deeply ashamed and terrified people will find out how far down he has sunk in recent months, though he is not yet willing to give it all up. The truth behind Nilton's job is a secret at the NGO, and I am one of the few people in our social circles who knows what he's up to.

As Nilton shakes my hand to leave and pats me on the back, one of the local gangsters walks over to our little group. Unlike some of the soldiers from the gang, who occasionally stroll by holding Uzis or AK-47s, Dunga is unarmed. Instead, he has a clipboard in his hand and is going over the schedules for a soccer tournament that is starting up tomorrow at the court. He shows the list to Nilton, who occasionally volunteers as a referee. The two nod their heads as they discuss which teams are coming in, from where and at what times. Dunga is seventeen and a lookout for the gang. He's well-liked in Cachopa and considered to be one of the friendlier people from the cartel, one with solid communication skills who's good at managing the quadra.

Silvana stands waiting for the two to finish to say one last thing to Nilton. As we talk, though, a group of five or six soldiers from the gang pull up alongside us. They have pistols strapped their belts, machine guns in their hands and are wearing knapsacks—presumably full of munitions or other work-related materials. The soldier's leader clasped hands with Dunga. "Faith in God!" the two merrily shout out. Moving on a few steps further to lean up against the chain link fencing, the gangsters get in position to watch the party, much as police might do in other neighborhoods.

Silvana gives me a look of irritation. I know that she wants to get away from Dunga and head back down to the party. It doesn't matter that he is personally a very likable guy or that the Cachopa gangsters are the people renting the soccer court to her family for the birthday party. She's never particularly liked or trusted any of the people associated with the drug gangs. When she was a little girl, drug traffickers killed her father over a small amount of money he owed for drugs. Later, when she was fifteen, the drug traffickers didn't help her in an urgent moment of need, when a drunken neighbor murdered her favorite uncle in broad daylight. It had all been the result of a neighborly dispute that could have been resolved simply and without incident.

One day, Silvana's little cousin's kite had accidentally flown onto a neighboring rooftop. When her uncle had scrambled across the short wall dividing their homes, the drunken neighbor had become enraged. The two men, who already previously didn't like each other, exchanged heated words. Things escalated and the inebriated man struck Silvana's uncle in the face. Later that day, the neighbor waited for Silvana's uncle outside his home, a broken bottle in hand. When her uncle eventually returned home, the drunken man used the broken glass to cut him through the jugular vein.

On her way home from school that night, Silvana had found her uncle on his side bleeding in the narrow alleyway that led to her house. She put her hand over the cut to try and stop the blood, but it was messy. Her fingers kept slipping off, causing the blood to spurt out like a stream from a water gun. As he lay there and slowly died, Silvana's uncle instructed her to keep his little boy away from him. When he passed, she was devastated and traumatized. Despite the fact that Silvana had never liked the gangsters, she decided to seek them out anyway. At their boca-de-fumo headquarters, she pleaded with the drug traffickers to punish the murderer. They didn't want to get involved, though. It was not their problem, they told her. Not long after, the murderer moved away from

Rocinha and was never heard from again.[16]

16 In 2004, the infamous Dudu da Rocinha escaped from prison and returned to Rocinha with a band of gangsters. Commandeering several cars along the streets below, part of his group drove up into the favela in from the neighboring community of Vidigal. Another group came from above on foot through the forest. The gangsters killed several people that night, including Jefferson, another Rocinha gang member in charge of the Cachopa football court at the time. He had been a reasonably well-known skateboarder in Rio, even appearing on national television once or twice. After his knee injuries, though, Jefferson took up working for the cartel. After he mistook the invading force as part of the Rocinha gang from another area of the hill, even greeting them enthusiastically, the invaders briefly took him captive. Jefferson had been presiding over a party in the quadra on the eve of Good Friday, a major holiday in Brazil much celebrated in Rocinha. Jefferson pleaded with his captors, letting the rival gangsters know he was a father. There on the Rua da Raia—steps away from the Cachopa court—they killed him anyway.

9

Trafficking Culture

My movement is socio-political[1]

My trafficking is cultural

My movement is socio-political

My trafficking is cultural

I'll tell you there's Black and White[2] young sir

Yes, there is, taking care

The favela is socialist, it gave me an overdose of consciousness

Religiousness, faith in God we carry in our hearts

Peace justice and liberty war for good without destruction

—"Cultural Traffic," by MC Bocão[3]

The quote above offers another poignant example of how various ideological strategies typically work together in the lyrics of a proibidão-style funk song that was a hit in Rocinha in the early 2000s. On one level, the song's MC, Mr. Catra, presents himself as a metaphorical

1 A double-entendre in Portuguese referring to the "selling of drugs" and a "social movement."

2 A double-entendre for "Black and White people" and "marijuana and cocaine."

3 Portuguese: "Meu movimento é político-social; Meu tráfico é cultural; Meu movimento é político-social; Meu tráfico é cultural...; Vou te dizer, tem preto e tem branco, seu moço; Tem sim, empenhado no seu bem-estar; A favela é socialista, me deu overdose de consciência; Religiosidade, fé em Deus trazemos no coração; Paz, justiça e liberdade, guerra pelo bem sem destruição" ("Tráfico cultural"). Full lyrics in Appendix A.

gangster who traffics revolutionary thought instead of drugs. His consciousness, represented as an outgrowth of the culture of the favela at the self-reflective level, is a blend of religion, revolution and a social formation built around drug trafficking. With an impressive economy of words, and slogans of the Comando Vermelho like "faith in God" and "peace, liberty and justice," the singer presents the core images associated with the power of Rio's criminal factions in the favelas of the city. It portrays religious sentiment, the commitment to the wellbeing of the gang and the community and the idea of the legitimate use of violence on the part of the drug traffickers. Also, the song involves that same double-entendre of the words "Black" and "White" as 'Rap do Patrão,' discussed above, which besides their racial connotation mean marijuana and cocaine, respectively.

In so doing, the song elevates the favela as an instance of racial democracy, smoothing over substantial racial differences that in reality do indeed persist in favelas—if somewhat less than other territories in Rio and Brazil—and rationalizes the economic base of the drug traffickers. This idea of racial democracy is especially crucial in the context of the legitimacy of the favela gang. On the one hand, despite the stubborn persistence of this view as a feature of the status quo ideology in Brazil, people in favelas are much less inclined to believe in this at the national level. The racial discrimination they so often experience from outside of their communities only reinforces such disbelief among favela residents. On the more localized plane of the favela, however, ideas of racial harmony between residents can be more convincing—especially given the intense stigmatization they endure from the mainstream society surrounding them. So in a sense, affirming racial unity within the favela is a way of saying that, contrary to their much-sullied image, favelas are in a sense more 'Brazil' than is Brazil itself.[4]

The song functions on two levels. On the first, it is a protest against police harassment, saying that police mistake favela youths for criminals, as part of the systemic racism plaguing Rio and Brazil more generally. It is also an affirmation that musicians, artists and activists are not drug traffickers but rather 'traffic culture,' in the sense of circulating it in an outlaw fashion as a form of resistance. In the context of the culture of proibidão in which it is presented, within the favela community, the song also serves as a proclamation of the social banditry of the favela gangs. In this way, the whole song can be taken as a sort of double-entendre that presents the "war for good" as both that of an artist as a countercultural intellectual, representing the revolutionary nature of the favela and that of the gangsters as actual warriors in a just revolt.

By talking about an "overdose of consciousness," the MC ironically flips one of the most negative images of the culture of drug use around and turns it into the central metaphor of quasi-spiritual liberation in the song. It is as if the power of mainstream, legal hegemony is so strong one needs to nearly die to break from its spell. The urban culture of the favelas of the time was already far more complex than the pre-modern, mostly rural cultures Hobsbawm discussed, and thus it was perhaps not surprising that the role of its outlaws would also be more complicated. As was the case in the pair of songs "Bandidos de Cristo" and "Rap do Patrão," this song, was evidence of the mixing of Hobsbawm's ideologically conservative 'social bandit' and the more radical millenarian.

4 For a nuanced critique of the ideology of racial democracy in Brazil, from the country's historical roots to contemporary debates about Affirmative Action and college admission, see Henry Louis Gates, Jr.'s excellent episode of his PBS series *Black in Latin America*, "Brazil: A Racial Paradise?" He also treats the subject in a book of the same title (Gates 2011).

Although not all proibidão songs of those times offered such dense and complex discursive formulations as 'Vamos traficar cultura,' most presented combinations and mixtures of similar various ideological strategies. In the remainder of this section, I will make some general comments about how funk's discourse on the role of the traffickers represented it as "action-oriented" and how it was "rationalized," "legitimated," "universalized" and "naturalized" in classic gangsta funk, using the categories borrowed from Eagleton's work on ideology (1991, 47-61). Next, I will look at strategies which presented the power of the traffickers as that of the representatives of a "unified" community, another category suggested by Eagleton, and the approach that is perhaps most indicative of the broader underlying ideology of their prestige. Although such a discussion will be repetitive and hopefully somewhat superfluous at this point, the complexities of the social formation of the favela and its relationship with the dominant order—an order it depended upon even as it reacted against and resisted it—merit such emphasis. Still, the scope of such a discussion is wide enough as to prevent anything more than an initial attempt and I will have to be content to suggest some of the major features of that ideology.

Action-oriented: In the case of the favela, it is apparent that the principal activity of the drug traffickers was the actual trafficking of drugs. Residents knew that these drug traffickers benefited from the sale of drugs and that, as residents, they had better not interfere with that activity. At the same time, the sale of drugs was seen by the population as somewhat of a necessary evil and that without it the traffickers would not be able to protect and help the community. As a result, many of the rules, motivations and prescriptions implicit in the control of the traffickers were related to activities that were beyond the scope of selling drugs per se. These rules reflected the consensus on power that existed in the community, for example, that the traffickers should be the police, judicial branch, welfare services and recreational coordinators of the favela. This did not mean that churches, NGOs, businesses and even the government could not provide some of these services as well, but that the traffickers were also expected to perform such actions in the interest of the community.

Similarly, the residents were expected to act within the same set of goals and rules. This expectation took on a form somewhat similar to the "10 Commandments of the Favela," that "thou shalt not inform the police," "thou shalt not steal," "thou shalt not rape," "thou shalt not murder," etc. Other rules were less dramatic but still quite real. One shouldn't play one's music too loud too late on a weeknight, be a deadbeat tenant, leer at women or make 'cat calls.'[5] Nor should one punch another resident or throw a sloppy hotdog in a local vendor's face.[6] Such rules, too, were

5 Once, my partner at the NGO, Socorro, was walking home from teaching at the small early childhood education center that she co-owned with our other partner, Vivi. Passing through the Valão area of Rocinha near her home, she noticed a workman from the Light power company leering at her. "Dama de vermelho," he commented to her as she walked by, "Lady in red." She was wearing a red dress that day. An armed 'soldier' from the gang happened to be nearby. He approached the man, machine gun in hand, and told him to respect the population. The workman turned pale and quickly apologized. When Socorro arrived at her home, where I was sharing lunch with her mother, Dona Raimunda, she excitedly recounted the story, beaming.

6 The reference to the hotdog is also based on a true story. Carlos, in his early thirties and the older brother of Charlys da Rocinha, was selling savory treats at a stand in the Passarela area at the foot of Rocinha. One day, a semi-drunken, abusive regular costumer threw a hotdog in his face, upset that it was not better tasting. Carlos, who was a skilled martial arts practitioner, dragged the man off to the boca-de-fumo (drug dealing stronghold). Carlos begged the local manager of the gang for permission to beat the abusive customer up. He told them he would never strike anyone without permission. The gang members denied his request but ordered the customer to stay away from Carlos. In a similar incident, one day Carlos was working at his stand with an open cut on the top of his hand. Suddenly, a drunken man who frequently slept on some stairs near the stand appeared, holding up the index finger of his right hand. On the tip of the finger was a blob of some sort of white-colored mucus. Before

sometimes made explicit in funk lyrics, as were the punitive activities of the drug traffickers in regards to those who broke them. In proibidão funk, emphasizing the array of guns and other weapons of the traffickers was a form of evidence that they had the means to carry out the enforcement of their rules.

Rationalizing: It may seem that in the sad, harsh reality of the favelas of Rio it would not be necessary to rationalize a social order built upon the sale of drugs. Positively, the population would be inclined to accept any semblance of order over chaos. Still, favelas are in many ways very conservative places, and many residents oppose drug use and oppose the rule of drug traffickers in their communities. In fact, many residents do not even approve of legal drugs like alcohol and cigarettes, especially members of the Evangelical Christian circles who make up about one in five favela residents. As a result of this situation, a part of the rationalization of the power of the drug traffickers involved a separate rationalization of the use of drugs themselves. This rationalization stemmed from ideas not limited to favela drug traffickers or those of Brazil generally but those that are rather widespread in contemporary international society—as they still are. Part of this is the notion that using drugs is democratic and individualistic; the individual consumer should have the right to choose his or her pleasure, just as with anything else in life. Individuals become consumers looking for a series of pleasurable moments and experiences that temporarily provide them with some degree or another

Carlos knew what was happening, the man wiped the substance across the open cut on Carlos' hand. Carlos grabbed the man by the collar and pulled back his arm, ready to punch the drunken man in the face. The drunken man, eyes wide in fear, raised up his left hand to reveal a tube of antibiotic ointment. Fortunately for all parties, Carlos realized that what he'd taken for mucus was in fact a pharmaceutical product. The drunken man was merely trying to help him.

of euphoria beyond their physiological and emotional needs regarding things like friendship, love and support.[7]

Another rationalization of drug use relevant to the culture of drug trafficking in Rio in those times was that idea that drugs were not so hazardous to one's health. According to this view, drugs could even be quite beneficial, and the fact that they were illegal itself was hypocritical. After all, alcohol, a drug that could be at least as dangerous as marijuana and cocaine, was legal. Furthermore, if an individual had a problem with drugs, it was his or her problem and it could not be blamed on the drug itself. Some argued that using drugs was somehow a subversive act of rebellion against the values of the dominant order, that it was part of a culture of brotherly love and anti-materialism, one quite contrary to the self-centered consumerism of the status quo. Drug use was related to the artistic and creative side of people, as a spiritual activity capable of freeing the mind and help a person think outside the box in ways which might make one a less passive subject for the traditional authorities.

7 In the mass-media dominated world of late-capitalism, the influence of this consumerist notion of 'happiness' and human life, in general, cannot be over-estimated. Still, it is not total and rather coexists, albeit incoherently, with competing notions of 'happiness,' such as those from the Greek and Judeo-Christian traditions, which would see happiness as independent of pleasure. One could say the Greek notion of happiness as *eudaemonia* was a sort of spiritual health comparable to physical health, a personal well-being that came with the balance of virtues. In Christianity, happiness could in some ways be described as the result of the experience of grace and love that come through salvation, usually conceived of as an internal experience. For both, the pleasures of euphoria are shunned as illusory and as potentially detrimental to 'true' happiness. Of course, in contemporary Brazil, there are a plethora of other notions of felicity besides, such as notions that have existed amongst Afro-Brazilian and indigenous peoples in the country throughout its history of ethnic and racial mixing—and even views shaped by Marxism and other influences in intellectual and cultural life. All these have mixed together alongside individual personal tastes and credos, as well as the psychological and neurological needs like those addressed by Lewis, Amini, and Lannon in *A General Theory of Love*.

Such ideas were not only a part of the countercultural revolutions of the late 1960s and early 1970s in places like the US, France and Brazil. The increasing legalization of recreational drugs today gives testimony to the growth of such thinking. Indeed, it seems clear that new attitudes about drug use should be adopted to help shift the focus away from the 'war on drugs' criminalization of drug users that has served to increase violence against favela residents and other minority communities around the world.

In case of funk music, there were constant references to the use of drugs: "Fui no Borel buscar uma trouxa" ("I went to the favela of Borel to buy a bag"), "Confesso pra vocês que gosto de fumar um bagulho" ("I admit I love to smoke a joint"), "Muita gente não sabia que no morro do Borel faço rap na maresia" ("Few people knew I made my rap music in the middle of pot smoke"), "Demorou formar o bonde do maconheiro" ("We got together our pothead gang of friends"), "Demorou formar o bonde do rastafari" ("We got together our Rasta gang of friends"), etc. While many of these references cast drug use in a positive light, especially that of marijuana, there are also a high number making fun of those who abused drugs, like drug addicts. The song "Bonde do che-cheiro," says, "A brizola faz a gente perder peso e não querer comer, mas depois vem aquela esticação, e quando ficar sem dinheiro vai ter que vender seu bermudão" ("Cocaine makes us lose weight and not want to eat, but then you get strung out and when you go broke you gotta sell your shorts"). Such humor at the expense of the addict was not meant as a global condemnation of drug use, in general, but rather more of a warning. In a sense, it also served to deflect criticism about the evils of drug use by placing the blame on the individual abuser.

A rationalization that was more specifically related to the actual rule of the traffickers in favelas was the notion that, since the government didn't have a strong presence there, some local power needed to step in and provide the necessary services for the community. The selling of drugs was a necessary evil that benefited the residents of the favela, in this light. Besides, this rationale suggested, the drugs were less often sold to residents than to mostly to wealthy people from outside of the community. These were the same people who benefit from the fact of economic disparity in the first place and who weren't doing much to alleviate the problem.

I think, too, that a critical aspect of the acceptance of the power of the drug traffickers by the communities they controlled was a certain fatalism, or at least a deep sense of frustration, in regards to the notion of power in general. Poor people in Brazil at the time often did not have high expectations from government and were indeed very much used to corruption and violent abuse from would-be authorities. There was an accepted notion among poor people in Brazil that the vast majority of wealth and power in the country has been acquired through dirty dealings of one kind or another. From this point of view, the notion that the local power of the favela was built upon the sale of illegal and potentially dangerous substances was not so different. In other words, the illegitimacy of power in Brazil historically helped to legitimize the power of the drug traffickers in the specific case of their rule of the favelas. Unfortunately, this dynamic is still all too common in the present.

Legitimating: By discussing above how an MC gave advice to gangsters and made fun of them, I have already touched upon some essential features of the legitimating ideological strategy in proibidão funk. The goal of this strategy was to get the public, understood as bandits and non-bandits alike, to begin to measure and judge itself according to the internal value system of the consensus on power and the rule of the drug traffickers. For example, to the extent a person refrained from informing on the police not out of fear of the violent reaction of the boca-de-fumo but because he or she thought it is morally wrong, the order had effectively legitimated itself with that person. Of course, all these ideological strategies were to some degree interdependent with the others. It would have been hard to get people to internalize the value system of the rule of the drug traffickers without also getting them to accept the actions that oriented the community or without them seeing the order of the gangsters as being natural and rooted in universal values.

The discourse on power in proibidão funk did not condemn a person for being a thief in for example Barra da Tijuca and Ipanema—wealthy neighborhoods not under the rule of the drug gangs—whereas robbing within the favela was expressly prohibited. One song from Rocinha was even dedicated to the thieves of the community and celebrated their thievery across the wealthy neighborhoods of the Zona Sul ("Bonde dos Ladrões," by MC Cordão de Ouro). No mention was made in the song of the prohibition against stealing within the community, but it was something that was widely understood and was indeed mentioned in many other songs, such as "10 mandamentos da favela." Even besides the 'rules' of the neighborhood, other cultural tendencies that were continuously reinforced and presented in funk could potentially become a part of the identity of people in the favela, be they gangster, funkeiro or otherwise. In any event, to efficiently legitimize the discourse of the power of the traffickers, the rules it professed must be presented as applying to everyone, regardless of their status within the favela community or whether or not he or she was a trafficker or a non-trafficking-affiliated resident.

Universalizing: That religious sentiment consistently expressed in proibidão, as discussed above, connected the power of favela drug traffickers to notions of love, faith, peace, justice and liberty: higher principles portrayed as guiding political, social and ethical life both in and outside of the social order of the favela. Even though the specific phrase "peace, justice and liberty" was a slogan of the Comando Vermelho, the words still carried meaning as references to notions of universal human good reaching far beyond that context. Humility was also frequently evoked as being a necessary quality in the drug traffickers themselves, a quality seen as giving them both the power and wisdom to survive and to help the community. Humility could also mean the idea that one should not forget who one was and what one's roots were. One should place loyalty to the community over personal interests. Such an emphasis on humility was a way of affirming the value of the people of favelas, gangsters and otherwise, and implicitly contrasting it with the stereotype common among Rio's poor that middle and upper-class people were arrogant. In this sense, the frequent declarations about the humility of the drug traffickers could be understood as a means of constructing them as Hobsbawm's social bandits who have been forced into being outlaws by the hypocrisy of the system. In any event, the rules of the favela were presented as being related to a higher authority based on a divine order of things that was applicable to all people at all times.[8]

Naturalizing: The culture of crime in proibidão funk consistently represented the community of the favela and its drug trafficker leadership as a family. The traffickers were not an invading force of people unconnected to the kinship ties and other social networks of the community. Instead, they were *crias* ('homeboys') locals brought up in the favela. As such, they represented the community and knew the population as intimately as everybody else living there. A typical funk song would refer to the manos, or brothers, in the gangs and would often mention cria.

8 In "Falso profeta," MC Manda Brasa, criticizes another proibidão MC who thinks he "é dono do mundo" ("owns the world") and needs to be humble and remember instead he is merely "filho do Dono" (the son of the owner"), or a mere child of God.

An example is a line from MC Vidigal's "Rap do Comando Vermelho," "É o bonde só de cria que só tem destruidor" ("It's the homeboys group that's just got killers"). The notion of brotherhood was also important, but more than a real kinship based on actual blood relations, the tribal family of the favela was formed by racial, class and geographical identities.

This favela identity, standing in contrast to that of the Brazil of the 'asphalt' as formal city, was something involving other ideological strategies besides naturalizing. Particularly crucial was the strategy of unifying, which I will treat below. This may have been one of the reasons funk songs so often included rhymed lists of the names of favelas or areas of favelas considered 'good.' For example, in the song "Rap da Rocinha," by MC Galo, he sung, "Galera da Cruzada, Santa Marta e o Pavão, Tabajara, Mineira e a Providência é sangue bom, Cidade Alta, Juramento, Catete e Vidigal" and so forth ("The gang from Cruzada. Santa Marta and Pavão, Tabajara, Mineira and Providência good blood, Cidade Alta, Juramento, Catete and Vidigal"). It may be that emphasizing the paternalistic structure of the traffickers' governance was another aspect of the naturalizing strategy in funk; this paternalism easily translated to the traditional tribal notion of power based on interpersonal relations mentioned previously as a part of the universalizing strategy. Also, the constant mention and brandishing of weapons can be seen as a naturalizing gesture in a society in which the weak were so accustomed to being dominated by the strong so that a show of strength made the rulers seem natural.

Unifying: One of the most central features of the ideology of the power of the criminal factions present in proibidão funk was the way in which it sought to build some common identity among people in Rocinha. In reality, the demographics of Rio's favelas were incredibly diverse and included people with great differences in terms of race, class, gender, sexual orientation, age, regional origin, religious views, profession and the like. In funk, one of the most influential characteristics of the unity of the people living under the power of the drug traffickers was, not surprisingly, their common geographic identity. No matter what region one was from, or what color or sex a person may be, the fact that he or she lived in a favela made that person a part of the family of the favela. As I mentioned in my comments on the naturalizing strategy above, this was one reason it was so typical to find lengthy lists of the names of favelas included in funk songs, lists that almost never included any wealthy neighborhoods.

In funk, the physical space of the favela was elevated over the space of the so-called 'asphalt' of Rio's formally urbanized city in a sort of semiotic inversion of the geopolitical map of the city of Rio de Janeiro. In the case of Rocinha, which was enormous and included several smaller areas within its limits, the lists of the areas and their inclusion in many songs strengthened the notion that it was one giant family. The same was true of the frequent boasts that it was that 'biggest favela' in Latin America, a boast often made both within the favela's own local culture of funk and without. The demarcation of territory and the notion of belonging to the family of the favela ultimately depended on the fact that it was a mostly informal system within a significantly hostile formal system. The racism and class-based discrimination felt by the people of favelas as lived experience helped to unify them in this way. If residents had not felt significantly excluded from and discriminated against by the larger society, the traffickers would have had a much smaller chance of gaining legitimacy, no matter how fearsome they might have appeared to be. If they had not viewed government 'authorities' as incompetent or unconcerned with their lives and if the police were not regularly killing innocent people, it would have been more difficult for the traffickers to achieve legitimacy.

Once again, the importance placed upon geographic space in the discourse of funk calls to mind the divided city model put forth by Zuenir Ventura in his book *Cidade Partida*, a poignant study of the question of citizenship and changes in the concept of the 'other' and its implications for the larger Brazilian society. As I stated earlier, the focus of the book was the 1993 massacre by police of twenty-one innocent people in Vigário Geral, a favela in Rio. It also told the story of the anti-violence social movement called Viva Rio which grew out of it, one which by the time of my study had grown into a very well-respected and large group of NGOs in Rio. Ventura's basic thesis was that Rio's society was undergoing an ever-increasing polarization into rich and poor groups. Additionally, the rich were becoming more and more terrified of the poor. The poor, on the other hand, were growing increasingly frustrated as the result of the lack of sufficient participation in society with which they were faced. Ventura eloquently stated the urgency of the problem of citizenship, connecting it with the growing level of violence in Rio.

Ventura's reading of the socio-political climate of the late twentieth century was strikingly reminiscent of the classic study of the Brazil of the coastal *litoral* ('regions') versus the Brazil of the 'arid hinterland' in *Os Sertões*, by Euclides da Cunha, mentioned above. In his analysis, da Cunha associated the coastal regions and the Republic with European influences and the notion of 'progress,' while the backlands people were presented as racially inferior and backward, a dichotomy da Cunha ambiguously supported even as he came to lament it and eventually denounce it. Ventura's model of the divided city points out a similar tendency on the part of the elites of Rio to see themselves, as did those of the coastal perspective, as white heirs of superior European culture. In contrast, they viewed the favelas and other working-class neighborhoods as being like the Sertão 'backlands,' with what they considered as a population of mixed-race, ethnically inferior barbarians.[9]

Even though his focus was the class issue, Ventura's work did suggest racial nuances in his class-divided city concept, as did that of da Cunha a hundred years earlier. The implication was that racial identity was also be becoming more polarized in Rio in similar ways. Problems such as racism and the social exclusion of the poor were not new, nor were they limited to the lives of people living in the favelas of Rio de Janeiro, but instead they were a fundamental part of the 500 years of history since the first Portuguese began arriving on Brazilian soil. The slavery and genocide of African and indigenous peoples so fundamental to the history of Brazilian civilization had resulted in a highly complex racial make-up in the country and equally complicated racism. There is an extensive tradition of thinking about the question of race in Brazil crucial for the consideration of this issue in the culture of the favela and I could not hope to do justice to a discussion of the topic in the present study.[10]

The racial component of the identity of the people of favelas is one that cannot be overstressed, though as a part of Brazilian racial identity it was as complicated as one would expect, and the culture of funk at the time may yield some clues. Yes, in the case of the ideology of the power of

9 An excellent commentary on the war of Canudos and the book *Os Sertões* is *Vale of Tears: Revising the Canudos Massacre in Northeastern Brazil, 1893-1897* (Levine 1992).

10 In fact, it will be better to leave the treatment of the intricacies of Brazilian race relations and their implications for funk and the culture of the favelas for the final section of this book, in Chapters 10 through 12. For the time being, I should clarify that the sort of 'blackening' of racial identity that I discuss below was not a process occurring merely at the level of political consciousness but instead as an emergent form of lived consciousness. This meant that while it may not have yet been as directly useful to the Black Movement in Brazil as some would have liked, as the basis of political mobilization, it was still an essential part of the social cohesion of the favela as a subculture.

traffickers in favelas as articulated in funk, race and class did often seem to be conflated in what one could term a process of 'blackening' of racial identity. This may explain in part why efforts at consciousness-raising by the Black Movement in Brazil were not yet finding greater acceptance in favelas. Still, if the construction of the identity of the favela resident was in some ways typical of Freyrian notions of 'racial democracy,' it was made in contrast to a parallel construct of "whitened" racial identity of the asphalt, as I hinted above.[11] In other words, the funk projects the favela as a non-white space and as a 'brown' one, instead just as it projects the middle and upper-classes as 'white.' In the case of funk and the identity of people in favelas, communities in which a widely mixed group of people of different racial types lived in proximity, it was not surprising that race and class should be conflated. An example is the following refrain from a song by MCs Leonardo and Júnior (who themselves are not black): "Eu quero mais

11 By 'Freyrian,' I am referring to the general theories of racial harmony and democracy espoused by Gilberto Freyre, particularly in his seminal work, *Casa Grande e Senzala: formação da família brasileira sob o regime da economia patriarcal.* According to this view, the intimate contact in Brazil of the European, Indigenous and African racial groups, particularly in the relationship between the children of the wealthy landowners and their Afro-Brazilian nannies, resulted in a somewhat unique situation in which less racism existed when compared to other countries. Freyre associated certain attributes of the human personality to the different races in a stereotypical fashion, for example, that intelligence came from the European influence and human warmth, musicality and sensuality came from African influence. Since the introduction of these ideas in the early 1930s, an introduction which occurred as a reaction to the even more racist notions of eugenics and attempts at *embranquecimento*, or the 'whitening' of the Brazilian population, Freye's ideas have come to occupy a central place in the Brazilian national ideology. More recently, the idea has been attacked precisely for the sort of racial hierarchy it presupposes as well as for masking and denying racial disparity in Brazil. Today, the success of Freyre's ideas has been considered one of the chief obstacles for the mobilization of the country's black movement, since even many people of color believe that Brazil is racially democratic. Once again, for a nuanced introductory treatment, see Gates documentary, *Black in Latin America*, "*Brazil: A Racial Paradise?*" and book of the same title (Gates 2011).

paz e amor, justiça, liberdade para o pobre, para o negro" ("I want more peace, justice and liberty for poor people and Blacks").[12]

Each favela had a unique history and there was a wide variety of demographic make-ups in various favelas, often related to the age of the community. Also, since most had sprung up and exploded in size within the previous forty or fifty years, the question of where people came from originally or where their parents came from was often a crucial part of an individual's identity and must also be accounted for in the unifying process. Older favelas, like Mangueira, for example, in Rio's Zona Norte, tended to have more Black residents, in part because the population was comprised of people who had histories in Rio and in part due to the immigration of large segments of people specifically from Bahia, which was especially important as an Afro-Brazilian center, in the late 19th and early 20th centuries. Newer favelas, such as Rocinha and the expansive Rio das Pedras, in Jacarepaguá, had boomed amidst the massive immigration of people from other places in the Northeast, usually from the dry region of the Sertão in states like Ceará and Paraíba, occurring in more recent decades. These regions further from the coast had a more racially mixed population. Further complicating the racial identity of favelas was the fact that they tended to be looked upon by the middle and upper-classes as spaces of racially inferior 'non-white' people. Of course, racism did exist in the favelas, too. For example, many Northeastern immigrants looked down on Blacks and even those who were very dark were likely to consider themselves as White, or at least *pardo* ('brown'). Ironically, as a consequence, some residents of communities like Rio das Pedras and Rocinha even thought their favelas were better than other favelas having more Blacks.

12 This song appeared on DJ Marlboro's 1995 *Samba Rap*, (Afegan Produções Artísticas 441079/2-482221).

The space of the favelas of the late 1990s and early 2000s as hybrid spaces of overlapping levels of pre-modern and post-industrial consciousness in which past Brazilian ideologies still held their ground and shared space with more recent ideological features. It seems possible, then, that both the classic 'whitening' influence and Freyrian 'racial democracy'—type thought would exist, despite the fact that they were in many ways antithetical. In other words, while a collective racial identity was necessary for the notion of the unity of the people of favelas as a group of mostly non-white people oppressed and discriminated against by the larger society, in reality, many negative racial stereotypes continued to operate within the social order of favelas. In Rocinha, for example, though it was common to find Black people in the gangs, the majority of higher-ups tended to be lighter in color.

The racial stratification of Rocinha reminded me a bit of Brazilian soccer at the time (and perhaps still today). On the one hand, people sometimes pointed to *futebol* as an example of Brazilian 'racial democracy' in action. The problem was, however, that most coaches were white and most players had white wives and girlfriends, two details very relevant to the subtleties of race relations and racial hierarchies in Brazil. If a person wanted to win a soccer game, or win a gun battle against the police, it was advantageous to field all the best players, regardless of race. Still, hierarchies did exist, and whereas a Black person might be socialized to be a foot soldier or football striker, society might teach him that he lacked the intelligence, moral authority or other necessary attributes to serve as leader.

If the Black Movement in Brazil has had trouble getting people to see the racial dimensions of Brazilian society, this may be in part because many of the poor non-white people in Brazil live in communities such as the favelas of Rio where the myth of racial democracy is still compelling. I don't mean that poor people believe Brazil itself is a racial democracy, in the mainstream, but that within the subculture of favelas there exists a society that is more racially equal. Such is not to say there was nothing countercultural in the assimilation project of the drug traffickers in the heyday of proibidão do funk. Although in ways it worked to smooth over differences between individuals members of the community, in offering a racial identity of the 'brownness' in favela communities, the culture of crime worked to solidify the allegiance of the population against the white dominant racial hierarchies of the mainstream Brazilian society of the asphalt. The construction of an ethnic and class identity in the favela as a territory of the African Diaspora remains a complex topic I will explore in greater depth in the remaining chapters of this book.

Rebels in the Backlands of the City

Oh, that night started with a gunfight
The favela was surrounded, you couldn't get out
And the children were scared
For the love of God, Daddy, get us out of here
And then a tear came down my face
I saw that my strength was coming from God
I only ask that young man that before he pulls the trigger
That he thinks about his kids before killing mine
But I just want to go into my house, young man, young man
And kiss my kids, kiss my wife
Have my daily bread, I just want to be happy"
—"My Rights," by MCs Santos and Agostinho[13]

Whatever the motives of Rocinha's drug traffickers on an individual basis, be they greedy—as Alba Zaluar would have it, or revolutionary, as Nêgu Tema claimed—they did work within the everyday culture of the favelas to legitimize their de facto power there. Although the illicit nature of their activities necessarily placed their rule outside of the formal system, the gangsters would never have been able to legitimize their control of the favelas if they had been entirely oppositional to the status quo. By this I am not referring to the de facto involvement of the police in drug trafficking typical of the workings of Rio's criminal factions in those times—and today—or that of elites at the highest levels of organized crime.

Though these two realities did work to reinforce the legitimacy of the drug traffickers, they were mostly incidental to the cultural hegemony of the factions in the favelas. That is not to say that the drug traffickers of Rio de Janeiro could have maintained their power without the complicity of state agents like police and politicians, or at least that they would not have been considerably less potent without the cooperation of these agents. Besides, the incompetence and corruption of state agents did serve to legitimize the traffickers further and in such ways as those suggested in the previous chapter, in the dialogue at the pizzeria, through their abusive treatment of people living in favelas.

What I do mean is that the hegemony of drug traffickers also depended upon a high degree of ideological complicity on the part of at least some favela residents. As I have suggested above, this culture of the

13 Portuguese: "Mas essa noite começou com tiroteio; Favela tava cercada, não dava pra sair; E a criançada tava com desespero; Pelo amor de Deus, Papai, tira a gente daqui; E aí então uma lágrima desceu; E vi que as minhas forças vinham das forças de Deus; Só peço àquele moço antes de apertar o gatilho; Que pense em seus filhos antes de matar os meus; Eu só quero entrar na minha casa, seu moço, seu moço; E dar um beijo nas criança, beijar minha patroa; Ter o pão de cada dia, eu só quero é ser feliz" ("Meus direitos"). Full lyrics in Appendix A.

favela was an extremely hybrid one in which many forms of consciousness overlapped and intermixed. As a result, the leadership of the favela—especially that of the drug traffickers—employed ideological strategies involving elements of pre-modern and post-industrial societies. So no matter how 'revolutionary' they might have seemed, the rule of the drug traffickers was mostly—as Hobsbawm might say—reformist, operating principally within a very traditionally mainstream Brazilian ideological framework. As I argued, in fact, in some ways some constructs of Brazilian identity were even more deeply ingrained in the minds of favela residents than in those of people of the middle and upper-classes, such as that of racial democracy. In ways, the social formation of the favela of Rocinha was a microcosm of at least some extremely conservative ideas of religion, race, class and gender. In the end, the ideological foundation of the power of the drug traffickers ended up being ambiguous, at once reinforcing the national hegemony even as it served to challenge and undermine it.

It may be for this reason that the middle and upper-classes had been able to live with the reality of the 'favelification' of their country for so long, at least in part. The favelas have not proven to be breeding grounds for revolutionaries, as such. Still, the revolutionary spirit of Brazilian hip-hop, notwithstanding Tema's comments above, did not seem to evoke such a viscerally negative response amongst people of the Brazilian middle and upper-classes as "did funk"—ironically. Perhaps the liberal ideals of hip-hop in Brazil calling for a complete restructuring of society were modern enough to make sense to folks from the middle and upper classes. Being a Revolution Through Words (Revolucão Através da Palavra, or RAP), it was likely to be even less scary. Indeed, from a mainstream point of view, Brazilian hip-hop is something significantly democratic and modern.

This is not true of the funk of the golden age of proibidão, which was infinitely less theoretical and future-oriented. In the end, as I suggested earlier, funk was not merely a 'Revolt Through Words' but much more the musical expression of the reality of a present and ongoing 'Revolt Through Firearms.' Ultimately, however, the same 'un-revolutionary spirit' that made the favelas tolerable for so long for the middle and upper-classes was what eventually began making them increasingly intolerable as proibidão funk and the culture of crime flourished there. Elites in Brazil could only tolerate the 'favelification' of the country as long as it did not spill over too much into their lives, as long as Nêgu Tema's "crimes of legitimate self-defense" didn't become too rampant. Such was because underneath the status quo attitude of looking the other way was a fear far greater than that of revolution—the fear of barbarism and the revolt of some pre-modern unconscious masses of backlands fanatics and cold-blooded gunmen.

The drug traffickers of the hills and favelas of Rio de Janeiro were demonized and romanticized, just as they stood in both pre- and post-modernity. They were social bandits who were oddly millenarian even as they were anti-revolutionary. As the city grew increasingly divided, the fear, neglect and complicity of the middle and upper-classes had allowed Rio's criminal factions to take root and grow to come to power and helped them to stay there. The poor, albeit reluctantly, turned those outlaws into their champions. As a result, the gangsters had come to occupy a crucial role in the administration of power in the larger Brazilian social order. It could be said that the War of Canudos, fought between federal troops and the followers of Antônio Conselheiro in the 1890's, was the great challenge after the monarchy for the Brazil of the First Republic. Now, the 'divided city' was proving to be the great challenge for the restored democracy in Brazil in the years after the military dictatorship.

One can argue that politicians and the other powers that be in any given society always have some degree of Machiavellian self-interest motivating them whenever they take the actions that they do. Others believe that human beings can at least sometimes act in the interests of the well-being of their communities. While I would not argue that Rocinha's drug traffickers were necessarily any different from other leaders, I would suggest that the notions of success and power they held were contingent on their experiences as people born and raised in the favela. Such gangsters were native residents of their communities, not an invading army, even as they were residents of Brazil. As a result, even their particular fashion of pursuing money and power did not take on the same form or entail the same values as that of people from the middle-class and elite segments of the population.

For example, even the highest ranking drug traffickers never expected to become the president of the Republic, a judge, lawyer, banker, engineer or doctor or even to go to college at all. He knew he would never have prestige in the larger society, nor did he expect to enjoy pleasures such as foreign travel and fine dining. To the contrary, he was aware that he would not even be able to move about freely within his own city but would instead be forced to either remain hidden within the favela or wear a disguise to occasionally escape its confines. Furthermore, once he became at all integrated within the world of organized crime, he knew it would be extremely challenging and dangerous to quit. Perhaps most importantly, the drug trafficker expected to die a violent, early death or at least to be locked up in prison for significant portions of his life.[14]

14 With regrets, I've decided to use the masculine pronoun here, as throughout much of my discussions of Rio's drug traffickers. Although vastly less common in those days even than now, there were occasionally women in the drug gangs, sometimes even in positions of leadership. See, for example, the story of Raquel Oliveira, a high-ranking female trafficker in Rocinha in the late 1980s, as told in her autobiography *A Número Um* (Oliveira 2015).

Such social disparities, even among criminals from different social classes, bring to mind a line from perhaps the all-time biggest song of the funk movement, the "Rap da felicidade," recorded in 1995 by Cidinho and Doca, of the Cidade de Deus neighborhood in Rio's Western Zone. The song, sung as a letter of appeal to the authorities, captured this sense of the poor people wanting justice and decent lives in the new democratic order. At the same time, it also implied the threat that if justice did not come from above, the poor would make it happen from below:

> I suffered in the storm, now I want the calm
> People, be strong, all you need to see
> If they don't do nothing there we'll do it all from here[15]

Proibidão Postscript

Although up to 2004 all proibidão songs in Rocinha had been associated with the Comando Vermelho criminal faction, this quickly changed when Dudu da Rocinha and fifty men invaded Rocinha from the favela of Vidigal in April of that year. That invasion, directed by higher-ups within the CV from within the Bangu prison, brought about the deaths of several people, including innocent residents and other bystanders. Eventually, police killed Lulu, the favela's much-loved crime boss—a death Dudu and his men celebrated with gusto. Still, they never did manage to gain control of Rocinha, and shortly afterward the surviving leaders of the gang there switched factions from the CV to the ADA,

15 Portuguese: Sofri na tempestade agora eu quero a bonança; Povo tenha força, só precisa descobrir; Se eles lá não fazem nada faremos tudo daqui. Full lyric in Appendix A.

ushering in a new age of organized crime in the favela—in which the cartel allied itself even more closely to police. The switchover from CV to ADA also ushered in a new age of proibidão there, since the old CV songs were banned. In the time immediately following the transition, proibidão songs from other ADA favelas were brought in and distributed to Rocinha gangsters and their friends on pirated CDs.

In short order, however, local MCs like Cordão de Ouro proved key in helping embrace the change and the new ADA cartel. As CV graffiti tags were scrubbed off the walls of the favela's alleyways, new slang also replace the old in both song and speech. Immediately afterward, the slang phrase "É nós!" ("It be us!"), associated with the CV was banned in the favela, as was the CV slogan "fé em Deus" ("faith in God"). "É nós!" was replaced, as people began to use an ADA slang expression, "É nós é o caralho! É a gente, mane!" or "It's be us, my ass! It's us, fool!" "A gente" is another way of saying "us," in Portuguese, with the added favela slang *mané* (which meant 'fool' but was used more like 'man,' 'dude' or 'homeboy').

Still, Rocinha was effectively cut off from the usual cast of characters at the bailes funk in the community, since it was no longer safe for MCs representing the CV in their songs to perform there. This was especially significant because, as the base for the crown jewel in the Rio drug trade, the Rocinha CV cartel had the funds to invest greatly in the culture of proibidão funk. Looking back, one wonders if this fragmentation in the Rio funk circuit may have marked the end of the golden age of live proibidão.

10

Musical Survival Tactics

Kiddy Funk at the Emotions Club

From high atop his father's shoulders, a toddler in a tank top sways to the pervasive beat of the music coming through the massive speaker stacks at the Clube do Emoções, located at the foot of the favela. It is early Sunday evening in the summertime, and the baile funk is packed with more than two thousand kids from eight to eighteen years of age dancing amid the swirl of lights and music that permeates the sweaty air of the enormous dance hall. This dance is a matinê, a type of baile funk in which alcohol is not served and is intended for underage children and adolescents. The young people in attendance dress in close imitation of the slightly older, drinking-aged crowd that will replace them here later tonight. Girls wear tiny skirts or skintight, stretchy jeans, with little, colorful bareback tops, while most boys are dressed in Bermuda surfer shorts, Gracie jiu-jitsu shirts and tennis shoes, many having close-shaved heads tinted a peroxide blond or even light orange. Some boys and girls are dressed more formally, with long pants and button-up shirts or even pastel dresses. The bone-rattling volume of the funk music at Emoções limits most conversations to short phrases spoken up close to the ear, handshaking and little kisses, as well as a good deal of eye contact and flirting. It isn't possible to speak with more than one person at a time. The music is so loud as to be physical, a sort of sonic massage in which the bass from the amps can be felt in the chest and the tiniest hairs on the body.

Though Emoções is at the edge of Rocinha, many of the young people present are from other favelas as well, such as Vidigal, just across the mountain from Rocinha, or Rio das Pedras and Cidade de Deus in the neighborhood of Jacarepaguá, several kilometers away in Rio's Western Zone. People mix about, greeting one another, seeing and being seen, dancing in pairs, small groups and short lines or clusters. Most keep to the open space of the middle of the club, either on the dance floor or next to the thirty-meter-long bar at the far end. Several others move about on the top floor balcony areas, leaning against the railing and watching the crowd below. More stand along the steep ramp leading down from the entrance and the security guards patting down a group of kids just coming through the security gates. Still others crowd around the vending carts outside Emoções in the Estrada da Gávea, Rocinha's busiest thoroughfare, between a line of a hundred or so parked motorcycles and the passing buses, cars and motorcycle taxis that wind in and out of the favela.

On stage is a singer in a camouflage shirt, sneakers and baseball hat, with a simple gold chain around his neck, commonly referred to in Rocinha as 'the greatest all-time singer of funk,' or even 'the History of Funk.' MC Cordão de Ouro, a Black man in his mid-twenties, is a local from Rocinha and a familiar presence at Emoções. He moves only very slightly, holding the mic straight out from his mouth, rattling off his rhymes like machine gun fire in his deep, somewhat raspy voice. In his songs, MC Cordão exalts the strength and unity of Rocinha's drug trafficking cartel and praises the residents of Rocinha for being smart and filled with joy and brotherly love. He sings about gangster friends living and dead and what people in the favela should do to avoid getting lost, or even killed, in a hard world of drugs, violence and poverty. In one song, the MC commends the local hoodlums and thieves who steal outside the favela—never inside, and in another, he pokes fun at the cocaine addicts who sell their Bermuda shorts for drugs. He sings about the history of funk, playing soccer on the beach and his beloved city of Rio de Janeiro—a paradise of funk. Toward the center of the stage next to his DJ stands MC Cordão's wife. She wears a small, aqua-colored Lycra top; her long hair pulled into a ponytail that reaches all the way down to her waist and her form-fitting, stretchy jeans. The radiant young Black woman sways modestly to the music, serenely proud of her famous and talented husband.

The sweatiness and smoke of the air intensify, the lights spin, and electronic sounds pulsate and hum. A long train of teenage boys winds its way through the crowd of dancers in the middle of the hall. In the thick of the mass of fans, the toddler on his father's shoulders moves his little body to the beat, just like his dad, as they both smile contentedly. The little boy makes a gun with his thumb and fingers and continues laughing as he gestures along with the digital gunshots of the MC's song—bang, bang, bang![1]

Musical Survival Tactics

At the core of Rio's funk is a utopian impulse, a desire to be lifted above the scarcity, vulnerability and dreariness of poverty and transported to a place of abundance, power and excitement through a collective

1 Although this scene contains elements that would have been typical of bailes funk in Rocinha throughout the golden age of bailes de comunidade in the favela, I observed the little boy on his father's shoulders making the gun with his hand at Emoções on January 13, 2002.

musical encounter in the baile funk. This utopian drive functions in ways specific to the context of funk as a musical culture practiced by young people living on the edge of poverty and in areas marked by intense violence, such as Rio's favelas and other impoverished neighborhoods. At its core, funk carioca is a transformational and countercultural practice through which these youths can experience unity and find a greater sense of strength and courage to resist the wearying effects of the harsh realities facing them on a daily basis. In Rio's bailes funk, a densely significant and complex musical encounter is enacted in which social norms are subverted and a politically charged and powerfully moral space-time is conjured up and sustained.[2]

Perhaps it may seem strange to talk about utopianism in a musical practice like funk carioca so often branded with words like 'violent,' 'pornographic,' 'childish' and 'tasteless.' In referencing utopia here, I do not mean to invoke the notion of theoretical plans for the creation of an ideal world, or even of a specific, conscious project of how to transform society for the better. I am thinking instead of utopia as the creation of a temporary collective space in which those gathered can lift one another above the limitations of their ordinary lives to an emotional state that enables them to feel what it is to live in a better world.

Even the famous death corridor-style dances of the early 1990s held such a utopian allure for many of the youths who attended them. In 1994's *Funk Rio*, the first documentary on funk carioca, a teenage funkeiro named Paulo gives testimony to such an effect. Explaining the feeling he gets just as the dance parties exploded into the semi-ritualized, collect-

2 Here I'm using "space-time" instead of merely "time" to convey the sense that the baile creates a temporal space as well as a physical one, one rooted in the here-and-now of the present moment.

ive hand-to-hand combat they were famous for, he says, "Imagine when you get that rush that hits you, that big feeling. It's like you're in another place, another world."[3] Indeed, it can be hard for outsiders to appreciate why such a dangerous moment would hold any such appeal, especially for those of different age groups and socio-economic classes. When one considers more familiar instances of fighting in music, like those in the mosh pits of punk rock or the *rodas* ('circles') of capoeira perhaps it seems less odd. Utopias are, of course, different for everyone and what may feel like heaven to one person may be hell for the next. In the end, what we experience as utopia is connected to our specific traumas and histories.

Paul Gilroy's work on cultural expressions of the African diaspora and its underlying moral, spiritual and political dimensions, especially in music, offers useful insights on the collective feeling of hope and power such practices evoke (Gilroy 1993, 72-110). Building upon W.E.B. Du Bois notion of "double-consciousness," Gilroy argues that a huge disjuncture arose between the emphasis on liberty and equality in the political ideology of the Enlightenment and the horrific collective experience of slavery. As a result, a form of double-consciousness developed among diasporic peoples as they struggled for survival in their transatlantic and international journeys.

On the one hand, they adopted much of the belief in the fundamental dignity of each human being and the necessity for society to progress into a socially just political order.[4] In other ways, though,

3 See *Funk Rio* (1994, 18:50-19:00). The original Portuguese is, "Imagina a hora que bate um daqueles pancadão, aquela emoção grande, a gente tá em outro lugar, em outro mundo."

4 Du Bois' notion of double-consciousness arose from what he viewed as the inner conflict of the "American Negro," as he wrote, between an African and an American soul. In the context of Gilroy's notion of the Black Atlantic, the concept of double-consciousness is expanded to be even more transnational, rooted in the tensions

Black Atlantic communities rejected the rationalistic impulse of Western thought, coming to privilege more relational modes of knowledge, power and being in the spirituality and emotionality of collective musical encounters. In the face of the terror of slavery and its legacy in social inequity, these diasporic communities adapted, reshaped and ironically reinterpreted Western cultural forms and practices into a utopian vision that fortified them with courage and energy as they struggled to thrive and survive. For Gilroy, the sharply countercultural tendency of such Black Atlantic cultures intensifies the utopianism of their activities and blurs together categories such as music and politics, playing and fighting and the religious and the everyday. Although he never directly engages funk carioca, Gilroy dedicates large portions of his study to the discussion of its close cousin, hip- hop. He is especially interested in reuses and reinterpretations made in hip-hop of diverse musical, linguistic and cultural elements—or 'found sounds'—they encountered. He focuses less on dance parties or performance dimensions of hip-hop and more upon cultural artifacts like lyrics and other texts.

Although Gilroy's views on the nature of utopia in African diasporic cultures are directly applicable to Brazilian funk in all its aspects, especially to its songs and music, to fully explore the utopianism of funk one must take into account the creation of a musical community in the space of the bailes funk themselves. Richard Dyer's perspectives on the utopian dimensions of entertainment are useful in moving beyond lyrical analysis to the experience of audiences in the broader sense (Dyer 1999, 371-381). The great originality of this work is condensed in the rubric he suggests for the specific ways in which the dystopian aspects of the lives of fans are

of Europe, Africa and the Americas beginning through the European colonialist project.

emotionally resolved in the entertainment experience (Dyer 1999, 376).

Another aspect of Dyer's work that makes it applicable to the study of funk—and Performance Studies more generally—is his insistence that music is the most 'felt' performance medium and therefore the mode of cultural production most closely related to utopian practices. The musical dimensions of practices like American musicals and Brazilian funk involve participants in extra-rational, intensely emotional experiences that embody utopian feelings through a series of nonrepresentational signs. For Dyer, signs like colors, texture, movement, rhythm, melody are even more fundamental to the utopian impulse of entertainment than the formal, representational ones, such as song lyrics and movie scripts (Dyer 1999. 373).

The utopianism of entertainment is, according to Dyer, a sort of escapist flight from the stark inadequacies of real day-to-day life, inadequacies that correspond to the failed promises of patriarchal capitalism in America. Dyer does not condemn this fugitive aspect of entertainment as a thing that necessarily breeds apathy, however, but instead suggests it stems from an unconscious, revolutionary urge. He writes:

> Two of the taken-for-granted descriptions of entertainment, as 'escape' and as 'wish fulfillment,' point to its central thrust, namely, utopianism. Entertainment offers the image of "something better" to escape into or something we want deeply that our day-to-day lives don't provide. Alternatives, hopes and wishes—these are the stuff of utopia, the sense that things could be better, that something other than what is can be imagined and maybe realized (Dyer 1999, 373).

Dyer's view on utopia and entertainment is exceedingly useful in considering funk. Even so, there is a much higher degree of co-participation between the performers and the audience in the encounters in Rio's bailes funk than in the musical films of Dyer's analysis. Because the involvement of audiences in funk is such an inseparable part of the spectacle—compared to that of moviegoers—it is necessary to expand his understanding of entertainment considerably for this case. Dyer considers entertainment a commercial mode of cultural production and contrasts it with performances in other economic contexts, such as tribal, feudal and socialist. Entertainment, he states, is "a type of performance produced for profit, performed before a generalized audience (the 'public') by a trained, paid group who do nothing else but produce performances which have the sole (conscious) aim of providing pleasure" (Dyer 1999, 372).

Such a division between production and consumption blurs somewhat in the baile funk. Despite the centrality of the song lyrics in funk, its most intensely utopian dimension is the one that comes together live and in full color in the space-time of the baile. In the staging of a baile funk, audience and performance meld together. An intensely participatory and highly interactive play occurs between the audience and the performance through which the baile enacts itself as a series of sounds, signs, movements and behaviors involving both musicians and other folks in attendance. Such communion is intensified by characteristics like the sorts of improvisation and call-and-response typical of bailes, as well as the tendency to borrow and reinterpret signs and sounds from other cultures. These aspects make the performance dimension of funk carioca similar to those of other less professionalized, more folkloric and carnivalesque forms of entertainment in Brazil, as well as to many Afro-Caribbean and African American musical practices.

Perhaps at this point, it's worth considering a bit more some of the fundamental differences between musicals as entertainment and the practice of funk. As I have argued, the infinitely higher level of active participation on the part of the audience in funk is the factor that most dramatically separates it from forms of passive entertainment like musicals, which more conveniently fit into traditional notions of the circuit of production and consumption. Funk can easily be seen as an example of what Puerto Rican sociologist Ángel Quintero Rivera has called *músicas mulatas* ('mestizo musical forms') and the tendencies of Afro-Caribbean culture with which he identifies them.[5]

Quintero Rivera identifies primary characteristics of músicas mulatas that overturn traditional divisions between things like performance and audience or production and consumption. Firstly, the act of composition itself is done with the intention that space will be left for vocal and musical improvisation, an improvisation that is understood as a vital part of the resulting communication between the performers and their audience. Second, the vocalist is expected to spontaneously ad-lib additional lyrics, sounds and gestures in his interpretation of the original composition. Also, improvisational musical breaks, such as *descargas* ('jam sessions') are built into the songs, and individual musicians of an extensive variety of instruments are given space to play and interact with the crowd and vocalist. Next, the public itself is an active participant in the performance of the music, clapping out syncopated beats with their hands, singing along with the songs (especially choruses), demanding energy from the stage and dancing.

One final characteristic he highlights is what he calls the *polivocalidad* ('polyvocality') of Afro-Caribbean musical forms through which extreme hybridity is formed. According to Quintero Rivera, sounds and instruments are strategically borrowed from European, African and

5 This explanation of the characteristics of músicas mulatas appears in chapter one of *¡Salsa, sabor y control! Sociología de la música tropical* (Rivera 1998, 35-92).

indigenous sources alike, and mixed with other elements appropriated from world popular and mass culture in a way that democratizes and overturns the hierarchy of instruments and voices. It is worth noting that these features, which Quintero Rivera identifies as typical of 'tropical music,' are in fact also typical of Afro-American music, as can be seen in varying degrees in the traditions of forms like gospel, blues, jazz and hip-hop.[6] According to Gilroy (16-17, 78), these tendencies are characteristic of the cultures of peoples of the African Diaspora in general, as I shall explore in the chapter twelve—especially call and response, or what he calls 'antiphony.'[7]

In the context of these observations, it is noteworthy that the baile funk is indeed a "baile," or dance, and not a "show," a characteristic making it fundamentally different from forms of entertainment like Dyer's musicals. It may be the case that Brazilians, in particular, like to participate actively in their entertainment. Such is apparent, for instance, to anyone who has attended a soccer game in Brazil—or watched the Brazilian national team in a World Cup match on TV—and seen the large numbers of fans beating on drums and calling out chants. In the case of funk, I would say that in a sense 'true funk' only exists in the space-time of the baile. Other instances of funk, such as listening to the music in the car or at home, are somewhat two-dimensional and crystallized moments of funk. They tend to work in reference to the more quintessentially funk culture of the baile, live and improvised in a community of

6 For a more detailed exploration of these tendencies in African American music, see *A Change is Gonna Come: Music, Race and the Soul of America* (Werner 1999).

7 Scholars frequently assert that Brazilian music shares such characteristics with forms of folk music throughout the Americas. McGowan and Pessanha add to the list by pointing out that music in the Brazilian context plays an extraordinarily crucial role in daily life..

funkeiros who are as much a part of the spectacle as the paid performers. Indeed, this is one of the reasons I refer to funk throughout this study as a practice, a culture or an expression and not just as a musical style.' Funk is an organic confluence of living signs, melding and mixing together in a flow of sights, smells, sounds and gestures. In this sense, the stage in funk ends up spilling out throughout the dance and among those in attendance, democratically overturning traditional divisions between the spectacle and the spectators and between production and consumption. As a result, the central locus of the consumption of funk, the baile, is also the principal point of the production of funk.

The mixture of consumption and production in funk may be a good part of the reason it is so unpopular among people who have never gone to a baile, as the necessity of this mixture limits the ability of the traditional consumer to even understand funk. True, there has always been a funk song or two that gains national popularity, like MCs Leonardo and Junior's "Rap do centenário," about the hundred years of the Flamengo soccer club, Claudinho and Buchecha's ultra-smooth and romantic "Nosso sonho," discussed above, Bonde do Tigrão's raucous "Cerol na mão" and Serginho's "Pocotó," the would-be children's song about a little horse that dominated Carnival across the nation in 2003. Still, access to these songs is not the same thing as access to funk, in the sense of the high level of audience participation that characterizes it. In truth, the baile funk, per se, has never consistently maintained national or even city-wide popularity throughout the social classes in Rio.

Even some poor people from neighborhoods other than favelas, such as the suburbs of the Baixada Fluminense, may have more limited access to the entire culture of funk. For one thing, the proibidão-style songs about the drug gangs and criminal factions are not played on TV and radio and in fact are often not played in nightclubs outside of favelas. A person exposed to the forms of funk that are more easily marketed by the mass media in Rio and Brazil will experience only a limited brand of funk, one primarily divorced from the improvised experience of the baile—and one which communicates the pleasure of the utopian dimension of funk to a much lesser degree.

Considering such limitations may offer some clues as to why, of all contemporary musical styles in Brazil, perhaps only sertanejo country music elicits anything like the degree of dislike, and even disgust, from non-fans as does funk (Stroud 2008, 186).[8] Sertanejo, in my opinion, is another example of utopian entertainment, one which projects an imagined simplicity of an idealized and noble rural life, implicitly contrasted to the noisy pace of modernized life. Sertanejo is another Brazilian musical style which has appropriated a considerable dose of American culture, that of country music, and a relatively simple level of musical virtuosity. This simplicity can make it somewhat unpleasant to a great many Brazilians who are not fans, yet, when it comes to sales, sertanejo is indisputably one of the most popular styles in the country. I would argue that the appeal of sertanejo consists beyond its musical merits, instead in the specific socio-historical and cultural context in which it is enjoyed, which entails a sort of 'pastoral return.' Such nostalgia is especially relevant in a country characterized by reasonably recent emigration

8 Another candidate for the least popular music outside its demographic is Brazilian Contemporary Christian Music. Taken as a group, funk carioca, sertanejo and Brazilian Christian music could be considered the triad of a sort of *Música Impopular Brasileira*, or *MIPB—Brazilian Unpopular Music*, to make a play on the term for the iconic Música Popular Brasileira (MPB). Sean Stroud argues that many of the would-be arbiters of music of quality in the country, such as journalists, critics and scholars from at home and abroad focusing on Brazilian music, reveal a decidedly middle and upper-class aesthetic bias when it comes to Brazilian music that makes it difficult for them to appreciate mass music—or even tolerate it.

from the countryside to the great urban centers and the accompanying fragmentation of the communities and values of rural life in the face of rapid modernization.

If sertanejo projects a 'pastoral return,' funk carioca is the somewhat corresponding 'city-dominated' utopian view. As is the case with sertanejo, ironically, in funk it is fans' very participation that enables them to derive pleasure from it. Because of this participation, funkeiros are likely to experience and interpret differently those same aspects of funk that make it intolerable to many non-fans—such as its multiple layers of violence, sexuality and playfulness. The question of who ends up liking funk and why is very complicated and indeed not merely a matter of social class. In the years of my study in the field in the late 1990s and early 2000s, even people born and raised in the favela would often remark, "Funk is entirely devoid of culture." Perhaps it was even the majority that held such a view. Many favela residents complained funk was misogynistic. On the other hand, even people from middle-class of affluent neighborhoods sometimes said, "Funk is a very sensual rhythm!"[9]

Earlier I explained that one of the reasons that I refer to funk in the golden age as a 'culture,' as opposed to merely a 'style' of music, was the high-level of audience participation in the production of funk as entertainment in the space-time of the baile. Another reason was that funk was so closely dependent on the specific cultural and socio-historic context in which it existed. Such was true both regarding funk's ties to the power of the drug traffickers and its relationship to the cultural legacy of

9 This quote comes from an interview with Penelope, a twenty-one-year-old middle-class salesperson at *Yes Brasil* in the Fashion Mall of São Conrado, beneath Rocinha, on February 8, 2002. In the original Portuguese, she said, "O funk é um ritmo muito sensual!" Despite her middle-class background, she considered herself a diehard funkeira.

poor people in Rio de Janeiro. Such a legacy was closely tied to Carnival and globalization mediated by tendencies of relational hybridity and the musical survival tactics of the African Diaspora. Funk as a culture and practice was also related to the specific inadequacies in the lives of poor people in the socio-political terrain of favelas in Rio de Janeiro. Thus, although in important ways language and social class were determining factors, the 'culture' of funk was not merely a question of a language or class barrier.

Funk and the Brazilian Dream

It is also important to consider differences between the ideological and sociohistorical contexts relevant to Dyer's American musicals and the culture of the bailes funk. In his study of American musicals, Dyer points to the failed promises of patriarchal capitalism and what he refers to as the 'American Dream.' Although the failings of capitalism are relevant to Brazil, the promises of what could be called the "Brazilian Dream" involve an understanding of what it means to be Brazilian, often called *Brasilidade* ('Brazilianness'), obviously making it different from American ideology. Though it is difficult to specify what exactly constitutes such brasilidade, certain characteristics are commonly identified with the Brazilian national personality. One is racial mixing. Along with this, one of the most controversial attributes associated with Brazilianness is a characteristically optimistic vision of racial harmony, often referred to in the Brazilian context as 'racial democracy.'

Along with such racial diversity, Brazilians have self-consciously embraced the sorts of transnational cultural hybridity and creolization common throughout the Afro-Atlantic world since the modernismo of the twenties. In Brazilian artistic and intellectual life, this tendency is often labeled *antropofagia* ('cultural cannibalism'). Another is the high priority given to carnivalesque popular cultural practices (involving euphoric gleefulness, playful inversion of gender and class roles and social contestation). Others ideological features of brasilidade include playful sensuality (often involving androgyny); nostalgia—often expressed by the ambivalent and ubiquitous Portuguese term *saudade*—and deep emotional affect more generally. Certainly, Brazilians have similarly embraced friendliness, cheer and musicality as part of the national identity.

Another is *malandragem*, a word that might be roughly translated as 'the art of the hustler.' Malandragem is the art of the resourceful rogue, the *malandro*, who is capable of using a mixture of qualities such as charm, street smarts, friendship ties and a hint of dangerousness to maneuver between formal and informal social spheres and to survive in the face of corruption and disparity. It's a cousin to the idea of the famous *jeitinho*. This term is hard to define, yet readily understood by most all Brazilians and even visitors to Brazil in the country only a short time. When a jeitinho comes into play, the implication is that a special exception to the rules has been made in favor of someone due to some personal consideration. In the face of absurd bureaucracy and the sorts of constant hassles that make daily life in Brazil so inconvenient for most people living there (as well as in business, government, healthcare, etc.), the jeitinho has become entrenched in the Brazilian ethos as a necessary escape valve and remedy. Ironically, however, like widespread malandragem, the prevalence of the jeitinho often serves to increase corruption and the tendency for people to seek their individual advancement and that of their family members and close friends over that of the larger society.

In many ways, these attributes of the Brazilian national personality have their origins in the cultural practices of the same sort of ordinary, working-class poor people as the ones from Rio's favelas that make up the funk scene. The traits of this Brazilianness have been gradually appropriated by the middle and upper-classes in the evolution of the Brazilian nationalist identity since before independence.

The harsh conditions of everyday life facing many of the country's poor, however, make it extremely difficult for them to experience the sort of racial equality, sensuality, humor and friendliness associated with brasilidade outside of the utopian spaces they create for themselves in cultural practices like funk. Such expressions, like funk, allow everyday people to re-appropriate and to reaffirm these qualities, even as they exaggerate and intensify them in new ways, making it possible for them to continue to use such strategies for their survival. In an effort to coin a term to encompass the processes of ideological re-appropriation occurring in popular practices like funk, I offer *re-brasilidade*. This term can be taken to convey the meaning of a reaffirmation of the sort of qualities associated with brasilidade mentioned previously. At the same time, it can denote an expansion of Brazilianness to include more considerable space for the aesthetics of poor communities like the favelas in the postmodern, globalized context of contemporary Brazil.

11

Utopias de Favela

From a cultural point of view, film theorist Richard Dyer's work on utopia and entertainment offers some helpful analytical tools useful for understanding how the frustrations of poor people in Rio with the inadequacies of their lives might prepare them to be able to connect to funk carioca. In "Entertainment and Utopia," Dyer begins by organizing social inadequacies into categories such as scarcity, exhaustion, dreariness, manipulation and fragmentation. He then goes on to identify the utopian solutions for these inadequacies that fans feel in entertainment experiences, such as abundance, energy, intensity, transparency and community (Dyer 1993, 376). Below, I'll apply his rubric to the bailes funk in favelas during the golden age of proibidão in the late 1990s, early 2000s. I'll also suggest one additional pairing hinted at by Paul Gilroy's analysis of the moral spaces created in Black Atlantic cultural practices—powerlessness and power. Since in practice these categories tend to overlap and blur together, other researchers will likely identify still further types.

Abundance

The conditions of scarcity experienced by most residents of the favelas of Rio de Janeiro in the late 1990s and early 2000s are well known, as are they today. Inadequate jobs, housing, healthcare, transportation, educational opportunities, public safety and access to other goods and services, these are some of the hardships facing them. At the same time, there was a wealth of human community in favelas in areas such as friendship and love, creativity and playfulness, beauty and sensuality, emotion and humor. In the space and moment of the baile funk, scarcity and poverty vanished and were replaced by an abundant feast in which food and drink flowed, and there were plenty of drugs and alcohol. Sex and romance were readily available. The specific characteristics of abundance in funk took on something of a 'favela aesthetic,' as opposed to one of, say, a middle-class nightclub. In a sense, in the space-time of the baile revelers embraced the ambivalent nature of the favela, elevating it and transforming it into a fantastic, idealized place in which the humanity and personality of the community were preserved even as the troubles of severe poverty it faced were overcome.

Such a transformation occurred even at the seediest and most criminal dances, such as a Friday night dance along the Valão, an ample, open sewage drain at the bottom of a favela near Rocinha. The smell and unseemly sight of this sewage canal and the shack-like houses and shops that surrounded it revealed the reality of poverty in the favela as well as just about any other aspect of the physical neighborhood. The presence of the gangsters throughout the dance—mingling with the crowd with their oversized weapons, selling drugs and counting money on tables in the middle of the dance—was another stark symbol of the fact of the social exclusion of the community. In the music and energy of the baile, however, everything was wholly changed as people drank, laughed and danced, wearing their tightfitting Gang-brand jeans and Bad Boy shirts, with Nike tennis shoe knockoffs, eating hot dogs and grilled meat on long, flimsy sticks. The signs of poverty were present; they even became central tropes in the aesthetics of consumption in the baile. But it was idealized poverty turned into a feast, devoid of hunger or scarcity.

Energy

The exhaustion experienced in the everyday lives of many poor people in Rio—so often stuck in long lines, under-resourced schools and low-paying jobs—was left behind in the experience of the baile. Instead, the crowd was filled with vigor and energy as people danced sensually, singing passionately amid the fiercely loud funk music. In contrast to the tiring routine of everyday life, the space of the baile was one of energy and relaxation. Bailes often started late, sometimes after one o'clock in the morning, and could go until dawn. Loud booming music, dancing, flirting and fighting were all energetic elements of funk dances and, despite the rigors of urban life, it was uncommon to see people yawning or even sitting down at a dance.

A good deal of the energy in the funk dance came from the music itself, not only rhythmically or even emotionally but also from a sonic standpoint. In the music, the constant chaotic and individual sounds of the city and the favela were drowned out by the music blaring from the wall of speakers and replaced by a restful and harmonious flow of pulsing music. It energized the crowd, as fans were filled with its rhythms and melodies, lifted up and swept away in the flood of throbbing bass pouring out of the subwoofers. That blanket of sound covered the fans with an irresistibly invigorating collective heartbeat.

A song that speaks to the energy of the baile funk is "Vai Lacraia," by MC Serginho (Sérgio Braga Manhães), singer of the funk hit about the little horse, mentioned above ("Minha Eguinha Pocotó"). In the staccato chant of "Vai Lacraia," he sings:

> Be careful with Cuca because Cuca will get you
>
> She'll get you here, she'll get you there

Be careful with Cuca because Cuca will get you
She'll get you here, she'll get you there[1]

In the earlier funk carioca scene of the mid-1990s, these verses first had become popular with the "Montagem Cuidado com a Cuca" ("Montage Watch Out for Cuca") by the Pipo's sound team (*equipe de som*). Known as the originator of the *montagem* style of funk carioca in the mid-1990s, Pipo's relied heavily on loops of samples of words and sounds instead of full song lyrics. Their slogan was "O Encontro da Massa," or "The Meeting of the Masses."

The Cuca song sampled in that version, "Cuidado com a Cuca," was from the 1977 TV series *Sítio do Picapau Amarelo*, based on the children's stories of Monteiro Lobato, which blended Brazilian folklore with world mythology and were published in the late thirties and early forties.[2] In the magical world of his "Yellow Woodpecker Farm," Lobato's Cuca was an evil witch with the face of a crocodilian caiman. He adapted her from an Iberian tradition of Cuca characters in folklore going back at least as far as medieval Portuguese stories of dragons, witches and other monsters which were said to come for poorly behaved children in the night. The 1990s, montagem-style funk version of "Cuidado com a Cuca" had a horror movie tone to it, mixing incantations of what seemed to be hexes with monochromatic harmonic progressions. In 2001, Cássia Eller's sinister-sounding version for that year's reboot of the TV series was a national hit, inspiring a new wave of funk versions.

1 Portuguese: "Cuidado com a Cuca que a Cuca te pega; E pega daqui, e pega de lá."

2 One online version of that 1977 TV shown song credits the great Bahian singer Dorival Caymmi as its composer, but I cannot confirm this (*Gabriel & Cia O Canal mais Cultural do Youtube!* "Dorival Caymmi: A Cuca Te Pega," YouTube, September 23, 2016. https://www.youtube.com/watch?v=_dRe1dNUlCI).

The version by MC Serginho intermingled the lines with the warning to "watch out for Cuca" with the words "Vai Lacraia." This second element was an appeal to his transgender male to female dance partner, Lacraia (Marco Aurélio Silva da Rosa), to perform her famously frenetic dance moves.[3] Lacraia's unique style of wiggly dancing reflected the meaning of her artistic name, which is the Portuguese word for a large centipede.[4] Besides the infectiously energetic dancing of Lacraia herself, the song contributed to the energy-giving dimension of the space-time of the bailes in the way it mixed the innocence and emotion of childhood with the sensuality of adulthood. The exhaustion of a life of poverty in Brazil routinely deprived children of their youthfulness. But the baile was a place of play in which childhood was reclaimed as an act of resistance to the dehumanization of the prevailing social order of the formal city. The baile was a perpetual Carnival relatively unhindered by the sorts of cooptation, commercialism and rule-oriented structure that had come to impact so many other expressions of popular culture in Brazil.

In bringing Cuca out to play in the stage character of Lacraia, the baile was transformed into a space of life in the here and now, in which needs could be met through improvisation, imagination, creativity and friendship. This change occurred not merely intellectually or with respect to ideas and symbols but in the body—and all the way down to a person's limbic core, physiologically. Lacraia became the supreme utopian figure

3 Lacraia was born a male but considered herself a woman, as is apparent MC Serginho's tearful eulogy upon her early death from tuberculosis (Maselli 2011).

4 An example of the duos' performance can be seen on the famous live Sunday afternoon auditorium-style TV show, *Domingo Legal*, in 2003. Renato Borges, *Mc Serginho e Lacraia ano 2003 Domingo Legal Dançarinos*, 2013. YouTube video, 9:21. https://www.youtube.com/watch?v=bSBtyaHgKps.

of the baile funk and a spirit guide calling on others to follow her into an alternative world.

It was very suggestive to mix the figure of a transgender person like Lacraia with a popularly known folk character representing such a dense knot of pejorative associations of feminine power. The performance that resulted was perhaps even more subversive of traditional social hierarchies than the figure of the social bandit. Though the notion of favela social banditry was countercultural in class terms, in many ways it embodied stereotypical views of masculinity, including the assumption of male leadership, emotional toughness and sexual prowess. In community dances and funk carioca more generally, however, gangsters and male-to-female transgender or transsexual persons were brought together in suggestive ways.

At one particular dance in the Valão in Rocinha on a Friday night in June of 2009, I was struck by the large proportion of cross-dressed people to armed gangsters in the crowd. Out of the perhaps five-hundred folks in attendance, roughly one-hundred were openly brandishing weapons, which they raised above their heads in a celebratory fashion as they danced and sung. Swaying to the beat alongside them, singing along and cheering, were roughly the same number of cross-dressed persons.[5]

5 Indeed, by 2009 it seemed the presence of male-to-female transgender or transsexual persons in bailes in Rocinha had increased since the golden age of the late 1990s/early 2000s. Popular culture changes quite quickly, of course. Because the ADA criminal faction replaced the CV in Rocinha in 2004, transforming the lyrics of funk songs and the sorts of MCs and other performers who came to the favela, it raises the question of whether or not specific factions tended towards identifiably different funk aesthetics (CV, TCP and ADA). Was ADA approved proibidão somehow friendlier towards members of the LGBTQ community and more receptive to them? In any case, it seems the baile funk was increasingly becoming a haven for transgendered people against the difficulties and persecution they so often faced in the mainstream world of Rio's asphalt.

In a sense, the baile became a space of ultra-masculinity and ultra-femininity, just as such categories were routinely turned on their heads and the divisions between them constantly blurred in a myriad of ways. Indeed, Lacraia was embraced by the public as a kind person with great heart and humanity, greatly missed after her untimely death in 2011 at the age of 34.[6]

Intensity

There was almost always some level of flashing lights, smoke machines and pyrotechnics used in bailes funk. The use of alcohol and drugs often further intensified the ambiance, making the dances drastically different from the dreariness and predictability of everyday life. Bailes usually began with a DJ playing prerecorded music, then moved on to performances by less known singers and dance groups, sometimes involving competitions by groups of local nonprofessional dancers and usually finished with the big name MCs at the end of the night. Despite these conventions, fans never precisely knew what would happen next in the baile as strangers kissed, fights broke out, and romance and danger filled the air.

In bailes taking place in clubs, where fights were more likely to

6 I'm grateful to Professor Seo Eun-hee, my colleague at Seoul National University, for her efforts to explain to me pronoun and other word use related to LGBTQ issues. Ultimately, my hope is for discussion of LGBTQ in funk carioca to be expanded beyond the admittedly limited scope of my comments in this section. Some of the resources she shared with me included the online glossary of terms from GLAAD, the Gay and Lesbian Alliance Against Defamation (see GLAAD), The LGBT Resource Center of the University of Southern California (see LGBT Resource Center) and *Transgender People* (Gilbert 2013).

break out—because armed gangsters were not present to prohibit such behavior—security guards regularly ejected hotheaded young men (and occasionally women) who got into altercations. These scuffles often caused people nearby to stop and pay attention. Now and then, these brawls would explode into mob scenes involving dozens or even hundreds of people that could bring the music to a halt. More often, however, the MCs would keep right on singing, vocally admonishing people to stop fighting. In short, the intensity of funk dances was great and even people who hated them seldom listed boredom as a factor for disliking the bailes funk.[7]

In the community dances taking place outside of clubs in the streets of favelas, the presence of armed drug traffickers added a further element of excitement and danger to the atmosphere of the dance. Furthermore, the lyrics of the many proibidão funk songs made mention of those criminals, the weapons they possessed and the deeds they carried out, as explored in earlier chapters. These verses made the gangsters, in a sense, as much the stars of the bailes funk as the DJs, MCs and dancers who officially performed. This association of the bailes funk with favela drug traffickers also serves to add intensity to the space-time of the dances.[8]

The following lyrics from the song "Sou da Rocinha" offer a quintessential expression of proibidão and a good example of its tendency to add intensity to the experience of the bailes funk. It was by MC Cordão de Ouro; the

7 As mentioned previously, semi-ritualized gang fighting had been a part of the spectacle further earlier in the history of funk carioca, such as the infamous and now defunct dance at the Country Club in Jacarepaguá and other dances of the 'death corridor' variety.

8 In addition to the many sources listed previously about proibidão funk in this context, Franco-American ethnomusicologist Gerard Béhague also referred to the patronage of bailes de comunidade by favela gangsters in his highly regarded writings on "Afro-Brazilian music" (Béhague 2000, 286).

MC described in the vignette about the matinê baile at the Emoções Club described at the start of the previous chapter. "Sou da Rocinha" was a version of a radio-friendly song that did not make specific mention of gangsters or criminal factions. The excerpt cited here, recorded live at a dance in Rocinha, included references to the favela's CV gangsters in 2002:

> I am from Rocinha and I don't make it easy
> For the Third Command to mess us up
> I am from Rocinha and I don't make it easy
> For the Third Command to mess us up
> I'm gonna shoot 'em with an AK, bang!
> Check out this next part, brother, I don't kiss nobody's ass
> Heavy weapons, check it out, nobody has 'em like Rocinha
> At the front of the gang is Bigode, Bill, Buiú
> Cavanhaque, 21, Marcelinho Marino, and 99
> Don't forget Magu, Domar, Dewilson, Molejo and Bel
> The others are in Heaven, Baiano, Batatinha
> My friend Serginho, the loyal Trola
> Finishing up, armed with AKs, Soldado, and Cabeção, Magu, Naiba
> See, Bill, I don't forget my friends
> Make the AKs sing!
> It's the gang that protects the Valão, let's hear it!
> I'm tired of saying it, but I have to explain
> If you mess with Buiú you'll take a bullet from an AK
> I'm tired of saying it, but I have to explain
> If you mess with Lelé you'll take a bullet from an AK
> If you mess with Buiú you'll take a bullet from an AK![9]

At the time "Sou da Rocinha" was recorded, the enormously popular Luciano Barbosa da Silva, known by the nicknames Lulu, Bigode and Magro, was in charge of the faction in Rocinha, before police shot him to death in April 2004. He was particularly successful in promoting a positive image for himself and his gang within the community, and indeed attained a level of popularity and support among the residents rarely matched in the history of Rocinha.

With the impressive arsenal of weapons listed and the mention of courageous gangsters both living and dead, the song made a bold declaration of the power of the Rocinha gang and a sounded a warning to rival criminal factions, the police and enemies from within the favela alike. Even so, the sense of fraternal spirit and loyalty underlying the song emphasized the worth of these gangsters in terms that went beyond their capacity for violence. Given the popularity of Lulu in Rocinha and his image as a social bandit, the power of the gangsters stressed by the song also carried with it the connotation that they were protectors and benefactors of the favela community. The suggestion was clear that they

9 Portuguese: "Sou da Rocinha e não dou mole; Pa Terceiro Comando querer me esculachar; Sou da Rocinha e não dou mole; Pa Terceiro Comando querer me esculachar; Vai tomar de AK, pa pum! Na continuação se liga meu mano não sou simpático a ninguém; Armamento pesado bote na sua mente, igual à Roça não tem; Puxa o bonde Bigode, Bill, Buiú, Cavanhaque, 21, Marcelinho, Marino e o 99; Não esquecemos de Magu, Domar, Dewilson, Molejo e o Bel; Os restantes estão no céu; Baiano, Batatinha, o meu amigo Serginho, Trola, o braço fiel; Para finalizar de AK na mão Soldado e o Cabeção, braço Magu, Naiba; Se liga, Bill, não esqueço dos irmãos; Bota o fuzil pra cantar! É o bonde que fortalece o Valão, quero ouvir; Tô cansado de falar mas eu tenho que explicar; Se mexer com o Buiú toma tiro de AK; Tô cansado de falar, mas eu tenho que explicar; Se mexer com o Lelé toma tiro de AK; Se mexer com o Buiú toma tiro de AK!" (Note, the song's refrain follows the melody of "El africano," first recorded in 1983 by the Colombian vallenato legend Calixto Ochoa—with Wilfrido Carmelo Martínez Mattos, known as 'Manduquito,' popularized by the Dominican merengue great Wilfrido Vargas in the following year with additional lyrics. Lyrics in Appendix A.

were willing to help the poor and weak and capable of doing justice for those who had been wronged or injured by their neighbors. Most of the drug traffickers mentioned in the song were, at the time, among the soldiers who protected the Valão area of Rocinha, considered the favela's leading boca-de-fumo and one of the most lucrative in all of Rio.[10] The song portrayed the boca of the Valão as a sort of castle or fortress and its gangsters as the brave and loyal warriors who protected both the drug den and, by extension, the larger social order of the favela of Rocinha.

On still another level, the song suggested a transferal of the bravery, cunning and street smarts associated with the drug traffickers as social bandits onto the other residents of Rocinha. In this sense, the "eu," or "I" of the refrain, as the MC yells, "I am from Rocinha and I'm tough," represented both the figure of the gangsters of the favela and the figure of the other people who lived in Rocinha not working for the cartel. This connection was strengthened by the sense of cooperation between gangsters and residents that existed in the paternal relationship between the two. The gangsters protected the residents in return for the silence of the residents and their refusal to inform rival criminals or the police about the gang's activities. The underlying message of the song was that residents of Rocinha should feel a sense of pride to be members of a CV community. They were somehow different from and better than residents of favelas elsewhere, the song implied, especially those controlled by other factions like the ADA and TCP. The implication was that there was power in the lives of people in Rocinha and that its residents all were a part of a legacy of courage and strength in which important decisions were made that affected the lives of thousands of people.[11]

10 Sadly, the boca-de-fumo has resurged in Rocinha since september 2017.

11 This pride also implied a feeling of superiority regarding favelas in other cities with-

Transparency

Besides being places of abundance, energy and intensity, the bailes funk were also spaces of very direct and spontaneous sorts of interaction that afforded fans a great deal of transparency in communicating and pursuing their desires. The transparent sexuality in funk worked against the social controls that encouraged individuals to veil or curb their needs for sex and romance, to rely upon reason and dialogue and to control their emotions and impulses in general, or what Dyer calls manipulation.

Besides being present in many lyrics of funk songs, the forthright and powerful sexuality of funk was apparent in the suggestiveness of the dance moves, courtship practices and overtly sexualized atmosphere of the bailes. Indeed, there was something almost orgiastic in the funk dances, as crowds of people hugged, kissed and rubbed up against one another in clothing that was often very tight, shiny and small. The loudness of the music itself forced people to talk right into the ear of the other person, bringing people into even closer contact. Dance steps and choreographies often imitated sex acts, as lines of men and women grinded against one another to the music with their hands on their knees or made other pumping and thrusting gestures. The aggressive style of flirting, with which members of both sexes approached each another, was another aspect of the prevalence of sexuality in the baile. It was not uncommon for men and women to kiss various partners in one dance, often people they did not previously know. Such behavior on the part of either

out criminal factions. If was not uncommon for Rocinha residents to brag amongst themselves, saying things like "Our crime is organized!" ("Nosso crime é organizado!"). Even people radically opposed to the criminal lifestyle, like Evangelical Christians, would make such statements.

was not considered reprehensible in funk culture. Such transparency embodied the kind of "open, spontaneous, honest communications and relationships" Dyer(1993, 377) associates with transparency .

Not surprisingly, funk lyrics often reflected and promoted this high level of sexual transparency in the space of the bailes funk. A subgenre of funk that was particularly relevant for the open, spontaneous, honest communications and relationships typical of funk culture was funk sensual, often called putaria, discussed above. This style, performed by male and female artists alike, involved frequent and explicit pornographic references, thinly veiled innuendo and sexual plays on words. Because many of the most graphic songs of funk sensual included words that most radio stations were unable to play, there were often alternative versions of these songs, as was the case of many proibidão songs. Indeed, the more risqué versions were sometimes available on bootleg compilations sold under the same 'proibidão' banner. The notorious "Vai, Serginho," by MC Serginho, in which the MC describes a slow descent of kisses starting at the woman's mouth and ending at her vagina, exemplified this tendency.

It's not difficult to understand why people would accuse funk of being misogynist, with MCs like Serginho singing that what he really wants to do is to "morder o seu grelinho" or "bite your little clitoris." While critics of funk often accuse funk carioca of misogyny, though, all the female funkeiras I interviewed over the years did not agree.[12] On several occasions, I asked female fans (all teenagers or in their early twenties) about the use of funk slang terms like *cachorra*. It means 'female dog,' though it does not transmit

12 As mentioned in chapter one, for more on putaria, especially the debates as to whether or not the female MCs should be considered organic feminists, see Caetano, "My pussy é o poder: representação feminina através do funk: identidade, feminismo e indústria cultural," *Funk-se quem quiser* (Lopes 2011, 151-210) and Moreira, "Bitches Unleashed."

the same connotation as the US slang, 'bitch,' which in English implies a mean, unpleasant woman. Those female fans responded by saying that one could not understand funk by isolating terms outside the context of the larger scene, which was fairly egalitarian and inclusive in regards to gender, they claimed. Neither should the term be conflated with American culture, but rather should be understood as something like 'little doggie.'

The term cachorra, these young women emphasized, was used as a reference to a playful role that could be assumed by women in the baile. It was in contrast to the more traditional female role of the Brazilian social hierarchy, identified as *gatinha* ('kitten' or 'little kitty'). In mainstream Brazilian slang, a *gato* is a handsome man and a *gata* is an attractive woman. In the funk dance parties of the times, male and female MCs alike would yell out both options to the crowd. "Gatinha! Miau! Cachorra! Uau Uau!" or "Little Kitty! Meow! Little Doggie! Ruff ruff!" It was as if those were two options for female identities or behavior. Despite the troublesomeness of such a limiting formulation, the young women pointed out that funk somewhat objectified both sexes. This mutual objectification placed them at the same level as the men, they said. Being on the same level as men made them feel empowered. Funk provided women chances to be hunters, too, and aggressors, they insisted. It gave them the same right as a man to view a member of the opposite sex as an object of consumption to be obtained.[13]

13 My friend Aline, who was twenty one in 2002 and a middle-class student of Brazilian Literary Studies from Rio's Barra da Tijuca neighborhood, made such an argument during a debate about sexism in funk at the Congresso dos Estudantes de Letras do Estado do Rio de Janeiro, in Volta Redonda, in November of 2001. Subsequently, various formulations of this attitude were expressed during subsequent interviews by young women who attended bailes funk in Rocinha, including Clisna (January 3, 2002, age twenty), Cleide (January 13, age fifteen), Fernanda and Barbara (January 13, 2002, ages fourteen and seventeen), Denise and Silvana (February 5, 2002, ages

One MC who embraced the cachorra female funk identity was Tati Quebra-Barraco, whose name translates as something like 'Tati Bust-the-Hut.' From the nearby favela Cidade de Deus in Jacarepaguá, in Rio's Western Zone, Tati made a name for herself through songs involving highly transparent and playful sexual innuendos. To this day, she remains perhaps the most enduring and widely known female entertainer in funk. Almost all of her songs have played with the objectification of men and the liberation of the female libido.

In the late 1990s and early 2000s when Tati first became famous, almost all of her songs were of the variety known as montagem, relying heavily on stuttering electronic beats and sampled loops, as well as lyrics that were usually minimal and repetitive, almost mantra-like. Her repertory of songs from her self-titled debut album in 2000, released by Pipo's Records, and her 2004 CD *Boladona*, released on Link Records, offered numerous examples of the open, spontaneous sexuality for which she was famous, as can be seen in the following excerpts:

"Montagem Assadinha (69)" ("Sore and Hot [69]"):

> 69, chicken on a spit, we like it lying on our side

nineteen and twenty-one) and Nani (March 15, 2002, age sixteen). This view is also extolled in Denise Garcia's documentary *Sou Feia Mas Tô na Moda*, of 2005. Due to the ages of those interviewed and the controversial nature of this subject, I have left out the full names of young women cited here. One woman I interviewed, who wished to remain anonymous, did not share this view. She felt the young women and girls on the funk scene who held such views were fooling themselves. Her status as a psychologist and a Christian made her sympathetic to them, as did her working-class upbringing. Though she attended several funk parties with her boyfriend (a foreign researcher), she felt the open sexuality of funk exposed the young women to harm. As mentioned in Chapter 1, for scholarly treatments of this ongoing debate see Caetano, "'My pussy é o poder': representação feminina através do funk: identidade, feminismo e indústria cultural," *Funk-se quem quiser* (Lopes 2011, 151-210) and Moreira, "Bitches Unleashed."

If you can't take it, stop a little, it's burning, blow on it![14]

"Montagem Cardápio do Amor" ("Menu of Love"):

With whipped cream on that little body, I'm going to suck every bit of it

At mealtime if there's meat

Get your roasting spit ready and your sausage for later on.[15]

"Montagem Tchutchuco" ("Sexy Baby")

Take off your shirt, put it in, take it out, go in and out.[16]

More than merely appropriating an aggressive sexual posture considered traditionally male, by embracing her sexuality in this way, Tati enacted an empowering gesture of liberation of female sexuality in which a woman was free to pursue her pleasure as she desired. At the core of her libidinous point of view was a playful celebration of sexual domination through which she stimulated both her own gratification and the satisfaction of her man by turning the tables on him. Furthermore, by refusing passivity or emotional dependence on men and by negating the need to please them, Tati communicated a powerful sense of being untamable. In one song, she sung "I don't like little dicks," or "Não gosto de piru pequeno," then graphically describes what she does to the men she conquers or catches.[17] Tati transformed women into hunters and aggressors who had the same right as men to view a member of the opposite

14 Portuguese: "69 (the sex position, often called soixante-neuf), frango assado, de ladinho a gente gosta; Se tu não tá agüentando, pára um pouquinho, 'tá ardendo, assopra!" Lyrics in Appendix A.

15 Portuguese: "Com chantilly nesse corpinho vou lamber ele todinho; Na hora da refeição se tiver sua carne; prepara seu espeto e sua lingüiça pra mais tarde." Lyrics in Appendix A.

16 Portuguese: "Tira a camisa, bota, tira, entra e sai." Lyrics in Appendix A.

sex as an object of consumption to be obtained.

More still, she heightened the playfully combative nature of sexual relationships and brought about an intensification of the sensuality of the baile funk experience for all parties. Between songs, Tati calmly walked about the stage in tight jeans that clung to her slightly obese figure and a midriff that showed her belly fat. She often repeated a catchphrase that came to define her even as it made a refusal that a woman's worth is based on good looks: "Sou feia mas tô na moda!" or "I'm ugly but I'm in!" After Tati opened the way, a series of other female funk artists, such a Deise da Injeção, also from the Cidade de Deus, groups like Bonde das Loiras and Gaiola das Poupozudas and solo artist Valesca Popozuda had success performing similar songs. Still, it's worth noting that, by and large, they are considered more physically attractive than Tati. Indeed, in the years since, even Tati has undergone dozens of plastic surgeries and lost nearly as many kilos.

Community

In addition to what might be called the formal aspects of community formation, such as people being together in one place, having shared interests and engaging in collective activity, a significant element of the community formed in funk dances was one of racial and class dynamics. The country's deep-rooted, historical divisions along race and class lines had given rise to a sense of fragmentation in contemporary Brazil. Such disintegration was exasperated by the increasing breakdown of

17 The song references and samples the international hit from 1994, "Short Dick Man," by female rapper Gillette of the US, recorded with her group, 20 Fingers.

traditional forms of social interaction in many of today's postindustrial mass societies around the globe. This fragmentation was overcome in the experience of the baile funk through the creation of an intensely unified and vibrant musical community in which there were no outsiders, no rich and poor, no black and white. Instead the individual members of a *massa funkeira* ('funk crowd') formed an enormous collectivity of fans who swayed together to the beat as they danced and sung.

The repetitive nature of the dances was another aspect that transformed them into community spaces. As the fans got comfortable with the setting of a particular dance over a period of months or years, it became something like the square of a small town in the interior of the country. Indeed, in communities like favelas that rarely had any central squares or parks in which people from all over the neighborhood could come and socialize, the space of the bailes became one of the most critical alternatives, especially for young people. In the case of Rocinha, for example, it could be argued that the beach in São Conrado held this function and that many courtships and friendship ties were developed and maintained on the beach. In fact, the population of Rocinha had virtually taken over both São Conrado and Pepino beaches and the middle-class people from São Conrado were much less evident there (other than those involved in the hang gliding circles towards the far end of the beach). At night, the beach was less popular and the people of Rocinha met in thousands of other smaller places throughout the favela. There were some very small plaza-like clearings in houses, but typically nothing brought together as many people as the baile. The somewhat upscale Emoções could safely hold as many as 4,000 and the street dances in the Via Ápia could hold even more. In dances held during carnival, there were upwards of 5,000-6,000 people crowded into the relatively small street.

Although it was clear that the baile, and indeed funk culture in general, was associated with blackness and low-income communities, there was an anti-essentialism in them that embraced the characteristically Brazilian dream of racial harmony and democracy to a striking degree. Although the skin tone of the crowd in the baile was likely to be varying shades of brown, MCs, DJs, dancers and fans of funk are of a variety of colors ranging from Black to White. Even the music played was non-essentialist. In most bailes, blocks of other styles of urban music were played in addition to funk, such as hip-hop, pagode, and even hard rock. Whatever class and racial connotations these styles might have possessed tended to be ignored. All this is not to say that Black ethnic identity was lost in funk but rather that it eschewed any facile dichotomy. In a way, by not making Blackness a requisite for participation in the baile funk, funk culture invited all those in attendance, whatever color they were, to share in its essence as an expression of Black culture, suggesting a blackening of racial identity that ran counter to the historical tendency of Brazilian society to aspire to whiten itself.

Furthermore, unlike other social and cultural practices in Brazil, in which the poor were usually given an inferior place, the bailes funk create a space that inverted conventional social hierarchies and places them at the top. The funk aesthetic projected an understanding of social class in a manner that was similarly nonessentialist in its identity as an expression of Afro-Brazilian culture. People from other social strata were readily welcomed to participate in the funk world of the bailes, as long as they were willing to embrace the baile on its own terms and to hold aloft the vision of the idealized world of the favelas it sustains. This is even true for people from other countries, such as MC Gringo (Bernhard Weber), a German singer of Brazilian funk who later achieved great success. The same was true for Don Blanquito (Alex Cutler), from the US, who appeared a few years afterward. It was also the case for me, as a foreign resident, community activist and researcher. It's hard to imagine I would be as accepted in other youth scenes around the globe as I was in the funk circles of Rocinha, where I was typically embraced as a brother both before and after I became a 'researcher.'

As a result of such openness, the baile was one of the few places in Carioca society where middle-class and wealthy young people could have extensive contact with young, poor people on somewhat equal footing. Funk inverted the traditional social hierarchies in Brazil placing the rich on top, allowing so many wealthier adolescents and young adults who attended bailes to transcend the class and race differences that are so blatantly present in their daily lives. In this way, the culture of funk enacted a revolutionary new vision of Brazilianness in which the identity of the poor was central.

Power

It seems appropriate to add one more category of social inadequacies to Dyer's list. It is the utopian solution to the sense of powerlessness often experienced by poor people living in places like Rio's favelas—both politically and personally—as well as the sense of fear, frustration and despair they so often felt. Beyond the problems of the physical scarcity of resources typical of poverty anywhere, the feeling of powerlessness felt by people in Rocinha was rooted in the country's long-standing racial and class inequities and in the ongoing crisis of violence it faced. These conditions frequently threw poor people into traumatizing experiences like gang warfare and police repression. The utopian solution found in the encounter of the bailes funk ameliorating this was a source of empowerment available to fans in the baile as an emotional state endowing them with feelings of power, courage and hope. These feelings were accompanied by a sense of inclusion in the larger Brazilian society, not necessarily the Brazil of the middle and upper classes, but a Brazil of everyday people. It was an intensely Brazilian space of hyper-brasilidade, in all its racial openness, sensual playfulness, musicality, gregariousness and merriment. At the same time, it was a cosmic space that connected with people everywhere, especially young people from low-income communities in the Afro-Atlantic world and beyond.

The baile was a space of many forms of power, both collective and individual, starting with the incredibly loud funk music itself and the wattage and technology necessary to sustain it. The sheer, physical size of the crowd of funk fans coming together at the dance provided a sense of the power of the energy, creativity and soul of a large mass of people unified in dance and song. There was power, too, in the ability of both women and men to fulfill their emotional and corporal desires sexually and romantically.

In the contexts of many baile funks in favelas, there was an underlying sense of the power of the favela gangsters, who often brandished high-powered weaponry such as grenades and firearms as they attended or even sponsored the dances. Perhaps just as importantly, there was also a feeling of power in the space of the baile funk as it transmitted a sense of inclusion to individuals into the greater society as members of vibrant, human communities like Rio's favelas, exalted in the signs and sounds of the bailes as places of beauty, creativity, love, faith and culture.

Even though in the present context I am using the term 'power' in relation to 'powerlessness,' and therefore in a more ideological and psychological sense, in my view the power made available in community funk dance parties should also be understood as something corporal and physical. It is also related to community, discussed above. Indeed, the level of 'community' this power comes from is indeed a thing far beyond 'utopia,' as such. What I have in mind here is the physiological boast one gets through what in psychology is called limbic resonance and restoration, related to the idea of 'limbic realism' I referred to in the introductory chapter of this book. Thomas Lewis, Fari Amini and Richard Lannon describe the brain's 'limbic core' in the following way:

> A primordial area of the brain, far older than reason or thinking, creates the capacity that all humans share… the workings of this ancient, pivotal urge reveal that our nervous systems are not self-contained. Instead, our brains like with those of people closest to us, in a silent rhythm that makes up the very life force of the body. These wordless and powerful ties determine our moods, stabilize and maintain our health and well-being and change the structures of our brains. In consequence, who we are and who we become depend, in great part, on whom we *love* (Thmas Lewis, Fari Amini and Richard Lannon 2000, 167).

The baile funk should be understood in terms of such neurological intermingling between those present, in the collective presence of those making it up, as a time-space field emerging between them. Thus, the empowerment made available in the baile funk is not merely in symbols, lyrics or ideas—or through even music, dance, fashion, gestures, speech or other outward signs. Instead, power comes from collective being itself through this merging together into a total that is greater than the sum of its parts.

12

Mixes from the Margins

Vigário Geral, Rocinha and Vidigal
Coronel, Mutuapira, Itaguaí and Sacy
Andaraí, Iriri, Salgueiro, Catiri
Engenho Novo, Gramacho, Méier, Ihaúma, Arará
Vila Aliança, Mineira, Mangueira and Vintém
In the Posse and Maduereira, Nilópolis, Xerém
Or wherever
I will see you and admire your beauty
—"Our Dream," by Claudinho and Buchecha[1]

In this chapter, my plan is to round off my discussion of proibidão with some considerations about funk carioca in a broader sense as an expression of Afro-Atlantic culture. Throughout this study, I have avoided approaching funk carioca from a heavily comparative point of view alongside either Brazilian hip-hop, US gangster rap, Mexico's narcocorrido, reggaetón, world hip-hop, electronic music or other styles

1 From Claudinho and Buchecha's "Nosso sonho" ("Our Dream"). These verses are from the middle stanza, which poetically arranges names of favelas, low-income communities and neighborhoods of Rio de Janeiro with bailes funk. Portuguese: "Vigário Geral, Rocinha e Vidigal; Coronel, Mutuapira, Itaguaí e Saci; Andaraí, Iriri, Salgueiro, Catiri; Engenho Novo, Gramacho, Méier, Inhaúma, Arará; Vila Aliança, Mineira, Mangueira e a Vintém; Na Posse e Madureira, Nilópolis, Xerém; Ou em qualquer lugar; Eu vou te admirar." Full lyric in Appendix A.

of music in Brazil or around the world.[2] Instead, my emphasis has been on attempting to delve intimately into proibidão funk carioca as a local culture in Rio's favelas—especially in Rocinha at the end of the 1990s and early 2000s in what I consider to be the golden era of the bailes de comunidade. Such an approach has advantages and disadvantages. Hopefully, the portrait I have painted thus far has offered an up-close look into the dynamics of crime and community in the everyday lives of people living there. Still, such a tact has not left much space to explore the connections of funk to similar musical practices in the broader Afro-Brazilian, Black Atlantic or global contexts. With such considerations in mind, here I offer some initial comparisons with both carnival and hip-hop in Brazil at the time. Hopefully, others will be able to evaluate such connections more closely.

One of the threads that most obviously tie funk carioca together with other expressions of Afro-Atlantic cultures is the cultural mixing at its core. In the context of contemporary Brazil, it is rare for scholars to talk about such hybridity without framing it in terms of Brazilian modernismo of the twenties and the country's legacy of 'cultural cannibalism.' In his "Manifesto Antropófago" of 1928, Oswald de Andrade drew from the ritual cannibalism of the Tupi warriors before the arrival of Portuguese to Brazil to advance a combative posture of cultural resistance aimed at overturning the power relations between his country and the neo-colonial hegemony of Europe and the United States. The manifesto presented a series of lyrical, prose aphorisms announcing a revolution against a

2 Besides more obvious connections to gangster rap, fruitful comparisons can be made with Mexico's narcocorrido, especially for the combination of religious belief and imagery with expressions of the culture of crime so strongly present in both (Ramírez-Pimienta 2004; Ramírez-Pimienta 2011).

dominant order in Brazil built around the culture of White, rationalist Western civilization. Oswald wrote, "Só me interessa o que não é meu. Lei do Homem. Lei do antropófago" (Oswarld 1991, 65), or "I am only concerned with what is not mine. Law of man. Law of the cannibal." (Oswald 1991, 38).

Instead of slavishly accepting and imitating foreign cultures, Oswald argued, as a part of their ever-expanding, hybrid nature, Brazilians were to take what they liked from the cultures of Europe and the US, ingesting it, mixing it with their regional and national cultures and making it something new. Besides staving off foreign dominance, such a gesture was aimed at rising above the patriarchal capitalism at home, together with the ossified societal norms and psychological restraints that accompanied it. For countless intellectual and cultural vanguards in Brazil ever since, Oswald's anthropophagic idea has offered a compelling banner of defiance against the legacy of colonialism and contemporary foreign cultural hegemony.[3] Interpreters of Brazil, too, have pointed to its openness to cultural mixing as one of the most deeply-engrained features of its national personality, more often than not framing hybridity in terms of this cultural cannibalist tradition of modernismo.[4]

3 A great many authors from Brazil and around the world have considered the question of modernismo's cultural cannibalism and its relevance in making sense of Brazilian culture today. Recently, new understandings of anthropophagy and its heritage regarding issues of hybridity and resistance have arisen in fields like Performance Studies and Postcolonial Studies. See Bishop-Sanchez' insightful essay, "On the (Im) possibility of Performing Brazil," in the book she co-edited with Albuquerque, *Performing Brazil* (2015, 677-683).

4 Another nuanced perspective on the inheritance of cultural cannibalism in Brazil today is "Biting the Meat, Spitting It Out," by Fernando de Souza Rocha, also from *Performing Brazil.* Seeking to understand hybridity in the current generation in Brazil, Rocha claims that a new scene has come about opposing the consumption of cannibalism with that of capitalism. He argues this scene has moved "beyond" cannibalism. The question is no longer one of "Tupi or not Tupi," as Oswald de Andrade originally framed it, but instead of "Tupi and not Tupi" (Albuquerque 2015, 1027-1028).

Another seminal work of modernismo, Mário de Andrade's *Macunaíma, o herói sem nenhum caráter* (*Macunaíma, a Hero without a Character*), published the same year, similarly proclaimed cultural mixing as the foundational feature of the Brazilian national identity. In the novel, its protagonist, Macunaíma, undertakes a fantastic and comic odyssey through a mythical world drawing from Tupi and other Native peoples in Brazil and from the modern landscapes of São Paulo. Symbolizing the amorphousness of the anthropophagic tendency of the Brazilian nation at the time of the book's writing, Macunaíma undergoes a constant metamorphosis during the course of his adventures. He even alters his race and personal character to suit changing needs and circumstances. Throughout the novel, the folk roots of the diverse mixture of everyday people in Brazil shift and change their qualities as they interact with the global influences of modernity. Macunaíma himself ends up with a personality that is 'sem nenhum caráter' ('without character'), even as his "character" forms precisely as the ability to create a hybrid culture for himself on the frontiers between Western rationalism and what Mário de Andrade considered as Brazilian primitivism.

Such literary creations indeed projected a compelling inversion of power dynamics between center and periphery. Their nationalistic tones have been helpful since in staving off the full onslaught of US and European privilege in the country.[5] Brazilian music scholars Charles Perrone and Christopher Dunn link the lineage of Oswald de Andrade's cultural

5 Another nuanced treatment of the question of hybridity, resistance and the heritage of modernismo is offered by João Cezar de Castro Rocha and Jorge Ruffinelli, authors of an essential collection of reflections on the topic in *Antropofagia Hoje?* Also see Luís Madureira, *Cannibal Modernities*, for his treatment of the subject from a postcolonial view that takes into account both Brazilian and Caribbean cultural movements.

cannibalism through the antiestablishment tropicália movement of the late 1960s and early 1970s to Recife's hyper-eclectic Manguebeat musical movement of the mid-1990s (Perrone and Dunn 2001, 19-20; 29-30).

It's tempting to connect the eclecticism of funk carioca to modernismo in a similar way.[6] It's worth pausing to consider, however, the matter from another of Perrone and Dunn's viewpoints in this context. They argue for the need to move beyond a nationally-minded perspective when addressing hybridity in the contemporary Brazilian context, pointing to Paul Gilroy's emphasis on the broader Afro-Atlantic world (Perrone and Dunn 2001, 25-30).

Hybridity, then, is not peculiar to Brazilian *modernismo*, funk carioca or even Brazilian culture in general but rather is something Gilroy defined as one of the most significant characteristics of the various cultures of the African Diaspora. Even so, one could argue that commonalities in the Afro-Atlantic aesthetics of pastiche and bricolage perhaps could be better understood as examples of the tactics of resistance of subaltern populations anywhere facing situations of struggle against domination. As John Fiske pointed out, in everyday life culture is more a question of "process" than "products." For him, popular culture should always be understood as a process of borrowing and reusing symbols and ideas. For Fiske, then, the question at the heart of the matter is not so much "who people *are*" as "what they *do*" (Fiske 1995, 323). One might argue, in this sense, that this process of hybridity is the domain of everyday life more than something Brazilian or even Afro-Atlantic, as something of what Fiske calls "cultures of making do."[7]

6 As I myself attempted to do in my doctoral thesis (Sneed 2003, 193-203).

7 Latin American historian Florencia Mallon made a similar point in one of our many discussions about my research for my doctoral dissertation in the early 2000s.

But is there not something distinctive about hybridity in the Afro-Atlantic context, specifically? For me, building upon Gilroy's ideas, relationality and the communal are crucial features of Black Atlantic cultural practices such as funk carioca.[8] For him, hybridity is more than aesthetic preference, in a Kantian sense. It is, instead, a means of connecting people to one another and the world around them. He writes:

> Antiphony (call and response) is the principal formal feature of the musical traditions. It has come to be seen as a bridge from music into other modes of cultural expression, supplying, along with improvisation, montage, and dramaturgy, the hermeneutic keys to the full medley of black artistic practices (Gilroy 1995, 78).

Gilroy's interests in Black music in the Afro-Atlantic context lie beyond "rampant, invasive textuality." Instead, ephemeral meetings in live time are the quintessential space-time of Black music.[9]

Historically, one might say, the practice of daily life in the Afro-Atlantic world has been about people doing life together in ways that mix the sacred and profane—in the music, dance, worship and fellowship of groups, gatherings, circles and community encounters. One must bear in mind, therefore, that such practices are not merely what people *do* but of what they *do together*. Further still, this relational, communal hybridity

8 Gilroy's view is compatible with Édouard Glissant's similarly relational notion of creolization, also helpful in moving past the more nationalistic view of the hybridity of Brazilian anthropophagy in the context of discussions of funk carioca (Glissant 1997).

9 Such a view of the primacy of music in human life is reminiscent of Anthony Seeger's classic ethnographic work on the Suyá tribe in Brazil. In *Why Suyá Sing: A Musical Anthropology of an Amazonian People*, Seeger stresses the role of music in the structuring of communal space-time in that society (Seeger 2004, 130-136).

is not merely pragmatic, in the sense of what people *do* or what culture *does*. It is also about who they *become* together as they do the things they do. It's about coexistence, in this way, ontologically—not in a fixed sense, but in a relational one.

Seen from this light, perhaps cultural cannibalism is of somewhat limited usefulness in understanding cultural mixing in Brazil, at least outside of modernismo. Firstly, it frames things too narrowly with a nationalistic perspective that is more than slightly passé. Just as importantly, the metaphor of killing and eating the other is far more objectifying than the encounters of everyday life tend to be in spaces like community dance parties of the funk in favelas. The relational hybridity at the heart of such encounters is moved by a more dialogically-oriented spirit, which perhaps one could better describe as "co-existentialist" than anthropophagic.[10] Thirdly, the anthropophagy of the modernists tended to focus mostly on signs, symbols, ideas and other readily identifiable textual and cultural artifacts. It did not attempt to take into account the live dimension of meetings and its implications for hybridity. In the end, mixing is more than ideological. It is not only linguistic but ontological, not just "mixing and thinking" or "mixing and talking" but also "mixing and becoming."

Paul Gilroy's pioneering work, *The Black Atlantic: Modernity and Double Consciousness* (1993), has become a constant reference for cultural critics dealing with issues of race in the West in general and scholars of Brazilian music in particular. Although the study is dense and difficult to read, it is thoroughly grounded in a broad range of examples from the vernacular of African American musical cultures from the time of slav-

10 I have made a similar argument in treating cultural mixing in the music of Chico Science e Nação Zumbi and Recife's Manguebeat of the mid-1990s (Sneed 2016, 92-94).

ery to global hip-hop today. Gilroy's vision encompasses Europe, North America, the Caribbean, Brazil and other parts of Latin America, though the actual examples in the book tend to limit themselves somewhat to the English-speaking world. He dedicates a great deal of space to the discussion of American hip-hop, for instance, as the quintessential form of the utopian character of African Diaspora cultures in contemporary society. He frames hip-hop as a radical artistic praxis problematizing the complicity of Western rationalism and Progress with the history of violence, slavery and genocide.

Gilroy argues that the experience of slavery gave rise to a "double-consciousness" among slaves and their descendants with regards to Western notions of rationalism and Progress. On the one hand, Enlightenment ideals such as liberty, equality and human rights have fueled the utopian impulse of the Diaspora experience and intensified the sense of the injustice of the world as it is. According to Gilroy, at the same time, Black Atlantic peoples have developed a "double-consciousness" through which they have recognized the complicity of those same ideals—and modernism, in general—with the institutionalized violence, racism and genocide that has characterized recent centuries.

For Gilroy, the double-consciousness of African Diaspora peoples manifests itself as a Black Atlantic counterculture for which the experience of slavery and the subsequent mixing together of diverse ethnic groups and cultures has left indelible marks. Under the oppression of slavery, music has taken the place of the written text of rationalist discourse as the principal form of identity construction and the transmission of wisdom. He writes:

> Black music's obstinate and consistent commitment to the idea of a better future is a puzzle to which the enforced separation of slaves from literacy

> and their compensatory refinement of musical art supplies less than half the answer. The power of music in developing black struggles by communicating information, organizing consciousness, and testing out or deploying the forms of subjectivity which are required by political agency, whether individual or collective, defensive or transformational, demands attention to both the formal attributes of this expressive culture and its distinctive moral basis.

Music, under such conditions, becomes is a powerful means of conveying a subversive utopianism that simultaneously rejects the world of the racist oppressor even as it expresses a feeling of what it would be like to live in a better one. As such, for Gilroy, the transformational collective life of Black Atlantic cultures offers an antidote to the cold, rationalistic control of modernity (Gilroy 1993, 36).

Beyond the emotional resonance offered by musical encounters, there is also a great deal of space in them for resisting the status quo through the use of humor, irony, double-entendre and the like. Combining these, the utopian dimension of African Diaspora cultural forms entail significantly more than 'escapism' but rather a sort of spiritualized power for resisting social injustice and reshaping the world. In the counterculture of Afro-Atlantic peoples, Gilroy argues, the purposefully fragmentary dramaturgical dimension of representation became one of the primary weapons for keeping the dream alive for a better world in the face of prejudice and violence.

The power of Black musical forms—from gospel and R&B to reggae and hip-hop—and their relevance for the American civil rights movement are subjects that have attracted much scholarly attention.[11] Simi-

11 *A Change is Gonna Come: Music, Race and the Soul of America* (Werner 1999) offers a thorough exploration of the subject, as well as an ample bibliography on the same.

larly, commentators of hip-hop have pointed to how it has empowered Black youth by turning the circuit of production and consumption on its head.[12] Some have claimed hip-hop is "… unarguably the most culturally significant style in pop, the genre that speaks most directly to and for its audience…the single most creative, revolutionary approach to music and to music making that this generation has constructed." (Light 2004, 138).

Gilroy is similarly enthusiastic about hip-hop as a locus for the Black utopian "politics of transfiguration" he associates with it, pointing to the "… deliberately fractured…" structure of its music. He writes:

> Acoustic and electric instruments are disorganically combined with digital sound synthesis, a variety of found sounds: typically screams, pointed fragments of speech or singing, and samples from earlier recordings—both vocal and instrumental—whose open textuality is raided in playful affirmations of the insubordinate spirit which ties this radical form to one important dimension of blackness (Gilroy 1993,104).

As did the cultural cannibal of Brazilian *modernismo*, the hip-hop artist of Gilroy's view subverts the authority of the dominant White European culture and constructs a fragmentary, countercultural identity through the use and ironic reinterpretation of such "found sounds." Throughout its history, the open playfulness and irony of hip-hop, along with its force as a countercultural discourse to modernity, have made it extraordinarily relevant to socially excluded communities in a variety of contexts. Furthermore, the privileged position of the US mass culture

12 See, for instance, groundbreaking *Black Noise: Rap Music and Black Culture in Contemporary America* (Rose 1994) and *Spectacular Vernaculars: Hip-Hop and the Politics of Postmodernism* (Potter 1995).

industry has guaranteed a high level of exposure for the hip-hop culture across the globe. Though he never mentions Brazilian funk in his study, it is a quintessentially Black Atlantic cultural form in the sense of Gilroy's work. Indeed, funk carioca is one of the most representative Brazilian cultural practices of the tendencies he identifies (Gilroy 1995, 104).

Though the culture of funk carioca in Brazil is considered separate from hip-hop, in the Brazilian context, funk's musical and cultural lineage mark it as part of the same universe. Funk carioca was born out of the movement of Black soul music in Rio throughout the 1970s and 1980s. As time passed more and more international and local influences were mixed into it in a process that led funk away from any essentialism, either racial or musical (Herschmann 2000, 279-283). Urban dance cultures such as hip-hop and techno were central in the development of funk, and the beats of early hip-hop DJs, like Afrika Bambaataa, and late-1980s DJs, like Battery Brain (Mark Rogers), could be heard practically unaltered in much of funk music through to the late-1990s. As songs emerged with lyrics in Portuguese, beginning in the early 1990s, more and more elements of Brazilian culture became a part of the Rio funk sound. Samba and Brazilian pop melodies were used, together with those of international hits. More and more Portuguese language samples were superimposed into the highly fragmentary musical montages of funk.

Digitalized rhythms of local instruments also added to the mix, like those of the single-string, musical bow percussion instrument known as the berimbau, one of the principal instruments of the Afro-Brazilian martial art and dance capoeira. As is often the case with the musical cultures of the African Diaspora, and indeed Brazilian pop music, absolute originality was less important than the meanings new versions of pre-existing sounds and symbols could be given and the feelings they evoked. At the same time, by aggressively embracing so many currents of local and international musical culture, funk carioca emerged as a very distinct and very Brazilian hybrid that was not only original but also very relevant to the specific conditions of the lives of the poor people in Rio de Janeiro who cultivated it.

The fact that US hip-hop was something of a parent of Brazilian funk did not mean that it was a purer form of African Diaspora culture. One could say that the "found sounds" of the culture of hip-hop were eventually found and absorbed by Brazilian funk (if not 'eaten,' in the vein of the cultural cannibal). Musical production in funk was similarly 'deliberately fractured,' yet funk producers were not content merely to be or become another regional adaption of global hip-hop. Instead of rapping, for example, funk MCs tended to sing. Similarly, though the figures of the DJ and the MCs were central to funk carioca, breakdancing and graffiti, two other elements commonly associated with hip-hop.

More important than any particular formal difference between American hip-hop and funk carioca, however, was the fact that people engaged in funk culture did not identify it as hip-hop—as did the folks of the Brazilian hip-hop scene of those days. Instead, they viewed their funk carioca as its own independent culture. Perhaps this distance in of itself was a testimony to the openness of both styles. It demonstrated the relevance of hip-hop to marginalized communities as a source of countercultural resistance and its adaptability to local contexts, even as it showed the ability of people from Rio to mold international currents into a new hybridized local culture that was self-consciously independent of any of its parent tendencies.

Funk Carioca and Hip-hop Brasileiro

Given the fact that funk carioca shares many of the same influences as early American hip-hop and has borrowed so much from it, it is significant that separate musical cultures arose in Brazil as funk carioca and Brazilian hip-hop. Since its beginnings in the Bronx in New York City in the late 1970s, various styles of American hip-hop have developed in different locations across the US, notably in New York, Los Angeles, Miami, Atlanta, Chicago, Memphis, Oakland, Houston, Detroit, Philadelphia and New Orleans, among others. Despite often being associated with subgenres and unique characteristics that set them apart, these various regional American styles have identified themselves with the broader context of hip-hop. In contrast, funk carioca and Brazilian hip-hop are considered to be two different, if not opposing styles, even though both are vibrant Afro-Brazilian electronic musical cultures embodying the kind of double-consciousness of Gilroy's views.

In Chapter 7 of this study, "Social Bandits in Funk," I briefly commented on the implications of Hobsbawm's understanding of primitive rebels for the funk carioca and Brazilian hip-hop, exploring the differences between the two movements as differences in the degree of revolutionary consciousness possessed by each. At the heart of funk, I suggested, was a sort of 'revolt' stemming from dissatisfaction with the traditional order. Brazilian hip-hop, as Negu Tema pointed out, possessed a more highly developed and radical revolutionary consciousness that made it a RAP, or "Revolução Através da Palavra" ("Revolution through Words").[13]

13 For a brief, but insightful overview of the different phases of hip-hop in São Paulo and, by extension, Brazil more generally, see *Hip-hop in São Paulo: Identity, Community Formation and Social Action* (Weller and Tella 2011, 188-204).

In his exhaustively researched and insightful ethnography *Ideologies of Marginality in Brazilian Hip-hop*, cultural anthropologist Derek Pardue echoes Negu Tema, stating that perhaps no other musical practice in contemporary Brazil has so self-consciously embraced a spirit of social criticism and subaltern pride the hip-hop movement of the industrial neighborhoods around São Paulo. He presents a compelling case that even though only a few rappers have attained status as nationally recognized talents, the impact of Brazilian hip-hop on local-level, grassroots activism in the city would be difficult to overstate. The culture of hip-hop in Brazil, for Pardue, presents a rare opportunity to understand the efforts of everyday people to resist oppression and transform society from the bottom-up (Pardue 2008, 17). It promotes an oppositional view that explores the longstanding contradictions through at the heart of Brazil's national identity, in terms like racial democracy, cordiality, tropicalism and tradition (Pardue 2008, 12).[14]

Given the higher degree of explicitly revolutionary consciousness in Brazilian hip-hop in the late 1990s and early 2000s, however, it is curious that compared to funk carioca it was far less demonized in the media, academic circles and the conversations of so many everyday observers. Perhaps this was because the references to violence in Brazilian hip-hop were generally less explicit than those appearing in funk. When violence was mentioned, it tended to be in a more militant fashion, as a fairly obvious protest or representation of the disenfranchisement of Blacks and other poor people. Alongside the socio-political and historic-

14 In the late 1990s and early 2000s, the groups and rappers perhaps best-known nationally included Racionais MCs, 509-E, Xis, Facção Central or Rappin' Hood from São Paulo, MV Bill and Marcelo D2 from Rio, GOG and Câmbio Negro from Brasilia and Faces do Subúrbio, from Recife.

al analysis of Brazilian hip-hop, it also presented a powerful message of personal responsibility and self-help that ended up something like a sort of musical meeting of Narcotics Anonymous. There were lots of stories of people rising above. The criminal culture celebrated was generally in the past tense, as a means of legitimizing rappers like Mano Brown and Edi Rock of Racionais MCs, Dexter and Afro-X of 509-E, MV Bill, Escadinha and Xis. The implication was that such figures had been transformed by the radicalizing mission of their revolution through words. Furthermore, the sexuality of Brazilian hip-hop was not only less than that of funk carioca, but in fact considerably less even than the sexuality of mainstream Brazilian culture and musical expressions such as Carnival, *axé* music and pop. Brazilian hip-hop was infinitely less sexualized than American hip-hop, too. When it came to drug consumption, only a few notable Brazilian hip-hop groups were known to celebrate smoking marijuana in their music.[15]

Two additional differences may help explain why these two similar but separate practices arose in Brazil. The first relates to the somewhat complicated matter of the degree to which both styles resist becoming what Gilroy calls "essentialist." For him, such essentialism is a tendency that narrowly defines and demarks the boundaries of cultural practice, unintentionally weakening its power as a tactic in the politics of transformation. One could make an argument that São Paulo hip-hop is more essentialist than funk carioca, not only racially but even stylistically.

15 A conspicuous example was São Paulo's De Menos Crime, whose song "Fogo na bomba" of 1998 was an anthem of the pro-marijuana sentiment of the day. In Brazilian rock, a great many bands projected a pro-marijuana stance, like Charlie Brown Jr., Planet Hemp, Chico Science e Nação Zumbi and Mundo Livre S/A. Though these bands incorporated hip-hop as a part of their musical mix, they generally were not considered to be hip-hop bands per se.

São Paulo's hip-hop tends to draw more explicitly from Black music and culture, whereas funk carioca borrows from virtually any type of musical form, independent of the racial and cultural connotations of its sources.

The second difference is the fact that hip-hop arose mainly in São Paulo and funk in Rio. Of course, in Rio MV Bill and Marcelo D2 came to the forefront of Brazilian hip-hop, and in the early to mid-2010s funk ostentação—the subgenre of funk carioca associated with conspicuous consumption—arose in São Paulo.[16]

During the golden age of proibidão community funk dances in Rio's favelas in the late 1990s and early 2000s, though, the division between Rio as the city of funk and São Paulo as the capital of Brazilian hip-hop was widely accepted. What was it about the two towns that brought about such a distanced evolution? Some have suggested, in in somewhat simplistic terms, São Paulo had a far more fragmented cultural landscape in which racial dynamics were more similar to those of the United States and the presence of ethnic groups and youth tribes was more pronounced (from punks to skinheads and indeed fans of hip-hop). Rio de Janeiro, on the

16 The São Paulo funk scene is by no means limited to funk ostentação. Indeed, it is a rich, complex musical expression deserving of a lengthy separate treatment of its own not possible within the confines of this book. The list of funk videography appearing in Appendix B includes a variety of documentaries and other videos exploring that scene, including a fascinating short called *No Fluxo* (Barreiros 2014). This video portraying new trends in dance, music and lyrics in the street parties featuring rows of cars with custom speakers playing new São Paulo funk (such as styles like *passinho do romano*). Another is *Documentário MC Zoi de Gato* (A Voz da Favela) (Lopes 2018), a do-it-yourself-style video telling the story of a singer considered by many to be the greatest São Paulo MC of proibidão, Zoi de Gato. His real name was Denner Antonio Sena da Silva and he was born in Vila Natal, in Grajaú, in the Southern Zone of São Paulo. Zoi de Gato started out singing proibidão at age ten or eleven and died in a car accident at age 16, in 2009. Since he passed away, I am using his real name. His best known songs include "Primeiro Comando" ("First Command") and "Fábrica de Bico" ("Gun Factory"), both sorts of homages to São Paulo's largest criminal cartel, the Primeiro Comando da Captial (PCC).

other hand, was a culturally more homogenous space, despite the enormous racial mixing and the stark differences in social class that characterized it.[17]

It also may have been significant that crime in São Paulo, too, was less 'organized' than crime in Rio. Criminal factions in São Paulo played a much less crucial role in politics and security in that city's favelas. The different character of criminal activity in the two cities was crucial since the musical practices of each were the outgrowths of the particular social organization of their respective environments. This may have been one of the reasons MCs of Brazilian hip-hop did not tend to sing about the power and justice of criminal factions in favelas as did their funk counterparts. Despite its power and prestige in São Paulo, the faction known as Primeiro Comando da Capital (PCC) was not typically referenced in hip-hop songs as was the Comando Vermelho in funk.[18]

There was not a wide-scale, parallel circulation of underground 'prohibited' recordings in hip-hop, either. Instead, the sort of crime typically represented in hip-hop tended to be 'disorganized crime,' in addition to being represented more in the spirit of lamentation than exaltation. In São Paulo's hip-hop, crimes were portrayed as symptoms of the violence and failings of the larger system. Overtones of social banditry then were

17 I do not wish to overemphasize this point, since I do not consider myself any sort of expert on São Paulo, Brazilian hip-hop or the thriving funk carioca scene that city. Prof. José Augusto de Rodrigues Souza, a political scientist from the Universidade do Estado do Rio de Janeiro (UERJ) and one of my first mentors on urban violence in Brazil, presented such an argument to me in personal communications in 1995. It's worth noting that much has changed since that time, such as the rise of São Paulo's criminal faction PCC, which today rivals the Comando Vermelho (CV) as one of the largest in Brazil.

18 In the culture of funk carioca in São Paulo, a subgenre of proibidãop did arise that proclaimed the PCC in similar terms as its cousin in Rio proclaimed the CV, TCP and ADA. See note 17 above.

considerably subdued. Survival in hip-hop became something entirely different from the Ten Commandments of the favela-style rules of organized crime in the favelas. Instead, it was more a question of allegorical tales of individual cunning and desperation in the no-mans-land of the São Paulo periphery.[19]

There were exceptions. One of the most graphic songs about crime in Brazilian hip-hop was "Isto aqui é uma Guerra" ("This Here is a War"), by Facção Central from São Paulo, released in 1999 on their album titled *Versos Sangrentos* ('Bloody Verses'). The group is considered one of the all-time leading groups of Brazilian hip-hop's gangster rap. Though the song and music video circulated on the air for some six months, even on MTV Brazil, it was eventually censored and the group was accused of promoting crime, violence and racism. The music video for the song was particularly graphic, depicting scenes of its merciless protagonists kidnapping people, robbing them or tying them up and killing them in front of their children. Rappers Dum Dum and Eduardo claimed the song and video were created in a spirit of protest, pointing out that one of the criminals portrayed in the video is dead at the end and his partner under arrest, implying that crime does not pay.[20]

19 In this light, it's interesting to consider New York hip-hop vocalist The Notorious B.I.G.'s 1997 song, "Ten Crack Commandments," which reflects a highly individualized notion of the cultural of crime quite different from that of funk carioca and the favelas of Rio de Janeiro. Christopher George Latore Wallace, also known as "Biggie Smalls" or simply "Biggie," was one of the all-time most iconic figures of US gangster rap. The song, off disc 2 of 1997's *Life after Death.* Though organized crime in São Paulo arose later than in Rio, however, by the early 2000s the Primeiro Comando da Capital, or PCC, was steering the culture of crime in that city in a more collectivist direction.

20 While it is tempting to attempt a more detailed comparison of 'Isto aqui é uma guerra' with Rio's proibidão and American gangster rap of that period, such is beyond the scope of this current project.

Another crucial difference between Brazilian hip-hop and funk carioca is that of the locus of each style. The utopian vision of Brazilian hip-hop at the time, for example, was not centered upon performance places like funk carioca's bailes funk. Instead, it projected a somewhat spiritualized vision of the interior world of the hip-hop artist as it existed in a recorded album. In a more geographical sense, it also prioritized the space of the *periferia* ('periphery') itself, which it held up in contrast to the *sistema* ('system'). It's also noteworthy that the favela, as such, was only a part of the more geographical spatiality of hip-hop in Brazil at the time. Instead, the periphery often evoked included many lower-income neighborhoods that were more formally integrated into the city, albeit precariously so. Still, there are parallels, of course. São Paulo's hip-hop affirmed a division between the alienating and racist system and the dangerous, yet brotherly periphery. Funk carioca often presented a dichotomy between the cold and dehumanizing *asfalto* ('asphalt') of the formal city and the familiar *comunidade* ('community') of Rio's favelas .

In the third chapter of his book *Ideologies of Marginality in Brazilian Hip-hop* (2008), Derek Pardue departs from his previous explorations of race and gender from earlier in his book to explore the question of space in these terms. First, he examines the evolution of the periphery as a discursive category of urbanization encompassing regional migration, crime, unmapped communities and long-term do-it-yourself home construction by low-income residents. Next, he analyzes hip-hop's use of periphery as a semantically charged symbol of cultural insurgency. That very same self-made construction style, called *auto-construção* in Portuguese, for Pardue represents the geographic inversion hip-hop performs that inverts the derogatory connotation of periphery from the mainstream perspective. Instead, it is the more affluent, formally urbanized areas of the city that are vilified in hip-hop as territories of the icy, dehumanizing sistema. That oppressive space of the system, Pardue states, is held in contrast with the greater humanity of the marginal periphery as home and as, "… a primary source for informação and transformação" (Pardue 2008, 30).

Interestingly, besides the more general notion of 'periphery,' another more specific spatial reference for Brazilian hip-hop was that of prisons. Indeed, some of the seminal hip-hop productions in Brazil in the late 1990s and early 2000s was produced in and around prisons. Such was the case of the brilliant albums of 509-E, recorded from inside São Paulo's notorious Carandiru prison, *Provérbios* 13, from 2000 and MMII DC (2002 Depois de Cristo), from 2002. Another prominent example was that of Escadinha (José Carlos dos Reis Encina), the infamous Rio crime boss-turned-hip-hop missionary who was incarcerated from 1985 until his murder in 2004. In 2000, he released *Brazil 1: Fazendo justiça com as próprias mãos* (*Brazil 1: Making Justice with Our Own Hands*), a classic compilation that included several of the outstanding rap talents of the day along with Escadinha's spoken track, "Introdução" ("Introduction").[21]

This album presented an anti-drug, anti-crime message—making it a quintessential example of the sort of musical meetings of Narcotics Anonymous I mentioned above. This prison-based spatiality further emphasized the distance between the impoverished physical reality of the rapper and the dream of a better world. The mind was a considerable part of the place of the utopian dimension of Brazilian hip-hop, one which nostalgically projected into the past and imagined what the world could be as the body endured the harshness of life in the present. The psychological landscape of the prison in ways connected that

21 The compilation includes classic figures of activist hip-hop in Brazil, like Racionais MCs, MV Bill, Dexter and Afro-X of 509-E (under the name of Linha de Frente on the CD), Câmbio Negro and GOG, Thaíde e DJ Hum, Xis, Consciência Humana, Visão de Rua, Guerrilha Urbana, and A-Man.

inward-reaching, spiritual dimension of Brazilian hip-hop with the oppositional spatiality of the periphery.[22] Not surprisingly, in funk carioca prisons were a constant theme. But they were represented more in the light of social banditry, either regarding suffering or the connections they had to the history and reality of Rio's cartels like the CV, ADA and TCP. They were less about the representation of personal transformation from the thug life to the life of a Black activist, as was the case in Brazilian hip-hop.

The performative dimension of hip-hop, for groups like São Paulo's seminal Racionais MCs, became somewhat sacred in this context, and much less humorous, sensual and playful than in funk. It is for this reason that Brazilian hip-hop was almost not even 'entertainment,' in the sense that it so dramatically deemphasizes the dimension of pleasure. Instead, it was more musical activism. As the result of its hardcore, somewhat Manichean prison aesthetics, which de-emphasized pleasure and instead spiritualized the utopian impulse, Brazilian hip-hop sacrificed some of the playfulness and sensuality characteristic of hip-hop in the US—and indeed of Black Atlantic musical and other cultural expressions typically. This is not to say that pain and suffering had not always been a part of the Diaspora experience, nor that a powerful sense of solidarity-based entertainment was not fundamental to Brazilian hip-hop. The fact remains, however, that Brazilian hip-hop was a much more self-contained and essentialist culture than either American hip-hop or

22 Luciana Burlamaqui's documentary *Entre a luz e a sombra* ('Between Light and Shadow') (2009) offers a rare, up-close look at the interactions between hip-hop in São Paulo and the city's prisons. It focuses on the story of rappers Dexter and Afro-X, childhood friends and cellmates who exploded in popularity with their seminal group 509-E. In an unexpected twist, the film explores Dexter's relationship with Sophie Bisilliat, an actress from a white, middle-class background who met him after years of volunteering in Carandiru prison.

Brazilian funk. Members of the hip-hop community typically rejected funk carioca on the grounds it was complicit with the system by promoting consumerism, violence and the objectification of women.

In contrast, in funk carioca the music of Racionais MCs and MV Bill was commonly played at bailes funk, and their music was often sampled in funk recordings. On the other hand, Brazilian hip-hop tended to limit its beats and samples to self-consciously Black music, mostly from Brazil and the US. Indeed, it did not even sample American hip-hop songs very often. That funk has produced a figure like Mr. Catra, one of the most enduring funk MCs of all-time, is also a testimony to the eclectic nature of funk. Catra was extremely versatile, performing songs that showed an influence of several styles of Black music, from R&B to gospel. When he performed or recorded hip-hop, Catra was accepted by the hip-hop community as a legitimate member. When he sang on the funk scene, he was a bona fide funkeiro. In contrast, no significant hip-hop artist crossed the lines between styles in that way or regularly referenced funk carioca musically.

When it comes to Brazilian hip-hop and funk carioca in the late 1990s and early 2000s, Blackness was crucial in both cultures—though in different ways. The São Paulo scene—as were adepts of hip-hop in cities like Rio and Brasilia—was more explicitly Black, just as the sources of music it borrowed from and referenced tended to be self-identified as Black music. Rio funk, on the other hand, tended to be less explicitly Black. It was also more inclusive of musical influences and found sounds from around the world. In both cases, when lighter skinned MCs, DJs and dancers—or even fans— were involvedthey generally could be considered as legitimate. This was especially easy if they were from low-income backgrounds or the neighborhoods associated with the styles, like Rio's favela and São Paulo's periphery. In a sense, a person's status as being from a poor, urban background gave him or her a certain blackness-by-proxy.

In the case of funk, such inclusiveness even extended to White, middle-class Brazilians and foreigners to the extent they were able to convincingly align themselves with funk's favela aesthetic in some way. There was an awareness of difference in race and ethnicity in funk, too, but it was quite a blurry line. Going through the photos of bailes funk and daily life in Rocinha in this book may help readers appreciate the complexities of race in funk carioca. This was something I experienced personally as a middle-class, White man from another country. I was also three or four years older than the majority of MCs in Rocinha at the time, like MCs Manda Brasa, Cordão de Ouro, Júnior and Leonardo, in turn, themselves already older than most fans at the dances. I found it surprising how little people made of such differences. Indeed in US hip-hop, and in academic culture, such differences of positioning are at the center of crucial debates.[23]

Due to this lack of racial essentialism and the hybrid nature, and high degree of incorporation of world cultural currents evident in both styles, both have been at times accused of being imports from the United States and criticized within Brazil as less authentic forms of national culture. Looking at them in terms of Gilroy's theories, though, the absence of such essentialism becomes a sign of the vitality of these practices as Afro-Atlantic cultural forms and of their capacity to offer avenues for the resistance of Diaspora peoples. Gilroy states:

> My point here is that the unashamedly hybrid character of these black

23 Though I felt it beneficial at the time to focus on commonalities instead of differences, in subsequent years, I have found it increasingly necessary to recognize my own limitations as an interpreter of funk carioca. I have attempted to address these limitations throughout this book.

> Atlantic cultures continually confounds any simplistic (essentialist or anti-essentialist) understanding of the relationship between racial identity and racial non-identity, between folk cultural authenticity and pop-cultural betrayal (Gilroy 1995, 99).

In a sense, such absence of racial essentialism contributed to the vitality of Brazilian hip-hop and funk carioca as practices of everyday life in resisting the conditions of social exclusion and violence facing so many Blacks and low-income people in the country. Their openness and fluidity helped them expose the class and racial fissures hidden by facile concepts such as "Brazilian music" and any overly simplistic North versus South dichotomy. As a result, the non-essentialist character of these practices served to further weaken the hegemony of both the local national dominant order and the culture of modernity in general.

Sometimes poor people in Brazil are criticized as focusing too much on music, style, and entertainment and not enough on formal social activism and political mobilization (Hanchard 1994). Indeed, there is an urgent need for more explicit action. Still, the double-consciousness of modernity that Gilroy ascribes to African Diaspora cultures gives the poor residents of Rio's favelas a multifaceted political soul to match the duplicitous reality of state and criminal power in their communities. In the long run, for people to vote, protest, strike, sue, study, volunteer or otherwise participate in the formal democratic state, they need to remain alive. Beyond survival, people need to take heart, to care for themselves, their loved ones and those around them in the larger society. Beyond mere subsistence, people need resilience to retain their full humanity, something for which music and community can help even more than direct forms of political engagement.

For Afro-Atlantic aesthetics, historically, the acts of resistance of everyday people are often less easily identifiable as 'political,' according to the Western rationalist understanding of the term. Often seemingly innocuous cultural activities like musical practices embody powerful moral dimensions with real effects and consequences in political life. Gilroy describes these moral dimensions in terms of the utopian impulse that drives them. "In the simplest terms," Gilroy (1995, 36) writes, "by posing the world as it is against the world as the racially subordinated would like it to be, this musical culture supplies a great deal of courage required to go on living in the present." Perhaps Black people and other poor people in Brazil, and other countries as well, have not managed to elect as many Black politicians as one might like, nor sufficiently mobilized themselves to change laws that would further advance the cause of equality. Nonetheless, through cultural practices African Diaspora groups such as those involved in funk and hip-hop in Brazil have managed to survive hundreds of years of violence and to preserve their fundamental humanity throughout their history of oppression, keeping the dream of reaching ever closer to the promised land alive.

My Name is Carnival

The potential of carnival in Rio as a countercultural practice—and one involving poor people—is well-documented. As the result of a gradual but steady process of commercialization and status quo appropriation, however, carnival by the turn of the millennium had come to occupy a position of diminished importance with regard to the lives of poor people in Rio. The ironic and subversive spirit of Carnival had been transferred to other cultural forms that have become the new spaces of the utopian impulse among the poor, in expressions such as funk (and, I might suggest, in the Pentecostal Christian movement). While it still had a degree of relevance for poor youths in Rio de Janeiro, funk culture had primarily replaced the space of the carnival in Rio as the principal leisure activity of poor young people both in content and form. Indeed, many of the observations made by Mikhail Bahktin in his widely influential theories of the carnivalesque renaissance of European society—that it presented a satirical, mocking provocation to the legitimacy of conventional social hierarchies—applied to the culture of funk. Indeed, one could argue that throughout its history, funk had come to provide a place in which to express energies and needs often suppressed in modernized life, displacing and inverting normative social hierarchies.

To this day, carnival continues to thrive in Rio de Janeiro, where it is a vital and relevant part of the cultural life of the city for people from all socio-economic classes. I would not argue that Carnival had been wholly replaced by funk as the quintessential space for Rio's poor, but instead that its significance as a utopian practice for them had become much reduced. The new generation had found a powerful outlet in Rio's funk scene. Still, the cultural terrain of the favela was hugely varied, as I have argued, and was made up of an enormously ample variety of musical practices and styles. In fact, something of a cross-fertilization occurred in the 1990s between funk carioca and the samba music associated with Carnival. Many samba schools playfully experimented with the inclusion of funk beats in the rhythms of their drum lines. Likewise, aspects of samba impacted funk songwriting, as did those of its direct descendants, pagode and axé music. As a result, funk drew upon *samba de enredo* melodies, finding inspiration in the *sambandido* ('bandit samba') of Bezerra da Silva and copied dance moves from Gera Samba and Companhia do Pagode, both of which became national crazes.[24]

Different from its beginnings as a marginalized and even illegal practice of mostly Afro-Brazilians, throughout the twentieth century the culture of Carnival had gradually become a status quo culture until it was eventually the musical style most readily associated with the Brazilian national identity, both at home and abroad. A far-reaching result of this was that the space of the poor, although still acknowledged as the backbone and root of Carnival, had become increasingly limited in its de facto celebration. In no small degree, Carnival had been taken out of the street, contained and commodified. This commercialization was noticeable during Carnival at Rio's *Sambódromo*, a sort of street/stadium where the big parades take place. There wealthy people and tourists had the best seats, often in company box seats or along the actual avenue at the street level. While the cast of personalities present in the parades itself still included many people from favelas or who were traditional figures of the world of samba, more and more attention was focused on the White stars of the Globo and other Brazilian television networks, singers and musicians and the like. Carnival had become synonymous with the world of big Brazilian entertainment and was somewhat of a who's who of the dominant Brazilian popular culture.

Furthermore, stars of alternative cultural practices in Brazil, such as hip-hop singers or funkeiros, were not often highlighted in Carnival and were unlikely to appear on top of a float in the parade. It may be that the relatively newfound popularity of Carnival in the Northeastern city of

24 Interactions between funk and samba were also apparent in the album *Samba Rap*, produced by DJ Marlboro. It matched consecrated *sambistas* of Rio's *escolas de samba* with the new generation of funk performers. On the funk side, it included Claudinho and Buchecha, Leonardo and Júnior, Marquinhos and Dollores, Mr. Catra and Dr. Rocha and others. On the samba side, Jorginho do Império, Dominguinhos do Estácio, Gera, Haroldo Melodia, Preto Jóia, Paulinho Mocidade and Carlinhos de Pilares (DJ Marlboro. 1995. *Samba Rap*. MP3 Audio, Afegan Produções Artísticas 441079/2-482221).

Salvador over the previous two decades had occurred as somewhat of a reaction to the commercialization of Rio's Carnival, resulting from the desire to bring Carnival back to the streets and back to the people. But by 2000, the Bahian Carnival had become primarily another big-money entertainment culture, too, and most ordinary people still didn't have enough money to be in the parades of the *blocos-afro*, for example, as the groups for street parades were called. In Rio de Janeiro, as was the case throughout the country, the culture of small street *blocos* was regaining popularity. It was a similar effort to reclaim Carnival as a non-commercial practice, although these efforts seemed to come as much from the middle-class as from poor people living in places like favelas.

Because such a wide-scale process of co-optation and commercialization had not occurred in funk carioca, the utopian dimensions once available to poor people in Carnival still existed in that cultural expression. The experience of watching unattainably beautiful and famous people enjoying themselves on the TV screen in Carnival—or even live at the parades in the Sambódromo—did, of course, offer some degree of utopian escapism for the spectator. But this was infinitely less powerful than the chance to participate in the spectacle itself to the degree provided by a baile funk, in the sense of Quintero Rivera's mixture of audience and performance discussed in Chapter 10. As I argued in that chapter, in funk the audience became the stars, just as was once the case with Carnival. Audience members become the *destaque*, as the people on the floats in the Carnival parades are called.

In terms of Richard Dyer's characteristics of utopia in entertainment, too, Rio's Carnival in the late 1990s and early 2000s rated as less powerfully utopian than funk. The 'abundance' that was still present in Carnival had become less potent as a utopian symbol for the poor. Such abundance was no longer theirs but instead had come even to alienate people who were 'not invited to the party,' so to speak. In a similar way, the energy and intensity offered in the experience of Carnival were considerably reduced for many poor people, because one would have had to be involved in the event to feel them with great intensity. The rigid codification of Carnival in the parades of the Sambódromo also made them somewhat predictable. Carnival was run and organized by official authorities and not gangsters brandishing guns in the middle of the performance. Carnival was in danger of losing its teeth, becoming a somewhat routine, safe practice in which the rules of regular life and the mainstream society were more consistently applicable.

As a platform for the presentation of the spectacle of the world of Brazilian entertainment, the Carnival of the day was full of marketing images and advertising to such a degree as to threaten to render it too greatly manipulative and consumerist. As such, it had also become considerably less "transparent," in Dyer's sense, than funk. Also, while there was a good dose of playfulness in regards to gender roles and sexuality in Carnival that did in some ways rub against the grain of bourgeois values, such had become overshadowed by the somewhat hedonistic objectification of women. Carnival did not transform the woman into a hunter in the way funk did. Instead, her sexuality often was constructed around a notion of femininity understood as a woman's ability to provide pleasure as as an object of sex and beauty. Likewise, Black feminine beauty in carnival often presented itself in more problematic terms of exoticism and racial inequality, especially as projected for mainstream audiences.

I do not want to overemphasize the cooptation of the Carnival of the late 1990s and early 2000s regarding sex and gender since it still provided space for a degree of countercultural femininity, social criticism, transgender play, equal rights and advocacy for gay and lesbian lives. Although less often emphasized than the attractive models in feathers and glitter, such sexuality was still an essential part of the irony and indeed utopia of carnival. Additionally, despite the growing control over the holiday by the status quo and mass media, and the enormous amount of money spent on advertising, it still offered at least some space for subversive ideas and the contestation of social values. My point here is that Carnival had become so generally neutral regarding race and class through this process of appropriation that its utopian dimensions for poor folks were severely restricted. Given this, Dyer's last category, "community," also found itself significantly weakened in the Carnival culture of the day.

Particularly noticeable was the 'Whitening' of carnival, as it became a space for the rich and famous, as well as for other affluent people and international tourists. Despite its roots as a form of African Diaspora culture, the capacity for Rio's Carnival to transmit or preserve much significance as a racial community had become so thoroughly diluted as to be practically impossible. Instead, a clear hierarchy of race had emerged in Carnival more attuned to the actual ethnic dynamics in Brazil—along with all the inequities they entailed—than to the imagined, utopian racial dynamics of a baile funk. Carnival was just multiracial enough to appear to represent the sort of racial harmony or racial democracy so fundamental to the Brazilian national ideology. All the shades of brown were visible in carnival, from the Native to the mixed race to Italian immigrants. Furthermore, many Afro-centric and indigenous themes continued to be chosen by the samba schools for their yearly parades.

Nevertheless, the representation of race in Carnival often occurred amidst hierarchies in which Whiteness becomes associated with progress and civilization and Blackness with a somewhat folkloric musicality and exotic, primitive sexuality. Despite the formal content of the parades—as sorts of subversive texts—the commercialization of Carnival ended up whitening the whole event in a de facto sense at the informal, non-representational level of performance. In other words, even though the composers and organizers of the various samba schools did come up with a great many subversive and ironic parades each year, much of the power of those parades as expressions of utopian culture was getting lost. To a significant degree, those representational, performative dimensions had given way to the primacy of textual aspect of Carnival as a media and advertising event of the dominant White order in Brazil.

In this light, it is interesting to consider the samba music and parades of Carnival culture at that time with respect to the characteristics of tropical Caribbean music suggested by Quintero Rivera. In many ways, Carnival could still be seen as an example of the sort of música mulata he describes, but the high degree of audience passivity inherent in the growing divide between performer and audience occurring in the commercialization of Carnival had altered it considerably. On the one hand, music composition was still made to allow for improvisation and singers still sought to spontaneously improvise and interact with their audience, as did musicians (particularly the percussion drum line). Also, the music was still extraordinarily polyvocal in the way described by Quintero Rivera. Finally, multiple levels of what he calls *timbres*, or 'tone-colors,' did intermix in the rich musical play typical of the sambas of Carnival.

Still, the level of interaction and real communication between the public and the spectacle was reduced in Rio's Carnival in those times. Most poor folks did not make it to the Sambódromo to watch the parades of Rio's big samba schools but instead tuned in on TV. Even if a person made it to the Sambódromo, he or she was still somewhat removed by being seated in the bleachers. People did sing and even dance a bit, but anyone expecting the sort of high degree of participation typical of street Carnival celebrations was in for a disappointment. On the other end of the spectacle, the emphasis on attractive, famous people on floats also restricted communication, which was typically was limited to smiles, waves of the hand, and jumping up and down, with little dancing. Due to the increasing divide between the public and the performance that occurred in the evolution of the practice of Carnival over the course of the 20th century, it had become somewhat less of one Quintero Rivera's músicas mulatas and instead more similar to the culture of American musicals studied by Richard Dyer.

The problem of mass commercialization and cooptation in the culture of funk carioca in those days was much smaller, even though people were making money in funk, too. Inevitably, some of the larger society's racial hierarchy still infected it, although to a lesser degree. Still, Rio funk was, by and large, offensive to middle-class sensibilities. It had been spared, therefore, anything but momentary flashes of status quo appropriations. The presence of DJ Marlboro (Fernando Luiz Mattos da Matta) on Xuxa's Saturday morning program Xuxa Hits during the mid-1990s comes to mind, in this sense. Different from Carnival, funk remained principally a space for the poor, mostly Black people who inhabited Rio's favelas and low-income areas. Bailes funk were quite inexpensive to attend—or even free in the case of the community dances. They were parties for everyone, even for the rich and white people living in elite neighborhoods of the Zona Sul.

Whereas Carnival appeared to be the realization of a culture of racial democracy, the culture of funk carioca offered its fans a much more intense utopian feeling of what it would be like to live in a world of racial harmony. The community created in the space of the baile was not one of any essentialist definition of Blackness, even though as a form of Diaspora culture it did enact a sort of 'Blackening' of racial identity upon this community. In this sense, funk carioca was something much more countercultural than was Carnival. The community created in the baile funk opened up a quintessential space for cultural inversions, as it turned taboos into totems and raised up the space of the favela to the realization of the dream of racial and class inclusion in Brazil.

13

Last Dance

Our music was of war; now it is of peace
About the gang fights, I don't sing anymore
Here there are no "bitches," only powerful women
Worshiping with this music, just good crews of the funk crowd!
- "Warrior from Hebron," by *Tribo do Funk*[1]

Anderson

It was late July of 2009, winter in Rio and a bit damp and chilly up the slopes of the Two Brothers Hill. Nem, the crime boss of the powerful Rocinha chapter of the Amigos dos Amigos drug cartel, had given orders for a baile funk to be held at the top of the favela, in the indoor giant cement court of the neighborhood samba school. It was to be an homage to Nem's friend and mentor, Lulu, his predecessor and one of the all-time most famous bosses of the Rocinha gang, slain by police five years earlier during the infamous 'War of Rocinha' in 2004. The party, set for the night of Lulu's birthday, July 21, would be free and open to all. Even though it fell on a Wednesday, people said it was going to be a colossal event.

1 Verses of the classic 2007 gospel funk "Guerreiro de Hebron," sung by Tribo do Funk vocalist DD Júnior (over a volt mix beat-based track, in the style of the 1990s). Portuguese: "O som que era guerra, agora é som de paz, Confronto de galeras, eu já não canto mais, Aqui não tem cachorra, só tem lindas varoas, Louvando com esse som, só tem funkeiro sangue bom."

At the time, I was back in Rocinha for a few months conducting fieldwork on space and resilience in gatherings in community organizations across the favela. Building upon my earlier studies of bailes funk, the new project focused on live events such as the *rodas*, or 'fight/dance circles,' of the Senzala association of the Afro-Brazilian martial art capoeira, meetings at the Leão XIII group of Alcoholics Anonymous and worship services at the charismatic Wesleyan Methodist Church. It also focused upon classes at our Instituto Dois Irmãos community center, nighttime gatherings in and around the PizzaLit pizzeria and the latest generation of gangster funk dance parties in the favela.[2] After having gone to an outdoor street dance along the sewage duct of the Valão area of Rocinha the week before and another in the Vila Verde area of the favela, I made plans to attend Lulu's birthday party. When the night came, I headed up through the twisting alleyways to the top of the hill.

Some thirteen years older since my first official fieldwork studying funk carioca in Rocinha—and nineteen years after my first stay there examining residents' views on the local drug traffickers—by 2009 much had changed in my life. In early 2002, I had cut off my ponytail and shaved off my goatee. In the next year, I had gotten married. After finishing graduate school in 2003, I'd been fortunate enough to find employment as a professor of Portuguese in the US, too. In my first semester working, I was baptized and became involved in a church for the first time in my life (though I had had my 'encounter with Christ' in Rocinha in 1992). Off part-time work and student loans for the first time in years, in 2004 my wife and I managed to buy a car. In 2008, our beautiful son was born.

Though I still loved funk carioca, various personal life crises along

2 I ended up featuring the first three spaces on this list in my documentary, *Atalhos e Encontros* (2012) (https://vimeo.com/49417397).

the way had caused me to be more aware of the difficulties of relationality, whether at the individual level of close friendships, in enormous crowds of youths meeting in musical euphoria or the fast-paced mass societies of our contemporary world. As human beings, I was coming to believe, we had a fundamental need for closeness and community. But there was also a violent side to human nature. Indeed, even the dynamics of belonging to one group as opposed to another often encouraged violence to those in other groups. In a sense, the favela metaphor of asphalt versus community, explored in chapter Three, could be viewed as an extension of our human tendency to divide ourselves into in-groups and out-groups. Even at the individual, personal level, we were caught between a rock and a hard place. We need others at a fundamental, even physiological level, yet whoever we are as people and whatever background from which we come, to some degree we all carry deep wounds inside of us that make it difficult for us to connect well with each other or to avoid harming each other. Our efforts to join together in friendship, it was becoming more apparent to me, does not automatically result in things like 'love' and 'community.' It is often the people closest to us that hurt us the most—and to whom we ourselves do the greatest harm. Social exclusion and violence only exacerbated such difficulties.

Just because funk carioca was a form of communication of everyday people, I was starting to conclude, there were no guarantees that it would automatically promote peace and healing, racial awareness or even simple release from the hardships of daily life. Indeed, compared to the other spaces I was immersed in with my new community studies research project, the bailes funk seemed particularly problematic. On the one hand, they were very accessible and open to people who would not easily be accepted elsewhere. On the other, it seemed to me that the favela street parties were perhaps not always as countercultural as I had once thought.

Often they could promote a certain superficiality, objectification and self-centered consumerism that were all too typical of mainstream society—in Brazil and anywhere else I had ever lived. Like an older brother, I started to worry about my younger friends and neighbors in and around the bailes. The celebration of violence, drug abuse and compulsive sexuality so present in the dances, if left unchecked, could be unhealthy for their emotional well-being—and at times even life-threatening.

I was particularly concerned about the upcoming dance party for celebrating the deceased Lulu's birthday, which was sure to have a higher than average number of armed gang members. I even told "Anderson"—the nineteen-year-old young man who had been helping me so much with my research—not to join me in attending.[3] I had known Anderson since he was a year old, a toddler just walking. Once, when he was just three, I had gone with him and two of his aunts to a children's birthday party. The four of us had joked around incessantly until a clown with her face painted entered the party to guide the children in some group games. Anderson went ballistic. Despite the woman's best efforts to win him over, Anderson went on crying hysterically to the point we needed to excuse ourselves and make an emergency exit. Like lots of kids—and even some adults—it turned out that my plucky little buddy suffered from an atrocious case of fear of clowns.

Over the years, Anderson and I had become extremely close. When he was nine, one day he came across a defenseless pigeon with a broken wing. It was hiding under a car, in front of the Catholic chapel in Rocinha's Largo do Boiadeiro plaza. The poor bird was terrified of the other

3 Even though "Anderson" authorized the use of his real name during that 2009 research stint, due to his age at the time (nineteen years) and the sensitivity of the subject matter, to better protect him I have opted not to use it here.

small children present, many of whom had been throwing rocks at it and were trying to finish it off. In a daring rescue, Anderson outmaneuvered the other kids to sweep in and capture it. Much to the chagrin of his mother, three aunts and grandmother, all of whom shared his small house with him, he kept the wounded bird at home until he could lovingly nurse it back to health. When it could fly, he freed it.

Over the years, countless times the two of us had watched cartoons, gone hiking, gone to the movies, played in the woods, spent time at the beach, played football, read books and eaten pizza at PizzaLit. No matter where we were, we joked around a lot and he always made me feel happy. It was because of Anderson that our NGO had started up English classes for children in 2000. When he was twelve, he helped me film my first daily diary-style documentary about Rocinha and our NGO. As he grew into a young adult, he showed a considerable talent for sports, especially street basketball. He also became deeply involved in youth projects like the Rocinha young people's waltz dance team, which traveled around Rio for competitions and even to neighboring states. To many people, Anderson was an incorrigible cut-up and irreverent prankster. To me, he was the kid brother I'd never had.

In 2009, as my impromptu research assistant, Anderson's help was proving invaluable. He was communicative and bright and seemed to know at least half of the residents of the favela. He had not, however, been able to study regularly or to hold any particularly promising job, not for lack of natural ability or charm but because of the instability and scarcity of necessary resources in his circumstances. He had a loving heart and an inquisitive mind and I was sure that he was going places in life. My dream was for Anderson to one day be one of our partners at the NGO, where he was already a constant presence. Whenever new volunteers came to the favela to work with us, he would take them under his wing, ceaselessly leading them up and down the narrow, steep alleyways of the favela to eat, explore, purchase a SIM card, or whatever it was they needed or wanted to do.

With him now being a young adult, Anderson's family was worried that he was falling in with the wrong crowd. Even though I was only going to the baile that night as a researcher—and not to 'make the scene'—I didn't want to be a bad influence in his life. I had a feeling that particular baile was going to be *barra pesada*, as people say in Brazil, which translates as something like 'dangerously hardcore.' I was merely going to stop by the party, I told Anderson, say hello to some folks there, observe for a while and head home early. There was no need for him to join.

Pyrotopia

As expected, the baile was packed, both inside the dance hall and in the area outside in front of it. Even Rocinha's main thoroughfare, the Estrada da Gávea, was teeming with people up along the Rua Um area near the Acadêmicos da Rocinha samba school. Arriving around midnight, I chatted with various MCs outside the main entrance to the dance hall, along with a few other neighbors whom I ran into. This time around, unlike in the years before, I did not go with my friends from across the favela, like Orlando, Cícero, Alex, Alan, Charlys, Renato Moreno, Debora and Dáni or Vítor. At age forty-one, I felt like an old guy who would stick out. So after following the flow in and out of the dance hall a couple of times, I found myself outside at a twenty-four-hour juice stand back along the bustling road beneath the dance party, along with a small group of kids who lived on the street.

Often, street children living in the formally urbanized parts of Rio take temporary refuge in favelas. There they are generally better accepted and free from the death squads of off-duty police that might seek to kill them.[4] The favela was a big community. Rua Um was far enough from Cachopa, where I still kept my residence in Rocinha, that I had never been to that juice place before. Though I had seen some of the others around, I had only previously spoken with one of those children. They were friends with some of the street kids I did know, like "Morcego" ("Bat") and "Boca do Túnel" ("Moth of the Tunnel"), named so because he was born in the back of a bus that was stuck in a traffic jam in the transit tunnel beneath Rocinha)—both of whom frequented the lower part of Rocinha near our non-profit community center. There were four street kids with me at the juice bar that night, ranging from about nine to twelve years old. As I treated them to a big pitcher of papaya juice with milk, sugar and oatmeal, an acquaintance named Rambo (Mário Lúcio Mendes) appeared.

The "Rambo of Rocinha," as folks called him, was an eccentric man in his late-forties, born in the state of Minas Gerais. He lived in a cave

4 The first time I had lived in Rocinha, in 1990, a community leader who had been a Rio police officer earlier in life befriended me. In a taped interview, he recounted to me that years before he had killed several young people who had committed crimes. It all started, he told me, when he had begun hearing rumors that his son had been seen holding up buses near Rocinha. He confronted his son, who denied the allegations. Suddenly, one day, the son was shot to death in the act of holding up a nearby bus with a handgun. Distraught and overwhelmed by grief, the man said, he, along with some fellow police officers, had embarked on a spree of murders of young men they arrested for various similar hold-ups. After killing the young men, around ten altogether over an extended period of time, he and his companions had taken their bodies to the woods at the top of the favela and buried them in clandestine graves. In ways, the community leader's murderous spree was similar to the 1993 massacre of street children at Candelaria, detailed by Ventura (1994). It is also comparable to the rise in favela communities of *milícias*, or illegal militias of off-duty police and firefighters recounted in Zaluar and Siqueira Conceição (2007). Over the years, several milícias have been linked with similar killings and other extra-judicial punishments.

above Rocinha, further up the Dois Irmãos granite rock face. Almost always dressed in fatigues, Rambo had shoulder-length, wavy black hair and a huge sawback military-issue survival knife strapped to his side. Rambo identified himself as an independent volunteer firefighter, though he was not officially employed or otherwise connected to any firehouse. Basically, the man was a local, grassroots superhero. He had come to the baile that night in case anyone needed any emergency aid or other assistance. A slightly sour odor hovered over him, whether from the dampness of his cave permeating his clothes or from sweat, I wasn't sure. Slowly sipping his beer, he told me about the tough personal time he was going through with his wife back in their cave. I was sad to hear of his troubles, but between Rambo and the four youngsters, I was glad to have a little company to help pass the time. Maybe I wouldn't have to go back into the dance, I mused. The music was so loud, anyway, that we could make out the words to the songs from our seats at the street-side juice bar.

Around 2:30 AM, though, I went back into the dance hall, surprised to see the flickering light of a video projector showing photos on a screen set up in the middle of the dance floor. There, to the rhythm of the music, it cast images of a smiling Lulu when he had been the leader of the Rocinha gang, with his and gold chains and various weapons, surrounded by young women and other men from the faction. There were also pictures of Nem, the current boss, as well as of Bem-Te-Vi, Lulu's eventual successor, also deceased, and several other well-known figures from the Rocinha cartel past and present. A few of those shown were still living, but many were dead.

Despite the memorial tone of the photos, the mood of the crowd was not somber but celebratory. In the multitude of over a thousand people, there were more armed gang members than I had ever remembered seeing before at other dances. Several times the DJs and MCs exhorted them to hold their guns up in the air, and there must have numbered over a hundred assault rifles, submachine guns, pistols and many other varieties of firearms. Eventually, I moved to the side of the dance floor and headed up the steps of a long stack of low-rising cement bleachers. If I was not going to be able to dance or to joke around with a group of friends while attending, from there I would at least be able to gain a better vantage point from which to make my observations.

Close to the top, I leaned back against the step behind me, determined to enjoy the music that one of the DJs was performing across the dance hall. Illuminated by flashing lights, he was improvising beats on his equipment in an inspired display of digital virtuosity. Nearby, three female dancers in skin-tight Lycra shorts and sports bras were selecting random men from the crowd to bring them forward into a lighted area near the stage. There the dancers playfully sat the men down in simple, armless chairs, where their hands were tied down and their mouths taped shut. Once the men were secure, the women began rubbing up on them to the rhythm, three on one, in a sort of modified lap dance that I would blush to describe here. I had seen this sort of group spectacle before at Emoções, at the foot of the hill. Even so, sitting there alone watching from across the room felt weird. Deciding then that it was about time to go home, I started towards the door.

Just then, a burst of machine gun fire rang out from just outside the dance. *Paparrá, paparrá, paparrá clack bum!* Then another. Then another. It sounded to me like it was all from the same gun.

A mass scream arose from the crowd. A human torrent suddenly pushed back through the door, rushing in a dense mass all the way to the rear of the club. Getting out wasn't going to be easy, I realized. So I headed back to the bleachers, climbing even further up this time and hunkered down to wait things out for a while. Getting up on high ground was not the safest option, in terms of the possibility of a potential stray bullet—the *bala perdida* ('lost bullet') of favela parlance—but by that point, I was too tired to care.

Twenty minutes or so later, around 4:30 AM, things seemed to have had settled back down. Although I had not been drinking, exhaustion was causing me to feel a bit light-headed and intoxicated. I headed for the door again to make another attempt at getting out. This time I made it. 'What a relief!' I thought.

As I walked past the hotdog and beer stands outside, I saw a familiar face. Mike do Skate (Michael Batista Tavares) was selling beer and cans of soda, all laid out on a blue plastic tarp. A fixture on the Rocinha scene, Mike made his living as a vendor, on the beach below in São Conrado or at bailes and other cultural events. In his early thirties, his cheerfulness and hardworking attitude made him well-liked within the community. It seemed to me that he knew everyone and exemplified the stubborn insistence of people in Rocinha to overcome their difficult circumstances. Born with only partial legs, Mike glided around the streets of the favela seated on a skateboard. To go up the hill, he would hold onto the bumpers of buses, vans and cars heading up the snake-like Estrada da Gávea road. To come back down, he would weave in and out of traffic on his skateboard, using an old Havaiana flip-flop as a brake. His arms were incredibly strong—as was his spirit.

Mike clasped my hand, taking care not to squeeze too hard as he warmly greeted me. He knew I didn't drink alcohol and offered me a swig of his water bottle, which I gladly accepted. I asked him about his kids and his girlfriend, and we chatted for a few minutes. After a short while, I was ready to head out.

All of a sudden, another burst of machine gun fire popped off from over behind us. *Papum! Papum!* It was in the open area in front of the samba school, just across from the place where Mike was selling his drinks. That was my cue, I thought. At that point, it was definitely best to *vazar*, as they would say, or 'make like a tree and leave.' As I headed past the crowd to exit the outdoor area in front of the baile, I saw a mob of people gathered around a young man. He was lying on the ground, apparently injured. Springing into action, Rambo had already arrived there and was waving his arms excitedly and yelling out orders. I couldn't make out the young man's face very well through the crowd or see many of the people standing around him. Whoever it was, it would not help to have one more person crowded in rubbernecking, I decided. Besides, I was beyond exhausted. I walked on past and exited the scene.

Two or three minutes later I stepped off the main street into the deserted back alleyways leading down the favela back to my home in Cachopa. I did not realize then that it would be the last time I would attend a baile funk.

The next day, I found out that two young men had been shot and killed at the dance. I learned about the first one from a close friend who was tight with the gang, and who had just gotten out of prison after a three-year sentence. From what he told me, a young gang member from another favela had been there working at the dance that night, as part of Nem's security detail. At one point, a higher-up trafficker had given the young outsider an order which he did not understand well. When the young man had been slow to move, the higher-up had pushed him with the tip of the barrel of his rifle, placing it right up against the younger man's forehead. The gun went off, apparently by accident, killing the young man instantly.

The second death was of a man that I will call "Marcelo," a close friend of Anderson, my nineteen-year-old little brother-turned-research assistant. Unbeknownst to me, Anderson had decided to come up to the dance from his home in the Valão, at the bottom of Rocinha. He had wanted to find me, he would later tell me. He had also wanted to have some fun with his friends. Marcelo, in his late twenties and married with two small children, had given Anderson a call. He'd told Anderson he'd been working hard lately and that he needed to get out some and have a good time, relax with friends and maybe meet a lovely young woman or two. The two had come up the hill on Marcelo's Honda Titan motorcycle sometime after two AM and were joking around outside the dance hall when the trouble began.

One of the drug kingpin Nem's high-ranking lieutenants from the Rocinha gang had been a rival of Marcelo since childhood. When he came across Anderson and Marcelo in the crowd that night, he called Marcelo out. After a short exchange of insults, the trafficker suddenly upped the ante. Without warning, he shot Marcelo in the chest with his assault rifle. A split second later Marcelo was lying on the dirt outside the dance, bleeding out. In a panic, Anderson frantically jumped atop him, trying in vain to stop the blood flow. When Rambo arrived a minute later, he also attempted, though had no better luck in stopping it. No one else could do anything to help the man, either, and minutes later Marcelo died in Anderson's arms, as Anderson cried helplessly.

Utterly distraught, Anderson pleaded for someone to call for assistance. More traffickers appeared and took away the murderer, who was summarily judged by the boss and exiled from Rocinha, I was later told. The killer had violated the Ten Commandments of the favela, people said, and he needed to leave the community, at least for a while. The traffickers also took away Marcelo's body. As for Anderson, his hellish night was far from over. After Marcelo had died, he went down to the Valão area to the man's house. At age nineteen, Anderson had to tell his friend's wife that her husband had been shot and killed. In desperate, agonizing tears, the woman begged him to do whatever he could to recover her husband's dead body for burial. Beyond exhausted, Anderson had gone back up to the top of the favela, where he'd spent the rest of the morning doing his best to negotiate the release of the body with members of the gang.

After hours pleading with the traffickers and waiting around at the boca-de-fumo, Anderson was told by the gang that Marcelo's body would not be turned over to him. It was evidence, he was told. Instead, they said they were going to *abafar o caso* ('cover things up') burying him in an anonymous grave in the jungle above Rocinha. Anderson had eventually walked back down to the Valão area at the bottom of Rocinha and informed the newly widowed mother of two that he had not been able to get her husband's body back for her. When he finally went home in the late morning, he collapsed in his bed, completely drained.

When Anderson finally woke up late the next day, he called me. We spent the evening together at a nearby mall outside the favela, sharing a meal and talking. He was shell-shocked, often trailing off in mid-sentence to stare blankly off to one side. He cried, too—even if it was less than I would have expected. I didn't know what to make of my feelings, either. Looking back now, I realize a good measure of guilt was mixed in with the weighty sadness filling my breast. Guilt about Marcelo and guilt about Anderson, too, along with guilt about plenty of other things I would not have been able to explain at the time. I listened to Anderson and told him I loved him. I gave him hugs. Towards the end of the night, obtusely, I bought him an expensive new basketball. I don't think that the basketball was of much help, and neither was I. I wish I had given him more hugs and stayed with him for much longer.

House of Mirrors

Regarding my feelings about Marcelo and Anderson the day after Lulu's dance party, honestly my most immediate concern was for Anderson. I was relieved that he had not been physically injured but knew that he had been deeply-scarred at the heart-level. I don't want to reveal too many more intimate details of his life up to that point or afterward but suffice it to say this was not his first or last tough experience in life. How would he cope with the pain, I wondered? My greatest fear for Anderson had always been that he would someday wind up in the Rocinha gang, and all these years later it remains my greatest fear for him. I'm sure that at the time of this incident, becoming a gang member was the last thing on Anderson's mind. Even so, a life of harmful episodes adds up—especially on top of other forms of abandonment, whether at the intimate, family level or a societal one. Trauma from such experiences sometimes makes people vulnerable to seeking refuge in groups like gangs and other harmful organizations.

Even if Anderson did manage to stay away from the criminal life, I was worried that he would suffer from other personal problems like anger, depression, insecurity, unhealthy relationships or addictions. I feared, too, that he would have trouble in his family life, studies and work. At the time, he was just getting started with his first real girlfriend, and the following year they had a son together. I knew that it was likely that the pain and trauma of losing his friend that night in that way would adversely affect Anderson in his relationships unless he were to get some help from a support group or other loving fellowship. I couldn't help but think it was going to take more than bailes funk for him to get that sort of healing.

Speaking of funk, of course, I also agonized as to whether my visit to Lulu's birthday celebration was a factor in bringing Anderson and Marcelo to the dance party that night in the first place. There was a distinct possibility that if I hadn't gone there that night, they might have found some other way to entertain themselves. I couldn't help but wonder if Marcelo's death had been somehow my fault. Anderson repeatedly tried to assure me that the two friends would have gone to the dance either way. Despite Anderson's best efforts and arguments, though, I still felt I might be at fault. It always makes me sick to think of Marcelo's young wife and kids, who were both still so small. Even today, I wonder how life has been for them growing up without a husband or dad, knowing he died so needlessly.

The situation also highlighted my differences from Anderson and his life in Rocinha, besides, as well as some of my personal limitations at that point in my life. First off, I had many resources for mental health, healing and recovery to which folks in Rio's favelas generally have less access. In my church and at my university in the US, there were plenty of support groups, counselors, recovery ministries and psychiatrists. If they needed more help, people in those places could often even go into long-term residential programs. In Rocinha, and in Rio more generally, outside of cultural and community groups or religious practices, resources were scant. As I knew from my research into the AA and NA fellowships there, even free 12-Step programs had not significantly impacted the population, though there was a fledgling recovery scene.

As far as me being emotionally available to Anderson, myself, I knew I would only be around for another few days or so before I had to head up North to my wife's hometown of Belém do Pará, and then back to my full-time life in the States. We'd be in touch, I hoped, but I could not be there for him day in and day out as a stable older brother or father figure. More still, like anyone else, I was carrying my share of pain and trauma from my own life story, though at the time I was scarcely aware of it. In my own way, for most of my life, I had also felt abandoned and excluded, personally and socially. For almost two decades at that point, Anderson's family had graciously shared their faith and love with me. In the aftermath of Marcelo's death, I attempted to do the same with him. But I was severely distracted by my own worries and fears, with work at my university, at our non-profit and in my private life. Today, I believe the underlying sense of loneliness and disconnect I felt in those days was one of the forces driving me to seek intense immersion into community in Rocinha and even in the bailes funk.

Beyond the guilt and doubts I had regarding Anderson and Marcelo, I also had serious doubts about the potential impact of my research and writing about proibidão funk more generally. I wondered, for instance, if my efforts to pursue social justice by seeking to understand the bailes and the culture of crime in Rio's favelas might somehow produce an effect quite contrary to what I intended. In researching and writing about these topics, was I somehow glorifying the criminal lifestyle and violence? Was I somehow objectifying people or promoting superficial relationships in sex and love? I'd always view my research as complementing our work at our non-profit organization. But it was at least possible my frivolous search for adventure might be working against it to produce more desensitization than education.

Was I romanticizing proibidão or sensationalizing it, not just in writing but in being such an enthusiastic participant in the Rocinha funk scene? Was I sometimes a bad influence in the lives of young people? I had always thought of myself as a being more sincerely committed to peace and social inclusion than the average tourist, volunteer, social scientist or educator moving in and around the favela. I had to admit, though, that at some level I was not so different from any other outside visitor in Rocinha. Besides, getting regular praise and recognition for my activities in the academic community, in churches and the non-profit scene, I allowed my sense of grandiosity to swell. At times, I teetered on the verge of the White savior trope—and it wasn't pretty. Even today, these are not tensions I cannot neatly work out.

As I sit amidst the books and plants of my office today at the university to write, it occurs to me how different my life is now from my days living in Rocinha. People that meet me often say they are baffled as to how I could have ever conducted ethnographic research in one of Rio's favelas on a topic like Brazilian gangster rap. They sometimes ask how local people could accept a White, middle-class, American man like me. Wasn't it dangerous? Such questions are entirely sensible. Indeed, perhaps I should have concerned myself with such issues before taking on this study all those years ago or even when I moved to Rocinha for the first time back in 1990. Furthermore, when I first arrived in Rocinha, I was not a graduate student or trained anthropologist but mostly just a young person on something of a spiritual search. Though such a posture in ways allowed me to get personally involved at an emotional level, forming lifelong friendships, I can't help but think that my decision to avoid spending much time studying ethnographic methods and debates early on came with a price. I was unprepared for what I would go through and mostly unaware of the effects of living in Rocinha on me personally.

Looking back, I see there were extenuating circumstances on both sides that made it possible for me to connect so personally with the favela community and its funk scene. For openers, I see my experience in my teenage years as part of what led me to this area of study. Without going into too many details here, for about four years in my teens, I fell in with a rough crowd. When I continued to get in trouble over and over again,

I was introduced—entirely against my will—to a new, extremely diverse group of friends from a local community center. They eventually won me over, taking me in, loving me and guiding me as I got my GED (General Equivalency Development). Soon after my 18th birthday, I began taking classes at a local community college.[5] The journey left me with a soft spot for outcasts and a bit of practice looking past personal differences in my friendships.

When it came to my new life in Rocinha, I so hated being written off as a well-meaning foreigner that I did everything possible to allow myself to be transformed into a 'son' of the favela. I don't say this in the spirit of a recommendation regarding methodology but more as a confession. I wanted to be accepted and loved by the people around me, people I much admired and with whom identified. Early on in my life there, I tried to learn from my friends and neighbors—as from an adopted family—how to be more relational and people-centered, spiritual and non-rationalistic, yet street smart. So I almost never, ever spoke English, heaven forbid (unless I was teaching). I relished the sorts of praise I got from other residents that I was 'the most Brazilian foreigner in the country' or that I was 'already Brazilian.' I also relished it when close friends told me I was like a son or a brother. Indeed, until this day I still consider some of my closest friends in Rocinha practically family, like Anderson's relatives and others, as well.

On the Rocinha side, there was a certain openness and flexibility regarding diversity. My status as a foreigner was also a factor that often afforded me a certain degree of privilege and social capital. For many Rocinha residents, my foreignness also made me seem personally helpless

5 The GED is a sort of substitute for a high school diploma, though it is not generally perceived of as carrying the same prestige or social value.

and innocent, as well as distancing me from the blame for the social injustices around us. Even Anderson's grandmother told me once that I could bring as many foreigners to her home as I wanted, but please never to bring middle or upper-class Brazilians. I sometimes wonder how much more difficult it might have been for me to attempt a similar adaptation somewhere else, such as in the US. Often when people compare race relations between Brazil and the US, they point out that the situation is less fluid in the American context. Even so, I honestly believe that in most communities around the Afro-Atlantic world, including most of those in the US, willing outsiders like me can be accepted. Such would likely be the case with many other peoples, besides, though unfortunately not in all communities. Indeed, of all the places I've ever visited, Rocinha is one of the most open and accepting, especially in the favela's vibrant funk scene.

But there was another factor in my admission to the gangster funk community, and even to the favela, more generally—one I am only beginning to understand now. Yes, being a resident and community educator in Rocinha certainly had helped me to better understand the importance of music in the lives of the people there. But to be allowed into the funk community in the sort of intimate way I desired I needed to be 'funkified,' so to speak. Once I began immersing myself in the funk scene and the Rocinha nightlife, I found myself wanting to walk, talk and act like a favela hustler as much as possible. The *malandro*, a rough equivalent to 'hustler,' is a highly loaded term with tremendous significance for Brazilian culture. It is not easy to define, in any language. In short, it is the sort of 'bad boy' anti-hero celebrated in samba lyrics and other musical styles, like funk carioca. The malandro is associated with a combination of a degree of idleness, debauchery and charm—if not petty criminal activity. In its more popularized form, the malandro is a free spirit inclined towards a life of ease, living somewhat moment to moment amidst parties and other varieties of intense social interaction.

To be accepted into the funk subculture of the favela, I believed, I needed to allow myself to be changed and to bond with the other people in my new circles—not just aesthetically or ideologically but even physiologically and neurologically, at the level of the limbic core. In this spirit, I got a simple tribal tattoo of a semi-nude mermaid on my upper right arm. I also grew a goatee and long hair. I wore board shorts—the kind surfers wear—or capoeira pants, with lots of tank top muscle shirts, and was sure to stay tan. On my feet, I wore inexpensive flip-flops and Bamba tennis shoes. When it came to the gangsters, I had mixed feelings. Though I was on quite good terms with the gangsters in the Cachopa area where I lived, I mostly felt sad for the members of the gang. To me, they were the lost sons and daughters of the community. Some were psychopaths, besides, including one mid-level gang member who was said to drink a cup of blood from each person he murdered. But I also bought into the hype about the gangs, in no small degree, and the idea the drug traffickers had an ethical responsibility to behave as social bandits. For me, there were good gangsters and bad ones, a sentiment expressed in the popular criminal saying in Brazil that a good criminal must remain "o lado certo da vida errada" ("on the right side of the wrong life").[6]

I suppose, in ways, I was a big 'poser' and a 'wannabee.' But in another, I was, indeed, genuinely transformed. I somehow managed to listen to people and spent time with them in real friendships. Indeed, to this day I am immensely proud of Rocinha and the faith, charity and hope so many people there showed me. This love has strengthened my passion for social justice and the environment. But in allowing myself to become transformed in this way, I had become complicit with the social and cultural order of the drug gangs, especially regarding their gleeful celebration of the figure of the malandro and their supposed counter-cultural nature as defenders of the weak. And in the light of what happened to Anderson and Marcelo, it was coming back to me.

As a result of these mixed thoughts and feelings, I ended up putting off finishing and publishing this final manuscript for over a decade. For most of that time, I believed I was doing so mostly to avoid further staining the image of Rocinha and Rio's other favelas even further with representations of violence. Today I see, too, that also I was not yet ready to look in the mirror to see what this study said about me, as a person. Concerning what happened that night at that last dance party, it has been more difficult for me to work through my ideas and emotions. Indeed, this final chapter has been the most challenging of all for me to write, primarily as I have resisted the feeling I should have some tidy way to draw everything together. I do not.

In the end, this is a book about funk carioca and the people young and old of Rocinha—and favelas around Rio and other Brazilian cities. It's about Anderson, Marcelo and the other people who have lived the story and shared it with me along my own journey with funk carioca. My guiding principle has been to try and let people speak for themselves, as much as possible, as sons and daughters, brothers and sisters, neighbors,

6 This phrase is one of the central themes of *Abusado: O dono do morro Dona Marta*, by journalist Caco Barcellos. The biographical novel about the life and times of Marcinho VP (Márcio Marao de Oliveira), one of the CV's most articulate and socially conscious drug kingpins. Born and raised in the favela of Santa Marta, Marcinho VP was widely known for his revolutionary ideology and the welfare assistance he provided for residents. A key informant in the making of the famous documentary *Notícias de uma Guerra Particular* (1999), he was killed in Rio's Bangu III prison in 2003. The book is one of the most intimate and poignant portraits of the culture of crime in Rio. Since Marcinho VP's death occurred a mere two months after its release, many speculate it was a consequence of him revealing too much information about Rio's drug factions.

friends and even enemies. Crucially, I want to help make the "machine gun voices" of everyday people more audible than mine. Because of my profoundly personal involvement along the way, though, especially in events like the ones described above, my thoughts and feelings enter into this story, too.

Still, I do not want my private insecurities to prevent me from doing my best to let the everyday protagonists of the story of funk carioca in Rio's favelas be heard. Looking at the local context of the gangster dance parties in Rio's favelas provides a mirror, too, of the realities of Brazil today. It gives us a sort of MRI of the ongoing crisis of social exclusion and violence in the country and the contours of that crisis in terms like race, class and gender. In the broader scope, the mirror also reveals the contradictions of life in our contemporary world, too—socially, politically, culturally and even philosophically. The story of funk carioca is one for which the needs of the many outweigh the needs of the few in a struggle to resist outside groups and difficulties. Whether you are a gang member, student, shopkeeper, pastor or community educator, you are part of a collective and subject to the same basic rules and expectations. It is a story of life, in the fertility of funk's hypersexuality, and death, in the guns and violence of the gangster and police warriors.

On the surface, the core narrative of gangster funk often seems to pit one favela inside group against another favela outside groups. Usually, this entails pitting one criminal faction against another, as well. Similarly, it pits the inside group of favela residents against the outside group of the middle and upper-classes of mainstream Brazilian society.

At a deeper level, though, it is a story of the relational Afro-Atlantic world of community versus the dehumanizing colonialist and imperialist world of the dominant side of the Euro-Atlantic one. Beyond these more particular stories, however, at a deeper level still, the tale of funk carioca connects favela residents to the even larger inside group of youths around the world and even with the great human family. This gives Brazilian funk a utopian edge that points towards an improbable, yet powerful sense of hope for our greater coexistence. In the end, the story is ours, too, no matter where we are from or who we are.

Afterword

From dance party to dance party I met you,

It was singing rap that you looked at me,

I saw you go by looking into my eyes,

I told you, cutie, let's talk,

It seemed like a dream when I woke up,

All I found was a note.

- "From Dance to Dance," by MCs Leonardo and Júnior.[1]

'Funk carioca' means so many things to people in different favelas or cities—defenders and opponents alike. Moreover, it's in a constant state of change. New tendencies continuously arise in so many related areas: electronic beats and other musical aspects, dance moves, styles and trends, lyrics, slang, fashion, technology, market, space-time and so on. It changes, too, throughout the evolution of the social and cultural context in which it is practiced, and through the people who enact it. This has been true throughout the past forty-plus years of the evolution of funk carioca, from its beginnings in the 1970s in Black music from the US,

1 Lyrics by Renato Moreno, from the LP *De Baile em Baile* (1995), released by the Columbia label). Portuguese: "Foi de baile em baile que eu te conheci, Foi cantado rap que você me olhou, Olhando em meus olhos vi você passar, Te disse, gatinha, vamos conversar, Paparecia um sonho quando acordei, Somente um bilhete foi o que encontrei."

through the adoption of electronic music in the early 1980s, to the rise of the corridor-style mass fights in the dance parties of the late 1980s, and so on.

Even as funk carioca changed and evolved, something about it allowed people continue to consider is as 'funk' throughout its history.[2] In the 1990s, when Portuguese lyrics became the standard, people sang songs speaking out against fighting at the baile. They sought to raise awareness against racism and discrimination, too, began to praise the figure of the favela gangster and to sexualize the music more explicitly. Into the 2000s and 2010s, as funk spread from Rio to surrounding state capitals like São Paulo, Vitória and Belo Horizonte, more and more subgenres emerged—less popular ones like Gospel funk and mega-popular ones like funk ostentação ('swag funk'), which relied heavily on YouTube to present a materialist fantasy of inclusion through consumption to new generations of funkeiros across Brazil.[3]

The fact that funk carioca has never died off but instead has continued to thrive and expand is remarkable. By way of comparison, plenty of other vibrant musical styles have arisen across the horizon of the global youth scene which have come and gone, like punk rock or new wave. Their legacy continues, to be sure, but few people consider themselves as part of those scenes today. As of yet, however, nobody

2 Since much recent scholarship cited in the preface and opening chapters of this book includes references to such changes, I have chosen to limit new citations here. I would add though that recent developments in the culture and practice of funk carioca have been well-documented in the videography. A list of funk carioca documentaries spanning a quarter of a century can be found in Appendix B.

3 For an exploration of the rise of São Paulo's ostentação style, see *Funk ostentação—O filme* (2013), directed by Barreiros together with iconic producer and music video director Konrad Dantas, known as KondZilla. The following year a film on the same topic was released by Sidney Mariano, called *Funk ostentação—O sonho* (2014).

is talking about 'post-funk carioca,' the way one refers to post-punk. Instead, Rio's funk appears in ever-evolving and new permutations, much to the chagrin of its critics.

In the past few years, there has been something of a move away from this overpowering emphasis on cyberspace to return funk carioca back to the streets. A tremendously popular new dance style has been born in funk based around homespun dance moves like Rio's 2008 *passinho foda* (translated roughly as '*effing* amazing dance step'), which combined old-school international dance moves of performers like Michael Jackson with Brazilian dance styles like funk, forró and frevo. This dance style was born at the bailes funk and video-recorded in neighborhood dance battles on the rooftops of favelas, later disseminated on the Internet.[4]

Today, such moves are part of the mainstay of a new form of street baile in São Paulo called the *fluxo*, or 'flow,' in which people dance moves like the *passinho do romano* ('Roman step') in front of booming speaker stacks in the backs of cars, lined up in an endless row. Aside from dancing, crowds of people meet, dance, flirt, eat, drink and show of f their moves in these fluxos.[5] Naturally, YouTube and other sources of social media continue to increase the distribution of funk across these cities, throughout Brazil and even internationally, as well as giving countless dancers, singers, producers and DJs a platform through which to become stars, both online and on the ground. Indeed, no commentary on funk carioca today would be complete without mention of mega-successful YouTuber KondZilla (Konrad Dantas). Over the course of a mere decade,

4 Emílio Domingos' fascinating A *batalha do passinho* (2012) portrays competetions of passinho-style dancing in Rio de Janeiro.

5 Renato Barreiros' *No Fluxo!* (2014) offers vistas of the world of São Paulo's fluxo street funk scene, complete with interviews with a wide cast of participants, from street vendors to MCs and other music insiders.

this thirty-year-old self-made funk mogul born and raised in a favela in coastal São Paulo State has helped radically reshape the landscape of funk carioca. Firstly, through the hundreds of high production-quality music videos he has directed and produced, KondZilla has provided Brazilian funk with a never-before-seen visual aesthetic and style. Perhaps even more crucially, he has endowed funk with an unprecedented degree of exposure—in Brazil rivaled only by its sertanejo-country music scene. He now has 51.9 million subscribers his YouTube channel, making it one of the ten most popular in the world—and second most popular music channel anywhere (Darlington 2019).

It would be difficult to overstate the impact of KondZilla on contemporary funk carioca. After helping popularize São Paulo's funk de ostentação style in the early 2010s, more recently he has helped redirect funk carioca into even more popularly accessible subgenres like *funk romântico* ('romantic funk') and *funk dançante* ('danceable funk'). Already, a crop of YouTube competitors has risen in the wake of his success (GR6 Explode, for instance, currently has 25.5 million subscribers). In August of 2019, KondZilla even launched a critically acclaimed Netflix Original series, *Sintonia*, centered around São Paulo's funk scene, drug-trafficking and working-class Christianity in the lives of young people living there.

Back in Rio, young people in the city's favelas and other working-class neighborhoods have continued to update and innovate funk carioca, as something of an underground answer to the more capitalist pulse of the São Paulo scene (Larozza and Maxx 2019). Just as with early proibidão, community dance parties have been at the heart of this revival. At weekly festivities like the Baile da Gaiola in Vila Cruzeiro, in Penha, in Rio's Zona Norte, and the Baile da Nova Holanda, in the Complexo da Maré, figures like DJ Polyvox (Diogo Lima), DJ Rennan da Penha (Rennan Santos da Silva) and Mangueira's DJ Iasmin Turbinha (Iasmin Soares) have risen to a rarely before seen stature of funk stardom (Eiras and Bernardes 2019). Along with lyrical and vocal talents like MC Kevin o Chris (Kevin de Oliveira, also a composer and producer), these DJs have developed a quicker paced, more aggressive style of funk carioca known as 150 BPM. It's also known as *ritmo louco* ("crazy rhythm") and *putaria acelerada* ("accelerated whoredom"). Whereas previously most funk songs played at one hundred and thirty beats per minute (BPM), these new artists are pushing the threshold, sometimes up to and beyond one hundred and seventy (Molinero and Brêda 2019).

These and other online funk media entities in Rio have combined radio and local access television broadcasting with Facebook and other social media to promote the music, too. Programs such as Roda de Funk ("Funk Circle"), created by 3N Produções in São Gonçalo, in the Rio area, have also served as a means of documenting and archiving the contributions of past MCs, DJs and other funk personalities more active in the pioneering days of funk carioca before the growth of social media and commercial videography. Many of the artists from the golden age of Brazilian gangster funk treated throughout this book have made appearances on the program, which are available online. Together with their counterparts in São Paulo, Rio's new generation of YouTubers and other social media players have helped attain unprecedented visibility and popularity for funk carioca, not only throughout Brazil but across the globalized world."

Not surprisingly, with such a variety of funk expressions over the years, even those who identify as fans of funk often are at odds. Such can be confirmed by merely reading through the comments of but a few tracks on social media associated with the style. You'll find people from ten, twenty and thirty years ago complaining that today's funk is mindless garbage—though they generally use far stronger words than that to describe it. Funkeiros from merely five or six years ago say that the passinho foda dance steps popular in Rio in the late 2000s, which focused more on mostly on the movements of the feet, were so much better than the passinho do romano style of today, with its added emphasis on hand and arm gestures.

Similarly, advocates of *funk de raiz* ('roots funk') generally disdain the supremely pop variety of *novo funk melody* ('neo-funk') of mega-successful artists like São Paulo's MC Guimê (Guilherme Aparecido Dantas) and Rio's Anitta (Larissa de Macedo Machado). Anitta is one of Brazil's most prominent musical stars today, more in the mold of international divas like Beyoncé, Shakira or Rihanna than straight up funk carioca. Indeed, within the splits and divisions between different subgenres and periods, it is not uncommon for funk supporters to dislike the culture of one or another style of funk as much as the proponents of Brazilian hip-hop ever did funk carioca as a whole. Apparently, with funk—like anything else—what is ugly, offensive, violent, hypersexualized anti-music at one time or to one person is the beautiful or liberating stuff of dreams at another or to somebody else.

Recently, I asked a group of undergraduate students here at Seoul National University in Korea to watch a series of documentaries and read some articles about funk carioca. In preparation for our in-class discussion, their task was to write out a few *ID* questions ('identification') and a couple of *OP* ones ('opinion') about the material to go over together in small groups. On the day of class, as I made my way around the room listening in on their conversations and checking off their homework, I noticed one student had written only one question: "What is funk carioca?" The student, on exchange from her home university in Europe, was usually one of the most challenging thinkers in the class. Taken aback, I imagined at first that she had not prepared very well for the day's discussion, if at all. What did she mean by asking what funk carioca was? Wasn't it evident from the films and articles? I discreetly quizzed her a bit about the matter off to one side, however, and quickly realized that the student had gone over all the material. Quite carefully, in fact. She'd merely been shocked by what she'd seen in the documentaries, she told me, and didn't quite know what to make of it. Hers was an honest question, it turned out. And a bit of a philosophical one.

Champions of funk carioca and detractors alike often make claims about it in moral, political, cultural and ideological impact by making statements such as "Funk is culture!" ("Funk é cultura!") and "Funk is trash!" ("Funk é lixo!"). For me, it's more interesting to think of funk carioca relationally as interpersonal communication and as language. As such, it doesn't make sense to talk about its moral and ethical dimensions apart from those using it—or, perhaps even more critically, apart from the uses those folks make of it. It wouldn't make much sense to claim that all instances of a language like English, Portuguese or Korean were 'culture,' for example, at least not in the sense above as something automatically humane or liberating. Nor would it make sense to claim that all uses of a language were 'trash.' Languages and other forms of communication can be used to spread lies and misinformation, at personal, group and societal levels, just as they can be used for transparency and speaking truth. Of course, one can use them for promoting community, respect and love just as one can use them to encourage hostility or indifference.

For me, funk works in much the same way. It does not automatically bring people into the here and now of a community encounter. Yes, there is an underlying moral narrative built into the baile de comunidade that the needs of the many outweigh the needs of the few. The context of the collective resistance to the racial and social exclusion all too commonly lived by members of favela communities serves to bolster such a story further. From the start, this affords funk carioca with great potential as a force for unity and inclusion. Furthermore, beyond its ideological dimensions, when the baile does come together as a communal encounter, it can be a potent source of collective life and healing—along the lines of the paradigm of coexistence at the heart of this book. The favela street dance party can be a place of limbic resonance, regulation and revision but it can still also become a vehicle for violence, objectification and superficiality.

At times, the potential for community in funk can be problematic, since intense utopianism can work like a painkiller or mood-altering drug, covering over our needs for more profound community and friendship. Being naïve about such matters can make us vulnerable to people who don't genuinely care for our safety and wellbeing, no matter what the hype. These tensions between our needs for community and our tendency towards violence, both within our groups and without, reveal a predicament at the core of our social being. Our requirements for interconnectedness are not fanciful or romantic but rather physiological. Indeed, in essential ways, such needs and our abilities to meet are more real than our sociological theories or any ethnographic or other types of research. Yet, in attempting to satisfy such needs—as human beings with an innate capacity for violence that this is only intensified through social injustice and personal flaws and wounds—we all too frequently end up getting hurt or inflicting damage on those around us.

Regarding funk as an expression of language, in any event, is helpful in framing it as a community practice. Funk carioca is not merely some sort of 'content' but rather an interpersonal relational process—and one that blurs distinctions between song and speech. Often when we discuss language learning in the university setting, we refer to it in terms of 'acquisition.' We say that the learner acquires the language. But perhaps it's worth thinking about language learning in the opposite direction, too, as what we could call "double-acquistion." Perhaps it is not only the learner who acquires the language but the language, also, that acquires the learner. Beyond our capacity to use languages, we should think of them as cybernetic organisms made up of technology—in the words and structure of a language—and a collective mind, which uses that technology in inter-relationally, in 'presence.' Similarly, beyond its words, a language is also a bridge between collective consciousness and the collective matter of the bodies of those using it. Such a 'presence over content,' relational view of language undoubtedly offers a possible avenue of exploration, for linguists and philosophers alike.

In any case, our conventional view on language learning as acquisition reveals a Western notion of knowledge that tends to be overly object-centered. The epistemologies of the Afro-Atlantic world include alternative perspectives, many of which are communal, relational and musical, as discussed throughout the body of this book. Viewing funk carioca as a language, from such a relational point of view, one can acknowledge its potential as an expression of Afro-Atlantic resistance—and of the resilience of everyday people everywhere—without ignoring its possible pitfalls.

Thinking back on my student's question now, it strikes me as more difficult to answer than one might first presume. Initially, to me, the question "What is funk carioca?" appeared to be one of our class's 'identification' questions, simply soliciting a definition or some piece of information. It was more in the vein of our 'opinion' questions, however, requiring critical thinking. At an even deeper level, still, it occurs to me that profoundly understanding a complex, living musical expression like funk carioca requires much more than either information or analysis. Even reading articles and books–like this one–listening to music and watching videos and documentaries, at best one can get an introductory glimpse. We should take extra care, therefore, not to assume we understand or know more than we do. Indeed, despite my many years in close proximity to funk carioca, I'm not sure I can say that I have ever fully understood it. To whatever extent I have grasped anything about funk carioca, I'm sure I have not been able to communicate my understanding very completely anyway, even in the most vivid and lucid passages of this book. So now, as I write this afterword, I'm left asking myself, along with my student, "What the heck *is* funk carioca, anyway?"

As a point of departure in answering such a question, perhaps it's worth bearing in mind that, in the end, one can never fully 'know' a cultural practice like the bailes funk of Rio outside of the shared collective here and now of a live moment, as a communal encounter. A baile is not merely textual, such as a short story, poem or novel. Nor is it merely a performance, as a text written in bodies and other objects. There are dimensions of a baile beyond ideology—and even psychology—that are spatial, temporal and even physiological. As such, our ability to 'understand' a baile in the past tense is severely limited. One has to be immersed in it in the present.

Furthermore, one's presence requires something more than physically occupying the space of the dance party, as one takes notes or otherwise observes from a stance of impartial objectivity. To more fully apprehend the reality of a favela street dance party, one must relationally join into community with those around him or her. One's limbic core must become emotionally and even neurologically intermingled and entangled with others who are doing the same. Knowing, in this sense, is not so much a question of some experience had or object used, about any 'content' acquired or of which one becomes aware. It's about being immersed in relationship, in ways that change those who meet, in 'presence.'

Perhaps this is an analogy of how a language acquires a learner, in the sense I suggested above. It also frames the question of my own involvement in the culture of Brazilian gangster funk in ways similar to those I suggested in the last chapter of this book. To the extent a person is assimilated into a specific space-time and practice, he or she will necessarily succumb to the elements that make it up, all of which are not healthy or conducive to peace and coexistence. Eventually, therefore, we must reckon with the fact that we become somewhat complicit with whatever violence is inherent in it.

The communal impulse has always been a crucial component of the music and culture of funk carioca—be it in proibidão or other subgenres—all the way through to the present age of social media. This is evident in the evolution of funk carioca across the years past the rise of the proibidão funk that has been the focus of much of this book to its characteristics and tendencies more recently. What I hope is that even from the brief sketch of this evolution above—and throughout the book, more generally—it will be evident that even in the conventional sense of 'knowing,' from an informational or analytic point of view, it's hard to pin down precisely what funk carioca is.

In any case, just as the music has changed with time, trends in scholarly research shaping the ideas that went into writing this book also have come and gone. I've changed, too, over the course of more than two decades. More precisely, while I started with lyrical analysis to unpack the culture of crime in funk and its utopianism, in time I have become more interested in performance and the live event and questions of music, place and community. As I reflect on my long, strange trip researching funk, it occurs to me that this book has grown in stages much like the auto construction-style that has characterized the rise of favela communities of Rio de Janeiro. Throughout the various phases of the project, tier upon tier has been added as I have built upon my past work and that of others throughout so many changes in the evolution of funk carioca.

Bailes funk like the ones described in throughout this book are more than expressions of the power of the favela community to define and create its unique sound, aesthetic and identity. In a sense, too, those bailes are the favela heightened, or the transformation of the favela sounds and realities into music. I regret that space limitations throughout the previous chapters have left less room for the inclusion of more descriptions of bailes funk, song lyrics and the voices of everyday fans and residents of the favelas than I would have liked. Still, I hope that I have been able to transmit something of the energy and creativity of Rio's funk culture at the end of the 1990s and beginning of the 2000s—and of the people who lived it.

Appendix

Appendix A

Classic Proibidão Lyrics

In the late 1990s and early 2000s, during the golden age of proibidão in the *bailes de comunidade* in Rocinha and other favelas in Rio, MCs of funk carioca who included specific gang references or other portrayals of criminal violence in their songs risked persecution and arrest, just as they do today. Such MCs could be found in violation of two laws of the Brazilian Penal Code: Article 286 makes it illegal to incite people to violence, while Article 287 prohibits making an apology of crime. Most of the proibidão songs addressed throughout this book, therefore, were never played on the radio or sold in stores but instead were circulated informally on cassette tapes, CDs and MP3s by street vendors or house to house. Sometimes if an MC had a radio-friendly song, he or she often made an illegal version of the song that was played live at favela dance parties and sold through clandestine outlets. Often MCs brought their prerecorded beats to the show for singing along. The DJ just played them or mixed them with other sound effects and musical samples. So it was easy enough for the DJs providing the music for the baile to make reasonably high-quality recordings right through the equipment being used in the show.

As I have mentioned in this study, some singers have experienced legal troubles for the content of their song lyrics, such as MCs Leonardo and Júnior, who are not even proibidão style performers. Others, such as MCs Frank, Max, Tikão, Dido and Smith in 2010 have been arrested and also jailed (Palombini 2013). MC Galo of Rocinha was also arrested. Even much more mainstream acts outside of funk sometimes experienced legal problems for their music. Two notable examples were the rock group Planet Hemp, famous for its apology for the use of marijuana, and hip-hop artist MV Bill, who portrayed armed drug traffickers in his seminal video for 'Soldado do morro.' Still, within the culture of funk carioca, such 'purges' were usually momentary, often occurring on the heels of a crisis like the Tim Lopes murder, discussed in Chapter 5. Even so, in the late 1990s and early 2000s, it was not very common for police to confiscate proibidão CDs, give fines to vendors or harass funk singers. In 2002, I asked an officer from Rio's Military Police, whom I encountered near the beach in the Leblon neighborhood of Rio, as to whether or not he would arrest anyone over proibidão. He told me that he liked such music, personally, and that he frequently bought proibidão CDs for his kids!

In this appendix, I include three types of songs from the late 1990s and early 2000s. The first, titled "Classic Proibidão," is made up of selected songs associated with the genre, whether or not they were, in fact, illegal. All names of MCs listed are fictitious. Because all of these songs were collected in Rocinha, a Comando Vermelho community during most of the years of my fieldwork, none of them speak for or praise either the Terceiro Comando Puro (TCP) or the Amigos dos Amigos (ADA) cartels. Indeed, Rocinha was a privileged location for funk carioca at that time, since the CV was the largest faction and the Rocinha branch of the CV was generally the wealthiest one. I suspect the Rocinha drug traffickers generally had more money to invest in bailes funk than those of allied favelas. One song that represents this well was recorded live in 2002 at a birthday party for Lulu (also known as Bill, Bigode and Magro). In the song, five of the most popular proibidão MCs of the time (including three included in this appendix) perform a free-style homage to the crime boss, connecting Rocinha to other bands of CV drug traffickers in various favelas across Rio. The song, which I have not included below, is currently available online under the title "Mc Mascote, Mc G3, Mr Catra , Duda, e Gil - Rima na Hora [Ao Vivo] [ROCINHA] (Proibidao Antigo)."

After Rocinha switched to the ADA in 2004, a host of new ADA songs emerged, many of which were recorded and distributed within the favela. It was a period of even more significant commercial isolation, musically, than had been the previous one (since the CV MCs were not allowed to come to Rocinha). It was a period in which some new MCs appeared and many old ones switched allegiance to the new faction (such as MC Cordão de Ouro). Indeed, that transitional phase is deserving of its own carefully detailed study.

The second group of songs I've included, titled "Classic Sensual Funk" is a collection of verses from musical/lyrical *montagens* ('montages') and other lyrics. These songs often appeared on the same CDs as songs about gangs and violence. Though I have not studied the sensual side of funk closely in this book, I have included these songs for various reasons. For one, they are representative of the tendency in funk carioca at the time to use heavily sexual lyrics and metaphors. Second, though songs by male MCs focusing on sex, like MC Serginho and Mr. Catra, were also popular, the sensual funk genre was equally dominated by females, either as MCs or as groups. Of the female Rio funk artists of the day, the three MCs or groups I have included were perhaps the most influential. One was Tati Quebra-Barraco. I also include a musical 'duel' between Taty Quebra-Barraco and MC Serginho. The lyrics are the longest in this entire Appendix and are perhaps the most sexually explicit, yet they present in a compact, if incomplete way the field of negotiations of gender roles at paly at the time. It also contains verses from his famous 2002 hit "Vai Serginho."

Another was Deize Tigrona, whose name means 'Deize the Tiger' (after being earlier known as Deize da Injeção, due to the success of her most popular song). Finally, I include the all-female group Gaiola das Popozudas, whose name essentially means something like 'La Cage aux Big Butt Women,' referring to the drag nightclub from the musical *v*. Gaiola das

Popozudas featured Valesca Popozuda, who later rose to considerable national fame. Regarding this last group, although they got their start in 2000, most of their popularity came during the mid-2000s and 2010s. The song listed below is from 2005. Many songs by Tati, Deize and Valesca have been explored by scholars like Adriana Carvalho Lopes (2011) and Mariana Gomes Caetano (2015). These two scholars in particular have taken up somewhat opposite positions on the would-be organic feminism that such singers are often said to espouse.

The final grouping of songs in this appendix, "Five Classic Funk Songs," is comprised of lyrics of legal songs that were ground-breaking hits in the mid-1990s and defined and influenced many of the characteristics of the Rio funk of the time (of both the mainstream and prohibited varieties). Since such songs and their lyrics are readily available online, I have only included five. I have listed the dates of their first issue to place them in the context of the development of the genre.

While transcribing lyrics for this appendix, no attempt has been made to make emendations. In the place of words that could not be deciphered due to lack of sound clarity, ellipses have been added. In cases in which I purposely omit words to protect specific people, I've replaced them with the symbol '###.' Though in my esteem these artists deserve recognition for their art, I have chosen to omit their names to help them avoid any potential legal problems. In any case, since it is currently quite easy to find much of their material online, including almost all these songs, I hope that this list can still contribute to their recognition, without causing them trouble.

I. Classic Proibidão

MC Cordão de Ouro (from the favela of Rocinha)

- "Sou da Rocinha"
- "Vacilou, levou"
- "Venho alerter"
- "Papum, papum"
- "Bonde do chi-cheiro"
- "Bonde dos ladrões"
- "Bonde da fé"

MC Manda Brasa (from the favela of Rocinha)

- "Bandidos de Cristo"
- "Quem comanda a favela da Rocinha"
- "Somos vermelho"
- "Hoje eu sonhei"

MC Bocão (from the favela of Borel)

- "Vende um X-9 pra mim"
- "Terror da boca"
- "Cadê o esqueiro"
- "Simpático"
- "Tráfico cultural"

MCs Santos and Agostinho (from the Cidade de Deus)

- "Bota preta"
- "Cuca louca"
- "Rap da CDD"
- "Meus direitos"
- "10 mandamentos da favela"

- "Rap das armas (Versão commando)"

MC Vidiga (from the favela of Vidigal)

- "Avisa lá"
- "Menino sofredor"

MC Eddynho (from the favela of Borel)

- "Rap da cadeia"
- "Terceiro fraco"

MC Ruger (from the favela of Rocinha)

- "Seus alemão safado"

MCs Phillipe and Eddynho (from the favela of Borel)

- "Rap do Borel/Versão Comando"

II. Classic Sensual Funk

Tati Quebra-Barraco (of Cidade de Deus)

- "Montagem assadinha/69"
- "Montagem pidona"
- "Montagem cartão magnético"
- "Montagem cardápio do amor"
- "Montagem bota na tcheca"

Tati Quebra-Barraco with MC Serginho

- "MC Serginho vs. Tati Quebra-Barraco"
  (also available online as "Proibida")

Deize Tigrona (aka, Deise da Injeção, of Cidade de Deus)

- "Injeção"

Gaiola das Popozudas (with vocalist Valesca Popozuda)

- "Fiel é o caralho"

III. Five Classic Rio Funk Songs

- 🎧 "Rap da Rocinha" (MC Galo, 1991)
- 🎧 "Rap da Felicidade" (MC Cidnho and Doca, 1995)
- 🎧 "Rap da liberdade" (MCs Willian and Duda, 1995)
- 🎧 "Rap das armas" (MC Leonardo and Júnior, 1995)
- 🎧 "Nosso sonho" (Claudinho and Buchecha, 1996)

I. Classic Proibidão

🎧 MC Cordão de Ouro (from the favela of Rocinha)

"Sou da Rocinha"

Sou da Rocinha não dou mole pra Terceiro Comando
querendo esculachar, vai tomar de AK papum
Sou da Rocinha não dou mole pra Terceiro Comando
querendo esculachar, Bota o fuzil pra cantar!

É bonde que fortalece o Valão, quero ouvir, papum papum
é o bonde que fortalece o Valão, vamos lá
A união dos irmãos, que eu venho falar quem quiser venha formar
Para andar lado a lado com o bonde tu não pode vacilar
O ritmo é frenético é disposição nosso bonde é boladão
Plantado dia e noite fortemente armado, aqui na área do Valão
Bota o fuzil pra cantar,
é o bonde que fortalece o Valão, quero ouvir
Sou da Rocinha não dou mole pra terceiro comando
querendo esculachar, vai tomar de AK
Sou da Rocinha não dou mole pra terceiro comando
querendo esculachar

Na continuação se liga meu mano não sou simpático a ninguém
Armamento pesado bote na sua mente, igual a Roça não tem
Puxa o bonde Bigode, Bil, Buiú, Cavanhaque, 21, Marcelinho
Marino, e o 99 não esqueçam de Magu

Domar, Dewilson, Molejo e o Bel os restantes estão no céu
Bahiano, Batatinha, o meu amigo Serginho,
Trola o braço fiel para finalizar de AK na mão Soldado e
o Cabeção, braço Magu, Naiba,
se liga Bil não esqueço dos irmãos,
Bota o fuzil pra cantar!
É o bonde que fortalece o Valão, quero ouvir
Tô cansado de falar mais eu tenho que explicar
se mexer com o Buiú toma tiro de AK
Tô cansado de falar, mais eu tenho que explicar
se mexer com o Lelé toma tiro de AK
Se mexer com o Buiú toma tiro de AK

"Vacilou, levou"

Vacilou, levou, o comando é vermelho
se cagüetar, levou o comando é vermelho
Se não fechar, levou o comando é vermelho
fazer o queixa, levou o comando é vermelho

Se tu é CV na mente anda com o fuzil na mão
vem comigo a chapa é quente, o comando é vermelhão
Vem no clima da Rocinha, no ritmo do morrão
é a comissão de frente garantindo a contenção

Mas vacilou levou, o comando é vermelho, cagüetou velou
o comando é vermelho
Se não fechar levou, o comando é vermelho, se bulir levou

o comando é vermelho
Sigo fortemente armado de AR e de G3, lança-granada
e traçante é a turma da sem lei
Se os vermes pintar na pista, de ralelê vão ficar
desço o bonde do morrão, de cigui e de AK

Cagüetou levou, o comando é vermelho, vacilou levou,
o comando é vermelho
Se bulir levou, o comando é vermelho, vacilou levou
o comando é vermelho
Mas se liga laufranhudo no que agora eu vou falar
Vê se bota na cabeça usa chapéu quem sabe usar
Tem o bonde da Rocinha querendo jogar na mala
Mr. M simpatia vai de pedra lá vai bala
Se cagüetou levou, se tu bulir levou, se fazer queixa levou
mais vacilou levou, o comando é vermelho
A Rocinha é CV e comanda não é comandado,
mando um alô pra Mineira, Pavãovizinho e Canta Galo
a Grota e a de Deus, o Borel e a Varginha, Vidigal
Andaraí e o bonde da Fazendinha
Formiga, a Nova Holanda o Serra pra completar o Falete
o Fogueteiro e o Turano e a Cruzada

Vacilou levou, se cagüetar levou, o comando é vermelho
se bulir levou, o comando é vermelho, vacilou levou

sou da Rocinha não dou mole pra terceiro

comando querendo esculachar
Vai tomar de AK, papum,
sou da Rocinha não dou mole pra terceiro
comando querendo esculachar
Bota o fuzil pra cantar

"Venho Alertar"

Tô bolado, tô bolado,
tô bolado, tô boldado!

Maluco venho alertar, só mesmo vendo pra crer
Se não vive pra servir, não serve para viver
Porque no mundo do crime ganhar respeito e poder
Mas o final deste filme eu tô cansado de ver
Periferia é mil grau
Pra quem tem conceito forte
A todos os do bonde do mal
Violento conta com a sorte

O que os olhos não vêem o nosso coração não sente
Por isso a sociedade anda sempre contente

Já na revolta com a vida querendo lançar os panos
Não é preciso ser inteligente pra ver
o que acontece com os manos
Maluco na revolta, a molecada começa a roubar
De menor vai parar lá na FEBEM

De maior vai parar lá no DACA
Neurose aí violento
Já tô te ligando a fita
Pa tu ficar por dentro e não perder a vida
É só lazer tu tá ligado
E tá bolado só pra variar
Terrorista de salão Pikachu,
melhor amigo não contrariar
só para variar a mente, maluco, legalizou
por que eu sou o Galo da Roça
e os amigos abalou
eu tô em pé sem cair, tô deitado sem dormir
preparado sem fazer pose
é o bonde dos MC

Eu sou daqueles antes que bem só do que mal acompanhado
Se não faz tua cara, não atrase meu lado
Pense bem no que você tá dizendo pra não
bater com a língua nos dentes
Pra X-9, cagüete, maluco, descarrego o pente
Ande sempre pelo caminho certo
Não queira ser mais do que ninguém
Já vi muito mano esticado no chão
por querer ser grande também
fama, dinheiro e poder, claro que todo mundo tá de olho
mas como diz o ditado quem vai pela cabeça dos outros é piolho

"Papum, papum"

Cheguei da batalha bolado
Se liga em que aconteceu
Quando eu cheguei no morro
soube que mataram um amigo meu
E eu fiquei revoltado
Vim pra Rocinha formar
O Bigode sentiu firmeza e jogou no meu peito um AK
Papum, papum,
Com a pistola 45, um fuzil lança-granada
E tu vem com os irmãos formando o bonde da pesada
Eu sou negão e tô bolado Não tenho arrego, não
E vou descer com o meu bonde
E vou quebrar os alemão
Quero ouvir só de AK

La la iá, estufa o peito vou furar
La la iá e só passa tracante no ar
La la iá estufa o peito vou furar
La la iá e só passa tracante no ar

E o tempo vai passando Com o comando eu fechei
E tá tudo dominado É o bonde dos sem lei
Na favela da Rocinha O comando é consagrado
Se mexer com nosso bonde vai sair todo furado,
Papum, papum,
Or irmãos estão na pista

Sem neurose sem caô Nosso bonde é sinistro
é o bonde quebra-quebrou
O catuque já foi dado eu não vou mais repetir
Tenho um grande conceito Sou local MC
Quero ouvir só de AK
La la iá estufa o peito vou furar

"Bonde do chi-cheiro"

Essa vai pra rapaziada que gosta da
Alcione, tutti-frutti, escama de peixe
Gal Costa e muito mais, né
Aquela branquinha , bonde do chi-cheiro.
E meu irmão vou te dar umas dicas aí, boca do Valão, ta ligado né
Pó de cinco de dez, tem o pó de vinte que é bom pra caralho, hein

Ei ô bonde do chi-cheiro, vou dar um teco maneiro
na área do Valão, como é bom
Ei ô bonde do chi-cheiro, vou dar um teco maneiro
eu vou ficar é pancadão, pancadão
A brizola faz a gente emagrecer, faz a gente perder peso e não querer comer
Mais depois vem aquela esticação, se não tiver dinheiro vai
ter que virar um ladrão
Mais depois vem aquela esticação, se não tiver dinheiro vai
empenhar o seu cordão
Vamos lá fungador, se tiver de sola cheira, cheira, cheira
você não vai dispensar não, não, não

Tu vai cheirar a noite inteira até ficar pancadão
Tu vai vender sua bermuda e o seu quepe da cantão
Tu vai vender sua panela e o seu relógio e o fogão
cheira,cheira, cheira

Ei ô bonde do chi-cheiro, vou dar um teco maneiro
na área do Valão, como é bom
Ei ô bonde do chi-cheiro, vou dar um teco maneiro
eu vou ficar é pancadão, pancadão
A brizola faz a gente emagrecer
faz a gente perder peso e não querer comer
Mais depois vem aquela esticação
se não tiver dinheiro vai ter que virar um ladrão
Mais depois vem aquela esticação
se não tiver dinheiro vai empenhar o seu cordão
Vamos lá fungador, se tiver de sola cheira, cheira, cheira
você não vai dispensar não, não, não

"Bonde dos ladrões"

Um alô mané, é bonde do ladrão que gosta de
roubar um carro forte,
Fazer um seqüestro neurótico, tá ligado né mane
roubar um banco
E as menozadas que gosta de meter ums toca fita ta ligado né
A peça é essa ta ligado né, rapazeada hamm, então vai

A letra desse rap vai pra geral se ligar,

eu falo dos amigos que se amarram em roubar
Na área do Valão os ladrãos são sangue bom
vai em Botafogo Ipanema e Leblon
Na Barra da Tijuca o bonde vai geral
vai de pino, vai de lixa e até de pica-pau
Quero ouvir, quero ouvir, já roubou, demorou de bá
demorou de bá O Valão, Roupa Suja demorou de bá
solta o pancadão DJ pra galera delirar
Depois de sacudir eles vão se divertir
vão comprar é roupa nova, para o baile vão curtir
Bermuda da Ciclone ,Camisa da Toulon
quepe importado e um tremendo relojão
Mizuno, Nike, Kenny, tá ligado também é tradição
Quem usa essas peças Roupa Suja e Valão

Quero ouvir, quero ouvir, já roubou,
demorou de bá, demorou de bá
Mais demorou de bá,
agora meus amigos se ligue que eu vou falar
O nome dos amigos que se amarraram em roubar
Vem o amigo Liu, que é um cara sangue bom
vem o ######, #####,#####,##### (etc.)
E o ##### que pilota de montão, faz Miura, Catete e até grande fu
Quero ouvir, quero ouvir, já roubou, demorou de bá, demorou de bá

Não beba whiskey, beba Nescau
não fume cigarro a maconha é três reais

Não beba whiskey, beba Nescau
não fume cigarro a maconha é três reais
É na palma da mão o bicho vai pegar,
eu estou idignado vou fumar um classe A
Estico ra ta tá, mantando eu vou ficar,
se liga rapazeada que o bicho vai pegar
Formiga de tamanco não sobe parede não
nem perna de barata é serrote não
Barata viva não atravessa galinheiro,
porque o Galo esta lá e é um cara maneiro
Paz na mente e na consciência seu cabeça de bosta
rio que tem piranha jacaré nada de costa
Se fui pobre não me lembro se fui rico me roubaram
morena trás o esqueiro pra acender meu baseado
Já fui lá e já voltei, foi com meu cigarro,
morena trás o esqueiro pra acender meu baseado
Já fui lá e já voltei, passei ali por perto,
sangue bom faz o canudo que eu vou bater um teco
Sangue bom faz o canudo que eu vou bater um teço
vai dar um vai dar duas você vai ficar esperto

"Bonde da fé"

Recordação é viver, e o bom da vida é curtir
sonhar me dar mais prazer
Por isso eu canto tão feliz, alô rapazeada esse é o bonde da fé
Com Gordinho, Cassiano e Fernandinho e Dedé
Alô rapazeada esse é o bonde da fé, da fé, da fé

Mas com Gordinho, Cassiano e Fernandinho e Dedé
Pra mim é um grande prazer contar a sua história
Falar de amigos guerreiros que não me sai da memória
Vi Buzunga, Geraldete, Zé do Queijo e Bolado, com Ademir
Nelson Batina não dá pra ficar parado
O Cadi, Mario Heleno, Naldo e o Tibiriri a Rocinha
tem conceito e eu não vou sair daqui
Tão contente eu vi Vicente, Generoso e o Ademir
com Henrique e o Zequinha o Yoyo e o Parazim
O meu rap está rolando é da fé que emoção,
ai meu Deus tanta tristeza quando eu canto esse refrão

Recordação é viver, e o bom da vida é curtir,
sonhar me dar mais prazer
Por isso eu canto tão feliz, alô rapazeada esse é o bonde da fé
Com Gordinho, Cassiano e Fernandinho e Dedé
Alô rapazeada esse é o bonde da fé, da fé, da fé
Mas com Gordinho, Cassiano e Fernandinho e Dedé

Roberto e o Sabará, o Aranha no sapatinho
com Gato do Vidigal o Rafael e o Xiquim
Vi comprido Jorge Chefe, o Pet fez uma presença
o Luciano e o Bicudo não queriam violência
O Pantera, Santo escreve melodia e o Ramon
chegou com Paulo Caxanga, Rachini e o Molecão
Vi Bilisca com São Jorge, Beto, Falcão com Lelé, Dimenor
Brasileirinho, Carne Seca deu no pé

O Pitanga com o Zano, Lula fez a formação acordei
com tio Cefo, ó Deus e vi que era ilusão

Recordação é viver, e o bom da vida é curtir,
sonhar me dar mais prazer
Pó isso eu canto tão feliz, alô rapazeada esse é o bonde da fé
Com Gordinho, Cassiano e Fernandinho e Dedé
Alô rapazeada esse é o bonde da fé, da fé, da fé
Mas com Gordinho, Cassiano e Fernandinho e Dedé
Pra mim é um grande prazer contar a sua história
Falar de amigos guerreiros que não me sai da memória

MC Manda Brasa (from the favela of Rocinha)

"Bandidos de Cristo"

(Note: In the recorded version, MC Manda Brasa sings with another MC listed by online versions today as his former musical partner. Here we'll call him MC Jack Swing)

[MC Manda Brasa]
Demorou!
[MC Jack Swing]
Vamos lá, heim? Vamos esquentar assim... Botando pro alto, Botando pro alto de 762, pistola Glock, pisto UZI e HK vocês vão se amarrar.
[MC Manda Brasa]

Bandidos de Cristo, tem muita fé em Deus
Para esta vida tem que ter muita disposição
Pergunte pro Patrão
Eu perguntei
O bom patrão me respondeu
Tem que seguir esta lição
Porta granada e escopeta, e defender o nosso morrão
Não quero ver, não quero ver
Os irmãozinhos virando as costas pro morrão
Somos Vermelho, vocês também, quero ver
Vamos dar tiro de montão

"Rap do Patrão"

Vou subir, vou subir, vou subir o meu morrão
Com um alô pra os amigos
E um abraço pro patrão (× 2)

Um alô pro Bangu Um, Água Santa e Bangu Três
Onde vive os irmãozinhos, que saudades de vocês
Quando subo a favela e passo naquele lugar
Que o Patrão tirava onda dá vontade de chorar
Mas eu tenho fé em Deus e na pura santidade
Que em breve eu verei o Patrãozinho em liberdade
Pra gente zuar juntinho pelas partes do morrão
Desejando a liberdade dos amigos sangue bom

Um alô para os fregueses do meu Rio de Janeiro

Vai de preto ou vai de branco é do puro brasileiro
Pra quem são da Zona Norte, Zona Oeste ou Zona Sul
Zona Leste também vem, pelo jeito vai dar um
Um abraço pros amigos que protege as favelas
Obrigado pela força que vocês dão para ela
O vapor, o fogueteiro, o gerente e o ladrão
E a todos os soldados que protege o Patrão

O Rebelde ficou bolado e fez uma reunião
Quero todo mundo armado lá no alto do morrão
Fogueteiro AR-15, o gerente de G3,
o vapor vem de pistola, eu vou falar só um vez
os soldados do meu bonde vêm de 762
os olheiros de traçante, o aviso é dois em dois
o contexto quando é sangue, os amigos reconhecem
Rebelde vem no comando de AK-47

"Quem Comanda a favela da Rocinha"

O Bigode é quem comanda a favela da Rocinha,
quero ouvir! Rocinha! Geral! Tá ligado, né mané

Com vários bondes, vários bicos fazendo a conteção, pesadão
A nossa base é no alto do morrão
Só irmãos, nós somos 100% Vermelhão

Com o Bigode
não tenta que vai levar um sacode

sem neurose, são vários bondes vindo de caça android
vê se pode, Rua Um, Valão e 99
com a Rocinha, tá ligado, ninguém pode

A Vía Ápia, a Paula Brito, Cachopa,
Fundação, Terreirão,
Os bondes prontão sempre de AK na mão
boladão, observando a sua vacilação
fé em Deus para o Comando Vermelhão

"Somos vermelho"

Somos Vermelho até o osso,
É paz, justiça e liberdade
eu tô trepado até o pescoço
E o bonde está demais
Por isso a gente é fé em Deus
e o comando cresce mais
Aqui quem sabe é nós
Se caia chuva ou faça sol
Defendo a favela nem se for a vida inteira

E o X-9 a gente quebra na ladeira, irmão
E o X-9 a gente quebra na ladeira, irmão,
Do meu quartel vejo a praia,
Rocinha é minha área
Fim de semana e pura diversão
Tô fortemente armado e o CV preparado

Tá ligado

"Hoje eu sonhei"

Vamos lá, hoje eu sonhei viajando no Valão
ia ter um baile bom no lugar onde eu morava

Minha Rocinha estava enfeitada,
o DJ era o Buzunga, locutor era o Bolado
Mas de repente chegava o Ronaldo
com sua metralhadora no pescoço pendurado
Aí então eu fiquei muito animado,
ao ver toda aquela gente sorridente do meu lado
É, sem perceber chegou Tebererê minha
perna ficou bamba não vou mais sair daqui
Quero ouvir, Mario Heleno, Zé do Queijo e Osnê
Geraldete e o Cândi já passaram por aqui
Mais derepente eu vi Vicente e Ademir,
o Herinque com Zequinha, o Yoyo com Parazinho
Bebendo um choppe com amigo Bagulhão
que saudade dessa gente Rocinha recordação

Ai, ai meu Deus eu não posso acreditar,
isso mais parece um sonho me da vontade de chorar
Recordações me explique por favor
onde está toda essa gente, diga meu nosso senhor
e logo depois, chegou o Fernandinho
com Gato do Vidiga Rafael e o Chiquinho

Sem esperar desceu o bonde lá da Um
vi Comprido e o Pet, Jorge Chefe e mais um
Era o Bicudo que não deu pra conhecer
quando ele chegou junto foi que eu pude perceber
Até o Pantera, Santos, Cleber e o Ramon
foram parte desse sonho
foram muitos sangue bom
Ouvir dizer que o Cassiano estava lá,
o Lecão e o Bilisca mas ficaram de vagar
Melhor ficou pintou o Lula e o Zana
Raxini e o Vere dança com Paulo Caxanga
É , olhei pro canto vi seu Jorge e Lelé
com o seu velho charuto perguntei como é que é
Logo em seguida, imagina eu vi Dedé
Brasilerinho, Beto Fal, mas estavam de rolé
Léo de Menor, o Pitanga, Carne Seca
que saudade lá do bar, tio Celson era o cabeça
Deixo um abraço do fundo do coração
o amigo de Leandro eternamente o Padrão
Eu sou o Galo, sou contente ator aqui
eu não posso me esquecer do Lobão e do Gordinho
Sem desejar, o Bigode é sangue bom
quando arde o coração para o Bil que é meu irmão
É , vamos lá, oi demorou de bá, segura DJ

🎧 MC Bocão (from the favela of Borel)

"Vende um X-9 pra mim"

- Aí, cidadão, é o arrego.
- Qual é, Chefia, de novo? Porra. Tá maluco.
- Pois o salário tá bravo, né?
- Ah, quer dindin, então vende X-9 para mim.

Tá ligado
O, tá mandado, já voltou mas tá queimado

Se faz de amigo, só faz de conta
Sujeito safado tem que apanhar
Por causa dele o meu mano morreu
O plantão, todo o trabalho, ele enfraqueceu
E causou muitas mortes deixando infeliz
Famílias dos mano que eram raíz
Os moradores já querem pegar
Até grampearam o seu celular
O patrão já tá preso e mandou avisar
Sua sentença já vamos executar
É com bala de AK

Cachorro, se quer ganhar um dindin
vende X-9 pra mim, vende X-9 pra mim
Cachorro, cachorro, me entrega esse canalha
Deixa ele bem amarrado, pega o dinheiro e rala

Sujeito safado já sabe de cor
O endereço contato lá do DPO
Comédia fodido que entrega o irmão,
Se pego esse verme não tenho perdão
Pago quanto for, mas me dá o canalha
Eu vou comer esse verme na bala
De qualquer modo não vai escapar
Eu tenho para ele uma bolsa de AK

"Terror da boca"

Se liga nessa então, se liga hein, é mais ou menos assim, ó
Pra quem não conhece a disci, eu vou te apresentar
A disci é disciplina basta você aguardar
violar as cosias dos outros não fortalece em nada
Quando a gente não pensa é com a vida que paga
e na disciplina eu não deixo pra depois
Se Leonardo da Vinci porque eu não posso dar dois
E tô ficando na onda sem vacilação
Mr. Catra só dá papo reto, consciência meu irmão
Mr. Catra só dar papo reto, consciência meu irmão
e o terror de boca é chupeta, não adianta chorar
e quando a chapa esquenta ele pede colo querendo mamar
Terror de boca é chupeta, não adianta chorar
e quando a chapa esquenta ele pede colo querendo mamá
Vem mamar, vem mamar, ajoelhou você tem que rezar
Vem mamar, vem mamar, na ponta do bico do meu AK
Vem mamar, vem mamar, ajoelhou você tem que rezar

"Cadê o esqueiro"

Só um esqueiro, um esqueiro, DJ

legaliza Sem neurose, sem neurose, na humilde eu vou assim, ó

Ooooó, ó cadê o esqueiro, demorou formar

o bonde dos maconheiros (× 2)

De doideira, me deu uma louca vou abrir a boca

e falar do preconceito dessa sociedade escrota

Fiz tudo que faço, e do que faço eu me orgulho

Confesso pra vocês gosto muito é de fumar um bagulho

Tu não gostar tá um direito seu, agora não vem discriminar

o direito de fumar que é meu

Fumo e fumo mesmo, assumo pra você

e de chiar, meu Deus, nunca vi ninguém morrer

Como pode fazer mal, isso me deixa feliz

se eu experimentei foi porque eu sempre quis

Se sou assim não depende disso,

se eu sou assim é porque eu tô de bem comigo

Mas se tu não tá não é bom experimentar

porque não é com uma planta que você vai solucionar

Os seus problemas e nem melhorar o seu astral

pense nisso amigo cai na real

Ooooó, ó cadê o esqueiro, demorou formar

o bonde dos maconheiros (× 2)

Pára, pára tudo

Deixa acontecer naturalmente eu não quero não você chorar

Deixa que o amor encontre agente nosso caso vai eternizar

"Simpático"

Então, então, sem neurose, sem caô
com marra de cão vem um vacilão de bobeira no movimento
Sei que tá mancado a massa está sacando
tamo ligado no procedimento
Simpático ao brutro, não é do justo,
dos irmãos se desfaz errado vira certo, se acha esperto
Só fortalece que tem mais, o tempo é o remédio,
o proceder se mostra no dia a dia
A caôzada a simpatia já ta virando epidemia
Eu falei uma vez, tô bolado e novamente vou falar
pra cura safado o ator tá ligado, vacilão é bala de AK
Por isso que eu digo, toma cuidado
meu bonde bolado é um perigo
Comédia fudido, garoto metido é cartucheira de bandido
Porque ele vive na sombra do patrão
agradar vagabundo é sua profissão
Confunde ganância e ambição simpatia comédia vacilão
vive na sombra do patrão, agradar vagabudo é sua profissão
Confunde ganância e ambição simpatia comédia vacilão

Quem é? O simpático para de formar caô! Para de arrumar caô.
O simpático para de formar caô! Para de arrumar caô. (× 2)

"Tráfico cultural"

Pintam na sua frente
Abordando o negão sebá

Pergunta se esta portando
Por isso vai lhe interrogar
Ofendem, são intolerantes
Marginaliazam, só pra variar
Dizendo
"favela é local suspeito Por isso eu vou lhe revistar"
E responde sebá
Meu movimento é político-social, meu trafico é cultural (× 2)
Vem comigo, Vamos traficar cultura
Desentoca as peças marca atividade o negócio é plantar
Vamo lá, vamo lá vamos traficar cultura
Desentoca as peças
Marca atividade o negócio é plantar
Vou te dizer, tem preto e tem branco moço
Tem sim, empenhado no seu bem está
A favela é socialista me, deu overdose de consciência
Religiosidade, fé em deus, trazemos no corção
Paz, justiça e liberdade
Guerra pelo bem sem destruição
Pra você ver, pra você ver
Pra você ver, tem que plantar pra colher

MCs Santos and Agostinho (from the Cidade de Deus)

"Bota preta"

Parado na esquina sabe o que aconteceu, sabe o que aconteceu

Mais de dez D20 lá na Cidade de Deus
E é por isso que os amigos de plantão botaram pra cantar
E fizeram realidade o Rap do parrá pá pá
Seja no outono, primavera ou no inverno eu,
eu mais ou menos assim
Vou caçar os vermes até nos quinto dos inferno
E é por isso que vou botar
o meu tocão e vou botar a minha luva
E é por isso que as mulheres dos caninhas todas vão ficar viuvas
Tá ligado neguinho, é, tiro de nove, de doze e bereta
cadê vocês bota preta
Você na frente eu atrás só fazendo claquebum
DJ, cruz credo, isso dá um caô fudido

"Cuca louca"

Tá ca a cuca louca, tá lêlê da cuca,
A Rocinha é Comando na veia,
se quiser tomar tem que vir de bazuka

762- nós tem, AK- nós tem, G3- nós tem, Desert também (× 2)
lá na Rocinha eu vou dizer como é que é
o bagulho é sinistro, shock, pode levar fé, por quê,
facão amolado, bico afiado, somos soldado
Pavãozinho descontrolado
E tem menor bolado

"Rap da CDD"

Lá onde nasci tem que saber viver,
estou me referindo à minha CDD
Malandro desde pequeno sempre em busca da paz
Nós somamos, dividimos mas de menos jamais
A nossa união é coisa natural e a simplicidade é mesmo divinal
Mas se tu tá de mancada, você ver virar raíz,
mexe e morre pela boca
Chapado se liga eu vou dizer como é que é
Coração de vagabundo bate na sola do pé
E se o Gato passar, não se assuste não
E se a chapa esquentar é cobrança, irmão
E se tu quer jogar, vê se joga no Espelho
O Gato é preto a chapa é quente e o Comando
Quero ouvir o chapadão cantando assim

"Meus direitos"

Mas essa noite começou com tiroteio
Favela tava cercada, na dava pra sair
E a criançada tava com desespero
Pelo amor de Deus, Papai, tira a gente daqui
E aí então uma lágrima deceu
E vi que as minhas forças vinham das forças de Deus
Só peço aquele moço antes de apertar o gatilho
Que pense em seus filhos antes de matar os meus
Eu só quero entrar na minha casa seu moço
Ter o direito de ir e vir Dar um beijo nas crianças

Beijar minha patroa
Ter o pão de cada dia, eu só quero é ser feliz
É triste amigo a gente chegar do trabalho
E ser esculaxado por um motivo que eu nem sei
O rico sente pena, mas sentir pena é fácil
Ninguém passou na pele a humilhação que passei
Aos poderosos eu lanço um desafio
Viver um dia de pobre e o pobre um dia de rei
Mas eu só peço a esse moço por favor
Antes de bater na cara, respeite o trabalhador
E aquela praça onde a violência
Acabava com a festa da minha adolescência
Muita coisa mudou, mas eu posso te contar
Que hoje são meus filhos que não podem lá brincar
Pois a metralhadora que ainda interrompe
Ameaça jovem, velho, criança, mulher e homem
O problema que era deles, passa a ser problema meu
Ter que aturar uns caras que nem sabem quem sou eu

"10 mandamentos da favela"

Vou falar agora vê se não bate biela
Os dez mandamentos que tem dentro da favela
O primeiro mandamento é não cagüetar
Cagüete na favela não pode morar
O segundo mandamento, já já eu vou dizer
Com a mulher dos amigos não se deve mexer
O terceiro mandamento eu vou dizer também

E levar no brindão e não dar volta em ninguém
O quarto mandamento, não é difícil de falar
Favela é boa escola mas não se deve roubar
O quinto mandamento, boladão estou
Vou rasgar de G3 o safadão do encharcador

"Rap das armas (Versão commando)"

Vamo lá
Parrapapapapapá papá papá
Parrapapapapapapá papá papá
Paparrá Paparrá Paparrá clack BUM
Parrapapapapapapa papá papá

Morro do Dendê é ruim de invadir
Nós, com os alemão, vamo se divertir
Porque no Dendê vô te dizer como é que é
Aqui não tem mole nem pra DRE
Pra subir aqui no morro até a BOPE treme
Não tem mole pro exército civil, nem pra PM
Eu dou o maior conceito para os amigos meus
Mas morro do Dendê também é terra de Deus
Vem um de AR-15 e outro de 12 na mão

Vem mais dois de pistola e outro com 2-oitão
Um vai de URU na frente, escoltando o camburão
Tem mais dois na reta-guarda, mas tão de Glock na mão
Amigos que eu não esqueço, nem deixo pra depois

Lá vem dois irmãozinhos de 762
Dando tiro pro alto só pra fazer teste
De INA-Ingratek, Pisto-UZI ou de Winchester
É que eles são bandido ruim, e ninguém trabalha
De AK-47 e na outra mão a metralha
Esse rap é maneiro, eu digo pra vocês
Quem é aqueles cara de M-16
A vizinhança dessa massa já diz que não aguenta
Nas entradas da favela já tem .50
E se tu toma um pá, será que você grita
Seja de .50 ou então de .30
Mas se for Alemão eu não deixo pra amanhã
Acabo com o safado dou-lhe um tiro de Pazã
Porque esses Alemão são tudo safado
Vem de garrucha velha dá dois tiro e sai voado
E se não for de revolver eu quebro na porrada
E finalizo o rap detonando de granada

Parapapapapapapapapa, valeu
Paparapaparapapara clack bum

MC Vidiga (from the favela of Vidigal)

"Avisa lá"

Avisa cambada de alemão, que o bonde vai
partir a qualquer dia

Vai chegar o comando vermelhão
não adianta esculachar nossas famílias
Avisa que Roça vai chegar para botar o morrão na disciplina
Tá ligado que o bonde do Valão,
é Rocinha fechando com Vidiga

Avisa lá, avisa lá, avisa lá que sou Comando Vermelho (× 2)
Então, avisa cambada de alemão,
que o bonde vai partir a qualquer dia
Vai chegar o Comando Vermelhão,
não adianta esculachar nossas famílias
Avisa que Roça vai chegar para botar o morrão na disciplina
Tá ligado que o bonde é só bicão,
é a Rocinha formando com Vidiga

Avisa lá, avisa lá, avisa lá que sou Comando Vermelho (× 2)
Fafá de Belém,você é sangue puro,
é responsa tem que vir formar com nós
Mais tem que ser vermelho, vermelhasco,
vermelhusco, vermelhante, vermelhão
Se liga sangue bom, não seja um demente,
o Comando é chapa quente
É melhor pensar direito, se tu tá afim de formar com a gente
Meu coração, é vermelho, e vermelho é o nosso morrão
Eo, eo, eo se liga Mr. M não vem perder a linha
Morro doVidiga fechando com Rocinha
Vermelhão, Vidigal o bonde é sinistro o bonde tá na moral

Vermelhão nossos irmãos o bonde da Rocinha
é pura disposição, disposição, disposição

"Menino sofredor"

Era um menino sofredor que um dia se revoltou
E foi formar com irmãos da boca, do tá tá tá ele gosto do
tu tu tu ele adorou, muito mais do rá ,tá, tá, tá (× 2)
Eu quero ouvir, vem pro CV, pega uma pistola
e vem formar na boca
Mas consciente que aqui chapa é quente
e essa guerra é louca, louca (× 2)
Então vem, vem, vem pro bonde vermelhão,
tem que ter disposição
Se não tem peça pra forma vem de machado e o facão
Vem, vem, vem pro bonde vermelhão, tem que ter disposição
Se não tem peça pra forma vem de machado e o facão
Eu quero ouvir sangue bom

MC Eddynho (from the favela of Borel)

"Rap da cadeia"

E aqui no Valão, aos demais amigos
que se encontra na luta do dia a dia
Tá ligado, da Rocinha, alô Valão,
alô Via Apia, alô Rua Um, já é, é nós na fita
Tá ligado, vivo somos traídos, presos esquecidos

mortos só deixamos saudades é paz , justiça e liberdade
Vivos somos traídos, presos esquecidos
mortos só deixamos saudades é paz , justiça e liberdade
Morro do Borel o Potal do Catrabi
Formiga o Salgueiro, a Rocinha é aqui
Morro do Borel o Potal do Catrabi
Formiga o Salgueiro, o Valão é aqui
DJ seja burro use e abuse dos irmãos, ram ram ram
Encendeia, encendeia, encendeia, encendeia, encendeia (× 2)
Gosto de cantar pros manos, muita gente não sabia,
É no morro do Borel que eu faço rap na maresia
E na indiana shock no prédio Maracai,
Quando eu olho pra você, Valão, rola pra mim,
Não é melhor e nem pior, não temos pena não temos dor,
É lá de Pernambuco é bom, é a cabrobrooó, rei lá
No morro do Borel, chapadão na Rua São Miguel
e na Conde de Bonfim,
Formiga, Usina e Cachambi, lá rei laá,
No morro do Borel, chapadão na Rua São Miguel
e na Conde de Bonfim,
Formiga, Usina e Cachambi, se liga de processor,
esse rap está demais,
Como disse o pensador, que veio com o cachimbo da paz!
E continua a queimação, o alfe falando na minha mão,
depois que eu torrar eu toco para o Valão
No morro do Borel, chapadão na Rua São Miguel
e na Conde de Bonfim,

Formiga, Usina e Cachambi, lá rei laá,
No morro do Borel, chapadão na Rua São Miguel
e na Conde de Bonfim,
Formiga, Usina e Cachambi,
um alô para os funkeiros, com orgulho recebemos
Foi no morro da Barrão que eu conheci o ouro preto
Termino esse rap shock, aí chapadão, repetir,
sou do morro do Borel sou eu Duda MC

"Terceiro fraco"

Vejo o Terceiro está tão fraco e tão triste
Fica sem graça essa aventura de invadir
Mas o Comando é fortemente preparado
Para encarar tudo que possa, somos CV
Vejo o Terceiro caminhando sem destino
Não vende nada, até no meio da multidão
Mas o terceiro vai acabar é brevemente
Deixe eles verem quem está de frente então
Comando Vermelho, tudo é tão bonito
Comando Vermelho, é a pura disposição
Com o Comando, fico no paraíso,
Com pistola e vários bico
No Borel, morro do Chapadão

🎧 MC Ruger (from the favela of Rocinha)

"Seus alemão safado"

Alô, rapaziada,
Vamos sacudir, né, mano,
Humildemente, chapa quente na Rocinha,
Vamo lá, geral, cantar com MC Fornalha
Mais ou menos assim…

Se tu invadir e ficar de bam bam bam
Vai tomar de fuzil ou de pistola e de sadam
Por que o bonde não é papo furado, então eu digo
E fortemente preparado de fuzil e de AR-15
o Ruger 223 eu não posso esquecer
oi canta AK, canta G3, mas o G3 e uma arma potente
o bonde forte da Rocinha anda armado até os dentes você vê

olha só seus alemão safado
se invade a Rocinha vai sair todo furado
mas olha só, seus alemão safado
a Rocinha e o Comando e nunca vai ser comandado

Se tu é um alemão, ou então um policia,
Melhor não invadir a favela da Rocinha,
Por que se tu invadir tu vai ficar de Bigode
Se vir de peito aberto
E so tirao de caca androide

Demorou, por que o bonde nao deixa a desejar
Solta o pino da M9 e manda os alemão pular
Então olha a granada que é sempre alisada
Para todos os alemãos que ficarem de mancada
Dizendo vai invadir a favela da Rocinha
Então eu digo, e, só não pode perder a linha
Por que se perder a linha não vai encontrar mole não
Por que .30 e de 50
Oi na Roça tem de montao

Olha só seus alemão safado
A Rocinha é o Comando e nunca vai ser comandado
Olha só seus alemão safado
Se invadir a Rocinha vai sair todo furado

Tá ligado, né, mano,
é o Comando e nunca vai ser comandado,
Fé em Deus, Paz, jusitiça e liberdade
É nós memo, alô, rapaziada presente
um alô pra geral, sem neurose, é nós memo
MC Fornalha, humildemente, vai escutando a seqüência
que a Rocinha é chapa quente
tá gostando? A Rocinha
é nós memo, mano

MCs Phillipe and Eddynho (from the favela of Borel)

"Rap do Borel/Versão Comando"

Vou mandar esse rap com toda felicidade
Gente, essa letra é a pura realidade
Escuta massa funkeira, preste muita atenção
no rap que vai tocar e tem a consideração
pensa na eternidade não arruma confusão
paz, justiça e liberdade, muito amor no coração...
Para aqueles que se foram, nesse céu tão lindo
podes crer, eu sei que eles estão na paz!
Liberdade para todos nós, DJ!

Oi demorou pra abalar!
La la la ô, la la la uê,
chega de ser violento e deixa a paz renascer
la la la ô, la la la uê
paz, justiça liberdade, eu sou Borel somos CV

Se liga minha gente em o que nós vamos falar
é de um morro tão querido e a letra vão abalar
Isaí e Tico do Comando Vermelho
Paz, justiça e liberdade neste morro abalou

Agora minha gente nós vamos falar
o nome daqueles amigos que estão naquele lugar
é um lugar tão triste, tão triste e tão cruel

nós estamos falando é dos amigos do Borel...
olha coração, jamais vou te deixar
então por isso o Borel pede a liberdade já
o morro está tão lindo e não falta nada não
só está faltando é a liberdade dos irmãos.

II. Classic Sensual Funk

Tati Quebra-Barraco (of Cidade de Deus)

"Montagem assadinha/69"

69 frango assado, de ladinho a gente gosta (× 2)
Se tu não tá agüentando pára um pouquinho, tá ardendo assopra
69 frango assado de ladinho a gente gosta (× 2)
Se tu não agüentando para um pouquinho, tá ardendo assopra
Tá ardendo assopra, tá ardendo assopra,
fica de joelho faz um biquinho e chupa minha........(piroca) (× 2)

"Montagem pidona"

Bota na cara, bota na boca, bota onde quiser (× 2)
Bota tudo, huu e faz gostoso huu, bota tudo, huu e faz gostoso huu
Uma salada thola baby, ahaaaaaaaaa, huu huu,
Bota na cara, bota na boca, bota onde tu quiser,
Boca na cara, bota na boca, bota onde quiser
Bota tudo, huu e faz gostoso huu, bota tudo, huu e faz gostoso huu
Uma salada thola baby, ahaaaaaaaaa

Bota tudo, huu e faz gostoso huu, bota tudo, huu e faz gostoso huu

"Montagem cartão magnético"

Abre as pernas mexe e gira, abre as pernas mexe e gira,
já viu como é que faz (× 2)
O mané bateu com o carro, quis me levar pro mato
É na suíte do Mirante que eu quebro o meu barraco
Lugar luxuoso não entra mané, só sobe de carro que ver subir a pé
Se liga na Tati o rítimo é frenético
pra você abrir a porta só com cartão magnético

"Montagem cardápio do amor"

Cardápio do amor, cardápio do amor
Cardápio do amor, cardápio do amor, tu tem que saborear
Com vários tipos de delicias você tem que provar
Se pedir café completo, tu vai comer todinho
com chantilli nesse corpinho vou lamber ele todinho
Na hora da refeição se você quer sua carne prepara seu espeto
é só lingüiça pra mais tarde

"Montagem bota na tcheca"

Bota na theca, bota na theca, bota na theca
vem garotinho, theca theca
Bota na theca, bota na theca, bota na theca, ahaa ahaa ahaa
Bota na theca, bota na theca, bota na theca
vem garotinho, theca theca

Bota na theca, bota na theca, bota na theca, ahaa ahaa ahaa
Bota tudo, e faz gostoso, vem garotinho
Bota tudo, e faz gostoso, ahaa ahaa ahaa..

🎧 Tati Quebra-Barraco with MC Serginho

"MC Serginho vs. Tati Quebra-Barraco" (also available online as "Proibida")

Então quebra o meu quebra o meueu quebro o teu caralho (× 4)

Não gosto de peru pequeno
Eu gosto é de xereca grande (× 2)

Eu quero é sexo querida (× 2)

Eu vou te dar um papo mais vai ser engraçado
se não quiser leite de peito vem me dar leite de saco então

Então eu vou mandar pra ela
Tenho tenho leite longa vida
tenho leite de saquinho
No jacaré e no mango
o leite sai de canudinho
não se compra no mercado
não se tira de uma vaca
só toma de canudinho

é o leite de minhápica
Chaca chachaca chacha
cachaca na buchaca

Vou te dar um papo baixo baixo
babaxo babaxo bame éuéu

Não não gosto de peru pequeno! Valeu
Abre as pernas, faz beicinho
eu vou morder o seu grelinho Vai Serginho Vai Serginho (× 2)

Vai Tati!

Abre as pernas mexe e giraaaaa
Abre as pernas mexe e gira
já viu como é que faz (× 2)

o mané bateu com o carro, quis me levar pro mato
é na suite do mirante que eu quebro o teu caralho

lugar luxuoso não entra mané
só sobe de carro, quero ver subir a pé
se liga na Tati, o ritmo é frenético,
pra você abrir a porta só com cartão magnético

Joga a dinamite do meu lado

Puta que pariu!

Quebraram teu barrco foi maior decepção
Chegando lá a mulher era um canhão
Fedia no suvaco e na xereca também
Tá ligado mano é a mulher do frankstein

Bate na palma da mão (× 3)
a mulher era um canhão

Quando ela tirou a roupa os peitinho foi no chão
a bunda tava arriada mano que decepção
joguei a dinamite a dinamite não explodiu
quero que a mulher canhão vai pra puta que pariu

Mais joguei a dinamite a dinamite não explodiu
quero que a mulher camnhão vai pra puta que pariu

Goza na boca goza na cara goza onde quise

Quando eu gozar você grita eu dou-lhe um murro nas costas
cuidado pra não sujar o meu pinto de bosta
Eu mato qualquer uma cumpadre

Eu vou beijar a tua boca
vou morder o seu queixinho
Vai Serginho

Vai Serginho (× 2)

Valeu!

Puta que pariu
foi tomar bezetacil!
Demoro (× 3)

Uh tá na moda! (× 4)
toca pra mama na horta!

Valeu!

Eu mandei mamar na horta
você falo que não
agora sua safada
você vai mamar no chão
Jesus!

Vou mandando o meu rap
vou cantando com respeito
Sabe o que eu quero mesmo
É gozar bem no seus peitos

Abre as pernas faz beicinho
eu vou morder o seu grelinho
Vai Serginho (× 3)

Agora sua safada
você vai mamar no chão
Então
Chão, Chão, Chão, Chão,
Chão, Chão, Chão, Chãochão

Não adianta de qualquer forma eu esculacho
fama de putona só porque eu como seu macho! (× 2)

Quando eu meto eu meto forte bota tudo
Quando eu meto eu meto forte e tá gostoso
Te dou varias catucadas bota tudo
Te dou varias catucadas e tá gostoso
Jesus!

Deize Tigrona (aka, Deise da Injeção, of Cidade de Deus)

"Injeção"
Quando eu vou ao médico
Sinto uma dor
Quer me dar injeção
Olha o papo do Dr.
Injeção dói quando fura,
Arranha quando entra
Doutor, assim não dá,
Minha poupança não agüenta!

Tá ardendo, mas tô agüentando,
Arranhando, mas tô agüentando
Tá ardendo eu tô agüentando!
Arranhando, eu tô agüentando! (× 2)

Ai, doutor, que dor!!
Ai, médico, que dor...(× 2)

Ai... Ai...

Tá ardendo, mas tô agüentando
Arranhando, mas tô agüentando (× 2)

Gaiola das Popozudas (featuring vocalist Valesca Popozuda,artistic name of Valesca Reis Santos, born in Rio's Irajá neighborhood, as well as dancers Rose Mendes, Daniele and Pryscila Silva—song released 2005)

"Fiel é o caralho"
Aí, sua encubada!
Você fala que é fiel
Fica cheia de gracinha
Mas eu já te dei o papo
Que a pica dele é minha
Falou que ia me pegar
Você vai tomar no cu

É o bonde das amantes
Caçadoras de piru

Fiel é o caralho!
Você é empregadinha
Lava, passa e cozinha
Mas a pica dele é minha

Falou que ia me pegar
Você vai tomar no cu
É o bonde das amantes caçadoras de piru

Já saí com o alex
E já namorei o rodrigo
Mas no final da noite
Vou comer o seu marido

Você fica nervosa
Fica toda irritadinha

Mete o dedo no cu
Pois a pica dele é minha! Fiel é o caralho

III. Five Classic Rio Funk Songs

"Rap da Rocinha" (MC Galo, 1991)

Quando eu saí de casa só saí com a intenção
É de chegar no baile e as equipes dando som
Com os grandes DJ que também é emoção
Com as equipe maneiro agitando galerão
Quero ouvir

Olelê, olalá, a Rocinha pede a paz pro baile não acabar
Olelê, olalá, a Rocinha tem conceito
em qualquer morro que chegar Só você! Só você!

É que eu sou da Rocinha e estou curtindo o clima
Da maior favela da América Latina
Zona Leste ou Zona Oeste, Zona Norte ou Zona Sul
A favela número um, a rosa da Zona Sul

E pra quê tu dá porrada? E pra quê tu dá paulada?
Pra quê soco na cara?
Isso é maior mancada
Pra quê brigar, se o futuro é amar?
É que hoje você pega e amanhã vão te pegar
A Rocinha não quer ver você caído nesse chão
Com a cara cheia de tiro e com formiga de montão
Nem andando de ambulância tampouco de rebecão
Vem pro baile meu amigo c'as equipes dando som

Mas se liga meus amigos no que agora eu vou falar
O nome das áreas que vocês vão se amarrar
Vêm a Rua Um, a Rua Dois, e a Rua Três
E também a Rua Quatro não esquece de vocês
Cachopa, Fossinho, Vila Verde e Terreirão
Cidade Nova, Curva do S, Fundação
Via Ápia, Paula Brito e Boiadeiro
Roupa Suja e o Valão sempre têm que vir primeiro
Não esquecemos também do 99, meu irmão
É que fica do outro lado mas faz parte do morrão

Mas se liga, sangue bom, ou então preste atenção
E agora vou falar as galeras sangue bom
Galeras da Cruzada, Santa Marta e do Pavão,
Tabajara, Mineira e a Providência, sangue bom
Cidade Alta, Juramento, Catete e Vidigal,
Leme e o Galo, olha aí o Serra Coral
Verde e rosa a Mangueira, a Primeira Estação
Morro dos Prazeres e a Coroa é sangue bom
Jacarezinho, Formiga, Macaco
Sapê, Borel, Chácara do Céu,
Serrinha, Pedra Lisa, Estácio e Acari
Iriri, Icomprida e Andaraí
Niterói, meu amigo, olhaí o Tuiuti
Não podemos esquecer do morro do Boa Vistão
que lançou aquele rap e agitou o galerão

"Rap da Felicidade" (MC Cidnho and Doca, 1995)

Eu só quero é ser feliz
Andar tranqüilamente na favela onde eu nasci
E poder me orgular e ter a consiência que
o pobre tem o seu lugar Fé em Deus, DJ

Minha cara autoridade não sei o que fazer
Com tanta violência eu sinto medo de viver
Pois moro na favela e sou muito desrespeitado
A tristeza e a alegria aqui caminham lado a lado
Eu faço uma oração a uma santa protetora
Mas sou interrompido a tiros de metralhadora
Enquanto os ricos moram numa grande e casa bela
O pobre é humilhado esculachado na favela
Já não agüento mais esta onda de violência
Só peço a autoridade um pouco mais de competência

Diversão hoje em dia não podemos nem pensar
Pois até lá nos bailes eles vêm nos humilhar
Fica lá na praça que era tudo tão normal
Agora virou moda a violência no local
Pessoas inocentes que não têm nada a ver
Estão perdendo hoje seu direito de viver
Nunca vi cartão-postal que se destaque uma favela
Só vejo paisagem muito linda e muito bela
Quem vai pro exterior da favela sente saudades
O gringo vem aqui e não conhece a realidade

Vai para a Zona Sul para conhecer água de coco
E o pobre na favela passando sufoco
Trocada a presidência uma nova esperança
Sofri na tempestade agora quero a bonança
O povo tem a força só precisa descobrir
Se eles lá não fazem nada faremos tudo daqui

🎧 "Rap da liberdade" **(MCs Willian and Duda, 1995)**
Liberdade para todos nós DJ!
Demorou pra abalar

Lalalaô, lalalauê
Chega de ser violento e deixa a paz nascer
Lalalaô, lalalauê
Funkeiros sangue bom somos Borel até morrer

Se liga minha gente no que nós vamos falar
É de um morro tão querido e a letra vão abalar
Lá no Borel amigo é união, paz e amor
Na comunidade vai pra gente abalou
O morro mais humilde o bairro Tijucão

Porque meus amigos nós somos todos irmãos
Lá é como uma família, é gente de montão
No morro e na favela só tem gente sangue bom
Porque meus amigos, lá na comunidade
Nós fazemos festas em troca de amizade

É uma destas festas para os morros sangue bom
Para poder fazer amizade com outros irmãos.

Agora minha gente o Willian e Duda vai falar
Do morro mais humilde o endereço eu vou te dar
É uma rua linda, é na Rua São Miguel
Nós estamos falando é do morro do Borel
Olha meus amigos, muitos lá se foi
E isto entristeceu foi muita gente e também nós dois
Foram muito amigos que foram pra o céu
Por isso William e Duda pede a paz pro Morro do Borel
Viemos cantar, para poder lembrar
Um pouco dos amigos que se foi pra nunca mais voltar
Pois o nosso mundo é azul igual o céu
É um lugar do mundo está o Morro do Borel

Massa Tijucana escute o que vamos falar
Dos nomes mais bonitos que agora vamos citar
Morro do Borel, o Amor e a Mineira
Nova Holanda, e Vigário, Antári e a Mangueira
Morro da Galinha, Cruzada, Abolição
Andaraí, Rocinha, Iriri é o Estadão
….. Paúna, ….., Gardênia Azul
Turano, Vila Kennedy, eu falei um por um
Jacaré, Manguinho, …... e Ar de Deus
Nós cantamos esse rap no Unido, ele quase esqueceu
Põe a zoação gente, pulando até suar

Gente, nos escutar pra eles pedir pro baile não parar

Não vamos esquecer os amigos MCs
Que no Rio de Janeiro estão cantando por aí
Garrincha e Julinho, Dande e Tafarel
Ai, que bonito gente o Willian e Duda do Borel
Olha meus amigos, eu vou mandar também
Tem MC Mascote e MC Nemêm
Infelizmente, shock, o rap vai parar aqui
Eu sou MC William, eu sou Duda, MC
Valeu

"Rap das armas" (MC Leonardo and Júnior, 1995)
O meu Brasil é um país tropical
A terra do funk, a terra do carnaval
O meu Rio de Janeiro é um cartão postal
Mas eu vou falar de um problem nacional

Metralhadora AR-15 e muito oitão
A Entratek com disposição
Vem super 12 de repetição
45 que um pistolão

FMK, m-16
A pisto UZI eu vou dizer para vocês
Que tem 765, 762 e o fuzil da de 2 em 2

Nesse país todo mundo sabe falar
Que favela é perigosa, lugar ruím de se morar
É muito criticada por toda a sociedade
Mas existe violência em todo canto da cidade
Por falta de ensino falta de inforação
Pessoas compram armas cartuchos de munição
Se metendo em qualquer briga ou em quualquer confusão
Se sentindo protegidas com a arma na mão

Vem pistola Glok, a HK
Vema intratek Granada pra detonar
Vem a caça-andróide e a famosa escopeta
Vem a pistola magnum, a Uru e a Bereta
Colt 45, um tiro s"o arrebenta
E um fuzil automático com um pente de 90
Estamos com um problema que é a realidade
E é por isso que eu oeço paz, justiça e liberdade

Eu sou o MC Júnior, eu sou MC Leonardo
Voltaremos com certeza pra deixar outro recado
Para todas as galeras que acabaram de escutar
Diga não a violência e deixe a paz reinar.

"Nosso sonho" (Claudinho and Buchecha, 1996)
Gatinha, quero te encontrar, vou falar, sou Claudinho
menina, musa do verão, você conquistou o meu coração
tô vidrado eu hoje sou, um Buchecha apaixonado

Naquele lugar, naquele local era lindo o seu olhar
Eu te avistei, foi fenomenal, houve uma chance de
falar.Gostei de você, quero te alcançar
Tem um ímã que, fez o meu hospedar.
Nossas emoções, eram ilícitas, que apesar das
vibrações,Proibiam o amor em nossos corações
Ziguezaguiei, no vira-virou
Você quis me dar as mãos, não alcançou
Bem que eu tentei, algo atrapalhou
A distância não deixou
Foi com muita fé, nessa ilustração
Que eu não dei bola para a ilusão
Homem e mulher irem em versão
Bate forte o coração
Tumultuado o palco quase caiu
Eu desditoso, e você se distraiu
Quando estendi as mãos, pra poder te segurar
Já arranhado e toda hora vinha uma
À impressão que o palco era de espuma
Você tentou chegar, não deu pra me tocar

Nosso sonho não vai terminar desse jeito que você faz
Se o destino adjudicar, esse amor poderá ser capaz, gatinha.
Nosso sonho não vai terminar desse jeito que você faz
E depois que o baile acabar, vamos nos encontrar logo mais
Na Praça da PlayBoy ou em Niterói
No Fazenda, Chumbada ou no COI.

Quitungo, Guaporé, nos locais do Jacaré
Taquara, Furnai e Faz Quem Quer
Barata, Cidade de Deus, Borel e a Gambá
Marechal, Urucânia, Irajá
Cosmorana, Guadalupe, Sangue-Areia e Pombal
Vigário Geral, Rocinha e Vidigal
Coronel, Mutuapira, Itaguaí e Saci
Andaraí, Iriri, Salgueiro, Catiri.
Engenho Novo, Gramacho, Méier, Inhaúma, Arará.
Vila Aliança, Mineira, Mangueira e a Vintém
Na Posse e Madureira, Nilópolis, Xerém
Ou em qualquer lugar
Eu vou te admirar

Nosso sonho não vai terminar desse jeito que você faz.
Se o destino adjudicar esse amor poderá ser capaz
Nosso sonho não vai terminar desse jeito que você faz
E depois que o baile acabar, vamos nos encontrar logo mais

Os teus cabelos cobriam os lábios teus
Não permitindo encontrar os meus
E você é baixinha, gatinha eu vou parar

Mas tudo isso porque eu me sinto coroão
Tu tens apenas metade da minha ilusão
Teus doze aninhos permitem somente um olhar

Nosso sonho não vai terminar desse jeito que você faz
Se o destino adjudicar esse amor poderá ser capaz
Nosso sonho não vai terminar desse jeito que você faz
E depois que o baile acabar, vamos nos encontrar logo mais
Nosso sonho não vai terminar

Appendix B

Funk Carioca Videography

Askew, Charile. 2018. *Vai Anitta*. Netflix.

Barreiros, Renato. 2014. *No Fluxo!* JAB Produtora.

Dantas, Konrad and Barreiros, Renato. 2013. *Funk ostentação—O filme*. Kondzilla.

Domingos, Emílio. 2012. *A batalha do passinho*. Osmose Filmes.

_____. 2018. *Passinho de Favela*. Osmose Filmes.

Garcia, Denise. 2005. *Sou feia mas eu tô na moda*. Toscographics.

Goldenberg, Sérgio. 1994. *Funk Rio*. Centro de Criação de Imagem Popular (CECIP).

HBL, Leandro and Pentz, Wesley. 2008. *Favela on Blast*. Mad Decent.

Johnsen, Andreas. 2004. *Mr. Catra: The Faithful*. Rosforth.

KondZilla. 2019. *Sintonia*. Netflix.

Larozza, Felipe and Matias Maxx. 2019. *Por dentro do funk 150 BPM*. Vice Brasil.

Lopes, Kelvy, DJ Tyrim and Digão. 2018. *Documentário Mc Zoi de Gato* (*A Voz da Favela*). Estúdio Rec.

Mariano, Sidney. 2014. *Funk ostentação—O sonho*. Benditas Filmes.

Meirelles, Fernando. 2003. *Cidade dos homens*. "Episode 1." *Sábado*. Written by Fernando Meirelles and George Moura. Rede Globo/O2 Filmes.

Mellin, Rafael. 2010. *90 dias com catra*. Mellin Vídeos/Grupo Sal.

Portella, Juliana. 2015. *As galeras*. MGR Audio e Imagem.

Reis, Marcelo. 2013. *Esculacho*. Bagulium Loquo Est.

Bibliography

A

Albuquerque, Severino J. and Kathryn Bishop-Sanchez, eds. 2015. *Performing Brazil: Essays on Culture, Identity and Performing Arts*. Madison: University of Wisconsin Press. http://doi.org/10.3138/md.2016.59.2.249.

Alvito, Marcos. 1996. "A honra de Acari." In *Cidadania e violência*, Gilberto Velho and Marcos Alvito eds., 147-64. Rio de Janeiro: Editora UFRJ.

_____. 1998. "Um bicho de sete cabeças." In *Um século de favela*, Alba Zaluar and Marcos Alvito eds., 181-208. Rio de Janeiro: Fundação Getúlio Vargas Editora.

Aquino, Ruth de. 2011. "O homem que enfrenta os facínoras: Xerife com fama de incorruptível, pacificador das favelas e ídolo popular, o gaúcho José Mariano Beltrame conquistou o Rio e de Janeiro. Algo pode ameaçá-lo?" *Revista Época*. October 14, 2011. http://revistaepoca.globo.com/tempo/noticia/2011/10/o-homem-que-enfrenta-os-facinoras.html.

Araújo, Samuel. 2006. "A violência como conceito na pesquisa musical; reflexões sobre uma experiência dialógica na Maré, Rio de Janeiro." Trans. Revista Transcultural de Música, 10(1): 1-25.

_____. 2006. "Conflict and Violence as Theoretical Tools in Present-Day Ethnomusicology: Notes on a Dialogic Ethnography of Sound Practices in Rio de Janeiro." Ethnomusicology, 50(2): 287-313.

Araújo, Vera. 2002. "*Favelas proibidas aos PMs." O Globo, June 23, 2002.*

Arce, José M. Valenzuela. 1997. "Rebeldia urbana: tramas de exclsuão e violência juvenil." In *Abalando os anos 90-funk e hip-hop: globalização, violência e estilo cultural*, Micael Herschmann ed., 136-62. Rio de Janeiro: Rocco.

Arendt, Hannah. 1969. *On Violence*. New York: Harcourt Brace.

Arias, Enrique Desmond. 2001. "Crime, Violence, and Democracy: the State and Political Order in Brazilian Shantytowns." PhD diss., University of Wisconsin-Madison.

Arias, Enrique Desmond. 2006. *Drugs and Democracy in Rio de Janeiro: Trafficking, Social Networks and Public Security*. Chapel Hill: University of North Carolina Press.

Armstrong, Piers. 2001. "Songs of Olodum: Ethnicity, Activism, and Art in a Globalized Carnival Community." In *Brazilian Popular Music and Globalization*, Charles Perrone and Christopher Dunn eds., 177-91. University Press of Florida: Gainesville.

Avelar, Idelber. 2001. "Defeated Rallies, Mournful Anthems and the Origins of Brazilian Heavy Metal." In *Brazilian Popular Music and Globalization*, Charles Perrone and Christopher Dunn eds., 136-60. University Press of Florida: Gainesville.

______. 2011. "Mangue Beat Music and the Coding of Citizenship in Sound." In *Brazilian Popular Music and Citizenship*, Idelber Avelar and Christopher Dunn eds., 1-27. Durham: Duke University Press. DOI: https://doi.org/10.1215/9780822393603.

Avelar, Idelber and Christopher Dunn, eds. 2011. *Brazilian Popular Music and Citizenship*, Durham: Duke University Press.

Avnon, Dan. 1998. *Martin Buber: The Hidden Dialogue*. Lanham: Rownman and Litterfield.

B

Babenco, Hector. *Carandiru*. 2003. Sony Pictures Classics.

Baker, Eduardo. 2013. "Ensaio por uma criminologia perspectivista." Master's thesis, Universidade do Estado do Rio de Janeiro.

Barcellos, Caco. 2003. *Abusado: O dono do morro Dona Marta*. Rio de Janeiro: Record.

Barreto, Bruno. 2008. *Última parada 174*. Empire Film Group.

Batista, Carlos Bruce Sirimarco. 2010. "Da criminalização do funk à militarização do espaçoda pobreza." Master's thesis, Universidade Cândido Mendes.

Batista, Carlos Bruce Sirimarco, ed. 2013. *Tamborzão: olhares sobre a criminalização dofunk*. Rio de Janeiro: Revan.

Bary, Leslie. 1991. "Oswald de Andrade's 'Cannibalist Manifesto.'" *Latin American Literary Review* 19 (38): 38-47.

Béhague, Gerard. 2000. "Afro-Brazilian Traditions." *In The Garland Handbook of Lat-*

in American Music, Dale A. Olsen and Daniel E. Sheehy eds., 272–287. New York: Garland Publishing.

Belmiro, Danielle. 2014. "'O Rio virou uma marca a ser vendida': O deputado estadual Marcelo Freixo critica a gestão atual da capital turística do Brasil." *El País*, June 7, 2014. https://brasil.elpais.com/brasil/2014/06/07/politica/1402158279_444490.html.

Bill, MV, and Celso Athayde. 2006. *Falcão: Meninos do tráfico*. Rio de Janeiro: Objetiva.

Bill, MV, Celso Athayde and Luiz Eduardo Soares. 2005. *Cabeça de porco*. Rio de Janeiro: Objetiva.

Bishop-Sanchez, Kathryn. 2015. "On the (Im)possibility of Performing Brazil." In *Performing Brazil: Essays on Culture, Identity, and the Performing Arts*, Severino J. Albuquerque and Kathryn Bishop-Sanchez eds., 15-38. University of Wisconsin Press. Kindle Edition.

Bocskay, Stephen. 2017. "Undesired Presences: Samba, Improvisation, and Afro-politics in 1970s Brazil." *Latin American Research Review* 52 (1): 64-78. https://doi.org/10.25222/larr.71.

Bocskay, Stephen A. 2012. "Voices of Samba: Music and the Brazilian Racial Imaginary, 1955-1988." PhD diss., Brown University.

Bravo, Virgilio and Limbal, Loira. *Estilo hip-hop*. 2009. Estilo Hip-hop Productions.

Browning, Barbara. 1995. *Samba: Resistance in Motion*. Bloomington and Indianapolis: Indiana University Press.

Buber, Martin. 1947. *Tales of the Hasidim: Early Masters*. Schocken, New York. Transl.

_____. 2010. *I and Thou*. Translated by Ronald Gregor Smith. Mansfield Centre: Martino. First published 1937 by Scribner and Sons (New York).

Burlamaqui, Luciana. 2009. *Entre a luz e a sombra*. Zora Mídia.

C

Caceres, Guillermo, Lucas Ferrari and Carlos Palombini. 2014. "A era Lula/tamborzão: política e sonoridade." *Revista do Instituto de Estudos Brasileiros* 58, no. 1: 157–207. http://dx.doi.org/10.11606/issn.2316-901X.v0i58p157-207

Caetano, Mariana Gomes. 2015. "My pussy é o poder: Representação feminina através do funk: Identidade, feminismo e indústria cultural." Master's thesis, Universidade Federal Fluminense.

Caldeira, Teresa Pires do Rio. 2000. *City of Walls: Crime, Segregation and Citizenship in São Paulo*. Berkeley: University of California Press.

Cândido, Antônio e J. Aderaldo Castello. 2005. *Presença da literatura brasileira: História e antologia–II. Modernismo*. 14th ed. São Paulo: Bertrand Brasil.

Carvalho, Janaína. 2012. "Rocinha inaugura UPP e terá 100 câmeras para monitorar comunidade." *G1*, Semtember 20, 2012. http://g1.globo.com/rio-de-janeiro/noticia/2012/09/rocinha-com-upp-tera-100-cameras-para-monitorar-comunidade.html.

Cecchetto, Fátima Regina. 1998. "Galeras funk cariocas: os bailes e a constituição do *ethos* guerreiro." In *Um século de favela*, Alba Zaluar and Marcos Alvito eds., 145-66. Rio de Janeiro: Fundação Getúlio Vargas Editora.

Chazkel, Amy. 2011. *Laws of Chance: Brazil's Clandestine Lottery and the Making of Public Urban Life*. Durham: Duke University Press.

Crooks, Larry. 2001. "Turned-Around Beat: Maracatu de Baque Virado and Chico Science," In *Brazilian Popular Music and Globalization*, Charles Perrone and Christopher Dunn eds., 233-44. University Press of Florida: Gainesville.

Cunha, Euclides da. 2001. *Os Sertões*. 2nd ed. São Paulo: Ateliê Editorial.

Cypriano, André. 2001. *O Caldeirão do Diabo*. São Paulo: Cosac & Naify.

D

Daflon, Rogério. 2011. "Obras do PAC ladeira abaixo: Na Rocinha, construção de planos inclinados, creches e mercado está parada." *O Globo*, July 19, 2011.

Dantas, Pedro. 2002. "Cesar Maia pede decretação do Estado de Defesa." *O Globo*, June 24, 2002.

Darlington, Shasta. 2019. "How KondZilla Took Funk Out of the Favelas and Into the Mainstream." July 18, 2019. https://www.billboard.com/articles/news/magazine-feature/8520345/kondzilla-brazilian-favela-funk-konrad-dantas-interview.

Davis-Rodrigues, Corrine. 2002. "Favela Justice: A Study of Social Control and Dispute Resolution in a Brazilian Shantytown." PhD diss., University of Texas.

Davis-Rodrigues, Corrine, and Enrique Desmond Arias. 2005. "The Myth of Personal Security: Criminal Gangs, Dispute Resolution, and Identity in Rio de Janeiro's Favelas." *Latin American Politics and Society* 48 (4): 53–81.

Dent, Alexander. 2009. *Rivers of Tears: Country Music, Memory and Modernity in Brazil.* Durham: Duke University Press.

Diógenes, Glória. 1997. "Rebeldia urbana: tramas de exclsuão e violência juvenil." In *Abalando os anos 90–funk e hip-hop: globalização, violência e estilo cultural*, Micael Herschmann ed., 112-33. Rio de Janeiro: Rocco.

Draper III, Jack. 2010. *Forró and Redemptive Regionalism from the Brazilian Northeast: Popular Music in a Culture of Migration.* New York: Peter Lang.

Dunn, Christopher. 2001. *Brutality Garden: Tropicália and the Emergence of a Brazilian Counterculture.* Chapel Hill: University of North Carolina Press.

Dyer, Richard. 1999. "Entertainment and Utopia," in *The Cultural Studies Reader*, 2nd ed. Simon During ed., 371-381. Routledge: London and New York.

E

Eagleton, Terry. 1991. *Ideology: An Introduction.* London: Verso.

The Economist. "Rio's Post-Olympic Blues: Feuding Gangs and Empty Coffers Are Pushing up the Murder Rate," 2017. *The Economist.* October 5, 2017. https://www.economist.com/news/americas/21730054-feuding-gangs-and-empty-coffers-are-pushing-up-murder-rate-rios-post-olympic-blues.

Essinger, Sílvio. 2005. *Batidão: Uma história do funk.* Rio de Janeiro: Record.

Extra Online. "Tiroteio na Rocinha deixa um morto e um ferido." 2018. *Extra Online.* May 14, 2018. https://extra.globo.com/casos-de-policia/tiroteio-na-rocinha-deixa-um-morto-um-ferido-22681925.html

F

Facina, Adriana and Carlos Palombini. 2017. "O Patrão e a Padroeira: momentos de Perigo na Penha, Rio de Janeiro." *Mana: estudos de antropologia social* 23 (2): 341–370.

Facina, Adriana and Adriana Carvalho Lopes. 2012. "Cidade do funk: Expressões da diáspora negra nas favelas cariocas." *Revista do Arquivo Geral da Cidade do Rio de Janeiro* 6, 1: 193-206.

Faiola, Anthony. 2001. "The Fierce Beat of Shantytown Chic: In Rio, Funk Scene Thrills and Alarms." *Washington Post*, July 11, 2001, C7.

_____. 2002. "Brazil's Elites Fly above their Fears: Rich Try to Wall Off Urban Violence." *Washington Post*, June 1, 2002, A1.

Faiola, Anthony and Anna Jean Kaiser. 2018. "A once-trendy Rio slum is now 'at war' The murders in a popular Brazilian favela reflect rising violence in a country in crisis." *Washington Post*, January 5, 2018. http://www.washingtonpost.com/sf/world/2018/01/05/this-trendy-rio-favela-appeared-in-a-hollywood-kids-movie-now-the-bullets-are-back/?utm_term=.3412a75dd35b.

Fernandes, Nelito, and Martha Mendonça. 2010. "O mundo real do Coronel Nascimento." *Época*, October 2, 2010. http://revistaepoca.globo.com/Revista/Epoca/0,,EMI176445-15228,00-O+MUNDO+REAL+DO+CORONEL+NASCIMENTO.html.

Ferréz. 2000. *Capão pecado*. 2nd ed. São Paulo: Labortexto Editorial.

Fiske, John. 1995. "Popular Culture." In *Critical Terms for Literary Study*, 2nd ed. Frank Lentricchia and Thomas McLaughlin eds., 321-335. Chicago: University of Chicago Press.

Flores, Philip J. 2005. *Addiction as Attachment Disorder*. Lanham: Jason Aronson.

Foucault, Michel. 1985. "Des Espaces Autres." *Architecture, Mouvement, Continuité* 5: 46-49.

Freixo, Marcelo. n.d. "Por que as UPPs não chegam para todos. Marcelo Freixo, Deputado Estadual." Marcelo Freixo. December 17, 2011. http://www.marcelofreixo.com.br/site/noticias_do.php?codigo=104.

Freyre, Gilberto. 2003. *Casa-Grande e Senzala: Formação da família brasileira sob o regime da economia patriarcal*, 48th ed. Rio de Janeiro: José Olympio.

Friedman, Maurice. 1976. "Martin Buber and Asia." *Philosophy East and West*, 26 (4): pp. 411-426

Friedman, Maurice. 1955. *Martin Buber: The Life of Dialogue*. Chicago: University of Chicago Press.

G

G1. "Operação 'Choque de Paz' na Rocinha irá Bloquear acessos na madrugada: ação terá apoio das Polícias Civil, Militar, Rodoviária, Federal, e Marinha. Autoestrada Lagoa-Barra, Niemeyer, Estradas do Joá e Canoas fecharão," 2011. *G1,*` November 14, 2011. http://g1.globo.com/rio-de-janeiro/noticia/2011/11/operacao-choque-de-paz-na-rocinha-ira-bloquear-acessos-na-madrugada.html.

_____. "Eu era ruim, conta escritora que chefiou boca de fumo na Rocinha, Raquel Oliveira foi mulher de Naldo, chefe do tráfico nos anos 80. Ela conta sua história em um livro que narra um amor bandido." 2014. *Fantástico, G1*, July 12, 2014. http://g1.globo.com/fantastico/noticia/2014/12/eu-era-ruim-conta-escritora-que-chefiou-boca-de-fumo-na-rocinha.html.

_____. "Desde setembro, a cada 3 dias, uma pessoa morreu na Rocinha em confrontos entre PMs e traficantes. Em 4 meses, 37 pessoas morreram. Entre elas, 35 que a polícia diz ser ligados ao tráfico de drogas," 2018. *G1*, January 26, 2018. https://g1.globo.com/rj/rio-de-janeiro/noticia/desde-setembro-a-cada-3-dias-uma-pessoa-morreu-na-rocinha-em-confrontos-entre-pms-e-traficantes.ghtml.

Galinsky, Philip. 2002. *Maracatu Atômico: Tradition, Modernity and Postmodernity in the Mangue Movement of Recife Brazil.* New York: Routledge.

Garotinho, Anthony, Luiz Eduardo Soares, Barbara Soares, João Trajano Sento-Sé, Leonarda Musmeci and Silvia Ramos. 1998. *Violência e criminalidade no Estado do Rio de Janeiro: Diagnóstico e propostas para uma política democrática de segurança pública.* Rio de Janeiro: Hama Editora.

Gates, Henry Louis Jr. "Brazil: A Racial Paradise?" *Black in Latin America.* PBS, (Aired May 4, 2011).

_____. 2011. *Black in Latin America.* New York: New York University Press.

Gay, Robert. 1994. *Popular Organization and Democracy in Rio de Janeiro: A Tale of Two Favelas.* Philadelphia: Temple University Press.

Germino, Dante. 1990. *Antonio Gramsci: Architect of a New Politics.* Baton Rouge: Louisiana State University Press.

Gilroy, Paul. 1993. *The Black Atlantic: Modernity and Double-Consciousness.* Cambridge, Mass: Harvard University Press.

Glenny, Misha. 2015. *Nemesis: One Man and the Battle for Rio.* Toronto: Anansi International.

_____. 2017. "One of Rio de Janeiro's Safest Favelas Descends into Violence, the Latest Sign of a City in Chaos." *The Intercept*, September 26, 2017. https://theintercept.com/2017/09/25/rocinha-favela-rio-de-janeiro-violence/.

Glissant, Edouard. 1997. *Poetics of Relation.* Translated by Betsy Wing. Ann Arbor: Michigan University Press.

Globo.com. "Reforço na segurança,"2005. *Globo.com*, October 31, 2005. http://g1.globo.com/bomdiabrasil/0,,MUL816367-16020,00-REFORCO+NA+ SEGURANCA.html.

Goldstein, Donna M. 2003. *Laughter Out of Place: Race, Class, Violence and Sexuality in a Brazilian Shanty.* Berkeley: University of California Press.

Gouveia, Julianne. 2018. "Nota de pesar: Nêgu Tema, lenda do hip-hop carioca." *Agência de Notícias das Favelas*, January 31, 2018. http://www.anf.org.br/nota-de-pesar-negu-tema-lenda-do-hip-hop-carioca.

Guillermoprieto, Alma. 1990. *Samba.* New York: Random House.

Guedes, Maurício da Silva. 2007. "A música que toca é nos que manda: um estudo do 'proibidão.'" Master's thesis, Pontifical Catholic University of Rio de Janeiro.

H

Hall, Stuart. 1999. "Encoding, Decoding." In *The Cultural Studies Reader*, Simon During ed., 507-517. London; New York: Routledge.

Hanchard, Michael George. 1994. *Orpheus and Power: The Movimento Negro of Rio de Janeiro and São Paulo, Brazil, 1945-1988.* Princeton: Princeton University Press.

Harvey, David. 1973. *Social Justice and the City.* London: Edward Arnold.

Hebdige, Dick. 1993. "From Culture to Hegemony." In The *Cultural Studies Reader*, Simon During ed., 357-367. London: Sage Routledge.

Helena, Letícia. 1995. "Rap exalta lema do Comando Vermelho," *O Globo*, September 22, 1995.

Herschmann, Micael. ed. 1997. *Abalando os anos 90- funk e hip-hop: Globalização, violência e estilo cultural.* Rio de Janeiro: Rocco.

Herschmann, Micael. 2000. *O funk e o hip-hop invadem a cena*. Rio de Janeiro: Editora UFRJ.

Hobsbawm, Eric. 1963. *Primitive Rebels: Studies in Archaic Forms of Social Movement in the 19th and 20th Centuries*. New York: Prager, First published 1959.

Hodes, Aubrey. 1972. *Encounter with Martin Buber*. London: Allen Lane/Penguin.

Holub, Renate. 1992. *Antonio Gramsci: Beyond Marxism and Postmodernism*. London: Routledge.

J

Júnior, Antônio. 2016. *Fuga da Rocinha*. Mákina Cultural.

Junqueira, Eliane and José Augusto Rodrigues. 1992. "Pasárgada revistitada." *Sociologia: Problemas e Práticas* 12 (Fall): 9-18.

Jornal do Brasil. "Apreensão: sete homens são presos com drogas," 1999. *Jornal do Brasil*. September 10, 1999.

_____. "O brinde musical dos traficantes." 1999. *Jornal do Brasil*, November 17, 1999.

L

Leeds, Elizabeth. 1988. "Cocaína e poderes paralelos na periferia rbana brasileira: ameaças à democratização." In *Um século de favela*, Alba Zaluar and Marcos Alvito eds., 233-276. Rio de Janeiro: Fundação Getúlio Vargas Editora.

_____. 1996. "Cocaine and Parallel Polities on the Brazilian Urban Periphery: Constraints on Local Level Democratization." *Latin American Research Review* 31 (3, fall): 47-84.

Levine, Robert M. 1992. *Vale of Tears: Revisiting the Canudos Massacre in Northeastern Brazil, 1893-1897*. Berkeley: University of California Press.

Lewis, Thomas, Amini, Fari, and Lannon, Richard. 2000. *A General Theory of Love*. New York: Random House.

Light, Alan. 2004. "About a Salary or Reality? Rap's Recurrent Conflict." In *That's the Joint!: The Hip-hop Studies Reader*, Murray Forman and Mark Anthony Neal eds., 137-146, New York: Routledge.

Lima, William da Silva. 2001. *Quatrocentos contra um: uma história do Comando Vermelho*. 2nd ed. São Paulo: Laortexto.

Lins, Paulo. 1997. *Cidade de Deus: Romance*. São Paulo: Companhia das Letras.

_____. 2002. "Quem são os culpados?" *O Globo*, June 16, 2002.

Lopes, Adriana Carvalho. 2011. *Funk-se quem quiser: no batidão negro da cidade carioca*. Rio de Janeiro: Bom Texto.

Ludemir, Júlio. 2002. *Meu coração no commando*. Rio de Janeiro: Record.

_____. 2004. *Sorria, você está na Rocinha*. Rio de Janeiro: Record.

_____. 2013. *101 Funks que você tem que ouvir antes de morrer*. Rio de Janeiro: Aeroplano.

Lurie, Shoshanna. 2001. "Funk and Hip-Hop Transculture: Cultural Conciliation and Racial Identification in the 'Divided City.'" *Brazil 2001: A Revisionary History of Brazilian Literature and Culture, Portuguese Literary and Cultural Studies*, 4/5 (1): 643-659.

M

Machado, Fernanda. 2014. "Mostra exibe documentários sobre funk com entrada gratuita no. SESC Palladium: De quarta até sábado, serão exibidos sete filmes mostrando a cultura e contexto social em torno do estilo." *Portal Uai*. May 27, 2014. https://www.uai.com.br/app/noticia/cinema/2014/05/27/noticias-cinema,155117/mostragratuita-exibe-documentarios-sobre-funk-no-sesc-palladium-a-par.shtml.

Madureira, Luís. 2005. Cannibal Modernities: Postcoloniality and the Avant-garde in *Caribbean and Brazilian Literature*. Charlottesville: University of Virginia Press.

Maio, Alexandre de and DJ Fábio. 2000. "Edi Rock: O Proceder," *Rap Brasil* (3), 3.

Matta, Roberto da. 1977. "Carnaval como rito de passagem." In *Ensaios de antropologia Estrutural*, Roberto da Matta ed., 19-66. Petrópolis: Editora Vozes.

_____. 1997. *Carnavais, malandros e heróis: Para uma sociologia do dilema brasileiro*. Rio de Janeiro: Editora Rocco LTDA, 1997.

Mattos, Carla dos Santos. 2006. "No ritmo neurótico: cultura funk e performance 'proibidas' em contexto de violência no Rio de Janeiro." Master's thesis, Universidade Estadual do Rio de Janeiro.

McCann, Bryan. 2004. *Hello, Hello Brazil: Popular Music in the Making of Modern Brazil*. Durham: Duke University Press.

_____. 2006. "The Political Evolution of Rio de Janeiro's Favelas: Recent Works." *Latin American Research Review* 41 (3): 149-163.

McCoughlin, Beth. 2012. "Rio's Funk Parties Silenced by Crackdown." *BBC News, Latin America and Caribbean*, May 4, 2012. http://www.bbc.co.uk/news/world-latin-america-17657122.

McGowan, Chris and Ricardo Pessanha. 1998. *The Brazilian Sound: Samba, Bossa Nova and the Popular Music of Brazil*. Philadelphia: Temple University Press.

Meirelles, Fernando and Lund, Kátia. *Cidade de Deus*. 2002. O2 Filmes.

Medeiros, Janaína. 2006. *Funk carioca: Crime ou cultura? O som dá medo. E prazer*. São Paulo: Editora Terceiro Nome.

Moreira, Raquel. 2014. "Bitches Unleashed: Women in Rio's Funk Movement, Performances of Heterosexual Femininity, and Possibilities of Resistance." PhD diss., University of Denver.

Mundo Real. "Corruption and the Paradox of the UPP in Rocinha and Rio de Janeiro." 2012. *Mundo Real*, March 26, 2012. http://1mundoreal.org/corruption-and-the-paradox-of-the-upp-in-rocinha-and-rio-de-janeiro-2.

Murphy, John. 2001. "Self-Discovery in Brazilian Popular Music: Mestre Ambrósio." In *Brazilian Popular Music and Globalization*. Charles Perrone and Christopher Dunn eds., 245-57. University Press of Florida: Gainesville.

MV Bill, 2006. *Falcão: Meninos do tráfico*. Rio de Janeiro: Central Única das Favelas.

MYTFI. "La police prend contrôle de la plus grande favela du Brésil," 2011. *MYTFI*. November 3, 2011. http://videos.tf1.fr/jt-we/bresil-vaste-operation-de-police-dans-la-plus-grande-favela-du-6819714.html.

N

Neuwirth, Robert. 2002. "Rio Drug Gangs Forge a Fragile Security," *NACLA: Report on the Americas* 36 (21), 32-37.

Neuwirth, Robert. 2005. *Shadow Cities: A Billion Squatters, A New Urban World*. New

York: Routledge.

Novaes, Dennis. 2016. "Funk proibidão: música e poder nas favelas cariocas." Master's thesis, Universidade Federal do Rio de Janeiro.

O

O Dia. "Ex-chefe do tráfico na Rocinha é preso na Zona Oeste." 2011. *O Dia*, November 29, 2011. https://odia.ig.com.br/portal/rio/ex-chefe-do-tr%C3%A1fico-na-rocinha-%C3%A9-preso-na-zona-oeste-1.378910.

O Globo. "Juizado não consegue fazer a fiscalização," 2002. *O Globo*. June 16, 2002.

_____. "O Rio está perdendo a guerra contra o tráfico?" 2002. *O Globo*, June 16, 2002.

_____. "Apreendidos CDs piratas e de apologia ao tráfico," 2002. *O Globo*, June 24, 2002.

_____. "Presidente de Associação de Moradores da Rocinha é Morto: Wanderlan Barros de Oliveira, o Feijão, Já Foi Apontado como Suspeito de se Associar ao Traficante Nem," 2012. *O Globo*, March 26, 2012. http://oglobo.globo.com/rio/presidente-de-associacao-de-moradores-da-rocinha-morto-4417077.

_____. "Intervenção anuncia o fim de 12 UPPse mudanças em outras sete unidades. Algumas unidades serão absorvidas, e área será patrulhada por homens de UPP vizinha." 2018. *O Globo*. April 26, 2018. https://oglobo.globo.com/rio/intervencao-anuncia-fim-de-12-upps-mudancas-em-outras-sete-unidades-22631936.

Oliveira, Denise. 1999. "Sucesso bandido: policiais acusam cantor de rap de pregar o crime," *Jornal do Brasil*, September 11, 1999.

Oliveira, Raquel. 2015. *A Número Um*. Rio de Janeiro: Casa da Palavra.

P

Padilha, José. 2002. *Ônibus 174*. Zazen Produções.

_____. 2007. *Tropa de elite*. Zazen Produções.

_____. 2010. *Tropa de elite 2*: *O inimigo agora é outro*. Zazen Produções.

Palombini, Carlos. 2013. "Funk proibido." In *Dimensões políticas da justiça*, Leonardo Avritzer, Newton Bignotto, Fernando Filgueiras, Juarez Guimarães and Heloísa

Starling eds., 647–657. Rio de Janeiro: Civilização Brasileira.

_____. 2014. "Funk Carioca and Música Soul." In *Bloomsbury Encyclopedia of Popular Music of the World* 9, David Horn and John Shepherd eds., 317-325. London: Bloomsbury.

Pardue, Derek. 2008. *Ideologies of Marginality in Brazilian Hip-hop*. New York: Palgrave MacMillan.

Penglase, Ben. 2008. "The Bastard Child of the Dictatorship: the Comando Vermelhoand the Birth of Narco-Culture in Rio de Janeiro." *Luso-Brazilian Review* 45 (1): 118-145.

Perlman, Janice. 1976. *The Myth of Marginality: Urban Poverty and Politics in Rio de Janeiro*. Berkeley: University of California Press.

_____. 2010. *Favela: Four Decades of Living on the Edge in Rio de Janeiro*. Oxford, New York: Oxford University Press.

Perrone, Charles. 1989. *Masters of Contemporary Song: MPB, 1965-1985*. Austin: University of Texas Press.

_____. 1992. "Axé, Ijexá, Olodum: The Rise of Afro- and African Currents in Brazilian Popular Music." *Afro-Hispanic Review* 11 (1-3): 42-50.

_____. 1996. *Seven Faces: Brazilian Poetry since Modernism*. Durham and London: Duke University Press.

Perrone, Charles and Christopher Dunn, eds. 2001. *Brazilian Popular Music and Globalization*. University Press of Florida: Gainesville.

Potter, Russell. 1995. *Spectacular Vernaculars: Hip-Hop and the Politics of Postmodernism*. Albany: State University of New York Press.

Q

Quintero Rivera, Ángel. 1998. *¡Salsa, sabor y control! Sociología de la música tropical*. Havana: Casa Fondo Editorial de las Américas.

R

Ramírez-Pimienta, Juan Carlos. 2004. "Del corrido de narcotráfico al narcocorrido:

Orígenes y desarrollo del canto a los traficantes." *Studies in Latin American Popular Culture* 23: 21-41.

_____. 2011. "El narcocorrido religioso:Usos y abuso de un género." *Studies in Latin American Popular Culture* 29: 184-201.

Randel, D. Michael. ed. *The Harvard Dictionary of Music*. 4th ed. Cambridge: Harvard University Press, 2003.

Rebelo, Marques. 2000. "509-E enquadra a sociedade." *Rap Brasil* 3.

Rocha, Fernando de Souza. 2015. "Biting the Meat, Spitting It Out: Twenty-First-Century Cannibalism." In *Performing Brazil: Essays on Culture, Identity, and the Performing Arts*, Severino J. Albuquerque and Kathryn Bishop-Sanchez eds., Madison: University of Wisconsin Press. Kindle.

Rocha, João Cezar de Castro and Jorge Ruffunelli. 2011. *Antropofagia hoje?: Oswald de Andrade em cena*. São Paulo: É Realizações.

Robb Larkins, Erika. 2018. *The Spectacular Favela: Violence in Modern Brazil*. Berkeley: University of California Press.

Rohter, Larry. 2003. "As Crime and Politics Collide in Rio, City Cowers in Fear," *New York Times*, May 8, 2003. http://www.nytimes.com/2003/05/08/world/as-crime-and-politics-collide-in-rio-city-cowers-in-fear.html.

Romo, Simon. 2011. "Rio Slum Is 'Pacified' in Advance of Games," *New York Times*, November 13. 2011. http://www.nytimes.com/2011/11/14/world/americas/authorities-take-control-of-rios-largest-slum.html?_r=1.

Rose, Tricia. 1994. *Black Noise: Rap Music and Black Culture in Contemporary America*. New Haven: Wesleyan University Press.

_____. 1997. "Um estilo que ninguém segura: Política, estilo e cidade pós-industrial no hip-hop," In *Abalando os anos 90: Funk e hip-hop, globalização, violência e estilo cultural, trans. Valia Lamego*, Micael Herschmann ed., 190-212. Rio de Janeiro: Rocco.

Russano, Rodrigo. 2006. "Bota o fuzil pra cantar! O funk proibido no Rio de Janeiro." Master's thesis, Universidade Federal do Estado do Rio de Janeiro.

R7. "Policial do batalhão de choque é morto após troca de tiros na Rocinha. Essa foi a nona morte na comunidade ocupada desde meados de fevereiro," 2012. *R7*, May 4, 2012. http://noticias.r7.com/rio-de-janeiro/noticias/policial-e-baleado-apos-troca-de-tiros-na-rocinha-20120404.html.

S

Salles, João Moeira and Lund, Kátia. 1999. *Notícias de uma guerra particular*. Video-Filmes.

Sansone, Livio. 1997. "Funk baiano:Uma versão local de um fenômeno global?" In *Abalando os anos 90: Funk e hip-hop, globalização, violência e estilo cultural*, Micael Herschmann ed., 166-187. Rio de Janeiro: Rocco.

_____. 2001. "The Localization of Global Funk in Bahia and in Rio." In *Brazilian Popular Music and Globalization*, Charles Perrone and Christopher Dunn eds., 136-160. University Press of Florida: Gainesville.

Schechner, Richard. 2004. "Performance Studies: The Broad Spectrum Approach." In *The Performance Studies Reader*. 2nd ed., Henry Bial ed., 7-9. London: Routledge.

Scheper-Hughes, Nancy. 1992. *Death without Weeping: The Violence of Everyday Life in Brazil*. Berkeley: University of California Press.

Schwartz, Mark. 1999. "Planet Rock: Hip-hop Supa National." In *Vibe History of Hip-hop*, Alan Light ed., 361-365, New York: Three Rivers Press.

Schmidt, Selma. 2003. "Estudo aponta mais 49 favelas na cidade: Novo levantamento aerofotogramétrico da prefeitura mostra que o Rio já tem 752 comunidades carentes," *O Globo*, April 20, 2003.

Scott, James C. 1985. *Weapons of the Weak*. New Haven: Yale University Press.

_____. 1990. *Domination and the Arts of Resistance: Hidden Transcripts*. New Haven: Yale University Press.

Scruggs, Greg. 2011. "Hurricane BOPE to Make Landfall in Rocinha." *Rio on Watch.org*, November 12, 2011. http://rioonwatch.org/?p=2492.

Seeger, Anthony. 2004. *Why Suyá Sing: A Musical Anthropology of an Amazonian People*. Urbana: University of Illinois Press.

Skidmore, Thomas E. 1974. *Black into White: Race and Nationalism in Brazilian Thought*. New York: Oxford University Press.

_____. 2010. *Brazil: Five Centuries of Change*. 2nd ed. Oxford: Oxford University

Press.

Smith, Ronald Gregor. 1937. "Translator's Introduction." Buber, Martin. 2010. *I and Thou.*. Mansfield Centre: Martino Publishing.

Sneed, Paul. 2003. "Machine Gun Voices: Bandits, Favelas and Utopia in Brazilian Funk." PhD diss., University of Wisconsin-Madison.

_____. 2007. *Rocinha: Em casa no Morrão* (*Rocinha: At Home on the Big Hill*). Two Brothers Foundation.

_____. 2007. "*Bandidos de Cristo*: Representations of the Power of Criminal Factions in Rio's *Proibidão* Funk." *Latin American Music Review* 28 (2): 220-241.

_____. 2008. "Favela Utopias: The *Bailes Funk* in Rio's Crisis of Social Exclusion and Violence." *Latin American Research Review* 43 (2): 57-79.

_____. 2012. *Pacificação da favela: Encontro com Pai Almir* (*Favela Pacification: Encounter with Pai Almir*). Lawrence, Kansas: Casa Zero Produções.

_____. 2012. *Atalhos e encontros* (*Pathways and Encounters*). Casa Zero Produções.

_____. 2016. "Chico Science +20: Coexistencialismo versus Canibalismo no Manguebeat." *Latin American Music Review* 37 (1): 92-114.

_____. 2018. "Space and Relationality in Rio's Favelas: *Asfalto* and *Comunidade*." Revista Asiática de Estodios Ibero americanos 29 (3): 61-93.

_____. 2019. "The Coexistentialism of Chico Science and Brazil's Manguebeat." Latin American Research Review, 54(3), 651–664. DOI: http://doi.org/10.25222/larr.451.

Soares, Luiz Eduardo. 1994. *Violência e política no Rio de Janeiro*. Rio de Janeiro: Editora Relume Dumara, 1994.

Soares, Luiz Eduardo, André Batista, Rodrigo Pimentel. 2006. *Elite da Tropa*. Rio de Janeiro: Objetiva.

Soares, Luiz Eduardo, André Batista Rodrigo Pimentel, and Claudio Ferraz. 2010. *Elite da Tropa 2*. Rio de Janeiro: Nova Fronteira.

Souza, Percival de. 2002. *Narcoditadura: o caso Tim Lopes, crime organizado e jornalismo investigativo no Brasil*. São Paulo: Labortexto Editorial.

Sparks, David Hatfield. 1992. "Gilberto Gil: Praise Singer of the Gods." *Afro-Hispanic Review*, 11 (1-3): 70-75.

Strauss, Neil, 2001. "A New Dance Music Steps Out of the Favelas," *New York Times*,

February 11, 2001.

Stroud, Sean. 2008. *The Defence of Tradition in Brazilian Popular Music: Politics, Culture and the Creation of Música Popular Brasileira*. Hampshire: Ashgate.

T

Tabak, Bernardo. 2011. "Maior favela do país, Rocinha discorda de dados de população do IBGE. Segundo censo 2010, há 69.161 habitantes no local. Associação de moradores afirma que há mais moradores na favela." *G1*, December 21, 2011. http://g1.globo.com/rio-de-janeiro/noticia/2011/12/maior-favela-do-pais-rocinha-discorda-de-dados-de-populacao-do-ibge.html.

Taylor, Diana. 2003. *The Archive and the Repertoire: Performing Cultural Memory in the Americas*. Durham: Duke University Press.

Teles, José. 2000. *Do Frevo ao Manguebeat*. São Paulo: Editora 34.

Turner, Victor. 2007. "Liminality and Communitas." In *The Performance Studies Reader*. 2nd ed. Henry Bial ed., 89-97. London: Routledge.

TVIG. "Cresce o número de favelas no Rio de Janeiro." 2011. *TVIG*, November 1, 2011. http://tvig.ig.com.br/noticias/brasil/cresce+o+numero+de+favelas+no+rio+de+janeiro-8a49802c2b4a9df2012b4babc6671e4b.html.

U

UOL Notícias. "Morador morre e outro é baleado após confronto entre PMs e criminosos na Rocinha," 2018. *UOL Notícias*, May 14, 2018. https://noticias.uol.com.br/cotidiano/ultimas-noticias/2018/05/14/um-morador-morre-e-outro-e-baleado-apos-confronto-entre-pms-e-criminosos-na-rocinha.html.

V

Varella, Drauzio. 1999. *Estação Carandiru*. São Paulo: Companhia das Letras.

Velho, Gilberto and Marcos Alvito eds. 1996. *Cidadania e violência*. Rio de Janeiro: Editora FGV.

Vasconcellos, Fábio. 2010. "Pesquisa mostra alta aprovação das UPPs em favelas, sejam pacificadas ou não." *O Globo*, December 12, 2010. http://oglobo.globo.com/rio/pesquisa-mostra-alta-aprovacao-das-upps-em-favelas-sejam-pacificadas-ou-nao-2911694.

Ventura, Zuenir. 1994. *Cidade partida*. São Paulo: Companhia das Letras.

Vianna, Hermano. 1988. *O mundo funk carioca*. Rio de Janeiro: Jorge Zaluar Editora.

_____. 1995. *O mistério do samba*. Rio de Janeiro: Editora J. Zahar.

_____. 1996. "O funk como símbolo da violência carioca." In *Cidadania e violência*, Gilberto Velho and Marcos Alvito ed., 178-187. Rio de Janeiro: Editora UFRJ.

_____. 1997. "O movimento funk." In *Abalando os anos 90: Funk e hip-hop, globalização, violência e estilo cultural*, Micael Herschmann ed., 16-21. Rio de Janeiro: Rocco.

_____. 2003. *Galeras cariocas*. Rio de Janeiro: Editora da UFRJ.

W

Waiselfisz, Julio Jacob. 2008. "Sumário executivo: Mapa de violência dos municípios, brasileiros." Brasília: Latin American Technological Network.

Weller, Wivian and Marco Aurélio Paz Tella. 2011. "Hip-hop in São Paulo: Identity, Community Formation and Social Action." In *Brazilian Popular Music and Citizenship*, Idelber Avelar and Christopher Dunn eds., 188-204. Durham: Duke University Press. DOI: https://doi.org/10.1215/9780822393603.

Werneck, Antônio. "Uma juventude perdida no tráfico," *O Globo Online*, June 24, 2002.

Werner, Craig. 1999. *A Change is Gonna Come: Music, Race and the Soul of America*. New Baskerville: Plume.

Williams, Raymond. 1977. *Marxism and Literature*. Oxford: Oxford University Press.

Williamson, Theresa. 2012. "A Missed Opportunity in Rio." *New York Times Opinion Pages*. April 2, 2012. http://www.nytimes.com/roomfordebate/ 2012/04/02/are-the-olympics-more-trouble-than-theyre-worth/brazil-is-missing-an-opportunity-to-invest-in-the-favelas.

_____. 2012. "Brazil is Missing an Opportunity to Invest in the Favelas," *Rio On Watch*. April 2, 2012. http://rioonwatch.org/?p=3367.

Winnant, Howard. 1992. "The Other Side of the Process: Racial Formation in Contemporary Brazil." In *On Edge: The Crisis of Contemporary Latin American Culture*, George Yúdice ed., Juan Flores, Jean Franco. Minneapolis: University of Minnesota Press.

Worms, Jamie Lauren. 2010. "Social Exclusion in the Low-Income Communities of Rio de Janeiro." *Diversitates* 1 (1): 1-22.

X

Xavier, José Messias and Marcos Nunes. "Cartel forneceu 300 fuzis para o tráfico da Rocinha," *Extra,* March 30, 2003.

Y

Yúdice, George. 1994. "The Funkification of Rio." In *Microphone Friends: Youth Music and Youth Culture*, Tricia Rose and Andrew Ross eds., 193-217. New York: Routledge.

Z

Zaluar, Alba. 1994. *Condomínio do diabo*. Rio de Janeiro: Editora UFRJ.

Zaluar, Alba and Isabel Siqueira Conceição. 2007. "Favelas sob o controle das milícias no Rio de Janeiro: Que paz?" *São Paulo em Perspectiva* 21, no. 2: 89-101.

Zaluar, Alba and Marcos Alvito, eds. 1998. *Um século de favela*. Rio de Janeiro: Fundação Getúlio Vargas Editora.

Zimbalist, Jeff and Mochary, Matt. *Favela Rising*. 2005. HBO/Cinemax Documentary.

Acknowledgments

Heartfelt thanks to my friends in the favela of Rocinha, in Rio de Janeiro, Brazil, and the many folks elsewhere who have helped me along the way to carry out the research for this book and write it. It's difficult to mention by name all those who've helped me with this project along the way, be they residents of Rocinha, fellow researchers, students, teachers, relatives or other friends. Still, the passion for living and learning these friends have shared with me is a critical part of this book. I hope that the impact of our experiences together will be evident to any of them that might have occasion to read it. Perhaps it goes without saying if I hadn't had such kind friends and connections, especially in Rocinha itself, I never would have gotten anywhere near the sort of intimate view into the everyday life behind the music they made possible.

Thanks to Eliane Brasil, Seu Flávio, Dona Maria, Bete, Flavinho, in the Rua Um area. In Cachopa, my gratitude to Seu José Ferreira Marinho and Dona Josirene (it was in their home that I had my "encounter with Jesus" in 1992), along with their children Cileide, Josivaldo, Waldirene, Sarah, Thanks also to Apolônio, Dona Helena, Seu Antônio, Zezinho, Dona Ivonete, Pai Almir Gomes, his percussionist Rogério, Seu Pedro, Seu Rodrigo, Marcelino, Inés, Daniel, Danielle, Sílvio, Seu João, Rodrigo, Alfonso da Curva do S, Zezé da Fundação, Tatiana, Hugo, Jefferson, Rogério (nephew of Dona Helena), Lula, Alan and his older brothers Carlos and Charlys (of Charlys da Rocinha fame), to name but a few. In the Valão area of Rocinha, I thank Dona Raimunda, Seu José, Maria do Socorro Andrade Martins (Socorro, Maria Andrade), Margarida, Cleonice, Antônia, Erick Andrade Gonçalves, Viviana Rodrigues da

Silva (Vivi), Marcelo, Wesley, MCs Leonardo and Júnior, their mother Dona Carminha, Lucas Valentim and Luciana.

Across Rocinha, thanks to MC Renato, composer Renato Moreno, hip-hop rapper Nêgu Tema, MC Galo, MC Dollores, Wagner, owner of the Emoções club, and the many bouncers and DJs who worked there, Orlando Santos for his invaluable help transcribing many of the live recordings of underground 'prohibited' songs found in the appendix of this book, Clisna, Cleide, Fernanda, Bárbara, Leandro, Alex, Cícero, Denise, Silvana, Penélope, Vítor, Aline, Débora, Náni, Maikon, Philipe, Clêzinho, Michelle Rodrigues Andrade, Eduardo "Kadu" Souza, Seu Pereira (Everindo da Silva Pereira, president of the União Pró-Melhoramentos dos Moradores da Rocinha, or UPMMR, in the early 1990s), Antônio "Chaolin" Ferreira de Mello (president of the UPMMR neighbors' association in the late 2000s), Wallace Pereira da Silva (president of the Associação de Moradores e Amigos do Bairro Barcellos, or AMABB, another of the favela's neighbors' associations in the late 2000s), Luiz Cláudio de Oliveira, or "Claudinho da Academia" (deceased president of UPMMR, mentioned above, Rio de Janeiro State alderman and business owner in Rocinha), Paulo César Martins Vieira, or "Amendoim" (former president of AMABB, athlete and television personality) and Alan Jorge (comedian and occasional taxi driver).

Thanks to Bocão (from the Escola de Surfe), Aurélio Mesquita (from Companhia Teatral Roça Caçacultura community theater group), Yolanda Demitri (Afro-dance teacher/activist), Marcos Burgos (US-born activist/researcher and co-founder of the NGO Mundo Real), Father Thierry Linard de Guertechin (of the Nossa Senhora da Boa Viagem parish in Rocinha and professor of Sociology at PUC), Seu João, Maria Benedita da Silva Rodrigues, Professor Francisco, Danielle, Seu Martins (José Martins de Oliveira, one of Rocinha's most prolific community leaders/activists for the past fifty years), Karoline Martins, Aline and Bianca Andrade Martins (daughters of Socorro, mentioned above), Ana Luisa Bezerra Bastos, Luciano dos Santos, Dona Olaide, Seu Raimundo, Ilca and Alex. Thanks, too, to Leticia Lima, from PUC, and her family, Dona Nazaré, Seu Jumar, Márcio, Raquel and Nadia, from Jacarepaguá in Rio's Western Zone.

I also thank the community groups that supported my research, such as Rocinha's Grupo Abadá (of the Afro-Brazilian martial art capoeira), especially its leader, Renato "Taturana" de Souza, and his students, in particular Galega, Juma, Javali, Tico, Mosqueteiro, Selvagem and Canjica. Thanks to the Pentecostal church Igreja Metodista Wesleyana da Rocinha, especially Pastor Maurício, the family of José Ferreira Marinho (mentioned above, known at church as "Irmão Marinho"), Vinícius, Carol, Fábio, Rodrigo, Néia, Irmã Francisca, Hilquías, Daniel, Letícia, Larissa, Rayssa, Camila and Sara Morena. I'm also grateful to the two local groups of Alcoholics Anonymous, Grupo Leão XIII and the Grupo Rocinha, including Seu Zeca, Sandra, Ailton, Adilson, Zé da Brama, Vicente and Geraldo.

From the Two Brothers Foundation/Instituto Dois Irmãos, Vivi and Socorro (Maria Andrade, mentioned above), Consolação Lucinda, Washington Ferreira, Orlando Santos (mentioned above), Sergi Rivero Navarro, Bruno, Leila, Elli, José Luís, Sérgio Soares Almeida (who even ceded us our first office in 2000 inside the office of his restaurant, the enormously popular PizzaLit), Edite, Bruno Albino, Cláudia, Thatianne Santos, Joanna, Suede, Daniel de Oliveira, Robert Neuwirth, Gabe Ponce de Leon, Diego Deane, Nick Zimmerman, Toby Weisslitz, Chris Cuminsky, Benjamin Gleason, Rafael Berríos, Theresa Williamson, Mônica Guimarães, Mark, Ali, Anthony, Helena, Markus Stradler, Mike, Erika Robb Larkins, Doug, Moisés, Nini and Jackson Cliliano Gomes,

Corinne Davis-Rodrigues, Greg Scruggs, Filipe Balestra, Luciano dos Santos, Andréia Magalhães, Evan Rubin, Elizabeth Wagner and Rebekah Santos, Alain Poulin, Jesus Salas, Pedro dos Santos, Nadjla Sahyoun Bowie, as well as many others. Thanks, too, to the friends from the early days of Two Brothers in Madison, Wisconsin, such as Jacob Jesson, Brianna Carrigan, John Fieno, Enrique Desmond Arias, Thomas Mitchell, Isabel Mhula Boyd, Alan Kodzik, Joe Seitz, Andrew Irving, Ricardo Vogt, Sam (DJ Papiluv), Carlos Quintana, Kimberly Durden, Bob Jubb. I've left off some names of people I don't believe wished to be mentioned, for various reasons. Regrets to any I have forgotten to include.

In academic circles, I thank Emil Piscitelli (Northern Virginia Community College), David Haberly and Herbert "Tico" Braun (both from the University of Virignia) and Jurgen Heye, Elaine Botelho Junqueira and José Augusto de Souza Rodrigues (all from Pontifícia Universidade Católica do Rio de Janeiro, or PUC-Rio). At the University of Wisconsin-Madison, special thanks to Professor Severino Albuquerque. In addition to being my advisor, he supported me in countless ways and has continued to believe in me through all the various ups and downs of the long haul of my career. It is impossible to measure what I learned from him. Indeed, if it were not for Severino, I would never have come to Madison in the first place, nor would I have stayed. Professor Florencia Mallon also made invaluable contributions as a reader for the original study which gave rise to this book. As my advisor for my Ph.D. minor in Latin American History, she offered me crucial guidance on this project since it was first conceived in one of her graduate seminars. My contact with her over the years afforded me a model for making my graduate studies personally meaningful through her approach to "history from the bottom up."

I am also grateful to the other members of that thesis committee, Professors Guido Podestá, Alda Blanco and Kathryn Sanchez, for believing in my project, reading and evaluating my chapters and helping me to carry out that crucial phase of this study. Classes that I took with Professors Mary Lou Daniel and Ellen Sapega in the Portuguese department, in Latin American history with Professor Francisco Scarano, and in Comparative Literature with Professor Luís Madureira were also important to my ideas as I worked on the original manuscript for this book.

Thanks, too, to the other colleagues and friends who helped me with journal articles, conference papers and invited lectures that have developed as continuations of the earlier research on Brazilian funk. Thanks to Carlos Palombini, one of the most penetrating and prolific scholars of funk carioca today, for graciously agreeing to write the much-needed preface to this book. My gratitude also goes to Professor Juan Carlos Ramirez-Pimienta (my colleague at San Diego State University and expert on Mexico's narcocorrido music), Professor Derrick Pardue (specialist on Brazilian hip-hop), Fernanda Selayzin Duarte de Souza, Greg Scruggs (mentioned above) and Rodrigo Russano.

Scholars of Brazilian and Hispanic American music who have helped me include Professor Alexander Dent, Professor Dário Borim and Professor Jack Draper. At the University of Kansas, Professor Jonathan Mayhew edited much of my writing in related articles and Stuart Day, Antônio Simões, Melissa Birch, Christopher Anderson, Maraci Aubel and Dovis Bravo Pollock provided intellectual and spiritual encouragement. Thanks to the photographers who offered their material for inclusion in the photo gallery section of this book, Evan Rubin, Gabe Ponce de Leon, Greg Scruggs, Nino Mason, Mingyo Seo and Sergi Rivero Navarro and to Korean-Brazilian painter Grandpa Chan (Chan Jae Lee).

Thanks, too, to the countless folks who helped with my related Rocinha video projects over the years, especially John Verbick (University of Oklahoma), John Vitaglione, Amy Olsen and Evan Rubin (all three of San Diego State University) and John Rinnert (University of Kansas). Thanks for Casi and the crew who put together the Brazilian funk album for international release, Pancadão do Morrão, put out by Flamin' Hotz records, for letting me have a small role in that project, as well as allowing me to write part of the liner notes. All of its 23 tracks are available online at their website with Kudos, making it one of the best and easiest ways for readers to begin exploring the music of the mid-2000s Rio funk scene.

In my most recent dialogues with colleagues, thanks to Hugo Camarinha, ethnomusicologist of the Museu Paraense Emílio Goeldi (MPEG) in Brazil, for his suggestions and enthusiasm. I also thank archaeologist Helena Lima, who sponsored me as a visiting researcher at that same institution in January 2017 to continue working on this project. Thanks, too, to the participants of the Café Com Ciência seminar there for their thoughts and encouragement, to MPEG's Professor Cândida Barros for granting me the use of her office in January 2016 and to Dominik Giusti for her write up about my work in the Diário do Pará. I'm also grateful to the many excellent scholars past and present for their studies of Brazilian funk, favelas, violence, community studies and everyday life in the Brazilian context, many of whom are referenced throughout this book.

Here in Korea, I wish to thank my students and colleagues at Seoul National University, especially the folks in our Department of Hispanic Language and Literature, but also those of the Institute of Latin American Studies (SNULIAS). The Center for Brazilian Culture in Korea (CCBC) and the Faculty of Humanities, too, as well as the many other colleagues, students and staff throughout have encouraged me in my time at this vibrant university. A special thanks to the colleagues and graduate students who have directly helped me with this project, like Professors Kim Hyeon-Kyun, Chung Dong-hee, David Wright, Charles La Shure and Lee Eun-A and students Lee Soo-jie, (Cristina) Ye Joo-yeon,

Hwang Yun-jin, Choi Hee-joong, Lee Dong-hoon (Alejandro), Choi Jungyu, Kim Yeong-yun (Valentina), Choi Jin-seol (Marisol) and Seo Min-gyo (Bebeto). An extra special thanks to Professor Travis Smith for his invaluable help proofreading the manuscript for this book. It is infinitely better for his revisions and suggestions. I'd also like to thank my friends and colleagues of the Center for Korean Studies at the University of Hawai at Mānoa, where I finished the final edits for this book during my sabbatical, especially Director Baik Tae-Ung, my research sponsor Dean R. Anderson Sutton, Kortne Oshiro-Chin and Graduate Student Kim Sulim.

Certain sections of this book first appeared in the The *Latin American Music Review*, in my article "Bandidos de Cristo: Representations of the Power of Criminal Factions in Rio's Proibidão Funk" (Volume 28, Number 2, 2007), and in the *Latin American Research Review*, in my article "Favela Utopias: The Bailes Funk in Rio's Crisis of Social Exclusion and Violence" (Volume 43, Number 2, 2008). Another appeared in the *Revista Asiática de Estodios Ibero americanos*, in my article "Space and Relationality in Rio's Favelas: Asfalto and Comunidade." (Volume 29, Number 3, 2018). Thanks to all three journals for permission to republish such material here and for the invaluable comments and suggestions of their editors and anonymous reviewers. Thanks to my colleagues at the University of Kansas for their support of this project, both financially and for helping shape my ideas during my years at that university. Thanks, too, to my colleagues at Research Affairs of Seoul National University (Division of Research Support) for the many forms of support I have received for my work on Brazilian music, notably the New Faculty Research Resettlement Fund (2014-2015) and the Future Basic Academic Field Support Project (2018).

Finally, I would like to thank my family for their love and support.

Thanks to my sisters in the US, Theresa and Jenifer, and my nephew, Patrick, and his wife, Amber. I also want to thank my parents, Earl (who passed away in early 2017, after having a special connection to this research from the beginning) and Barbara, for helping me in a million ways to carry out this research and to be the person I am. Thanks to my lifelong best friend, Tommy Goguen, too, and to my family in Brazil: Dona Lúcia, Jairom, Alinna, Jeylhielly, Antônio, Moisés and Luiza (and all the rest of you). Thanks to my wife, Jeyla, who put up with more than her share of hardships as I researched and wrote this book; I could never thank her enough for all her love and support. Last but not least, thanks to my son, Cael. For a ten-year-old like yourself, those golden years of funk carioca are ancient history. But your heart and your light make me want to share the stories more than ever. It's to you and your mother that I dedicate this book.

Index

C

D

E

F